FRENCH *for* LE SNOB

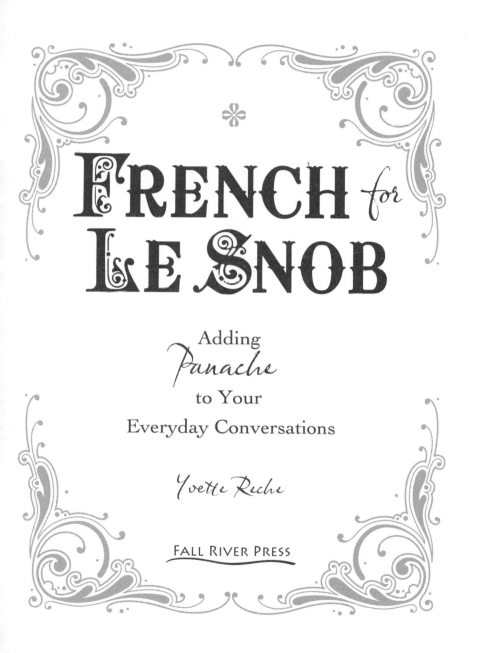

FRENCH *for* LE SNOB

Adding
Panache
to Your
Everyday Conversations

Yvette Reche

FALL RIVER PRESS

Book design by Christine Heun

Fall River Press
122 Fifth Avenue
New York, NY 10011

ISBN-13: 978-1-4351-0134-0
ISBN-10: 1-4351-0134-0

Printed and bound in the United States of America

1 3 5 7 9 10 8 6 4 2

CONTENTS

INTRODUCTION

> "The total number of French words
> adopted since the Middle English
> period was slightly over ten thousand,
> and of these, 75 percent are still in
> current use."
>
> — *A History of the English Language,*
> Albert C. Baugh and Thomas Cable

Anyone searching for *le mot juste* will find it in *French for Le Snob,* which is intended to make English speakers everywhere aware of the French loanwords and expressions that became part of the English vocabulary after the Norman sailed into England and won the battle of Hastings in 1066.

Shortly after the Norman set up shop in England, the French language became and remained the parlance of the rich and famous in the "Engle-land" for a long time. French was spoken by the upper classes, and it is not surprising that French loanwords are found when discussing areas in which people with education and wealth had an influence:

the arts, fashion and style, architecture, and food they enjoyed in exclusive social gatherings.

French for Le Snob is designed to enable sophisticated people to use the many French loanwords of the English vocabulary and to speak them with an impeccable French pronunciation. It will also review the origins of the English language, the development of American English, and about how French words invaded English speech.

French for Le Snob gives educated English speakers from all walks of life the ammunition they need to use the language in a learned, colorful, fun, and sophisticated manner in their daily interactions, including:

→ Chefs, people in the food industry, and all those who love to cook, eat, or entertain will find in the first chapter the French loanwords or expressions they need to impress their friends, neighbors, and guests.

With *savoir-faire, cordons bleus* will proudly announce the *Châteaubriand à point* served with crispy *pommes frites* and a Bordeaux *chambré;* a *salade niçoise* and a tasty, creamy Brie with a glass or two of Beaujolais; a delicious *crème brûlée,* followed by a Veuve Clicquot Champagne and of course, a *pousse-café.* All these French loanwords and many more are grouped under: hors-d'oeuvres, desserts, soups, sauces, meats and fish, vegetables, fruits, wines, liquors and aperitifs, cheeses, culinary terms, people, and places in **Chapter I**.

→ Writers, actors, musicians, dancers, and anyone interested in the arts and/or attending art events, will be able to choose *le mot juste* to discuss movies, theatre, artwork, or music.

With *élan* and a touch of class, art aficionados will talk about *trompe-l'oeil* paintings, *collage, assemblage, découpage, cloisonné, brise-soleil* designs, *pas de deux, cabriole,* and *objets d'art* they love. They will find all the words they must know to be sophisticated or snobs listed under: art terms, theatre, painting, literature, dance, and music, in **Chapter II.**

➤ Fashion designers and fashion editors, those who host or attend fashion shows, fabric store managers, and people everywhere who like clothes, fabric, and colors will be able to present or discuss the *en vogue* latest style. With *verve* and *éclat,* these experts will capture the gallery's attention as they describe the Coco Chanel "little black dress," the *bustier* worn by Madonna, *le déshabillé, le négligé* made of sheer *blanc de perle chiffon,* the *Bibi bonnet* or the *chapeau cloche.* These words and many others are organized alphabetically under: fabric, clothes, colors, and accessories in **Chapter III.**

➤ Anybody who wants to add *panache* to conversations will find the *bons mots* she must know in the above chapters and in **Chapter IV,** Potpourri of French Loanwords and Expressions. In the latter, a sophisticated English speaker can select French loanwords such as *à bas, au contraire, c'est la guerre, tout de suite, sans chichi,* etc., listed under Potpourri of French Loanwords and Expressions, or under French Loanwords by Categories: About Men, About Women, About Children, The Great Outdoors, Brouhaha, Up-to-Date or Not, and under French

Loanwords Alphabetically. She can also choose a few French words listed in the section For Francophiles Only.

HOW THE BOOK IS ORGANIZED

The introduction reviews briefly the origins of the English language, American English, and how French words infiltrated English.

Selected French loanwords and expressions, approximately 2,400, are alphabetically regrouped in five chapters, namely: Food, Arts, Fashion and Style, and Potpourri of French Loanwords and Expressions.

Each chapter is divided into the following sections:

French Loanwords: A vocabulary list of selected French loanwords with their English definitions. All French loanwords are in italics, for example: *au contraire mon cher*, etc. Also in italics are French words, followed by their English translation in parentheses, as for instance *l'art de vivre* (the art of living); other foreign words such as *macho*, or *crispus*; and book titles.

A pronunciation glossary offers snobs, Francophiles, intellectuals, bilinguals, *fanfarons, mondains*, and any combination of these categories the opportunity to speak these loanwords *à la française* with an impeccable French pronunciation.

Short Stories: Anecdotes or brief explanations about the origin of selected French loanwords. For instance, how *sauce Béchamel, croissant, crêpes Suzettes*, and *Champagne* came to be, or where *rond-point, chinoiserie, enluminures, papier mâché, trompe-l'oeil, brise-soleil, danse macabre and poète maudit, corset, crinoline, style Pompadour, Coco Chanel, femme fatale, and charivari* originated. In these short stories, people will find just enough information to appear cultured and cultivated while being the center of attention, and loving it. Those who know more than is told will have the opportunity to be pompous and dull intellectual snobs, if they can find an audience.

Be a Snob: Short French phrases, proverbs, and English phrases *à la française* are listed at the end of the first four chapters. These phrases are French expressions that contain one or more French word(s) and one or more French loanword(s) selected from the vocabulary lists. One example of such a phrase is *tout baba*, in which *tout* (all) is a French word and *baba*, a French loanword (See chapter I under Desserts). When a French person says "I am *tout baba*," (literally, "I am a total rum cake"), he means "I am completely stunned."

Anyone who enjoys being sophisticated or a snob can include any of these French phrases in her daily interactions. They are fun and easy to learn.

In the last chapter, the short phrases are made of French loanwords only. One example of such a phrase is *au contraire, mon cher* or *tout de suite, mon ami*, among many others. A cultured individual who uses these phrases may give the impression she speaks French when in fact she is speaking versatile, educated English.

Under "Be a Snob," anyone will find what she needs to show off, dazzle herself and her friends, the cashier at Walgreen's and the doctor's receptionist, her guests, and co-workers. *Pourquoi pas* (Why not), *mon cher*?

THE ENGLISH LANGUAGE

INTRODUCTION

> "The difference between the right
> word and almost the right word
> is the difference between lightning
> and a lightning bug."
>
> — Mark Twain (1835–1910)

One may be in a hurry to have the privilege and opportunity to be a snob, but it is nevertheless interesting to know a little about how French words came into the English language.

Some of the information here can also be useful to the snob when she wants to impress those who have no clue what the Germanic tribes or Roman and Norman invasions have to do with the English language, the second most spoken tongue in the world (Mandarin Chinese being first).

English is the vernacular of science, of aviation, and tourism; it is the language of diplomacy and business. More than half of all business deals are conducted in English, and one out of seven persons speaks English world-wide, either as a primary or as a secondary language.

ORIGINS OF THE ENGLISH LANGUAGE

> "English is the richest of the world's languages because it has borrowed freely from virtually every other language spoken on the face of the earth."
>
> —William and Mary Morris, authors of *Morris Dictionary of Word and Phrase Origins*

English is a Germanic language of the Indo-European family of languages, a name given to a large linguistic family that includes most of the languages of Europe, past and present, and many of the languages spoken in south-western Asia and India.

English has been used in Britain for more than 1,500 years and its rich and varied vocabulary comes mainly from two major sources: the Germanic and the Romance languages.

GERMANIC LANGUAGES

Two thousand years ago, Celt tribes had migrated from Central Europe to the British Islands, and consequently, the inhabitants of Britain spoke a Celtic language, the first Indo-European tongue to be spoken in England.

However, during the fifth century, the Celts were displaced out of Britain by Germanic tribes who crossed the North Sea and settled in the district of Holstein, the region that is now England. Supposedly, they had come to protect the Celts from their enemies at the request of Vortigen, a Celtic king, but instead, like the cuckoo *sans-gêne*[1] makes himself at home in the nest of other birds, they decided to stay. As they settled in the British Isles, they pushed away the Celts to Wales, Ireland, and Scotland where Celtic languages are still spoken.

Welsh and English are the official languages of Wales, one of the three countries that make up Great Britain, the other two being Scotland and England. More than half a million people speak Welsh in Wales and several hundred thousand speak it in England. Welsh is also spoken in the Chubut province, a small colony of central Patagonia in Argentina. *Penguin, crumpet,* and *flannel* are Welsh loanwords.

Irish Gaelic is the official language of the Republic of Ireland and is also spoken by some people in Irish communities in the United States, in Great Britain, and in Canada. Scottish Gaelic is spoken primarily in North Scotland, and in the province of *Nouvelle Ecosse* (Nova Scotia) in Canada. Among other words, Gaelic has contributed *brat, golf, leprechaun, shamrock, shanty, slob, slogan,* and *spunk* to the English vocabulary.

The vast majority of Gaelic speakers are bilingual in both English and Gaelic. However, the Gaelic language is endangered or extinct in some areas.

A variant of Gaelic is the Manx language that was spoken in the Isle of Man, located between England and Ireland. This language became extinct after the death of the last Manx speaker in 1974. A small group of Celts also went to the Brittany coast, in western France, where their descendents still speak a Celtic dialect called Breton to which we owe words such as *bar, bravo, job, plug, tan,* and *valet,* among others.

The main Germanic tribes that migrated to what is now England were the Angles, the Saxons, and the Jutes, collectively referred to as Engle in the eleventh century. These tribes brought their culture, their customs, and naturally, their language, with them. The Angles, named after Engle, their land of origin, spoke Englisc from which the word English derives; England is a contraction of Engle-land. The French word is *Angleterre: terre* (land) of the Angles.

By the fifth century, the language of the area conquered by the Germanic tribes was known as Anglo-Saxon (after the Angle and Saxon tribes). *Beowulf,* an epic poem of the eighth century, was written in the Anglo-Saxon language—or Old English—from which Dutch, German, and English developed. Words such as *Easter* (goddess of spring), *Tuesday, Wednesday, Thursday,* and *Friday* came from the Anglo-Saxon language, which is today an extinct speech.

Languages of the Germanic family that contributed loanwords to the English speech are: Dutch, German, Swedish, Danish, and Norwegian.

DUTCH LOANWORDS

From Dutch, the English language borrowed terms such as *ahoy, aloof, bluff, booze, boss, brandy,* and former Dutch colonies and today districts in New York, *Brooklyn,* and *Harlem.*

The word *Dutch* should not be confused with German *Deutsch*. Dutch is the language of the Netherlands (Nether-lands: the Lowland), also called Holland. Dutch is also spoken in the Netherlands Antilles, in the Republic of Suriname in South America. (Suriname was a Dutch colony from 1667 until its independence in 1975.)

GERMAN LOANWORDS

Pretzel, dachshund, edelweiss, Gestapo, hamburger, kindergarten, sauerkraut, vitamin, and *waltz* are just a few words we owe to the German language. German is naturally the national language of Germany, but it is also spoken in Austria, in Switzerland, and in the independent Principality of Liechtenstein, a state governed by hereditary princes. It is to be noted that the Swiss-German language is different from standard German and can be difficult for German-speaking people to understand (French, Italian, and Romansh are also spoken in Switzerland).

SCANDINAVIAN LOANWORDS

Scandinavian languages—also called Norse—belong to the North Germanic branch of the Germanic languages and include Danish, Faeroese, Icelandic, Norwegian, and Swedish.

The Scandinavian Union is divided in two parts: Scandinavia proper, which includes Denmark, Finland, Norway, Sweden, and the Faeroe Islands; and the Arctic region, composed of Greenland and Svalbard, a group of islands north of Norway, first discovered by the Norwegians in the twelfth century.

The English language borrowed *drip, dangle, fog, kidnap,* and *smile* from the Danish language. Danish (Dansk) is spoken by a little more than five million people in the constitutional monarchy of Denmark, a beautiful country of Northern Europe bordering the Baltic Sea and the North Sea. It is also spoken in Greenland, the Faeroe Islands, Iceland, and in some parts of the United States.

Norwegian, spoken in Norway has contributed *cog, fjord, rig, ski, slalom,* and *walrus;* and Swedish (called Swenska by the Swedes) has added among others, *boulder, dahlia, mink, moped, smorgasbord,* and *wicker* to the English vocabulary. Swedish is spoken by approximately eight million people in Sweden and by more than 300,000 people in Finland.

ROMANCE LANGUAGES

They are called Romance or Romanic languages, because they derive from the language spoken by the Romans, whose tongue was Latin, originally spoken in Latium, a region of central Italy where Rome is located. Although Italian is most common, Latin is still the official tongue of the Vatican City. At some point in history, the Romans spread their language as they built their Empire in the Western Hemisphere. Latin became and remained the vernacular of the English government and religious circles for approximately 400 years during the Roman occupation.

A distinction must be made between Classical Latin, the literary language of Plato, and Vulgar Latin, the language spoken in the streets. The word vulgar comes from Latin *vulgus,* meaning the mob, the common people. It is Vulgar Latin that Roman soldiers and colonists spread as they conquered other countries, and it is from Vulgar Latin that French and most other Romance languages derive.

In the fourth century A.D., the Roman Empire collapsed and people became separated and isolated, and perhaps a little confused, as were Noah's descendants in Babel when their tower collapsed. And although it was not a punishment for wanting to reach heaven, the Romans began to speak different languages, as it became the fate of people in Babylon.[2] In time, Latin, their language, evolved into individual Romance tongues. However, because of their common source, these languages have many similarities and their differences are often more phonetic than structural. Among others, French, Italian, Spanish, Portuguese, and Romanian words have enriched the English vocabulary.

FRENCH LOANWORDS

One of the most beautiful Romance languages, French has approximately 130 million speakers (*Le Petit Larousse Dictionary*), including more than 60 million people in *la belle* France. Like English it is spoken in many parts of the world. More than 70 million people speak it as a first language, and it is the co-official language in twenty-seven countries, including countries of Central Europe, in West Africa, the Caribbean, Canada, and Indochina. French is also one of the languages used officially by the United Nations.

Since many French loanwords are listed in *French for Le Snob*, none will be mentioned here. Except *voilà tout* for now!

ITALIAN LOANWORDS

Italian, one the most musical Romance languages, gave us many words— too many to list them all. *Bravo, brigand, umbrella, gondola, carnival, stucco, portico, Mafia, vendetta, fresco, fiasco, incognito, pizza, broccoli, volcano, spaghetti* (little strings), *vermicelli* (little worms), *pasta*, and *minestrone* are just a few terms that have spiced up English speech. Needless to say, more than 57 million people speak this romantic language in beautiful, picturesque

Italy. It is also a minority language in Switzerland and Austria, as well as in Somalia, Libya, and Ethiopia, which were once Italian colonies.

SPANISH LOANWORDS

According to Robert Hendrickson in *Encyclopedia of Word and Phrase Origins,* "there are probably five hundred words in American English borrowed from Spanish." Indeed, in California, Arizona, New Mexico, Florida, and Texas, many street signs bear a Spanish name. *Colorado* (red color), *armada, vanilla, marijuana, coyote, siesta, taco, tequila, sombrero, margarita, samba,* and *tornado* all are exotic words heard daily, particularly in many parts of the United States, the great melting pot and multiethnic society *par excellence.* Of course, Spanish is spoken in wonderfully scenic Spain and in many splendid and colorful Latin American countries.

PORTUGUESE LOANWORDS

Portuguese is spoken in Portugal, Brazil, Angola, and Mozambique, and from this Indo-European language we inherited words such as *apricot, fetish, albino, marmalade, veranda,* and *junk,* among others, thanks to Prince Henri the Navigator who sent Portuguese expeditions to the New World. Lisbon, the capital of this beautiful country on the Atlantic, was designated as Europe's Cultural Capital in 1995.

ROMANIAN LOANWORDS

Pastrami is Romanian, another important Romance language, spoken in Romania; *Dracula* (the snake) is another word from this great eastern European country on the Black Sea. The Romanian language is closer to classical Latin than the other Romance languages that are more related to Vulgar

Latin. Romanian is not to be confused with Romany, the Gypsy language. The Gypsies are the Roma of Hindu origin. The Roma have their own biological, cultural, and linguistic heritage and, traditionally, are nomadic people.[3]

HOW FRENCH WORDS INVADED THE ENGLISH LANGUAGE

Of all the Romance languages, French is by far the one that contributed the most words to British English. And it all began with the Norman invasion of England in 1066.

NORMANDY

On the northern coast of France, there is a province known as *Normandie*, a name that comes from the tribes that settled in that region in the ninth and tenth centuries. These were the Viking tribes, another word for Scandinavians and Danes, also known as Norse men. Hence *Normandie* became the name they gave to the region they conquered. Rollon, their leader, had made an agreement with Charles the Simple, King of France and, in 912, the Norse men obtained the right to occupy this part of France. Rollon became the first Duke of the Norman.

Very quickly the Norman adopted ideas and customs of the people they lived with and soon they absorbed the most important elements of the French civilization. They gave up their own language and spoke French. According to Albert C. Baugh and Thomas Cable in *A History of the English Language*, "At the times of the Norman Conquest, the civilization of Normandy was essentially French and the Norman were the most advanced and progressive of the peoples of Europe."

ENGLAND

Directly across from Normandy, lies England, then ruled by King Edward, called "the Confessor." It is to be noted that a strong French atmosphere pervaded the English court during the twenty-three years of Edward's reign. Indeed, the Dukes of Normandy received and sheltered him and his family when he was forced into exile. Later on, when he left Normandy to go back to England, he brought back with him Norman friends to whom he gave important places in the government of England.

KING EDWARD OF ENGLAND DIES

King Edward, whose long reign lasted twenty-three years, died January 5, 1066, without having produced an heir to the throne of England, and no wonder. Apparently, he had taken a vow of chastity before marrying Edith who was twice his age, and furthermore, it is said that a hunting accident had left him impotent. A successor to the throne of England had to be found. A rivalry for the crown began and ended with the battle of Hastings in 1066 and the end of Anglo-Saxon rule in England.

There were three pretenders to the throne of England after King Edward's departure. They were Earl Harold Godwinson, Earl of Wessex; William the Conqueror, Duke of Normandy; and Harold Hardrada, King of Norway.

FIRST CLAIMANT TO THE THRONE OF ENGLAND: HAROLD GODWINSON, EARL OF WESSEX

The leading claimant was Harold Godwinson, Earl of Wessex, one of the many kingdoms that formed England. He had been an advisor to King Edward and was a very powerful man in England. Harold Godwinson and the King were brothers-in-law as the King was married to Edith, Harold's sister. According to Harold, King Edward said to him on his deathbed, "I commend my wife and all my kingdom to your care." If in fact this statement was made, Harold had indeed the right to the throne of England, and *presto*, he took it. The very day Edward the Confessor was buried, Harold was shamelessly crowned King of England in Westminster Abbey, previously built by the deceased King. But on that same day, Harold's trouble began, because of William, Duke of Normandy, a distant cousin of King Edward who lived across the English channel.

SECOND CLAIMANT TO THE THRONE OF ENGLAND: WILLIAM, DUKE OF NORMANDY

His name was William the Conqueror, Duke of Normandy, and he too laid a claim to the English throne. William was born in 1027, or perhaps in 1026. His father, Duke Robert First of Normandy, also known as Robert the Devil, or at other times as Robert the Magnificent, had had a liaison with a tanner's daughter living in Falaise, a small town in the Calvados region, in *Basse-Normandie* (Lower Normandy).

The name of this *femme fatale* was Herleva, remembered as Arlette. One day she was washing clothes in the river, and Duke Robert happened to be in the neighborhood and fell in love with *la belle* Arlette. Soon after, William, his bastard son, was born out of this historical "roll in the hay." When William was eight years old, his loving father went on a pilgrimage and never came back. This is how William, also known as William the Bastard, became the new Duke of Normandy.

Apparently, in 1051, King Edward had also designated William to be his successor to the throne of England, as a favor for the hospitality he had been given at the Court of the Dukes of Normandy when he was in exile. And, supposedly, Harold Godwinson had previously sworn on the relic of a saint, a bone, that he would support William's right to the throne of England.

Rightfully, William of Normandy felt that Harold had defied the wishes of Edward and violated the sacred oaths he had made earlier. Without delay, he prepared to invade England, to destroy Harold, and become the next King of England. However, to complicate the situation, there was a third candidate to the throne.

THIRD CLAIMANT TO THE THRONE OF ENGLAND: KING OF NORWAY

He was Harold Hardrada, Viking King of Norway. Harold Hardrada was related to King Canut the Great, a Viking King of England from 1016 to 1032 and based on that very distant relationship, King Hardrada of Norway claimed that he, too, had a right to be the next King of England. He foolishly thought that England would be an easy target and without further ado he prepared to invade it, but was completely destroyed at Stamford Bridge. England was not to be a part of the Scandinavian Empire after all, and he went back to Norway.

WILLIAM THE CONQUEROR WINS THE THRONE OF ENGLAND

In September 1066, William the Bastard, Duke of Normandy, also remembered as William the Conqueror—because he was a fighter who had previously conquered Italy and Sicily—was preparing to conquer England. Earl Godwindson was occupied in the North fighting Hardrada when he heard that William was on his way to invade England. In the wink of an eye, he was on his way to fight him in the south. A memorable battle took place on a hill at Senlac, not far from Hastings, a harbor and seaside resort on the English Channel, and separated from Normandy by the Pas-de-Calais.

This encounter propelled the notion that one should never trust a Norman as their reputation is indeed to be cunning, to say "yes" when they mean "no." This is why a noncommittal, ambiguous answer is called *une réponse de Normand* (a Normand answer) in France. William used the trait to his advantage. He resorted to a ruse and ordered his Norman troops to feign retreat. *C'est la guerre!* Thinking the enemy was fleeing, a part of the English army went foolishly after them, but the Normans turned right back and a fierce battle started again during which Harold was apparently pierced in the eye by a Norman arrow. He died shortly thereafter.

The English, deprived of Harold, their leader, became disorganized. The Normans took advantage of the situation and William was left in possession of the field. He had won the battle of Hastings and eliminated his rivals.

On Christmas day 1066, William the Conqueror, Duke of Normandy, was gloriously crowned King of England in Westminster Abbey.

WILLIAM THE CONQUEROR DIES

Life is ephemeral. On September 9, 1084, William the Conqueror died in the monastery of Saint-Gervais in France. It is said that he fell off his horse while fighting. What else! His dead body was brought to Caen, a city in Normandy, 223 kilometers west of Paris. It is reported that during the funeral procession, a fire broke out somewhere in town and the people who carried his coffin dropped it in a hurry and ran to fight the fire—*le devoir avant tout* (duty first), something the Norman had learned from the French! After their work was done, they transported William's body to St. Etienne Cathedral in Caen. This beautiful Norman Romanesque structure was begun by William the Conqueror in 1067 and probably completed in 1087, just in time for his burial!

It was written up there *"sur le grand rouleau"* (on the large scroll), as Diderot[4] would have said, that it would be a bad day for William. Not only had he departed from the world but also one of his limbs broke while people tried to force his stiff body into a stone tomb built inside the cathedral. Apparently, such a foul smell emanated that everybody had to rush out to breathe some fresh air. The funeral ceremony was ended quickly in a very undignified manner. Nevertheless, William's body, with his broken limb, was placed again in the stone coffin to rest for eternity.

It turned out to be a short eternity, because a few centuries later Calvinists destroyed the tomb and William's dead body disappeared, except for one bone that somebody apparently managed to salvage. Eighty years later, another monument was built to rebury William's recovered thigh bone. But unfortunately, this new monument was totally destroyed again in 1793, during the French Revolution. Today, there is only a stone slab left to commemorate the life of William the Conqueror. The locals claim that the thigh bone is still under the slab.

William had been put to rest in Normandy where he had come from but the Norman continued to settle in England and this is how French words, slowly but surely, invaded the English language.

AFTER WILLIAM THE CONQUEROR

For more than two hundred years after the Norman Conquest at Hastings, French remained the language spoken by the upper classes in England. Cultured Englishmen were bilingual and biliterate. French became important internationally as the language of diplomacy. At first, those who spoke French were people of Norman origin. Later on, they married upper class people (love has no frontiers) and before long, the distinction between those who spoke French and those who spoke English was not ethnic but social. The language of the masses remained English, however.

Shortly after the year 1200, conditions began to change. A feeling of rivalry developed between France and England, ending with the Hundred Years' War (1337–1453), during which Joan of Arc heard voices from above, went to deliver Orleans to obey them, and sadly ended up being burnt alive in Rouen in 1431. The British lost this endless war at Castillon in 1453. However, in spite of the outcome of such a long fight, the French words that had infiltrated the English language during and after the Norman occupation became part of the language permanently, and as stated earlier, at least 75 percent of these words are still used today.

BAYEUX TAPESTRY

In France, the Bayeux Tapestry, also known as the Queen Mathilde Tapestry, is a Norman document that describes the Norman invasion of England and all the events that led to it. Queen Mathilde was the wife of William the Conqueror, who was King of England from 1066 to 1087. The Tapestry, however, was commissioned by Odo de Conteville, Bishop of Bayeux and half-brother of William. The Tapestry, embroidered on canvas, is 231 feet long and 20 inches wide. This embroidery made with eight natural wool colors is a picture story of the Norman invasion intended to educate the unlettered public. Today, the Tapestry is on display at *Le Centre Guillaume-le-Conquérant* in Bayeux, a city in the Calvados region.

FROM OLD TO MODERN FRENCH

If it is true that "a language is a systemized combination of sounds which have meaning for all persons in a given cultural community,"[5] it is also a fact that any language must change to express the ideas and needs of an era. Norman French of the eleventh century was indeed different from Modern French. French, as it is spoken now, has evolved from one stage to another, just as, according to some, humans walking the face of the earth today have evolved from the apes.

First, Old French was used to communicate from approximately 842 until about 1400. *Les Serments de Strasbourg (Oaths from Strasbourg)*, a treaty signed between Charlemagne's grandsons, was written in 842. It is one of the earliest texts of Old French, written and preserved. Then, Middle French was used during the fourteenth and fifteenth centuries. Finally, the Modern French period began in the sixteenth century and continues to the present day.

During the Norman occupation of England, the English vocabulary adopted French words from the Old and Middle periods of the French language, which, as time passed, evolved to Modern French. Naturally, the English speech of the eleventh century was not what it is today either. The English language also progressed from Old to Middle to Modern English and, like all languages, will continue to evolve.

HOW THE FRENCH LANGUAGE EVOLVED

When a country is born, it grows and changes because invaders, as they come and leave, alter the fabric, the culture, and the language of the territory they conquer. Therefore, any language is always the sum of the experiences of all the people who speak it at a given time.

Every school child in France learns in his first history book that: "*Autrefois, la France s'appelait la Gaule et ses habitants les Gaulois*" (A long time ago, France was called Gaul and its inhabitants were called the Gaulois). The Gaulois spoke Gaulish, a Celtic language. But Julius Caesar came with his soldiers and invaded Gaul and people began to speak Vulgar Latin, the language of their Roman conquerors. And later on, the Franks, a Germanic tribe, decided to chase the Romans out of Gaul (which they did) and the Gaulois had to switch to another language, the language of the Franks. The name Gaul was changed to France, and Vulgar Latin was replaced by Francien, the ancestor of modern standard French. This is how the French language evolved from the Old to the Modern version as it is spoken and used in the English vocabulary today.

The above is a quick and very simplistic overview of how Vulgar Latin spoken in Northern Gaul evolved into Modern French.

L'Académie Française, founded in 1635 by Cardinal de Richelieu to maintain the purity of the French language, will not prevent inevitable changes, and future generations will most likely need to coin another term to describe the evolution of the French language to its next stage.

AMERICAN ENGLISH

The word America comes from *Americus Vespuvius*, a latinized form of Amerigo Vespuci, an Italian navigator who lived from 1454 to 1512 and came to America, as would millions of people from everywhere. Indeed, people came to the New World from across the globe and brought with them a Babel of languages. English was one of many.

In the seventeenth century, colonists from England brought the English language to America. English has now been spoken in America for more than four hundred years. The first British colony in the New World was in Jamestown, Virginia, where the English settled in 1607. Approximately 104 settlers of different social classes arrived in America, and the few who were able to survive the harsh immigrant life created new words to describe their new life in a new world. They were faced with strange landscapes, unfamiliar wildlife and foods, customs, and diseases. Naturally, they had to borrow words from people who inhabited or explored the continent before them—from the Indians, from Spanish settlers who had adopted Indian terms themselves, and from the French.

Colonists other than the British also came to the New World. People from everywhere settled in various parts of America: French in Louisiana, Spanish in the Southwest, Germans in Pennsylvania, and Dutch in New York. Colonial Dutchmen were the first Yankees, a word derived from Jan Kees (cheese) and used as a derisive nickname for a Hollander.

Each immigrant group brought the customs and the language of their own country with them wherever they set up residence. As they integrated themselves in their new environment and learned English, they also spoke words of their own tongue or created new ones that were meaningful to their changed lifestyle. As a result, a colorful dialect developed and is heard wherever they migrated in America. Therefore, Americans should celebrate their language, one that is seasoned with local or cultural dialects.

Indeed, "Americans should all be bilingual," remarked a Los Angeles man during a PBS interview.

French words, mainly via Louisiana, and West Africa, through the importation of slaves, have influenced American English. *Armoire, bayou,* and *jambalaya* came into the language via New Orleans. *Goober, gumbo,* and *tote* are West African borrowings, first used in America by slaves.

Predictably, the American English vocabulary slowly became different from British English, and even though the British tend to hold the American speech to be a corruption of their own language, it is nevertheless a development of the language spoken in England, with its own identity and its own rich diversity.

We sometimes hear, "They speak English," or "They speak American!" In a sense, it is a true statement, but unfortunately, the implication is often that the former is the real thing, the correct way, while the latter is not. Different does not make it better or worse, only different. Of course, within the United States, we do not all speak American either; we speak New Yorker or Texan among others. This is true in France also. Parisians have indeed contempt for the *Marseillais,* the people from the South of France who communicate in their own creative and rich dialect with an accent that is not pleasing to the snobby Parisian ear. What Parisians tend to forget, however, is that it is not Paris but Anjou that is called *le berceau de la civilisation française* (the cradle of French civilization) where the purest French is spoken.

The American language—a potpourri of many languages, including French—began to be exported abroad during the nineteenth century. By the twentieth century, due to its economic, political, and technological prominence in the world, America became one of the greatest force contributing to the expansion of English throughout the world. Though, like British English, the American speech has inherited many French words, the most pervasive language that infiltrated itself into American English is undoubtedly Spanish.

Most French loanwords retained their French spelling in England, an indication of the extent to which French made its way into and influenced British English. In America, however, some words became Americanized and this is how *theatre* changed to theater, *centre* to center, *mètre* to meter, *catalogue, analogue,* and *dialogue* became catalog, analog, and dialog, and *moustache* changed to mustache.

NOAH WEBSTER

One man in particular believed fervently that there should be an American language with its own idiom, pronunciation, and style. His name was Noah Webster. He was born in West Hartford, Connecticut on October 16, 1758. His father was a farmer and his mother took care of the house, raising her two other sons and her two daughters. After graduating from Yale in 1778, Noah Webster taught school because he could not afford to study law. In 1789, he married Rebecca Greenleaf with whom he had eight children. And when he was forty-three years old, he started the first American dictionary because he strongly felt that all Americans should speak what some people call, sometimes with snobby contempt, American English. It took him twenty-seven years to complete the *Webster* dictionary with its 70,000 words. When he finished it in 1828, he was seventy years old. Noah Webster died in 1843.

CONCLUSION

Because English is international in origin and spoken worldwide, it has evolved as a global language. According to the *Encyclopedia Britannica*, "90 percent of the global language used to communicate on the Internet is English," which is the most widely taught foreign language and the most extensively spoken as a second language.

Inevitably, invaders alter the language and the culture of the country they conquer, and naturally, the Norman occupation of England had an influence in the evolution of the English language between 1066 and the late fourteenth century. Since then, however, French words have continued to enter the English vocabulary, and will continue to do so, just as English will keep on infiltrating the French language. Indeed, international interactions will not stop. On the contrary, contacts between people worldwide will increase because business transactions, cultural and political exchanges will be unavoidable and more and more frequent in a world that has become a "global village," as we hear it referenced all the time.

As time moves on, people's needs and lifestyles will change and so will the language they speak to express themselves in their various dealings. In every language, some words will become obsolete but new ones will be created to reflect new technologies, new trends in all aspects of life: art, food, fashion, etc. Therefore, the English vocabulary will continue to adopt loan-words from many languages, including French, since English speakers will keep on mingling, be it working and/or socializing, with people throughout the world.

As long as a language is spoken, it is alive, therefore changing. But wherever the English language is used, it shares a common heritage. Indeed, "A living thing is something that is always changing, yet always remaining essentially the same," said Georges Lowes; and Irish dramatist George Bernard Shaw (1856–1950) declared: "England and America are two countries separated by the same language." Therefore, English speakers everywhere will appreciate and take advantage of *French for Le Snob* to enhance their vocabulary. This will give them the tools to be snobby if they wish to be, or it will allow them to speak their mother tongue in a more sophisticated and literate manner if this is what they seek to accomplish.

FOOD

J'suis Snob, by Boris Vian

"*On se réunit*	We meet
Avec les amis	With friends
Tous les vendredis	Every Friday
Pour faire des snobismes-parties	For Snob parties
Il y a du coca	There is Coca-Cola
On déteste ça	We hate it
Et du Camembert	And Camembert
Qu'on mange à la petite cuillère"	That we eat with a small spoon

The above is an excerpt from *J'suis Snob* (*I am Snob*), a song written in the late 1950s by Boris Vian, a French singer and composer born in 1920 in Ville d'Avray in the Hauts-de-Seine region, a Paris suburb. Many of his songs ridicule the absurd behavior of fake people, i.e., snobs who eat cheese with a small spoon . . . an unthinkable crime in France.

Chapter 1

INTRODUCTION

French cuisine has always had a worldwide appeal and reputation. As such, many French food words were adopted in the English vocabulary during and after the Norman occupation of England. Many of these loanwords are used today in the vocabulary of Modern English.

Incidentally, the French word for food is *nourriture*, from *nourrir*, (to nourish); the familiar term is *la bouffe* (grub). The French use interchangeably *je mange* (I eat) or the slang *je bouffe*, (I grub), depending where they are, who they are, and to whom they speak. The expression *ils se bouffent le nez* literally means, "They eat each other's nose," and is interestingly expressed in English as, "They are at each other's throats." Either way, both are up to no good. The word *bouffe* is used in both French and English in the expression *opéra bouffe*, a musical comedy, a comic opera—quite a change from grub, no doubt.

The need for food is basic. People must eat to stay alive, as Molière[6] says it sensibly in *Le Bourgeois Gentilhomme*: *"Il faut manger pour vivre et non pas vivre pour manger"* ("One should eat to live, and not live to eat"). Socrates (469–399 B.C.) had the same idea long before, however: "Thou shouldst eat to live, not live to eat." He also said, "Bad men live that they may eat and drink, whereas good men eat and drink that they may live." Conclusion, if we all pay attention to what food and how much of it people put on their *assiette anglaise,*[7] we should find it easier to decide who is good or not.

Food words add cultural flavor to daily interactions, which is certainly the case in French and in English. In both languages, words such as *chicken, pig,* and *turkey* are often used to insult people. For instance, English speaking people will call you a meathead or pigheaded if you are a mule. The French call their own *une tête de lard* (a bacon's head) or *une tête de cochon* (a pig's head). In both languages a *cochon* (a pig) is a slob, and *un gros cochon* (a big pig) is a fat slob. *Un petit cochon* (a little pig) is a pervert in French or, like in English, an affectionate term for a sloppy child, a little piggy. Sir Winston Churchill, who understood human nature, liked *cochons*. He is to have said: "I like pigs. Dogs look up to us. Cats look down on us. Pigs treat us as equals."

In France, when you spot the *gendarmes* on the horizon, you scream, "*Voilà les poulets,*" literally, "Here come the chicken (the cops)," and you get out of the way, if you can. Let's not confuse the *poulets* with *une vache à roulettes* (a cow on wheels), referring to our friendly *flics* or *poulets* (cops) on wheels.

Scholars are familiarly called eggheads in English but in plain-spoken French you are a *grosse-tête* (a big head), and in snob land you become an *intello*, short for *intellectuel*, two French words that have nothing to do with food, but still mean that you are brainy. A brainless stupid person is called a turkey in America. In France a stupid woman is also *une grosse dinde* (a big turkey) or *une petite dinde* (a small turkey); a *dinde*, all the same. What have these turkeys done to us? A stupid man is a *dindon* (not a ding dong), or a *gros dindon* (a big turkey). The French also say of that same *gros dindon Quelle andouille* or *Espèce d'andouille,* (what a fool, what an idiot). *Andouille* is a loanword referring to a type of sausage made with chitterlings. Not very appetizing.

A nitwit is called a *cornichon* in France. *Espèce de cornichon,* as they say, which literally is: a kind of pickle, meaning *pinhead* or *lamebrain*. Again, not kind. A pickle is a troublesome child in English, although the word *cornichon* could be used since it is in the English vocabulary. A bad French movie is a *navet* (a turnip); the same bad movie is a *lemon* in English; of course a lemon is also a bad car or an idiot. The word *citron*, used in English to describe a sort of lime or lemon, is the French slang for *tête* (head). *J'ai mal au citron,* as the French say grumpily when they have a headache, which the reader is going to get if we do not move on to other things *tout de suite,* or almost *tout de suite.*

In this chapter, many of the French food loanwords are regrouped by categories and listed under: hors-d'oeuvres, desserts, soups, sauces, meat and fish, fruits, wines, liquors and aperitifs, cheeses, culinary terms, or people and places.

This first chapter can provide epicures, *chefs, gourmands, gourmets,* and gluttons everywhere the ammunition they need to be sophisticated English speakers, Francophiles or snobs, or all of the above as they see fit. They will speak the French words impeccably while they eat and drink. *Bon appétit* and *A la tienne, Etienne,* (cheers, Etienne) as they say on the other side of the Atlantic. Why Etienne? Probably because it rhymes. As we know, not only are most French *gourmets,* they are also poets. *En passant,*[8] when their glass is empty, the French say *cul sec,* a colloquial expression meaning literally, "bottom dry." If they drink too much, however, they will have to confess: *Je bois comme un trou* (I drink like a hole), that is, I drink like a fish.

Speaking of imbibing, why clink before drinking? Because it is the foreplay of the sacrosanct ceremonial of degustation[9] in which all the senses participate. But the practice also refers to a fifteenth century custom to avoid poisoning. In those far-away days, the signatory of a wine contract would bang his glass against the other signatory's goblet so that a few drops of his beverage would spill into the glass of the other fellow. If his business *compadre* drank the wine, the agreement could safely be signed.[10]

A reminder, however, if you travel in France you will hear the expression *à la tienne* (cheers) with or without Etienne, spoken between friends and relatives; the formal expression for cheers is *à la vôtre.* French people do not use (or did not use) the familiar *tu* (you) form, unless they have been friends for a long time or went to school together. As we know, the French language, like Spanish, has two forms to translate you: *tu*, familiar and *vous*, formal.

A ta santé (friendly), *à votre santé* (formal), or simply *Santé* is often used instead of *à la tienne* or *à la vôtre*. As they raise their glasses, the French also say: *A vos amours* (formal) or *A tes amours* (friendly), meaning, "Cheers. Let us drink to your loved ones."

DESSERTS

What's for dessert? It depends where you come from, or where you travel. Some people do not serve dessert; others do not eat it. What's wrong with them? In France, like in many other places, a dessert is always the proper exit to any great meal, particularly one that celebrates a special occasion, of which the French can find many. Of course, any self-respecting French hostess will always serve chilled (not iced) champagne with it or afterwards.

Apparently, Montaigne's[11] favorite dessert was goat cheese with grapes. This is an interesting and tasty combination appreciated by French people, although for many, a dessert worthy of the name must be nothing less than *choux à la crème* or pie *à la mode*. The latter is an American invention, however. If the French now eat hamburgers American-style, they still prefer their *tarte aux pommes* (apple pie) and their ice cream as separate desserts. *A chacun son goût.*[12]

Montaigne, who believed that *l'art de vivre* (the art of living) should be based on wisdom, tolerance, and common sense, ate with his hands—never with a fork. Montaigne lived from 1533 to 1592 and in those days, people accused you of *chichi* [13] if you ate with a fork. As such, he was probably a sensible man for not doing so. It is only by the mid-1600s that eating with forks was considered fashionable in England and shortly after that in France and by the early 1900s, in America.[14]

Almost anything we drink or eat has a past, therefore, so have desserts. Take for instance a *charlotte russe*. It was Carême who concocted this delicious treat in his restaurant, Rue de la Paix, in Paris. Marie-Antoine Carême (1784–1833) was a French cook known as "the king of cooks and the cook of Kings," and author of many great cookbooks. First, he called his creation, made with cake lining and filled with a Bavarian cream and fruits, a *charlotte à la parisienne* (a Charlotte Parisian style) but later on he dedicated it to the Russian Emperor Alexander and it became *charlotte russe*.

Marie-Antoine Carême was born in Paris in 1784 and died in 1833 at the age of forty-nine. He was buried in the cemetery of Montmartre in Paris. Carême's family was large and very poor but his talents as cook and pastry cook became noticed by Talleyrand, a French politician, who asked him to be his *chef*. Carême's works include *Le Pâtissier pittoresque* (1815), *Le Maître d'hôtel français* (1822), and above all, *L'Art de la Cuisine au XIX siècle* (1833), published in five volumes.

FRENCH LOANWORDS

Each word of the French loanwords listed below is followed by (m): masculine, or (f): feminine, indicating its gender. Loanwords that are not followed by either (m) or (f) are neutral, such as adverbs, locutions, or intersections. Learning the gender is puzzling to English speakers and can be frustrating. There is no other choice but to practice and remember, as is the case when one learns Spanish or German.

The indefinite article "a" is translated by *un* (m) and *une* (f). Some examples are: *un baba au rhum; une baguette.*

The definite article "the" is translated by *le* (m) and *la* (f). Some examples are: *le baba au rhum; la baguette.*

When a word begins with a vowel or an "h," the "e" of *le* and "a" of *la* are eliminated, as in *l'allumette* or *l'hôtel*, to make it easier to pronounce.

To complicate life, however, the French language has two kinds of "h": one called *h muet*, another called *h aspiré*. One must learn what is what and remember that the "e" of *le* or the "a" of *la* is eliminated only when the word begins with an *h muet* and kept when a word starts with an *h aspiré*. For instance, and God knows why, *héro* (hero) begins with an *h aspiré*, and one has to say *le héro*, not *l'héro*. Anyone interested in learning words beginning with either can consult the *Larousse Dictionnaire des difficultés de la langue française*, pages 196–197.

ALLUMETTE (f) Layers of puff pastry with a top layer of glazed sugar; a cheese straw in Great Britain; also French for *match*.

BABA AU RHUM (m) Light cake soaked in a syrupy rum.

BAVAROISE (f) A dessert made with gelatin and whipped cream and served cold; a *crème anglaise* with gelatin.

BEIGNET (m) Fritter sprinkled with icing sugar; sometimes served in restaurants in the southern United States. *Un beignet aux pommes* is a fritter with sliced apples inside.

BOMBE (f) Short for *bombe glacée*, a conical frozen confection.

BONBON (m) Candy or sweets, sometimes with creamy filling.

BOUDOIR (m) Lady's finger biscuit. *Boudoir* is also a woman's private sitting room.

BRIOCHE (f) Round-shaped pastry made with flour, butter, eggs, and yeast. The *brioche parisienne* (Parisian brioche) is made of two balls of dough; one big one for the body, a smaller one on top for the head.

BÛCHE DE NOËL (f) Yule log, a traditional Christmas French *gâteau* made of *génoise* and butter cream, decorated to look like a *bûche*, (a log).

CHARLOTTE (f) *Une charlotte aux pommes* is a light pudding with apples.

CHARLOTTE RUSSE (f) Whipped cream enclosed in a *brioche*, or sponge cake.

CHIFFON (m) Light and fluffy from being whipped, as in lemon chiffon pie filling.

CHOU (m) Short for *un chou à la crème*, cream puff; pastry filled with cream.

COMPOTE (f) *De la compote*: fresh fruits stewed with water and sugar; *de la compote de pommes* (stewed apples).

CONFITURE (f) *De la confiture* (jam); fresh fruits cooked with sugar. What the French call *confiture de gratte-cul*, literally, scratch-ass jam, is a jam made with haw, the fruit of wild rose.

CRÈME ANGLAISE (f) A vanilla custard.

CRÈME AU CARAMEL (f) Custard topped with caramel.

CRÈME BRÛLÉE (f) Burnt cream in which a cream or custard dessert topped with sugar is caramelized with a red-hot iron, or under the broiler.

CRÈME CHANTILLY (f) Vanilla whipped sweet cream; Chantilly cream.

CRÈME FRAÎCHE (f) Slightly sour-flavored raw cream.

CRÈME GLACÉE (f) Ice cream; see *glace* below.

CRÈME PÂTISSIÈRE Pastry cream; confectioner's custard.

CRÈME PRALINÉE (f) *Crème pâtissière* flavored with powdered *praline*.

CRÈME RENVERSÉE (f) A custard cooked in a mould, *renversée* (turned upside down), and topped with caramel.

CRÊPE SUZETTE (f) A thin pancake; the word *crêpe* comes from Latin *crispus,* meaning curly.

CROISSANT (m) A crescent-shaped flaky pastry.

DRAGÉE (f) Sugar-coated almond or hazelnut first mentioned in 1220. In France, *dragées* are traditionally given at baptisms, first communions, and weddings.

ÉCLAIR (m) Oblong pastry shell filled with a flavored custard, whipped cream, and covered with a flavored frosting; *un éclair au chocolat* (chocolate *éclair*).

ENTREMETS (m) Literally, between dish: *entre* (between) and *mets* (a dish). *Webster* defines *entremets* as a dish served between main courses or as a side dish. In France, non-sweet *entremets* such as *croque-monsieur* are served after the main course and before cheese. Sweet entremets, such as cakes, creams, etc., are often eaten as desserts. See under Short Stories: A la française.

FRANGIPANE (f) From Frangipani, Italian inventor of a perfume; a *frangipane* is a *crème pâtissière* with crushed almonds.

GALETTE (f) A thin, flat, round cake of various sizes made from oats, wheat, or buckwheat eaten with eggs, cheese, or honey.

GANACHE (f) Rich chocolate filling made with semi-sweet chocolate melted with cream used as filling for cakes, or chocolate drops. It was created in Paris at the Pâtisserie Siraudin in the 1850s.

GÂTEAU (m) Cake.

GÉNOISE (f) Light pastry made with sugar and whipped eggs; sponge-like *gâteau.*

GLACE (f) Ice-cream. The flavor usually follows as in: *une glace à la vanille, au café, au chocolat* (vanilla, coffee, chocolate ice-cream), *une glace panachée* (a *mélange* of various flavors); for beer drinkers *une bière panachée* is a *mélange* of beer and limonade. *Glace* is also French for *ice* or *mirror*. In France and in Québec, the French-speaking province in Canada, you can order and enjoy *une glace* or *une crème glacée*; the words are synonymous. If you happen to be in Lille, a city north of Paris, you can stop at Dagniaux (*glacier* since 1923) and purchase une *glace bimbo*, one of their specialty ice creams, made with a *mélange* of exotic fruits.

LANGUE DE CHAT (f) Tongue of cat; a tongue-shaped biscuit.

MADELEINE (f) A small, rich cake baked in a fluted tin.

MARRON (m) A variety of comestible chestnut. A horse chestnut is called a *marron d'Inde* in French, although it originated in the Balkans, it is a non-comestible horse chestnut. In France, street corner vendors sell *marrons chauds* (hot chestnuts) in winter months, much like we sell hotdogs in America all year long. One can hear the frozen peddlers shout: "*Chauds les marrons. Chauds,*" to attract customers.

MARRON GLACÉ (m) Glazed chestnut; a chestnut covered with sugar and glazed syrup. *Marrons glacés* were created during the reign of le *Roi Soleil* (the Sun King) Louis XIV.

MERINGUE (f) Egg white beaten stiff with sugar and baked until light brown.

MILLEFEUILLE (m) Literally, a thousand leaves; also called *Napoléon*, a pastry made of thin layers of puff pastry with a custard, a *crème pâtissière* or fruits, between layers.

MOUSSE (f) A sweet dish made with whipped cream, egg whites, and flavored; usually served cold; *Une mousse au chocolat* (a chocolate *mousse*).

NAPOLÉON (m) A pastry also called *millefeuilles* made with layers of puff pastry filled with jam or custard.

NOUGAT (m) *Du nougat*: a confection of sugar, honey, egg whites, and almonds or other nuts, stirred into a paste; specialty of Montélimar in Provence.

PARFAIT (m) A coffee-flavored ice cream. In France, a *parfait café* is a *crème glacée au café* or a *glace au café* (a coffee ice-cream) served in a dish; in Britain and the United States, a *parfait* is usually iced whipped cream or pudding, served in a tall, narrow glass. *C'est parfait* is French for "It's perfect."

PÂTE À CHOUX (f) Cream puff pastry; choux pastry.

PÂTE BRISÉE (f) Pie crust; short crust pastry.

PETIT-BEURRE (m) A crisp, rectangular butter cookie, such as Petit Lu biscuits.

PETITS FOURS (m) Also spelled with a hyphen, *petits-fours*; small biscuits or cupcakes served with coffee.

PIÈCE MONTÉE (f) Tall pyramid-shaped pastry often built with small cream puffs glazed together. A traditional wedding cake in France.

PLOMBIÈRE (f) Ice cream and *fruits confits* (crystallized fruits); a specialty from Plombières-les-Bains, a village in the Vosges mountains, in eastern France.

PRALINE (f) Confection made with grilled almond or hazelnut covered with glazed sugar; *praline* is used to cover cakes or fill candies.

PROFITEROLE (f) A small round ball of cream puff pastry filled with a custard, and covered with a hot chocolate sauce.

RELIGIEUSE (f) A small ball of puff pastry placed on a larger one and covered with a butter cream and decorated with icing. *Religieuse* is French for "nun."

ROULADE AU CHOCOLAT (f) From *rouler* (to roll); chocolate cake rolled and garnished with a chocolate cream.

SABLÉ (m) From *sable* (sand); shortbread from Normandy with a sandy texture.

SAINT-HONORÉ (m) *Gâteau Saint-Honoré*: flaky pastry cake covered with a *crème Chantilly* or a *crème Chiboust*.

SAVARIN (m) A crown-shaped cake soaked in rum or kirsch; another name for *baba au rhum*.

SOUFFLÉ (m) Puffed-up pudding; *un soufflé au fromage* (a cheese *soufflé*).

TARTE (f) Pastry shell filled with cream or fruits; in England a tart is a fruit pie with a top crust.

TARTELETTE (f) Tartlet; a small tarte.

TARTE TATIN (f) Pie made with caramelized apples and served upside-down. See Short Stories.

SHORT STORIES

BABA AU RHUM This cake was apparently named after Ali Baba, the hero of *Alibaba et les Quarante voleurs* (*Ali Baba and the Forty Thieves*), one of the many stories of the classic *Mille et Une Nuits* (*Thousand and One Nights*), a book that Stanislas Leszcsynski, King of Poland loved to read. While in exile in Lorraine, the King soaked a kugelhopf in syrup of Málaga wine from Spain because he found the cake too dry. *Pourquoi pas* (why not?). After all, the French dip their toasted bread or their *croissant* in their morning bowl of *café au lait*.

The kugelhopf is a specialty of Strasbourg. It was first created in the

1600s in Lemberg, a city called Lviv in Ukraine. The King's creation was called Ali Baba, like the hero of the story he also admired. Later, the wine was replaced by rum and the cake is known today as *baba au rhum*. The cake is called babka in Poland.

BRIOCHE According to the *Larousse Gastronomique*, the word *brioche* first appeared in 1404 and originally would have been made in Brie, a region in the Paris basin, hence *brioche*. However, it is now considered that the word *brioche* derives from *brier*, a Norman word, meaning "to grind;" French for *brier* is *broyer*. *Pain brié*, unsalted bread with a thick crust, is a specialty of Normandy. The best *brioches* are found in the towns of Gourmay-en-Bray and Gisors in Normandy. A *pain brioché* is a type of bread enriched with eggs and sugar.

Today, the French eat *brioche* as a dessert or for breakfast with a bowl of *café au lait*, particularly on Sunday morning. During the French Revolution, a crowd of hungry people marched to Versailles, complaining they had no bread to eat, to which Queen Marie-Antoinette, wife of Louis XVI, replied: "Let them eat *brioche*." The unpopular royal family was nicknamed *Le Boulanger, la Boulangère et le petit mitron* (the baker, the baker's wife and the baker's apprentice). Both the King and Marie-Antoinette died on the *guillotine*.

CRÊPES Simple but delicious, *crêpes* originated in Brittany where they are eaten in small restaurants called *crêperies* where only *crêpes* and *cidre* (apple cider) are served. In France, *crêpes* are traditionally made for *La Chandeleur* (Candlemas), February 2, and *Mardi Gras*, just before *le carême* (Lent).

This is what Anatole France, (1844–1924) French novelist and Nobel Prize laureate (1921) says about them in *Le Temps*: " . . . sprinkled with sugar and eaten hot, they form an exquisite dish. They have a golden hue and are tempting to eat. Thin and transparent like muslin, their edges are trimmed to resemble fine lace. They are so light that after a good dinner, a man from Agen is still willing to sample three or four dozen of them. *Crêpes* form an integral part of every family celebration. Served with white wine, they take pride of place on all joyful occasions."

Crêpes are a specialty of Agen (hence the man from Agen above), a small town on the Garonne River in the Southwest of France. The *pruneaux* (prunes) from Agen also have a worldwide reputation. French people in that region and elsewhere don't turn up their noses to a good *crêpe aux pruneaux* (a *crêpe* with prunes).

CRÊPE SUZETTE Many stories are told about its origin. One of them is that the *crêpes* were named after Mademoiselle Suzette, a French diminutive for Susan (Reichenberg) who was an actress playing a lady's maid at *La Comédie-Française* in 1897. In 1889, a chef by the name of Monsieur Joseph was making delicious *crêpes* in the Restaurant Paillard in Paris. Suzette loved eating them there, so it inspired him to dedicate his *crêpes* without a name to the lovely actress, and this is how they became *crêpes Suzette*. A story that makes good sense and a warming example of French chivalry.

Crêpes Suzette are paper-thin, flavored, and flamed with tangerine and Curaçao liqueur. Curaçao is a name that comes from *curacion*, a Spanish word meaning "cure," a good excuse to smother your *crêpes* with plenty of this exotic elixir to stay alive and well. Curaçao is the largest island in the Netherlands Antilles in the Caribbean Sea; the liqueur is made with *eau-de-vie*, (brandy) sugar, and bitter orange peels.

CROISSANT According to the *Larousse Gastronomique*, the *croissant* originated in Budapest in 1886. The Turks were attacking the city and had to dig underground trails to reach the town center. Bakers who made their bread during the night heard the noise and alerted the authorities. The Turks were defeated and the bakers made a pastry shaped as a crescent in memory of the emblem of the Ottoman flag. In France, this crescent-shaped pastry took the name of *croissant*. *Un café croissant* (coffee with croissant) can be ordered for breakfast and, like *brioche*, it is also dipped in a bowl of *café au lait*.

GALETTE French people eat *la galette des Rois* (Twelfth Night cake), on January 6 to celebrate the Epiphany, The Feast of the Three Kings. A flat bean is put in this traditional puff pastry *galette* and the person who has the piece of cake with the bean in it is king for the day and must choose his queen.

MADELEINE Some say that the name of this shell-shaped pastry comes from Madeleine Paulmier, a nineteenth century French *Cordon Bleu* cook to a rich man in the town of Commercy. On the other hand, the authoritative *Larousse Gastronomique* attributes the name to Jean Avice, a pastry chef in Paris who cooked for Talleyrand, a French diplomat (1754–1838). The *Larousse* also mentions another interesting and romantic story about this pastry. Apparently, in 1755, Stanislaw Leszcynski, Polish king, visited a castle in the town of Commercy in the Meuse province, in eastern France. He was served a cake made by a pretty peasant girl named Madeleine. He loved her pastry so much that he named it after *la belle* Madeleine. Of course, the *petit gâteau* was immediately *en vogue*, and everybody had to have it; they still bake it and love it today.

The *madeleines* were immortalized by Marcel Proust[15] in *A la Recherche du Temps perdu (In Search of Lost Time)*, also known as *Remembrance of Things Past,* published shortly after his death in 1922. Proust has one of his characters say: *"la petite madeleine trempée dans le thé fait revivre, par le rappel d'une saveur oubliée, toute son enfance"* (the little madeleine soaked in tea revives memories of his childhood, by reminding him of a forgotten flavor). This nostalgic French writer felt that one could find contentment and happiness in remembering simple things of the past. All his life, he suffered from chronic asthma and died of pneumonia November 18, 1922.

NAPOLÉON This pastry was not named after *le petit général,* (little general) Napoléon Bonaparte, whose remains have rested at les Invalides in Paris since 1840. The Invalides, *chef-d'oeuvre* of classical architecture, were built under Louis the XIV. It was initially intended to take care of wounded soldiers who had become invalid, hence the name. The *Napoléon* cake was created in Naples and should logically have been called *Napolitain.*

PRALINE This sweet, originally spelled *praslines,* originated in Montargis, a small town in *Bourgogne* (Burgundy), in eastern France. Lassagne (some thought his name was Clément Jaluzot) was a *chef* to the Duc César de Choiseul, Comte of Plessis-Praslin (1598–1675), and it is said that he created this confectionery. However, his helper reportedly is the one who mistakenly dropped pieces of almonds in honey and *voilà,* thanks to him, a new candy was born. This was a lucky error that allowed the Comte of Plessis-Praslin, who was a minister to Louis XIII and Louis XIV, to introduce the candy he loved to the French court. The *gourmandes* of the court liked it also and the confectionery was named *prasline* after him, though he had nothing to do with its invention. He only ate it. But *ainsi va la vie!* Today, the most authentic *pralines* are still sold at the Duc de Praslin by the *Mazet Confiseur et Chocolatier,* the Mazet Confectioner and Chocolate Maker Society.

SAINT-HONORÉ In 1846, pastry chef Chiboust created the *Saint-Honoré* pastry in honor of the Paris district where he worked, and because Saint-Honoré is the patron saint of Pastry *chefs* and bakers.

SAVARIN This cake, also called *brillat-savarin,* is a variation of the *baba au rhum.* It was made by Auguste Julien, a *Maître Pàtissier* who dedicated his creation to Anthelme Brillat-Savarin, famous French gastronome (1755–1826) who once wrote, "The destiny of nations depends upon what and how they eat," in *La Physiologie du Goût,* published in 1826.

TARTE TATIN It was the fate of two sisters, Caroline and Stéphanie Tatin, that they would create this pie in the late 1800s. They owned a restaurant in Lamotte-Beuvron, a small French town, 35 kilometers from Orléans,[16] a city located approximately 115 kilometers south of Paris. The story goes that hunters loved the Tatin sisters' wonderful pies and that they often stopped on their way home to eat a slice with a cup or two of black coffee. Accidents happen, and one day, somebody tripped while carrying a pie to their table. The pastry fell headfirst on the floor. The clumsy person—either Stephanie or Caroline—who had dropped the pie picked it up very quickly, hoping that nobody would notice, and served it upside-down, with the crust on top. Surprise! The hunters liked it so well that the Tatin sisters decided to make it that way from then on. This is how the topsy-turvy pie became known as the delicious and famous *Tarte Tatin.* The original *Tarte Tatin* is still served today at the Hotel Tatin in Lamotte-Beuvron.

FRUITS

An apple a day keeps the doctor away, dreamy idealists say. American cartoonist Jim Davis [17] has a different view on the subject. He wrote in *The Garfield Gazette*, now read worldwide by more than 220 million people, "Avoid fruits and nuts; you are what you eat!" Garfield, Davis's lazy fat cat follows his master's advice. He only eats lasagna, and plenty of it. The word fruit comes from Latin *fructus* meaning "enjoyment." Not only are fruits enjoyable but they are also good sources of vitamin C, fiber, and minerals. Fruits are healthy snacks or great desserts, for, "Every fruit has its secret," said D. H. Lawrence (1885–1930).

Some fruits must have very important secrets indeed. People everywhere believe that they can cure anything from acne to wrinkles. Fruits are exploited for their wonderful anti-aging, skin-scrubbing, toning, and relaxing properties. You want fruits on your head? Spread a Garnier Fructis shampoo on it. Would you like fruits on your walls? Fortunately, artists paint fruits or draw them, just to celebrate and immortalize their beauty; others write poetry and songs that make us appreciate how wonderful and colorful fruits are.

FRENCH LOANWORDS

ANANAS (m) Pineapple; Spanish native fruit.

BIGARREAU (m) Cherry shaped like a pear.

CERISE (f) Cherry.

CITRON (m) A yellow thick-skinned pear-shaped fruit used for its peel in baking. It is grown in Corsica and *Côte d'Azure* (The Riviera), in France.

FRAISE (f) Strawberry; *fraise des bois,* literally, *fraise* of the woods, wild strawberry.

FRAMBOISE (f) Raspberry.

GRENADE (f) *Pomme grenade*: pomegranate.

MIRABELLE (f) A type of yellow plum.

MUSCAT (m) A variety of grapes with a musky smell or taste.

NOIX DE GRENOBLE (f) Walnut from Grenoble, a city in the French Alps, sister city with Phoenix, Arizona, since 1989. *Noix de Grenoble* are grown in an *Appellation d'Origine Contrôlée* (A.O.C.) zone since June 17, 1938. According to the grower, "Three walnuts a day, seven days a week keeps your cholesterol under control."

PRUNELLE (f) A small yellow prune.

REINETTE (f) *Une pomme de reinette*: a type of apple in France, small with dry skin.

HORS-D'OEUVRES

Hors (outside) and *oeuvre* (the works), or main part of a meal. *Hors-d'oeuvres* are appetizers such as snails, *pâté, canapé*, olives, anchovies, cheese on crackers, etc., eaten at the beginning of a meal to whet the appetite, before *la pièce de résistance*, called *le plat de résistance* in France, is served. They are intended to create a festive atmosphere, not to fill the stomach to the point one can no longer eat and enjoy the rest of the meal.

FRENCH LOANWORDS

AMUSE-GUEULE (m) Literally, amuse-mouth: taste-tickler, a colloquial loanword for cocktail snack or munchies; olives, crackers and cheese, *canapés*, served before a meal with an *aperitif. Gueule* is French for the mouth of animals; vulgar for *bouche* (mouth) when speaking about people.

BOUCHÉE (f) A mouthful; from *bouche* (mouth). *Une bouchée à la reine* is a small shell made of flaky pastry and filled with vegetables or chicken in a mushroom sauce, baked and served as hot *entrée*; similar to *vol-au-vent* (see below).

CANAPÉ (m) A small piece of bread or a cracker spread with anchovies, *pâté*, cheese and served as an appetizer, as *hors-d'oeuvres*.

CROQUE-MONSIEUR (m) Toasted ham and cheese between two slices of thin crust bread and served warm as appetizer or as warm *entremets*.

CRUDITÉS (f) Assorted raw vegetables often served as *hors-d'oeuvres*.

ESCARGOTS (m) Snails.

HORS-D'OEUVRE (m) Appetizer.

QUICHE (f) A pie shell filled with *crème fraîche*, eggs, mushrooms, and pieces of ham, and baked until firm. *Une quiche lorraine* (A quiche from the Lorraine region).

VOL-AU-VENT (m) Literally, a fly in the wind, a round light shell of puff pastry whose creation is attributed to Carême; a small *bouchée à la reine*; the *vol-au-vent* various fillings are bound with a sauce; they are served hot as *entrée*.

SHORT STORIES

BOUCHÉE À LA REINE The first *bouchée à la reine* was made by Marie Leszcyinska, (1703–1768). Apparently, she had a good appetite for food and for life. She was the daughter of Stanislas Leszcynski, King of Poland. In 1725, she married Louis XV with whom she had ten children.

QUICHE LORRAINE The name *quiche* comes from *Küche*, a German word meaning pie. A *quiche* was a dish made in the provinces of Lorraine and

Alsace, in eastern France, as early as the sixteenth century. The crust was originally made with bread dough that is replaced today by a *pâte brisée*.

ESCARGOT Not much fun to be one when a chef decides to put you on the menu. He will make you starve for five or six days; then he will season you with garlic and herbs, throw you alive in boiling water or a *bouillon* and serve you as *hors-d'oeuvre*. You will delight his customers who are most likely unaware of the ordeal you had to endure. Indeed, you poor slow creatures, you eat plants all day, and since some may be poisonous and therefore kill people, something must be done to remove the poison out of your slimy body. One way of getting rid of it is to clean it out of you by making you fast and torturing you.

Bon appétit to escargots lovers, if you can still swallow them.

MEATS AND FISH

> "I have always eaten animal flesh
> with a somewhat guilty conscience,"
> admitted Albert Einstein.

Einstein is not the only one. Since the dawn of time, people everywhere felt that it was a crime to eat the flesh of animals. In ancient Egyptian mythology, for example, animism prevailed. People believed that animals had souls, and they worshipped animals. The bull Apis, for instance, was revered because it incarnated Ptah, the first god of all gods, the "Creator" of the world and all that was in it.

Jean Jacques Rousseau (1712–1778) [18] also wrote, "Greater eaters of meat are in general more cruel and more ferocious than other men." And William Shakespeare (1564–1616) felt the same way about it a century earlier. "He is a heavy eater of beef. Methinks it doth harm to his wit" (*Twelfth Night*). Meat lovers will shrug their shoulders, but everybody is entitled to his opinion. Nevertheless, if you are among those who will not eat meat for whatever reason, be content to learn the vocabulary below to understand what your carnivorous friends are talking about when they tell you they have enjoyed a wonderful *pâté en croûte*, or devoured the best *blanquette de veau* ever.

FRENCH LOANWORDS

ANDOUILLE (f) Sausage made with pork or veal intestines.

ANDOUILLETTE (f) Small *andouille* made with chitterlings, with tripes—the entrails.

BLANQUETTE (f) A dish of white meat and white sauce. *Une blanquette de veau* (a veal casserole).

BOEUF BOURGUIGNON (m) A casserole of beef cooked in red *Bourgogne* (Burgundy) wine.

CANARD (m) Duck; *canard à l'orange*. *Canard* is also a loanword for hoax or false report; it is slang for newspaper in French.

CHARCUTERIE (f) Ham, cold meat.

CHÂTEAUBRIAND (m) A steak *à la Châteaubriand*: thick tenderloin cut of beef into which a pocket is cut and filled with seasoning before being grilled.

CHAUD-FROID (m) Literally, hot-cold; pieces of meat, beef, or poultry, prepared on a hot stove but served cold as *entrée*, usually coated with a brown or white sauce.

CIVET (m) Stew of hare, rabbit, venison, and other animals cooked with onions and red wine; a *ragoût*. Civet (civetcat) is also defined as a cat-like animal of Central Africa in English dictionaries.

COQ AU VIN (m) Chicken cooked in wine, a dish probably prepared with a young *coq* (rooster). *Le coq gaulois* (Gallic cockerel) is one of France's emblems. *Gallus* is Latin for *coq* and for *Gaulle*, hence *coq gaulois*, symbol of the French fighting spirit. France was originally called *La Gaulle*. See Introduction under *How the French Language Evolved*. A *girouette* (weather vane) shaped as a *coq* (weathercock) can be seen on many church steeples or monuments in France. *Le coq du village* (the local Casanova), is the *fanfaron*, the boaster of the village, the *"m'as-tu vu"* (the have you seen me) as the French also say.

COQUILLE ST. JACQUES (f) Scallop.

CROUSTADE (f) A hollowed piece of bread filled with seafood or other ingredients. *Une croustade de homard* (a lobster croustade).

ENTRECÔTE (f) Literally, between ribs: *entre* (between) and *côtes* (ribs); boned prime quality rib steak.

ESTOUFFADE (f) Also spelled *étouffade*: a dish of meat cooked slowly with little liquid in a close recipient.

FILET DE BOEUF (m) A tenderloin.

FILET MIGNON (m) A tender cut of beef, usually served with mushrooms.

FRICASSÉE (f) A fricassee; meat stew.

GALANTINE (f) A dish of poultry, or *charcuterie* served cold in jelly, in *gélatine*.

GIGOT (m) Leg of lamb, or mutton.

GRILLADE (f) Grilled meat.

HACHIS (m) Hash; minced meat; a *hachis Parmentier*; see *Pommes frites* under Short Stories.

LANGOUSTE (f) Spiny lobster; a crawfish.

LANGOUSTINE (f) Norway lobster.

LARD (m) Lard; bacon.

LARDON (m) Pig's fat used in larding; *Une omelette aux lardons* (omelet with small pieces of lard). *Gros lardon* (fat slob) to a fat person; *petit lardon* (little brat) to a child.

MATELOTE (f) Also spelled *matelotte*, fish stew seasoned with red or white wine.

MÉDAILLON (m) A small, flat round or oval cut of meat.

MOULE (f) Mussel.

NAVARIN (m) A casserole of mutton or lamb with vegetables.

NOISETTE (f) A small, round piece of meat; *noisette* is also French for hazelnut.

NOIX (f) *Noix de veau* (a piece of veal cut from the rump).

ORTOLAN (m) Bunting; *ortolan* bunting; a rare bird officially protected in France; a delicacy that some people eat with Roquefort cheese.

PÂTÉ (m) Minced meat seasoned with herbs.

PÂTÉ DE CAMPAGNE (m) Country *pâté*; a coarse *pâté*.

PÂTÉ DE FOIE GRAS (m) Rich liver *pâté* made with fattened goose liver.

PÂTÉ EN CROÛTE (m) Pâté in crust, *pâté* baked in a puff pastry case.

PÂTÉ MAISON (m) *Pâté* made with the recipe of a particular *maison* (house) a particular restaurant.

PAUPIETTE (f) Minced meatballs; *paupiettes de veau* (thin slices of veal, stuffed, rolled, and baked); *paupiettes de veau* are also called *alouettes sans tête* (larks without heads).

PISSALADIÈRE (f) A Provençal open tart; a *tarte niçoise*, a dish garnished with onions, anchovies, and black olives; from Nice, a city in southern France.

POT-AU-FEU (m) Beef stew with vegetables.

POULE AU POT (f) A boiled chicken in a pot.

POULET (m) Chicken; *poulet rôti* (roasted chicken).

QUENELLE (f) Fried ball of minced chicken, veal, or fish, mixed with egg and bread crumbs.

RAGOÛT (m) A meat stew with vegetables.

RATATOUILLE (f) *Ratatouille niçoise* (a Provençal dish from Nice), a type of stew made with eggplants, zucchini, tomatoes, and onions cooked with olive oil.

RÉMOULADE (f) Spicy sauce, a *sauce piquante*, served with cold dish.

RILLETTES (f) *Pâté* made of seasoned minced pork, goose, or chicken.

RISSOLE (f) Minced meat or fish mixed with egg and bread crumbs and fried in a roll of flaky pastry.

RÔTI (m) Roasted meat.

ROULADE (f) Stuffed, rolled beef or fish.

SAUCISSE (f) Cured sausage; *saucisson*, a big *saucisse* already cooked, as in Salami *saucisson*.

TERRINE (f) A kind of coarse-textured *pâté* served in a *terrine* (a tureen).

TIMBALE (f) Minced meat, or pasta served in a *timbale* mould.

TOURNEDOS (m) Thick cut from a fillet of beef.

TOURTIÈRE (f) A kind of meat pie with a crust on top and filled with meat, a specialty of Québec, Canada.

TRIPES (f. pl.) Entrails; See: *à la mode de Caen* under Culinary Expressions.

TRUITE AU BLEU (f) Literally, trout in the blue: poached trout, a trout cooked with vinegar giving the fish a bluish color.

SHORT STORIES

CHÂTEAUBRIAND Chef Montmireil created this recipe in 1822, in honor of François René, Vicomte de Châteaubriand (1768–1848), a French writer and France's ambassador to England. Apparently, the steak was served to him for the first time at the French Embassy in London, but le Vicomte also ate it frequently at the Ritz where he owned an estate in the town of Ritz.

The Ritz is a luxurious and renowned chain of hotels founded by the Swiss Cesar Ritz (1850–1918). In Paris, the Ritz Hotel was designed by famed architect Jules Hardouin Mansard, who gave his name to Roof Mansard at the hotel. There is also the Hemingway Bar, named after the well-known writer who was an *habitué* at the Ritz. When Châteaubriand ate there, he would have a thick slice of tenderloin served to him with a *sauce Béarnaise*. Today, the steak is known as a steak *à la châteaubriand,* also spelled *châteaubriant,* from the town of Châteaubriant in the Loire Valley where the Vicomte owned another estate.

A TRUE FISH STORY Louis XIV liked to be entertained and to eat well. One day in April 1671, Prince of Condé invited him at his castle in

Chantilly. The *Roi Soleil* [19] and his *entourage* arrived at the Prince's mansion and festivities that were to last three days began. Chef François Vatel (1635–1671) was in charge of the menus and naturally, he wanted everything to be perfect. Honor is as sacred to a chef as it is to a soldier. Everything was going according to plan until the fish did not show. What was Vatel to do if the fish he had ordered was not delivered on time? The shame would be too much to bear. He became distraught and retired to his room, took his sword—not a kitchen knife *s'il vous plait*—a sword! The desperate man planted the weapon in the bedroom door and *toro!* He threw himself upon it. The fish was delivered a bit later, but Vatel would never know. He had impaled himself on the lethal instrument and died.

Madame De Sévigné (1626–1696), notorious *femme de lettres*, tells about his death in *Belles Lettres*, in a letter dated April 24, 1671. The Marquise de Sévigné, *née* Marie de Rabutin-Chantal wrote many letters about the mores of her time, especially to her daughter Madame de Grignan (1646–1705).

GIGOT The name *gigot* comes from French *gigue* (leg), an ancient musical instrument having a leg shape (*Larousse Dictionary*). A *gigot d'agneau*, (a leg of spring lamb) is a traditional meal in many French homes on Easter Sunday. Most French meat-eaters like it roasted medium rare and flavored with garlic. Lambs that are fattened in the *prés-salés* (salted meadows) near the Bay of Mont Saint Michel have a particular flavor appreciated by *gigot* lovers. Mont-Saint-Michel is a tourist islet, a famous landmark in the Manche district in France, where the Benedictine monks founded a prestigious abbey in 966, visited by tourists from everywhere.

PÂTÉ DE FOIE GRAS "Where ignorance is bliss, 'tis folly to be wise," wrote Thomas Gray (1716–1771).

This English poet's message in *Ode on a Distant Prospect of Eton College* (1742) is that it is sometimes better for a man to be blissfully ignorant of his fate. When it comes to how *pâté de foie gras* is made, it is perhaps wise to be ignorant, or one may stop eating it.

A barbaric technique is used to fatten the poor geese. Three times a day, hungry or not, the neck of the unfortunate creature is held and food is crammed into its gullet. The purpose of this uncivilized force-feeding technique is to enlarge the goose liver that is then used to make a *pâté de foie; gras* (fat) indeed! Goose liver *pâté* was very much appreciated by the Egyptians, the Romans, the Gauls, and today, by anybody who can eat it on French bread, *canapés,* or crackers as *hors-d'oeuvres.*

POULE AU POT The term is attributed to Henri IV, King of France (1589–1610) who it is said, spoke the famous words, "If God grants me a longer life, I will see that no peasant in my kingdom will lack the means to have a *une poule au pot tous les dimanches* (a hen in the pot) every Sunday," a tradition observed by many French, particularly in the country.

SAUCES

> "Woe to the cook whose sauce has no
> sting," declared Geoffrey Chaucer.

A good *saucier* quickly learns that a sauce can make or break a dish. As
Fernand Point (1897–1955), the father of *nouvelle cuisine*, knowingly stated
it in his cookbook *Ma Gastronomie*, "It is the sauce that distinguishes a good
chef, and the *Saucier* is a soloist in the orchestra of a great kitchen." What an
orchestra it can be when one thinks that there are more sauces than there
are days in a year. Most of them, however, are made from two basic sauces:
a brown and a white one. A few are listed below for the ambitious cook who
may as well listen to singer/comic Totie Fields's sensible conclusion, "I've been
on a diet for two weeks, and all I have lost is two weeks!" So, savor your
good homemade *béchamel, béarnaise,* your delicious *sauce hollandaise,* and a
rich *sauce au beurre noir.* They taste good and, eaten with moderation, can
do no harm.

FRENCH LOANWORDS

BÉARNAISE (f) *Sauce béarnaise; une béarnaise* is a thick butter sauce made
with egg yolks and wine, seasoned with tarragon, chervil, and ground white
pepper.

BÉCHAMEL (f) *Sauce béchamel; une béchamel* is a fine white sauce made of
cream, butter, and flour.

BEURRE NOIR (m) *Sauce au beurre noir* is made with butter melted until
it is brown.

GALANTINE (f) Sauce for fish and fowl; jellied meat.

HOLLANDAISE (f) *Sauce hollandaise* is made with butter, egg yolks, and lemon juice.

MARINADE (f) Mixture made with vinegar, wine, oil, herbs, and spices in which the meat is soaked before cooking to tenderize the meat and improve its flavor.

MAYONNAISE (f) Creamy salad dressing. The French still prefer their homemade mayonnaise to the store-bought variety.

MOUSSELINE (f) *Sauce mousseline* is a *sauce hollandaise* with whipped cream.

PIQUANTE (f) *Sauce piquante;* from *piquer* (to prick, to sting); a sauce stimulating to the taste.

POULETTE (f) *Sauce poulette* is made with butter, eggs, and lemon juice.

RAVIGOTE (f) *Vinaigrette* with a mixture of chopped chervil, chives, tarragon, and shallots.

RÉMOULADE (f) A type of spicy mayonnaise with mustard and herbs served as salad dressing.

ROUX (m) A mixture of browned flour with melted butter used to thicken sauces, soups, or gravies; *roux* (russet color); *un roux* (a red-haired man); *une rousse* (red-haired woman).

SOUBISE (f) *Sauce soubise* is a white onion sauce; the sauce is often served with eggs. From Charles de Rohan, prince of Soubise (1715–1787).

SUPRÊME (f) *Sauce suprême* is a rich cream sauce and a dish of meat served in this sauce.

TARTARE (f) *Sauce Tartare* is a mayonnaise with hard-boiled egg yolks, onions, and chives.

VELOUTÉ (m) A rich sauce of white stock, chicken or veal, thickened with a white *roux*.

VINAIGRETTE (f) French dressing made with vinegar, oil, and seasoning. À *la vinaigrette* or *en vinaigrette* (in vinaigrette).

SHORT STORIES

BÉARNAISE Why is the sauce called *béarnaise*? One theory is that the sauce takes its name from the Béarn region in France where Viscount of Béarn, future King Henri IV of France, was born. Another explanation is that the sauce was named after Lisette Béarnaise, his mistress. One thing is sure, *bons vivants* everywhere agree that a good *Béarnaise* is delicious with steaks, grilled fish, or chicken, whether it was named after Lisette or not.

BÉCHAMEL Chef François de la Varenne (1615–1678) is said to have created this basic "mother of white sauces" made with flour, boiled milk, and butter. He was a court *chef* during King Louis XIV's reign and dedicated the sauce to Marquis Louis de Béchamel (1630–1703), apparently, a handsome *gourmet* and art lover. Some are sure that it was Béchamel himself who created the sauce.

Béchamel was a financier who was also a steward of Louis XIV (1643–1715), whose stomach was found to be twice the size of a normal stomach when he died. The king may have been a glutton, but he could see the value in eating good food served with good sauces.

SOUPS

*"Je vis de bonne soupe et non de beau
langage."* (It's good food and not fine
words that keeps me alive.)

—Molière (1622–1673)
in *Le Bourgeois Gentilhomme*

Molière may have meant it literally that it was good soup that kept him
alive; after all he was French. In France, particularly *à la campagne,* a meal
is not a meal if it does not begin with a hearty soup. In some families, soup
is the main course, sometimes the only course of a meal. To many French
potage lovers, soup is *un plat* national (a national dish). They are not the
only ones to feel that way. In some restaurants in Guatemala, for instance,
black bean soup is the "national soup."

Gustave Flaubert did not seem to be fond of soup, however. One day
when he must have been in a bad mood, perhaps when he was writing *Madame Bovary* (1857), he said, "What an awful thing life is. It's like soup with
lots of hairs floating on the surface. You have to eat it nevertheless." Flaubert
lived in the old days, when French people used to say to their children, *"Si tu ne
manges pas ta soupe, tu ne vas pas grandir,"* a bribery meaning, "If you do not eat
your soup, you will not grow up."

Is soup the secret to being big and tall? No one would be taken aback to
read an article in the front page of *Le Figaro,*[20] informing curious French people
that, "According to a recent study, a surprising number of Frenchmen never
ate their Mama's soup." The survey, conducted by a group of researchers from

Berkeley, California, who spent one year in France enjoying *baguette, Camembert,* and *vin rouge,* also concluded that, "If given a choice, French children will eat *Petit Lu biscuits* and *bonbons au chocolat,* rather than *soupe à l'oignon.*"

FRENCH LOANWORDS

BISQUE (f) *Bisque de homard* (lobster bisque) is a thick, rich soup made with lobster meat or other shellfish, especially crabs.

BOUILLABAISSE (f) Dish made with fish and tomatoes, seasoned with spices and served with slices of bread.

BOUILLON (m) A clear broth, beef or chicken.

BOUILLON CUBE (m) A small concentrated stock used to make *bouillon.*

CONSOMMÉ (m) A clear soup made by boiling meat in water.

JULIENNE (f) A soup made with vegetables cut *à la julienne,* shaped like small sticks.

LA SOUPE DU JOUR (f) Soup on today's menu.

MADRILÈNE (f) *Consommé à la madrilène* is a clear soup usually served cold; Madrid style.

POTAGE (m) A thick soup made of vegetables; *le jardin potager* (vegetable garden).

SOUPE (f) Soup.

SOUPE À L'OIGNON (f) Onion soup; in some parts of France, people *à la campagne* used to eat a *soupe à l'oignon* for breakfast; some still do.

SOUPE PRINTANIÈRE (f) Made with spring vegetables. From *printemps* (spring).

VELOUTÉ (m) A creamy *potage,* such as *un velouté de champignons* (a cream of mushrooms); *un velouté d'asperges* (a cream of asparagus).

VICHYSSOISE (f) A thick cream soup of potatoes, leeks, and cream, often served cold; it takes its name from Vichy, a town in France in the department of Allier.

SHORT STORIES

BISQUE The word *bisque* comes from the Spanish province of Vizcaya that gave its name to the Bay of Biscay, where a dish made of spiced boiled meat or game was named *bisque.* Later on, crayfish became the principal ingredient of this dish that is often used to make a delicious, creamy fish soup.

SOUPE À L'OIGNON Since the Middle Ages, bistros in Paris were known for serving onion soup, very early in the morning, to the workers of les Halles or to visitors. Up to 1969, les Halles were colorful marketplaces in central Paris where wholesale food retailers were doing business. Les Halles have been moved to Rungis, in the outskirts of Paris.

BOUILLABAISSE Waterfront cafés in Marseille, in the south of France, are known for serving great *bouillabaisse,* a dish that dates back to antiquity. It is said that Venus made some sort of fish soup to feed Vulcan, her husband, so that he would fall asleep while she would spend time with Mars, the other man. It was thought that fish and herbs, especially saffron, could be used as soporific. *La bouillabaisse marseillaise* is the authentic *bouillabaisse* and originated in Massalia known as Marseille, (also spelled Marseilles), a city founded by the Greeks in 600 B.C. Fishermen in this beautiful port on the

Mediterranean Sea, west of the French Riviera, made this simple but tasty soup with a variety of fish to feed their family.

VEGETABLES

Légume is French for vegetable and *une grosse légume* is a bigwig. The French words *légumineuse* or *légumineux* are translated as legume and leguminous in English. For instance, *un petit pois* is *un légumineux* (masculine), in other words a *petit pois* is a leguminous, or a legume; *un haricot* is *une plante légumineuse* (feminine), that is, a *haricot,* is a leguminous plant. Confused in *petit pois* land?

Vegetable eaters are logically called vegetarians, a term that has been used for a while since apparently, Russian author Leo Tolstoy (1828–1910) claimed to be one. Some people, however, are scared of veggies eaters. What is music to some ears is cacophony to others. It is reported that Irish dramatist George Bernard Shaw (1856–1950) cancelled an invitation to a vegetarian gala. In retrospect his excuse was, "The thought of two thousand people crunching celery at the same time horrified me!" Interesting phobia.

Vegan, raw-foodist, and fruitarian are relatively newer words that reflect a trend followed religiously by people who have strong convictions about what they must eat to stay alive and well.

Not surprisingly, fruitarians eat fruits only, vegetarians eliminate all meat and fish from their diet; vegans not only cut all meats but all animal products from their menus as well, and that includes dairy, eggs, and gelatin. Fanatic vegans do not wear leather, silk, wool, or fur items. Naturally, raw foodists restrict themselves to *crudités*.

According to *Runner's World* magazine, most people are primarily flexitarians. A new word? Not to the Vegetarian Resource Group, a nonprofit veggie think tank based in Baltimore, Maryland, who concluded that, "Only two to three percent of Americans are strict vegetarians and 40 percent of us are flexitarians." In other words, most of us are "meat-eaters who dabble in vegetarianism." [21] This seems to concur with another survey made Somewhere by Somebody who determined that the average American devours an incredible amount of animal flesh in his lifetime. These carnivorous would eat more than ten cows, thirty pigs, ninety turkeys, and 2,200 chickens, not counting a thousand fish or so. Regardless of their denomination, vegetarians and the like all believe that *petits pois, aubergine, macédoine,* and many of the green leafy vegetables give the body optimal nutrition. Naturally and luckily for all, plant foods have protein, fiber, and a variety of micronutrients that we need to stay healthy. So, *vivent les legumes* (long life to veggies)!

FRENCH LOANWORDS

AUBERGINE (f) Eggplant; often used in Eastern and Mediterranean dishes such as *ratatouille* and *moussaka,* a Greek dish made with *aubergines,* minced meat, onions, tomato paste, and cooked in an oven.

CHAMPIGNON (m) Common mushroom.

CHANTERELLE (f) A wild yellow tasty mushroom, known also as *girolle* in France. This funnel-shaped mushroom is picked between June and October in coniferous forests.

CHOUCROUTE (f) Pickled cabbage; from German sauerkraut, similar to French *chou* (cabbage).

FRISÉE (f) *Chicorée frisée* (curly chicory) used in salad.

HARICOT (m) A bean; a leguminous plant.

MACÉDOINE (f) Salad of mixed fruits or vegetables cut in small pieces.

MANGE-TOUT (m) Literally, eat-all: a bean or pea eaten with the pods; also called sugar pea or sugar snap.

PETITS POIS (m) Also spelled *petits-pois* (with a hyphen), small green peas.

POMME (f) Short for *pomme de terre*, literally, apple of the earth (potato); *pommes frites*, or *frites* are French fries. In English a turnip is also called *pomme blanche*; *navet* is French for turnip.

RATATOUILLE (f) Vegetable dish made with *aubergines, courgettes*, tomatoes, and onions in olive oil.

ROMAINE (f) Lettuce with long leaves; romaine lettuce.

SALADE NIÇOISE (f) Made with tomatoes, hard-boiled eggs, and olives seasoned with olive oil and vinegar; the way it is made in Nice, town in the south of France.

TOPINAMBOUR (m) Jerusalem artichoke; a kind of sunflower with tubercles resembling potatoes that can be eaten as a vegetable.

SHORT STORIES

MACÉDOINE The name for this dish, made of a variety of fruits or vegetables, comes from Macedonia, the Empire of Alexander the Great, King of Macedon whose country was inhabited by people of various origins.

POMMES FRITES As O. Henry [22] (1862–1910) wrote in his weekly *Rolling Stones* magazine, "Our countries are great friends; we have given you Lafayette and French fried potatoes." However, some experts in the *pommes frites* origin may disagree because they are convinced that French fries were first made in Belgium. So be it, but assuming that America did not get the *frites* they consume at a rate of more than 5 billion pounds a year from the French, our two countries can still be great friends since they share, among other things, Lafayette, the Statue of Liberty, and Montesquieu. [23]

The word potato comes from *batata*, the Aravak Indian name for a vegetable that used to be cursed as evil poisonous food when it was first introduced in Europe in the 1590s. Today, food experts have established the potato as a nutritious and delicious vegetable that is rich in vitamin C, in many of the B vitamins, in iron, and above all, fat-free—a sacrosanct requirement today. It is also a good source of fiber if eaten with the skin.

The word *batata* became *patata* in Spanish, *potato* in English, and *patate* in colloquial French. As the French will say of a stupid person, "*Quelle patate!*" Literally, "What a potato," meaning, "What an idiot!" In Québec, the word *patates frites* is often used instead of *frites* or *pommes frites*.

In India, they have more respect for this versatile vegetable; they call it *alu*, a jack-of-all-trades. In Russia, and other countries, this amazing tuber is a second bread, the stuff of life for many people. Indians worshipped potato spirits and made pottery shaped as potatoes. Americans eat them in any shape, form, and quantity but they are not alone. The potato is served at almost every French meal. Naturally, Americans advertise their "made-in-America" potatoes and promote them any way they can imagine.

Idaho owes its international reputation as the Potato State to J. R. "Jack" Simplot, the potato king who proudly drove his Lincoln Continental displaying a very visible MR SPUD license plate. The colloquial word *spud* comes from the small spade that is used to dig the potato out of the ground.

Another creative and enterprising American by the name of Thomas

Hughes founded a Potato Museum on Capitol Hill in Washington, D.C., in 1983. The museum is now located in New Mexico, where Tom and his wife Meredith live. Anyone can make an appointment to visit the museum and look at some of the potato artifacts these two American *entrepreneurs* have collected over the years, as well as learn about the amazing history and properties of a vegetable misunderstood for too long, and underestimated and unappreciated by too many. Apparently, Protestants would not touch this evil, poisonous food because the word *potato* was not mentioned anywhere in the Bible. On the other hand, hungry Catholics resolved the problem by sprinkling the potatoes with holy water before eating them. *Nécessité fait loi* (necessity knows no law).

The International Potato Center founded in 1971, also known as CIP (its Spanish acronym), is situated in La Molina, outside Lima's capital of Peru where wild potatoes were cultivated at altitudes as high as 14,000 feet. The Center employs scientists in twenty-five countries and promotes the valuable *pomme de terre* (apple of the earth) as a means of fighting malnutrition worldwide. Unsurprisingly, it was the French who established the potato as a *gourmet* food. Antoine Augustin Parmentier (1737–1813) was a French pharmacist who was taken prisoner during the Seven Years War (1756–1763) and survived on potatoes while in prison in Hamburg, Germany. When this French army officer came back home, he managed to introduce the potato to Louis XVI and Marie-Antoinette who began to eat potatoes instead of cake. The queen even wore a bouquet of potato blossoms in her hair. Naturally, the potato entered the French cuisine. The *hachis* [24] *Parmentier* is not a *gourmet* dish, of course; it is a sensible way of using leftover meat. In *hachis Parmentier*, hashed meats are covered with mashed potato and baked in the oven.

Apparently, *pommes frites* first appeared in Paris in the 1840s but as mentioned previously, Belgium also claims that the idea of frying slices of potatoes in a pot of oil is theirs. All the same, *pommes frites* became a fast-food staple in the United States one hundred years later. Thomas Jefferson reportedly served them in the White House, though some believe it was American soldiers who were stationed in France and in Belgium during the First World War who brought back the fashion of eating them in America after enjoying them overseas. Regardless of whose idea it was and who made them first, Americans have eaten them ever since in astonishing quantities at McDonald's, Burger King, and Wendy's among other places.

MISCELLANEOUS FRENCH LOANWORDS

According to Talleyrand, a perfect cup of café should be:

"*Noir comme le diable*	"Black as the devil
Chaud comme l'enfer	Hot as the inferno
Pur comme un ange	Pure as an angel
Doux comme l'amour"	Mellow as love"

In the province of Kaffa in Ethiopia, there was a goatherder named Kaldi. One day, he saw his goats gamboling and prancing around a green bush laden with shiny red berries. Curious and daring, he ate a few. Soon after, frolicking and caracoling, he joined the goats' merry party. On his way home, he shared his exciting discovery with the monks. Monks are *bons vivants* and practical. They need to stay awake and alert to pray, make cheese and wine, and *enluminures*. So they, too, tested the devilish beans, throwing them in boiling water to make a brew that is now guzzled day and night worldwide, except perhaps in China, the land of tea drinkers.

Before drinking a *kahwah* (Arabic for coffee), people used to chew, rather than infuse, coffee beans because of their invigorating effects. Today, we buy chocolate-covered coffee beans to get the same results. "The more things change, the more they are the same."

Another coffee with a worldwide reputation is the Yemen Mocha that took its name from Mocha, a port city on the Red Sea in Yemen. Its exportation has decreased, but Mocha coffee is still processed today in Yemen as it was centuries ago. Brazil is the largest coffee producer.

Some people cannot live without coffee. "Without my morning coffee, I am like a dried up piece of roast goat," said the lovely—she had to be lovely—Lieshen in *Coffee Cantata (Kaffe Kantate)*, composed by Johann Sebastian Bach in the early 1730s. (See *Coffee Cantata* under Short Stories).

The French cannot wake up without their bowl of *café au lait* for *le petit déjeuner* (breakfast). They dip bread or *croissant* in it, and life begins. They often have un *café noir* after dinner, but of course they also have a *petit verre* after eating a *chiffonnade*, an *estouffade* with *fines herbes*, a *fricassée*, or *fruits de mer*. A *poussse-café* is a must after their last cup of *café bio* (abbreviation for *biologique*), a coffee grown without pesticides and fertilizer.

The French may drink a *café décaféiné* (decaf) before bedtime but during the day they prefer *un café noir*, also called *un petit noir* (black coffee). There are many places where they can stop to enjoy it in France: at a *café-restaurant, a café-bar, a café-tabac* (place where one can purchase cigarettes and read the daily newspapers), or at a *café-concert*, a music hall where the public can drink coffee and smoke. In a *café-théâtre*, coffee and beverages are served during a play in a live theater.

FRENCH LOANWORDS

ASSIETTE (f) *Assiette anglaise*, a platter of assorted cold meats; cold cuts. The term *assiette froide* (cold plate) is also used in France.

BAGUETTE (f) Bread shaped like a rod; *baguette* is also French for "stick" or "wand" as in *une baguette magique* (a magic wand).

BANQUET (m) An elaborate meal to celebrate an important event.

BOUQUET GARNI (m) A bunch of assorted herbs such as thyme and laurel for flavoring.

CAFÉ AU LAIT (m) Coffee with milk.

CAFÉ CRÈME (m) Coffee with cream; the French also call it *un cappuccino* as in the U.S.

CAFÉ LIÉGEOIS (m) Coffee or chocolate ice cream topped with *crème Chantilly* and served in a tall glass.

CAFÉ NOIR (m) Black coffee; also called *un noir* in France.

CHIFFONNADE (f) A dish made with shredded lettuce, raw or cooked in butter, and seasoned with chervil.

CHOUCROUTE (f) Sauerkraut; pickled cabbage.

CORNICHON (m) A tiny, sour, pickled cucumber.

COURT-BOUILLON (m) A seasoned stock made with water, vegetables, and wine (or vinegar) in which a fish is boiled.

CROQUETTE (f) *Des croquettes de pommes de terre* (potato *croquettes*) are small balls of paste mixed with mashed potatoes or chopped meat or vegetables, dipped in egg yolk, sprinkled with flour and deep-fried.

CROUSTADE (f) Hollowed bread or pastry with a filling.

CROÛTE (f) Crust, as in bread crust.

CROÛTON (m) Pieces of toasted or fried bread served with soup or salad.

CUISINE (f) Cookery as an art: *haute cuisine; nouvelle cuisine.*

DÉJEUNER (f) Lunch, as in *Déjeuner sur l'herbe* (1862), a painting by Edouard Manet (1832–1883).

DEMI-TASSE (f) A cup of small size for after-dinner black coffee. In *Normandie*, a *demi-tasse* is *un petit calva*, half-coffee, half-alcohol in a little *tasse* (cup); *calva* is short for *Calvados* (see under Liquors and Aperitifs).

DU JOUR (m) *Soupe du jour* is the soup the chef made for that particular day; not to confuse with *le couple du jour*, (the celebrity pair) everybody talks about in *le tout* New York.

ENTRÉE (f) A dish served after *hors-d'oeuvres* and before the main meat course; in America the *entrée* is the main course of a meal. The words *Entrée* or *Hors-d'oeuvre* appears on some French menus, indicating that you can order one or the other. For some people, both words have become synonymous, however; apparently many French people now eliminate one course to make life simpler. See "Short Stories, *A la française*" under Culinary Expressions.

FARCE (f) Stuffing; *tomates farcies* are stuffed tomatoes.

FINES HERBES (f) Fresh mixed herbs such as parsley, tarragon, chervil, and chives used in cooking.

FONDUE (f) A dish made with cheese such as *gruyère*, melted with white wine and eaten with small pieces of bread; *fondue* originated in Switzerland.

FRUITS DE MER (m) Literally, fruits of the sea; seafood.

GALANTINE (f) *De la galantine*: jelly from a mold of veal, chicken or other white meats boned, seasoned, boiled, and served cold in its own jelly.

GLACÉ Glazed, as *fruits glacés* (glazed fruits).

GRATIN (m) Topping of breadcrumbs and cheese; macaroni *au gratin* (macaroni and cheese).

GRATINÉ A dish cooked with a topping of breadcrumbs and/or grated cheese.

NATURE Plain.

OEUFS EN COCOTTE (m) Eggs in a cocotte: eggs and butter baked and served in individual *cocottes* or ramekins. In France, some people add *crème fraîche* and cheese to the eggs.

PAIN PERDU (m) Literally, lost bread: yesterday's bread soaked in eggs, sweetened and cooked in a frying pan.

PETIT PAIN (m) A small bread roll.

PETIT VERRE (m) A glass of liqueur.

PIÈCE DE RÉSISTANCE (f) In English, principal dish of a meal. In France people say: *le plat de résistance,* or *le plat principal.*

PLAT DU JOUR (m) Dish of the day; a specific dish featured on a restaurant's menu for a particular day.

POURBOIRE (m) A tip.

POUSSE-CAFÉ (m) After dinner liqueur, just after coffee; from *pousser* (to push). The term *chasse café (Webster's)* is not used in France; it is a literal translation of *chasser,* to chase the café.

PRIX FIXE (m) A meal consisting of several courses served at a total fixed price; opposite of *à la carte.*

RACLETTE (f) Cheese *raclé* (scrapped) and melted before an open fire; the soft melted part is eaten with bread or potatoes.

RÔTI (m) Roasted as in *poulet rôti* (roasted chicken), *un rôti* is a roast as in *rôti de boeuf* (roast beef).

TABLE D'HÔTE (f) Originally, a common table for guests at a hotel or restaurant. Today, a set menu at a hotel or restaurant served at a fixed hour and fixed price.

TISANE (f) An herbal tea.

SHORT STORIES

COFFEE CANTATA [25] Johann Sebastian Bach (1685–1750) composed mostly religious music, but he wrote Cantata No. 211, a satirical piece of music about Herr Schlendrian who promises to find a husband for Lieshen, his lovely daughter, if she pledges to give up coffee. But, as much as she wants a husband, Lieshen cannot give up, and will not give up, her coffee. Surely, many of us can relate. Name one chocoholic who can stop eating chocolate, the irresistible "food of the gods." The Theobroma cacao is a common cacao small tree, native to South America; Theobroma derives from the Greek *theos* god, and *broma* food, hence chocolate is "the food of the gods."

Below, is the aria to her favorite brew, Lieshen Aria:
"Mm. How sweet the coffee tastes
more delicious than a thousand kisses
mellower than muscatel wine
Coffee, coffee I must have
And if someone wishes to give me a treat,
Ah, then pour me out some coffee!"

WINES

Historical figures the world over agree on one thing—the virtues of wine. As most French will tell you with conviction, because they are taught early that to be happy you must keep a *juste-milieu* in everything you do, "Wine in moderation never did anyone any harm and many a great deal of good."

Napoléon, *le petit Général* (his nickname because, like most Frenchmen, he was not very tall) was practical about it: "*Pas de vin, pas de soldats*" (No wine, no soldiers).

Any *bon vivant* is likely to agree with Martin Luther's free spirited opinion: "He who loves not women, wine and song, remains a fool his whole life long."

Apparently, Luther (1483–1546), an ex-Augustine friar, had found a new calling.

And those who enjoy the moment and think later will gladly follow Byron's advice: "Let us have wine and women, mirth and laughter, sermons and soda-water the day after."

But of course, there are those who condemn such wicked philosophy because the Koran teaches that, "There is a devil in every berry of the grape." *Chacun son goût.*

In spite of naysayers, proof positive of the benevolence of wine is that it is the charge of some saints. If Dionysus, son of Zeus, is the Greek God of wine, Saint Vincent of Saragossa is one of the patron saints of wine growers; his feast is celebrated on January 22. He was a Spanish deacon whose remains are supposedly in Champagne.

St. Martin of Tours, who is the patron saint of beggars and horse riders among others, is also a patron saint of winegrowers. His *fête* is celebrated on

November 11 with plenty of drinking, at the risk of getting "St. Martin's sickness," an unforgettable hangover, the day—or days—after.

St. Martin, whose father was a pagan legionary, was born in what is now Hungary around 316. After joining the Roman army, Martin was garrisoned at Amiens, 132 kilometers north of Paris. One cold wintry day, a beggar asked him for alms and the penniless but warm-hearted Martin tore his red coat in two and gave him the other half. During the night, Martin had a beautiful dream: he saw Christ wearing the missing piece he had given to the poor frozen beggar.

Soon after dreaming this vision that he interpreted as his calling from above, he left the army, was baptized, and went to live as a hermit in Liguge, a small town near Poitiers, 329 kilometers south west of Paris. There, he founded a Benedictine monastery, evangelizing the pagans (country people), and made wine as a source of revenues and enjoyment because naturally, it is wise to test before you sell.

St. Martin died in 400 (or perhaps in 397), at the age of eighty-one. His body was enclosed in a stone sarcophagus and taken to Tours. The church, the tomb, and the relics were partly destroyed by the Protestants in 1562 and completely destroyed by the French Revolution in 1793, with the exception of two towers that are still standing. In 1860, excavations were made and fragments of the St. Martin's tomb were found and are now sheltered in the basilica, built by the Archbishop of Tours. Not only is Saint Martin credited for good deeds and performing miracles, but also for developing le Chenin noir grape that is now the *cépage* used to make the white wines in Touraine and Anjou.

The *Chenin cépage* was imported in 1445 by an abbot to Mount Chenin located in Touraine, a beautiful region in the Loire valley, also known as *Le jardin de la France* (the garden of France). The kings of France had many splendid castles built along the scenic river Loire; Amboise, Chambord, Blois, Chenonceau, Azay-le-Rideau are some among many others.

ABOUT WINES

The best French wines result from hard work and strict quality control. In France, winemaking is regulated by government laws that are set up by the *Appellation d'Origine Contrôlée* (AOC) *or Appellation Contrôlée* (AC) at the *Institut National des Appellations d'Origine* (National Institute of Names of Origin), established in 1930.

Europe produces three-quarters of the wine in the world. Unsurprisingly, the largest winery in the world is apparently E. and J. Gallo, located in Modesto, California.

The label on a bottle of wine gives useful information about its content. Among others, it should include: the name of the wine, its quality, the place where it is made, its vintage, the kind of wine, the name of the person or company who made it, and where it was bottled.

Mis en bouteilles (bottled) au Domaine (or au Château) means estate bottled, a wine made and bottled on the estate.

The term *Apellation d'Origine*, which is strictly regulated, applies to wines, spirits, and some cheeses. Four categories of appellation exist for wines made in France; they are listed below:

→ *Appellation d'Origine Contrôlée or Appellation Contrôlée,* abbreviated to AOC, a term used to speak of a high quality wine with a guarantee of origin, meaning that it is made in regions where the soil and climate have the proper requirements to produce the best wines. For instance: *Appellation Alsace Contrôlée*, a high quality wine made in Alsace, or *Appellation Sauternes Contrôlée*, etc. According to the *Larousse Gastronomique* there are more than 250 AOCs, "constituting the aristocracy of French viticulture."

→ *Vin Délimité de Qualité Supérieure*, abbreviated to VDSQ: It is a high quality wine coming from a specific area and made with strict production laws. Most of these regions are eventually promoted to AC status.

→ *Vin de pays* or *vin de terroir*: A quality wine made in a specific region (*terroir* is French for land) of France.

→ *Vin de table*, (table wine) the most basic wine made anywhere in France.

Premier Cru, Cru from French verb *croître* (to grow); *premier cru* literally means "first growth," it is a term indicating a wine of superior quality that has the characteristics of the *terroir*, (of the land) where it was made.

Grand Cru, (great growth) and *Grand Cru Classé* (classified growth), both refer to wines of exceptional quality.

ARÔME AND BOUQUET OF A WINE

The terms are often used interchangeably. However, *l'arôme* (aroma) is defined as the unique fragrance that emanates from a substance, for instance, from the skin of the grape used to make a wine. Each *cépage*, even by the same name, has its own aroma resulting from the soil and the climate of the region where it is grown, among other things. The aroma is the odor, the perfume, and the taste coming from one ingredient, for instance, *l'arôme du chocolat* (the aroma of chocolate).

Bouquet, on the other hand, is more complex since it is a combination of several aromas. The bouquet of a wine includes, among other factors: the specific aroma of the grape that is used to make it, the way this grape is fertilized and harvested, the fermentation process, the aging of a wine, and the way the wine is bottled and stored. Each stage generates a specific aroma. The *bouquet* is the whole smell of the wine. People swirl their wineglasses to allow various aromas contained in them to be released so they can taste, smell, and feel the *bouquet* as they savor their favorite brews.

FRENCH LOANWORDS

BLANC DE BLANCS (m) A sparkling white wine made with white grapes only. The word is used in many countries both for still and sparkling wines.

BOUQUET (m) The whole perfume of wine resulting from various aromas.

BRUT (m) Champagne brut (dry) or dry sparkling wine.

CARTE DES VINS (f) Wine list.

CHAMBRÉ (m) Room temperature; *chambre* is French for bedroom.

CHASSELAS (m) A fine white grape, grown in the small French village (171 inhabitants) of Chasselas, located in the *département* (district, territorial division) of Saône-et-Loire in the Bourgogne region.

CHÂTEAU (m) A large country estate giving its name to a wine made in its neighborhood as in Château Lafite, a red wine made in the Médoc region not far from Bordeaux.

DEMI-SEC (m) Medium dry.

DOMAINE (f) Private property that gives its name to the wine produced on its soil, as in Domaine René Manuel.

MÉTHODE CHAMPENOISE (f) A process that allows the wine to ferment in the bottle in which it is sold. A sparkling wine made in this way.

MOUSSEUX (m) A sparkling wine.

NOUVEAU (m) Beaujolais *nouveau*; *Vin nouveau*, wine from the new vintage.

PÉTILLANT (m) Slightly sparkling wine.

PINARD (m) Any basic or cheap wine; plonk; a *vin ordinaire*.

ROSÉ (m) Wine made with black grapes with some skins left during fermentation to give it its *rosé* color; also known as *vin gris*.

SAUVIGNON BLANC (m) White grape grown in Bordeaux, the Loire Valley, California, and other countries worldwide and used to make quality white wine.

TERROIR (m) *Goût de terroir*, literally (taste of the land); the specific flavor that a wine of quality takes from the soil and other local conditions, for instance from the weather.

VEUVE (f) French for "widow;" a word that is used as part of a proprietary name of a brand of Champagne, as Veuve Clicquot Champagne.

VIGNOBLE (m) A vineyard.

VINASSE (f) The residue in the manufacturing of wine; refers to a wine of inferior quality in France, what the French call *du pipi de chat* literally, (cat urine); insipid drink—often said of weak coffee and tea; *vinasse* is a cheap wine in America, plonk in Great Britain.

VIN BLANC (m) White wine.

VIN COMPRIS (m) Wine included in the price of a meal.

VIN CUIT (m) A sweet aperitif wine.

VIN DE PAILLE (m) Wine made from grapes that have dried on *paille* (straw mats) before being pressed.

VIN D'HONNEUR (m) A reception wine offered in honor of people for a special occasion; also the ceremony during which such wine is served.

VIN DOUX (m) A sweet, fortified wine.

VIN FOU (m) Literally, crazy wine: a white or *rosé* sparkling wine from the Jura region in France.

VIN GRIS (m) A *rosé* wine of eastern France; a *rosé*.

VIN JAUNE (m) A yellowish wine from the Jura region of eastern France.

VIN MOUSSEUX (m) *Un mousseux* is a sparkling wine.

VIN OEIL-DE-PERDRIX (m) Sweet dessert wine made from both red and white grapes, giving the wine the *oeil-de-perdrix* color (partridge's eye color); a *rosé* color.

VIN ORDINAIRE (m) Table wine.

VIN ROSÉ (m) *Rosé* wine.

VIN ROUGE (m) Red wine; *"un gros rouge,"* French for "a mediocre wine."

VIN SEC (m) Dry wine, with little sugar as opposed to a *vin doux* that is sweeter.

SHORT STORIES

VEUVE CLICQUOT Veuve Clicquot, one of the best-loved Champagnes in the world takes its name from *Veuve* (Widow) Clicquot, a lady who became known as *La Grande Dame de Champagne*. *Née* Nicole-Barbe Ponsardin in 1777, she married Monsieur Clicquot and was a widow in 1805. She was 27 years old. She took over the business and became very successful.

La Grande Dame de Champagne is made exclusively from Pinot noir and Chardonnay grapes grown in the vineyards she had purchased in the early 1800s. She died in 1866.

Vin Jaune This yellowish wine is the creation of the Black Nuns in Château-Châlon, a little village in the Jura region in France.

Vin Mousseux One of the greatest contributions to winemaking was that of Dom Pierre Pérignom (1639–1715). *Dom* is the Latin word for *Master*, or *Lord*, not to be confused with D.O.M. which stands for the Benedictine motto *"Deo Optimo Maximo,"* meaning "To God the greatest good."

Dom Pérignom (1638–1715) was a monk at the Benedictine Abbey in Hautvillers in the Champagne region. He became blind, which did not stop him from making white wine. Apparently, he developed a method of keeping bubbles in the bottle by replacing the traditional wooden bottle stoppers with corks imported from Spain, where his fellow monks had discovered their efficacy. This technique gave life to the sparkling wine called Champagne, which people drink all over the world to celebrate special occasions, preferably happy ones. Dom Pérignom died in 1715 and was buried in the church of Hautvillers. Celebrations are still given by the Champenois in Hautvillers to honor the monk, a great *vigneron* that contributed so much to the prosperity of their region.

RED AND WHITE WINES

Thanks to various studies and persuasive advertising, most people everywhere are now totally convinced—until a new study comes along—that a few glasses of red wine a day can significantly reduce mortality because this red elixir has a high content of antioxidant substances that can prevent cancer and heart attacks. That beats any pill. The same might soon be true of white wine. Apparently, a group of five researchers at the Center of Oenology[26] in Montpellier, France, is working at developing a new white wine, The French *Paradoxe*, which would have the beneficial properties of red wines. *Vive le Paradoxe!*

Wine is red because the red grapes that are used to make it are crushed with the skin and left several days to ferment in a vat. The pigment in the skin gives the wine its red color. White wine is made from either white or red grapes but the skin is removed before fermentation, allowing the wine to stay colorless and called "white." All wine lovers or *connaisseurs* enjoy *le bouquet* of the wines they drink.

Wines bear the name of the *cépages* that are used to make them. For instance, Cabernet, a red grape from the Gironde and Val de Loire; Chardonnay, a white grape grown in Burgundy and Champagne; Pinot noir, the black grape grown in Burgundy, Champagne, and the Loire Valley; Merlot, a red or white grape cultivated in the Bordelais, among others. These *cépages* (a *cépage* is a variety of grapes retained for AOC wines) are grown in many countries around the world where they are used to make local wines.

Only a few wine names—and terms about wines—are listed below. However, since it is "wines that maketh glad the heart of men," the list is long enough to make anyone glad and merry. Happily, wine snobs will now order more than one type of wines *à la française*, at the risk of annoying other people who like wine, period, with a French pronunciation or not.

The six main regions making wines in France are Bourgogne, Bordeaux, Champagne, Alsace, the Loire Valley, and the Rhône Valley. Wine names are listed in alphabetical order; they are always masculine: *le Bordeaux* or *un Bordeaux.*

Red wines are generally made in Bordeaux, Bourgogne, and the Rhône Valley and white wines in Bourgogne, the Loire Valley, and Alsace.

Some of the French wines found in the United States and other countries are listed below:

FRENCH WINES

ALSACE Dry white wine from northeastern France, made with German Riesling and Gewurztraminer grapes.

BEAUJOLAIS A light, fruity Burgundy red wine made from the Gamay grape that would have been planted in *Bourgogne* (Burgundy) in the third century by Roman soldiers.

BEAUJOLAIS NOUVEAU The first wine of the new Beaujolais vintage (vintage is the year in which the grapes were grown) bottled immediately after fermentation and consumed shortly after; a young wine.

BORDEAUX AOC wines from the Gironde, southwestern region in France.

BOURGOGNE *Un vin de Bourgogne*, (Burgundy wine) from eastern France; red Burgundy is made with the Pinot noir grape, among other varieties.

CHABLIS White wine from northern Burgundy made with Chardonnay grapes.

CHAMPAGNE Sparkling white wine made since 1695 in Champagne, a region located 90 miles east of Paris; Champagne is made in Reims and Epernay with Pinot meunier black grapes, Pinot noir, and white Chardonnay grapes. "In victory you deserve Champagne, in defeat you need it," said Napoléon. He had several of each. Apparently, Louis XIV (1638–1715) diluted Champagne with water.[27] This could have caused outrage serious enough to trigger a civil war. *Mettre de l'eau dans son vin*, literally to put water in one's wine, is a figurative French expression meaning to come down one peg or two. Indeed, a real Frenchman would not think of putting one tiny drop of water in his wine.

CHÂTEAUNEUF-DU-PAPE Dark red, dry wine produced in Château-neuf-du-Pape, a large vineyard area, located at the southern end of the Rhône Valley.

CLARET Also spelled *clairet*; it is a light-colored wine made in the Bordeaux region.

CLOS-VOUGEOT Red and white wines made in the Côtes de Nuit region in Burgundy.

CÔTES DU RHÔNE AOC wines produced in the Rhône Valley between Lyon and Avignon. Some well known among others are Châteauneuf-du-Pape and Hermitage. It was allegedly a Crusader returning from the Holy Land who created the latter.

GRAVES AOC wines produced in the Graves, in the Bordeaux region.

MÉDOC A red wine made in Médoc, a small town north of Bordeaux.

MEURSAULT A white wine made with Chardonnay grapes in from the Côte d'Or region in Burgundy.

MUSCADET Light, dry wine from the Loire Valley, made near Nantes with Muscadet grape.

MUSCATEL A strong, sweet, provençal wine made from the Muscat grape.

PINOT NOIR From *pin* (pine); the grape resembles a pinecone, hence pinot; a red wine made from Pinot *cépage* cultivated in Burgundy. Pinot blanc and Pinot gris are two of the white varieties made with the Pinot grape.

POMEROL *Grand cru* red wine produced in Pomerol, located near Bordeaux.

RHÔNE Red wines made with a variety of grapes: Syrah and Grenade among others in the Côtes du Rhône (the Rhône is a river), south of Lyon.

SAINT-EMILION A red wine from the Bordeaux region mostly made from Merlot and Cabernet franc grapes.

SANCERRE White wine made with the Sauvignon blanc grape in Sancerre, a town on a hill overlooking the river Loire Valley.

SAUTERNES A white Bordeaux dessert wine, made in Sauternes, a village south of Bordeaux.

VOUVRAY White wines and sparkling wines of the Loire Valley made from Chenin blanc grapes.

SHORT STORIES

BORDEAUX In 56 B.C., the Romans made wine in the Bordelais, the greatest wine-growing region in the world according to local people. Two hundred and forty-seven thousand acres of land are devoted to producing what most French people consider the source of longevity, of good health and happiness: the Bordeaux wines. No wonder that some French doctors prescribe a glass of Bordeaux for stomach ailments, and even for ulcers. In America most people don't mind drinking one glass or two of any wine since it is good for the heart, even though it may not be recommended for diabetes.

Bordeaux wines vary in quality from *vin de table* to famous *premiers crus* wines, such as Château Lafite, Château Latour, Château Margaux, or Château Mouton-Rothschild. Apparently, when Napoléon had to exile on the island of Elba, where he died in 1821, he requested eight bottles of Mouton-Rothschild; enough to drown his sorrows for a short while.

BURGUNDY Burgundies wines: "The Kings of Wines," are produced in Bourgogne, in eastern France. The Bourgogne region was settled by a Germanic tribe, the Scandinavian Burgundi barbarians in the fifth century. The greatest white burgundies come from the Côte de Beaune.

CHABLIS A small town in the Yonne region in eastern France. The *Chablisiens* (people of Chablis), produce the *Grands Crus*—the best Chablis of all. There are four categories of Chablis, in order of importance they are: *Chablis grand cru, Chablis premier cru, Chablis,* and *petit Chablis.*

CHÂTEAUNEUF-DU-PAPE The vineyards of Châteauneuf-du-Pape are in the Rhône basin in the Vaucluse region in France. The Grenache grape is used to make this dark red wine, formerly called wine of Avignon, a name it took from the ruins of the summer palace that the *Papes* (Popes), built during their stay in Avignon in the fourteenth century. The palace was destroyed by the Huguenots (French Protestants of the sixteenth or seventeenth centuries) and has been a ruin since 1552. In the nineteenth century the wine took the name Châteauneuf-du-Pape, from the region it was made. Strict production rules make Châteauneuf-du-Pape wine one of the best Rhône wines.

CLOS-VOUGEOT This is a wine created by the Cistercians Monks and produced in Bourgogne. The word *Clos* (enclosed, fenced), is a vineyard enclosed by walls or a fence. Vougeot is the name of a very small village named after the river Vouge. Vougeot is located in the Côte-d'Or region in Bourgogne. For centuries, Clos-Vougeot had a reputation for being the best of all Burgundies. This did not appear to surprise the Burgundians

Cisterians monks whose merry proverb was, *"Qui bon vin boit, Dieu voit"* (He who drinks good wines, sees God).

SAUTERNES Sauternes is a small village of 601 inhabitants in the Gironde region, southwest of Paris. It is said that Thomas Jefferson, who was the Ambassador to France from 1785-1789, declared that Sauternes was one of the best wines in France, but apparently he liked Champagne and Hermitage blanc even more.

LIQUORS AND APERITIFS

As early as the twelfth century, monks made *aqua vitea*: *eau-de-vie* (water of life) and used it originally, and still do in some parts of France, as a universal medicine to disinfect cuts and wounds or to cure sore throats and other maladies. But, they also drank it because, *"Boire du vin, c'est honorer Dieu"* (To drink wine is to honor God), preached Fénelon, a French prelate and writer (1651–1715).

Wise Frenchmen have an *apéritif* before a meal to stimulate their appetites and a liquor afterward to help digestion. Sensible living!

Benedictine monks made an amber-colored liquor that naturally, they called *Bénédictine*. Carthusian monks created *La Chartreuse*, a pale green liquor they still make today. In many countries of Europe such as France, Germany, Austria, Spain, Portugal, Italy, and in the United States (in the California Franciscan Missions, for instance) one is likely to notice and feel the strong association between wines and liquors, monks and monasteries. Indeed, monks have produced wines to earn a living, to celebrate Mass, and also to enjoy it as food for a very long time, leaving their footprints where they lived, prayed, and worked.

FRENCH LOANWORDS

BÉNÉDICTINE (f) Liquor made by the Benedictine monks in Fécamp, a town in Normandy; the liqueur is based on Cognac, herbs, and plants.

CALVADOS (m) *(calva) Calva* (familiar for Calvados) is apple brandy traditionally made in the Calvados region, a French district in Normandy. A glass of Calvados is also called a *trou Normand* (a Norman hole), in other words, a glass of alcohol that one takes during a copious meal to activate digestion in order to make *un trou* (a hole) in the stomach to put more food into it. Live it up today, pay the price tomorrow. Or, do it the American way: take a Tums.

CASSIS (m) A syrupy drink; a *liqueur*, often alcoholic, made with black currants and used to flavor drinks.

CHARTREUSE (f) Liquor or cordial, pale green or white.

COGNAC (m) French brandy named Cognac in 1783. It is made in the town of Cognac in the Charente region, in southwestern France.

COINTREAU (m) Orange flavored liquor made in Angers, a city in the Loire Valley, in western France; it is a *Triple Sec* liquor. *Triple Sec,* from *trois* (three) means three times distilled; *triple sec* is a sweet orange flavored *liqueur* made from dried orange peels in Curacao, a Caribbean island. Grand Marnier and Curacao *liqueurs* are also *Triple Sec.*

CRÈME DE CACAO (f) *Liqueur* flavored with cocoa.

CRÈME DE MENTHE (f) A peppermint-flavored *liqueur.*

CRÈME DE NOYAU (f) An almond-flavored *liqueur.*

DIGESTIF (m) A digestive, a drink taken after a meal to help digestion. *Adieu,* Alka Selzter!

EAU-DE-VIE (f) Literally, water of life: brandy.

FINE CHAMPAGNE (f) Old liquor brandy from the *grande Champagne* and *petite Champagne* vineyards.

GRAND MARNIER (m) *Triple Sec* liquor made with a blend of Cognac, orange peel, spices, and vanilla in Neauphle-le-Château, near Paris and aged in Château-de-Bourg in the heart of Charente region on the Atlantic.

GRENADINE Syrup made from pomegranate used for flavoring some alcoholic drinks.

MIRABELLE (f) A brandy made with *mirabelle,* a variety of plum.

NOYAU (m) A *liqueur* made of brandy flavored with the kernels of certain fruits.

PASTIS (m) Anise-flavored *liqueur* from the South of France.

POUSSE-CAFÉ (m) A liquor taken after a cup of coffee, at the end of dinner; the practice originated in France and was introduced in North America in the 1840s.

RATAFIA (m) A popular drink in Champagne made with grape juice and Champagne brandy, served with *hors-d'oeuvres* or desserts. Liquor or cordial flavored with the kernels of almonds or cherries, apricots, peaches; also called *ratifia.*

SHORT STORIES

CHARTREUSE The word *chartreuse* means charterhouse, or Carthusian monastery. According to the *Larousse Gastronomique*, the Chartreuse liquor was first made in Vauvert, near Paris, by Carthusian monks who later sent the recipe to La Grande Chartreuse, a monastery of Carthusians, approximately 20 miles from Grenoble in the French Alps, founded by Bruno Hartensfaust, born in Cologne about 1035. The monks still make the Chartreuse not far from the monastery, and the recipe is still their secret, although it is known that it is prepared from plants such as balm, angelica leaves, cinnamon bark, and saffron among others. Apparently, only three monks know the secret recipe and they can only speak to each other once a week. Impossible for anyone who likes to gossip!

CHEESES

Once upon a time . . . approximately 4,000 years ago, there was a lady, a fearless and beautiful Arab lady, who walked across the desert. According to a legend (embellished here), she had put milk in a pouch probably made from the stomach of a sheep or camel she had eaten. With her canteen strapped to her back with a rope made with plant fibers, she started her journey under the blazing sun. After a long while, she felt hungry and thirsty. She stopped, probably not under a tree, and opened the stomach-pouch. Surprise! The milk was gone. All she could see was a solid whitish yellowish lumpy mass. But she had nothing else to eat, so she bravely tasted the unappetizing coagulated matter. To her surprise, she loved it. When she arrived at her destination, she did what most women are supposed to do—she told everybody about her discovery. And this was the beginning of cheesemaking and cheesemongers all over the world.

Another legend, less imaginative but more practical, is told about how cheese was born. In the dawn of time, hunters got tired of hunting day after day and they began to rear cattle in pastures. They would put the cows' milk in containers and would tend to other chores. When the tired men came home after toiling all day, they found that the milk had become solid.

They tasted the stuff and liked it. The cheese industry was born. And this is why today there are more than 400 sorts of cheeses in France alone.

The French word *fromage* (cheese) has been used since 1180. The name comes from Latin *formaticus*, which has a Greek root *formos*, meaning *faiselle*, a French word designating some sort of recipient perforated to drain fresh made cheeses. Evidently, the word *formaggio* in Italian has the same Greek root.

Like wine, a cheese usually takes its name and its flavor from the area in which it is produced. Under the PDO (Protection of Designated Origin) system, a cheese name is protected against imitation. Such cheese is labeled in France: *Appellation d'Origine Protégée*, abbreviated as AOP.

Cheese is a living substance that keeps changing and continues to ripen even when it is refrigerated. This is why a Camembert keeps "running," once it is out of the box. A cheese tastes better when it is served at room temperature and in France, it is eaten with a crusty French bread, a *baguette* or a *ficelle*.[28] Some people eat cheese as dessert with grapes or other fruits, and of course, it is always served with wine—red, *rosé*, or white, depending on the type of cheese.

The French cannot think of ending a meal without a slice of cheese, nor could the (French) fox that began to drool when he saw Master Corbel perched in a tree, "holding in his beak a *fromage*".[29] The question is, what sort of cheese was it? This was the subject of a hot debate between two French little moppets one day that *Monsieur Ze* Inspector was visiting their school. Rufus said that it was a Roquefort. "*Mais non,*" said Alceste, "it was a Camembert." "Not at all," replied Rufus, "the crow would not have been able to hold it; it runs and it smells bad".[30] Debates continue and children learn how to agree to disagree.

Cheese provides protein, vitamins, minerals, fat, saturated fat, and cholesterol. Like all milk products, it is a good source of calcium but it can also be high in sodium and saturated fat and cholesterol. Cheeseholics who value their waistline and arterial lining may want to consume it with moderation, if they must and if they can.

Some of the French cheeses found in the United States are listed below. All cheese names are masculine.

FRENCH CHEESES

BRIE Cow's milk cheese made in the town of Brie: "The King of Cheese."

CAMEMBERT Cheese made in Camembert, a village in France from which the cheese was originally exported.

CHÈVRES Cheese made with goat milk.

CROTTIN A round goat's milk cheese appreciated by *gourmets*. From crotte (animal dropping); great cheese in spite of its unappetizing name.

FROMAGE BLANC A fresh, soft, white cheese.

FROMAGE FRAIS A soft curd cheese often used as a basis for desserts, also known in France as *un petit-suisse*.

GRUYÈRE Cheese first made in Switzerland.

MUNSTER Soft, creamy cheese with a strong smell and a tangy taste when fully mature; made in the town of Munster, in Alsace, France.

NEUFCHÂTEL A cow's milk, soft, white cheese produced since the Middle Ages in Neufchâtel, a town in northern France.

PARMESAN Parmigiano, cheese from Parma in Italy; Parmesan is the French word.

PETIT-SUISSE In spite of its name, this small round cream cheese has been made in Normandy since 1850; it is often served as a dessert with jam or fruits; *des petits-suisses* (plural).

PONT L'EVÊQUE Semi-soft cheese made in Normandy.

PORT SALUT Also known as Saint-Paulin and originally made by Trappist Monks. It is creamy but firm enough to slice.

REBLOCHON Semisoft, pale, yellow, creamy cheese with a nutty flavor.

ROQUEFORT A strong cheese with bluish mold made from sheep's milk in Roquefort, near the Spanish border.

SHORT STORIES

BRIE This cows' milk cheese with 45 percent fat content was first made in the thirteenth century. In 1814, it was crowned the "king of cheeses" at a European cheese tasting contest in Vienna. In 1997, Brie was awarded *la Médaille d'Or* (the Golden Medal). A Beaujolais or a Côte-du-Rhône wine can be served with Brie.

CAMEMBERT: THE CHEESE This cheese was served to Napoléon in the late 1700s. It has a rich, creamy taste and a strong smell. A red Burgundy can be served with Camembert. Marie Harel is supposed to have created this cheese and, as explained below, a monument has been erected in her honor in the village of Camembert.

CAMEMBERT: THE VILLAGE It is a very small village in Normandy, west of Paris. One of several stories about Camembert says that a long time ago, before the Norman settled in England in 1066, a man by the name of Mambert had bought some property in the village and called it Champ

Mambert, or *Campo Mamberti*. The name was later transformed to Camembert. In the village, *La Maison du Camembert* was inaugurated in 1992 and resembles a parted Camembert box from the outside.

There is also a monument in the village erected in honor of Marie Harel, the proclaimed creator of the cheese. According to the story, the statue was Joseph Knirim's idea. He was a doctor from New York who suffered from terrible stomachaches. One day, he visited Camembert and ate a lot of the village cheese. Surprise! His stomachaches disappeared. Logically, a Camembert overdose should have made him sicker or even made him die since he was already not well, but he claimed the Camembert cured him of his maladies. Grateful, he began to raise funds to build a monument to the inventor. It was erected in 1926, dedicated to Marie Harel on April 20, 1927, demolished by bombs during Second World War, and apparently rebuilt by funds generated by American and French Camembert lovers.

Today, there is a small park around it and people go on picnic with their Camembert, a French *baguette,* and plenty of *vin rouge* to enjoy life under the sleepy eye of the defunct queen of Camembert. There are other stories about this great cheese's origins but since the name was never registered, a judgment stipulated in 1926 that Camembert would not have an *appellation d'origine*. This explains why Camembert is mass-produced in France, as well as in other countries.

Camembert: Poetry by Brillat-Savarin

"*Camembert, poésie*	Camembert, poetry
Bouquet de nos repas	Bouquet of our meals
Que deviendrait la vie	What would life be
Si tu n'existais pas?"	If you didn't exist?

GRUYÈRE Gruyère cheese has been made since the twelfth century in the village of Gruyère in the canton of Fribourg, Switzerland, where the cheese is called Fribourg. In France, Swiss Gruyère is also called Fribourg. As early as 1762, the Académie française added the word Gruyère to its vocabulary and today there are many descendants of the real Swiss Gruyère, as for instance the Gruyère de Comté made in France. In Monroe, Wisconsin, Gruyère is made by Roth Käsee USA Ltd; the Company has a Master Cheesemaker certified in Gruyère and baby Swiss.

MUNSTER A cheese originally made in the seventh century by the monks in the village of Munster, located in the Vosges Mountains in France. The word *Munster* is a contraction of monastery. The monks ate the cheese they made but they also taught the local peasants how to make it. Today, most Munster cheese is made in factories with pasteurized cow's milk. A good wine to serve with a Munster is the local Gewurztraminer red wine, but beer is another choice since the town of Munster is so close to Germany, a country of beer drinkers. Munster cheese gained its A.O.C. in 1969.

PONT L'EVÊQUE It is a cheese named after a small town in Normandy where it was produced in the early 1600s. A red Burgundy or Cabernet Sauvignon is a good choice to enjoy with this soft cheese.

PORT SALUT Port Salut cheese is also called Saint-Paulin. Trappist monks made it first in the nineteenth century at the monastery of Port-du-Salut, a small town in Brittany. Trappists are monks of the Roman Catholic Order of Cistercians. They had to flee France during the persecutions of the Terror. In 1815, they came back to France and settled in Brittany in the village of La Trappe, eighty-four miles from Paris, and they continued to make cheese to earn a living.

RACLETTE The word comes from the French *râcler* (to scrape). *Raclette* cheese is made in the Alps, on both sides of the French-Swiss border. When eating a *raclette*, the cheese is placed over an open fire. When it begins to get soft, one must scrape it off and eat it with boiled potatoes, *cornichons,* and ham. A Sauvignon blanc can be served with it.

ROQUEFORT This cheese goes all the way back to the first century A.D. and it is made with the milk of sheep raised in the Causses region, in southern France. A mold called *Penicillium Roqueforti* is added to it, giving the cheese its blue spots. Roquefort is a crumbly, tasty, smelly cheese that goes well with a Burgundy or a Sauterne.

CULINARY EXPRESSIONS

To a gastronome, "The discovery of a new dish does more for the happiness of mankind than the discovery of a star," said Chef Anthelme Brillat-Savarin.

Obviously, the businessman in *Le Petit Prince* [31] did not care about such trivial pursuits. All he wanted was to discover one more star, and one more so that he "could put them in the bank," which puzzled the little Prince who had come from another planet and had trouble understanding the world of grown-ups. Regardless of one's feelings about a new dish or a new star, however, it is easy to be puzzled, and possibly overwhelmed, with all the dishes that can be made from the list below—unless you are a *chef.* Or perhaps, even if you are a *chef.*

FRENCH LOANWORDS

Expressions with *à la*, and *en* are feminine; expressions with *au* (contraction of *à + le*) are masculine.

Words such as *flambé, frappé,* and *farci* are adjectives used with masculine nouns. When used with a feminine noun they become *flambée, frappée, farcie.* The pronunciation is the same for both masculine and feminine.

A+ *la*, followed by the name of a region or country means in the style of a particular region or country such as *à la française*, French style.

A L'ALSACIENNE Alsace style: sauerkraut, ham, and sausages.

A L'AMÉRICAINE The American way: sliced lobster tail and truffles.

A L'ANCIENNE *Fricassée* garnished in the old fashioned way.

A L'ANGLAISE England style: boiled or roasted, coated with eggs and bread-crumbs, and deep fried.

A LA BONNE FEMME Homestyle; in a rustic manner; similar to *à la paysanne,* the dish is often served in the container in which they were prepared and cooked.

A LA BORDELAISE In the Bordeaux region style: a wide range of dishes including eggs, fish, or meat, cooked with Bordeaux wine.

A LA BOULANGÈRE Baker's wife style: basic dish of stock and braised onions and potatoes. In the old days not everybody had an oven in their homes and people went to use the *boulanger's* oven (baker's oven) in town to bake their food; hence *à la boulangère.*

A LA BOURGEOISE Braised meat garnished with vegetables.

A LA BOURGUIGNONNE Dish served with red Burgundy wine sauce; the most famous is *boeuf bouguignon,* beef garnished with small onions, button mushrooms, bacon, and cooked with *Bourgogne* (Burgundy) red wine.

A LA BRETONNE Breton style: meat (mutton shoulder or leg of lamb) garnished with fresh, white *haricot* beans.

A LA BROCHE On a spit; spit-roasted or *à la brochette.*

A LA BROCHETTE Cooked on a skewer.

A LA CARTE By the bill of fare; ordered as a separately priced item, or items, not as part of a *table d' hôte* meal from a menu.

A LA CRAPAUDINE Small birds trussed to look like a *crapaud* (toad); *crapaud* style.

A LA CRÉOLE After the fashion of the *Créoles*: savoury dishes often inspired by West Indian cuisine. In the United States, the term is used for Louisiana dishes influenced by French, Spanish, and African cooking.

A LA DIABLE Devilled; *le diable* is French for devil; usually spicy and hot.

A LA FLORENTINE Florence style: on a bed of spinach with a Mornay sauce.

A LA FOURCHETTE Of a meal requiring the use of a *fourchette.*

A LA FRANÇAISE In the French manner: meat usually served with asparagus tips, braised lettuce, *sauce hollandaise,* and small potatoes. *Service à la française*: see Short Stories.

A LA GRAND-MÈRE Grandma style (or rather *mammy* style as they say today): chicken casserole with pearl onions, sautéed mushrooms, new potatoes, parsley, lemon juice, and brown butter; dish similar to *à la bonne femme* or *en cocotte.*

A LA GRECQUE Greek way: vegetables stewed in olive oil, lemon juice, water, and seasoning, served cold as *hors-d'oeuvres* or *entrée.*

A LA HOLLANDAISE Boiled vegetables, poached eggs served with a *sauce hollandaise*.

A LA JAPONAISE Japan style: Garnished with Chinese artichokes (called Japanese artichokes in France) and potato *croquettes*.

A LA JARDINIÈRE From *jardin* (garden): garnished with various garden fresh vegetables cooked and arranged separately around a piece of meat or poultry.

A LA JULIENNE Cut into thin strips the size of matchsticks; after French chef Jean Julien who introduced the technique.

A LA LIMOUSINE Garnished with red cabbage as they do in *Le Limousin*.

A LA LORRAINE Lorraine style: potatoes sautéed in butter and braised red cabbage balls cooked in red wine.

A LA LYONNAISE In the Lyon style: sliced potatoes and fried onions seasoned with white wine.

A LA MADRILÈNE Madrid style: cooked with tomatoes.

A LA MAÎTRE D'HÔTEL *Sauce à la maître d'hôtel, à la maître d'h*: in *majordome* (major-domo) style; a sauce with butter, parsley, lemon, or as the *Maître d'hôtel* will order it to be cooked.

A LA MARINIÈRE Sailor style: seafood cooked in white wine; a *marin* is French for "sailor."

A LA MILANAISE Milan style: food dipped in egg, breadcrumbs, and grated Parmesan, and fried in clarified butter.

A LA MODE In the style of; also used to describe the specialty of a region, for in instance *tripes à la mode de Caen* (tripes in the style of Caen). In the United States, *à la mode* is used in pie *à la mode*, topped with ice-cream. In France, *boeuf à la mode* means braised beef with sliced carrots and onions. *A la mode* is also a loanword meaning "stylish." *A la mode de Caen* means in the Caen style (Caen is a town in the Calvados region in Normandy). Classic dish of tripe braised with onions, carrots, herbs, garlic, and white wine.

A LA NIÇOISE Nice style (Nice is a city in the South of France). Classic dish of chopped tomatoes sautéed in olive oil, garlic, capers, anchovies, lemons, and black Nice olives. *Salade niçoise*: a typical dish from southern France made with tomatoes, cucumbers, beans, black Nice olives, hard-boiled eggs, and anchovies.

A LA PROVENÇALE Provence style: a way of cooking in which tomatoes, garlic, and olive oil are always used to prepare a dish.

A LA REINE Queen style: prepared in some special, elegant, classic French way: a dish of chicken, mushrooms, truffles, and a *suprême sauce* with chicken stock and fresh cream.

A L'INDIENNE India style: boiled rice and curry flavored sauce.

A POINT Not overcooked or undercooked; just right.

AU BLEU Boiling fish in court-bouillon until the skin turns blue.

AU GRATIN Sprinkled with breadcrumbs, and/or grated cheese and browned as in *pommes de terre au gratin*.

AU JUS Served in its natural juice or gravy.

AU LAIT With milk; as *café au lait*.

AU NATUREL Plain.

BRAISÉ From *braise*, (live embers): cooked over live coals.

CHAUD-FROID A dish of cold cooked meat or fish in a jelly or sauce.

DAUBE *En daube*: way of cooking braised meat with a little wine and spices in a closed recipient; *boeuf en daube* (beef casserole).

EN COCOTTE Food cooked slowly in a *cocotte*, a pan with two handles and a lid.

EN CROÛTE Encased in a bread or pastry crust; *croûte* is French for "crust."

EN GELÉE In aspic.

EN PAPILLOTTE Filet of meat or fish cooked in a greased foil paper wrapper.

FARCI Stuffed: *tomates farcies*, filled with forcemeat.

FLAMBÉ Flamed: served with a sauce containing brandy or rum and set afire to flame.

FRAPPÉ Partly frozen, iced, cooled; chiefly of wine iced, chilled, or a drink served with crushed ice.

GLACÉ Iced, glazed up as in *marrons glacés* (See Desserts).

GRATIN (m) *Gratin de pommes de terre*: breadcrumbs and grated cheese topping.

GRATINÉ Cooked with a crisp topping or stuffing of breadcrumbs or grated cheese.

GRILLÉ Grilled; *pain grillé* is French for "toast."

LIAISON (f) Binding, thickening of soups or sauces using starch or egg yolks; nothing to do with *Les Liaisons Dangereuses* (*Dangerous Liaisons*), a novel by French writer Laclos (1741–1803).

MAIGRE Lean, low fat.

PIQUANT Pungent, sharp-tasting, spicy as in *sauce piquante*.

RÉCHAUFFÉ Reheated.

RISSOLER To brown in hot fat.

SAUTÉ Fried quickly and turned frequently in a little fat; sautéed.

VÉRONIQUE A dish (of fish or chicken) prepared and garnished with grapes.

SHORT STORIES

A LA FLORENTINE Apparently, we owe the term *à la florentine* to Catherine of Medicis (1519–1589), who introduced a dish cooked in the Florence manner to the Court of France. She was the wife of Henri II, King of France.

A LA FRANÇAISE It was le *Roi Soleil* (Sun King) who established a formal method of serving food called *le service à la française* (service French style) which, of course, became universally recognized as the civilized and elegant way of dining.

In France today, however, some people claim that the service *à la française*, as it used to be in the old days ten or twenty years ago no longer exists. On the other hand, more traditional people do not agree and according to them, people in some circles still celebrate special occasions with the traditional service *à la française*. There is always a transition period between old and new and traditions never disappear overnight; some never do or, like fashion, they reappear decades later.

It takes time to prepare a typical meal *à la française* and almost just as much time to eat it. Indeed, between each course, people talk and drink wine while they wait for the next dish.

A meal *à la française* requires many plates to be set. The top plate is removed after the first course is eaten, usually a potage. The second course is then served on the plate below, and so on, until the whole meal is eaten.

A typical meal *à la française* can (or used to) include the following:

1. A *potage*, sometimes more than one sort, is followed by *hors-d'oeuvres*.
2. *Hors-d'oeuvres* can be *crudités* such as radishes, celery, olives or *charcuterie* such as cold cuts of meat, *pâtés*, sausage, or small *quiches*.
3. *Hors-d'oeuvres* are followed by an *entrée*. *Entrées* are cold or hot and served before the main course of the meal. Cold *entrées* are slices of cold meats such as ham, hardboiled eggs, tomatoes, parsley, and olives *en vinaigrette*. Examples of hot *entrées* are *vol-au-vent* or *bouchées à la reine*.
4. After the *entrée*, the plate is removed to serve the main course. The main course, the *pièce de résistance*, called *le plat de résistance or le plat principal* in France, can be a roast, fish, or chicken with vegetables.
5. When the guests are done with the main course, they eat cheese served on a clean plate below. They can choose from several types of cheeses displayed on a *plateau de fromages* (tray of cheese).[32]
6. After *fromage*, the plate is removed again to serve *entremets*. *Entremets* that are not sweet are (or were) eaten before cheese. Today, however, people eat sweet *entremets* such as cakes, creams, sorbets, compotes, and fruits as desserts, followed by a *pousse-café*.

On regular days, most French still eat each course of their meal one after the other, usually on the same plate, except for dessert when they have one. For special occasions, however, it seems that traditional people still eat *à la française*. In the days not so far back, perhaps thirty years ago, when most French households did not have dishwashers, people and their polite guests (the ones that got re-invited) would spend half of their time eating and the rest of day washing dishes, cleaning, drinking more wine, talking, and having fun together.

People's lifestyles have evolved in France, as in most countries of the world. Generally, the table is set differently than it used to be in a typical service *à la française*. One large plate, called *assiette-déco*, (short for *décorative*) by some, *assiette de service* or *assiette de présentation* by others, is placed on the table with another plate on top of it for *hors-d'oeuvres* or the *entrée* since many French people now eat one or the other, except during special celebrations, such as weddings. After the *entrée*, the hostess removes the plate and places a clean, warm plate on the *assiette-déco* to serve the *pièce de résistance*. Then, she brings a clean plate for cheese, removes the *assiette-déco* and sets a clean plate for dessert. And to help digestion, she serves a *Triplesec* and a *tisane*.

A LA RUSSE During the late nineteenth century, Prince Alexandre Borisovich Kourakine, Imperial Russian Ambassador to Paris, introduced the Russian tradition of serving food. In the service *à la russe*, the dishes for each course are served from a side serving table rather than being set up on the table as it is in the service *à la française*. To drink *à la russe* is to empty your glass. Bottoms up! Throw the glass over your shoulder in the fireplace, or wherever you are still able to aim.

UTENSILS

Why eat with forks when God gave us hands? All over the world, babies know this. And in the Middle Ages, they knew that too, until wealthy people who always do things differently because they can afford it, thought of making forks, spoons, and knives.

Forks,[33] for instance, go back to the Greeks and apparently, by the seventh century A.D., royalties in the Middle East began to use them. Forks were brought to Italy in the eleventh century and in 1533, Catherine de Medicis, wife of the future King Henri II, brought them to France. It seems that the French were slow to accept forks because it was thought that using them was to act affected. In 1608, an Englishman named Thomas Coryate saw them in Italy and brought the first fork to England. By the mid-1600s, it was considered fashionable to eat with forks. Originally, forks were constructed with two tines. By the late seventeenth century they were made with four tines in France and by the early nineteenth century, the four-spike forks came to America.

Knives have been used since prehistoric times as weapons, tools, and eating utensils. In the Middle Ages in Europe, people brought their own knives with them to dinner because hosts did not provide cutlery for the guests. Knives were narrow and pointed so that people could grab food and eat it. In 1669, King Louis XIV prohibited the use of pointed knives on the street and at the dinner table; they were made illegal in order to reduce crime. At the beginning of the eighteenth century, knives were imported to America.

Spoons made of shells or wood were likely used in prehistoric times. Later on, they were made of various metals: gold for the royalty, silver for the wealthy, and no spoon for the poor. Around the fourteenth century, the general public could afford to eat with spoons because they were made of tinned iron, brass, or pewter, an alloy of tin and lead, brass, or copper.

Chopsticks were developed in China about 5,000 years ago. At the beginning, people cut their food into small pieces and ate it with twigs. Later, people used chopsticks made from bamboo because it was inexpensive. Cedar, sandalwood, teak, pine, and bone have also been used. The wealthy had chopsticks made from jade, gold, bronze, brass, agate, coral, ivory, and silver.

FRENCH LOANWORDS

BONBONNIÈRE (f) Container for *bonbons*; a candy box.

BROCHETTE (f) A small skewer or spit on which chunks of meat are cooked.

CAFETIÈRE (f) Coffee pot.

CARAFE (f) A glass recipient to serve wine or water.

CHINOIS (m) A fine-mesh conical strainer resembling and old *chinois* (Chinese) hat.

COCOTTE (f) A small round or oval cooking pan used to prepare dish described as *en cocotte* or *à la bonne femme*. See Culinary Expressions.

COMPOTIER (m) A *compote* porcelain bowl-shaped dish with a stem; also a fruits dish.

FOURCHETTE (f) A fork; the *fourchette* is also the wishbone of a bird, in both French and English.

MARMITE (f) Earthenware cooking-vessel.

MOUSSELINE (f) *Un verre mousseline (m)* , a wineglass made of very thin glass with ornamentation resembling muslin or lace.

PLAT (m) A dish.

PLATEAU (m) An ornamental tray or dish for table-service.

RAMEQUIN (m) Ramekin: a flameproof dish; also the food cooked in it.

RÉCHAUD (m) A dish in which food is warmed or kept warm, *réchauffé*.

RÔTISSERIE (f) A *rôtisserie* oven.

SERVIETTE (f) Table napkin.

SORBETIÈRE (f) Ice cream maker.

TERRINE (f) An earthenware fireproof vessel, especially one in which a *terrine de pâté* is cooked.

TIMBALE (f) Drum-shaped mold; also the food prepared in it.

PEOPLE

The origin of *Cordon Bleu* (bleu cord), goes back to 1578 when members of the Order of the Knights of the Holy Spirit, established by Henri III, wore a medal or a badge suspended on a *bleu cordon*. The Order was the highest of the Old French chivalry under the Bourbon Monarchy and the term *cordon bleu* became used later on to qualify an outstanding performance, particularly that of a *chef*.

Cordon Bleu is also the name of a school in Paris. The *Académie d'Art Culinaire de Paris*, founded in 1895, is teaching *l'Art de Vivre* (the art of living) to people who can obtain the *Grand Diplôme Le Cordon bleu* (Cordon Bleu Diploma) in nine months.

Twenty-five Cordon Bleu Institutes in fifteen countries are teaching the art of living well that begins with eating well. Apparently, Cordon Bleu Paris Ottawa Culinary Arts Institute, established in Canada's capital in

1988, claims they are the first Cordon Bleu School to operate outside of France.

Not everybody can claim to be a *cordon bleu*. And assuming that you don't want or cannot be one, you can, with a little work and practice, become *un garçon, un chocolatier,* an ordinary *chef* or *sous-chef.* And without any work at all, we can all be *gourmands*!

FRENCH LOANWORDS

The words below are all masculine: used with *un* (a or an), or *le* (the).

CHEF A head cook: from Latin *caput: tête* (head). A *chef* is sometimes called a *gros bonnet,* literally a big bonnet, a big hat. A *couvre-chef* is any hat that *couvre* (covers) the *chef* (one French word for head). See Chapter III under Hats.

CHOCOLATIER A maker or seller of chocolate.

CORDON BLEU A great *chef.*

GARÇON A waiter.

GASTRONOME A person who enjoys good food; an epicure.

GOURMAND A man fond of good food; *gourmande,* a lady who loves good food. In France a *gourmand* is not a *glouton* (glutton), one that eats everything in sight and plenty of it.

GOURMET A connoisseur of good food and good wines; an epicure.

MAÎTRE D'HÔTEL Informally called *maître d';* a dining room manager; food and beverage manager; a house steward; the major-domo.

NÉGOCIANT A wine merchant.

PÂTISSIER A pastry-cook.

PATRON The proprietor of an inn or restaurant.

PLONGEUR A person employed to wash dishes; from *plonger* (to dive), something they would undoubtedly rather do in a pool!

RESTAURATEUR A keeper or owner of a restaurant.

RÔTISSEUR From *rôtir* (to roast); a person in charge of all roasting in a restaurant and grilling and frying.

SAUCIER Cook specializing in making sauces; *a sauce chef*.

SOMMELIER Originally, it was the monk who took care of the linen, bread, and wine in a monastery; today, *le sommelier* is the specialist wine waiter who must know his wine and match it with the proper food.

SOUS-CHEF Literally, under-chef: second in command in a kitchen. Usually a *Saucier*.

TRAITEUR A caretaker; a person who runs a delicatessen selling prepared meals.

VENDANGEUR A grape-picker.

VIGNERON A person who cultivates grapevines.

PLACES

Before restaurants came into being, *chefs* were employed to cook for the royalties and the wealthy. The rest of the world ate their own cooking at home. But in 1765, Monsieur A. Boulanger had the clever idea to open the first restaurant in Paris, Rue des Poulies, known as Rue du Louvre today. His motto was, "Come unto me, all you whose stomachs are aching, and I will restore you." This reminds one of the American Jewish poet and novelist Emma Lazarus (1849–1887) and her famous poem *The New Colossus* (1883). "Give me your tired, your poor . . . ", which was engraved on a plaque in the Statue of Liberty to welcome poor, tired, hopeful immigrants.

Procuring food to the public was a new concept and was kept simple for a while, and mostly soups were served at the Boulanger restaurant. But as always, things change as they should, and in 1782, Antoine Beauvilliers founded *La Grande Taverne de Londres*, the first luxury restaurant in Paris that had a menu with a list of dishes available that were served at small tables during fixed hours.

Cafeteria, which the French spell *cafétéria* (to be contrary and resist the invasion of English words in their language), would have originated in San Francisco during the Gold Rush of 1849, featuring self-service. On the other hand, the *Larousse Gastronomique* says that the word appeared in France in the 1950s and came from Spain.

FRENCH LOANWORDS

AUBERGE (f) Inn.

BISTRO (m) Café in the United States; Parisian slang for small wine shop or restaurant where wine is served.

BOÎTE (f) A small French restaurant or *boîte de nuit* (a night club). *Boîte* is French for box, as in *une boîte de chocolat* (a box of chocolate).

BUFFET (m) A service of food from a sideboard or counter.

CABARET (m) A tavern.

CAFÉ (m) A place that sells drinks, particularly coffee, beer, wines, *aperitifs*, etc.

CHARCUTERIE (f) The shop where ham and cold meats are sold.

CUISINE (f) Kitchen; *faire la cuisine* (to cook); *je fais la cuisine* (I am cooking); *je fais ma petite cuisine* (I am doing my own thing).

RELAIS (m) In France, it is a café; a restaurant sometimes providing overnight accommodation.

RESTAURANT (m) From *restaurer* (to restore, to energize) the body. A *bouiboui* is French for a joint, a greasy spoon restaurant or a fleabag hotel.

RÔTISSERIE (f) A shop or restaurant where meats are roasted and sold.

SHORT STORIES

BISTRO Also spelled *bistrot,* the word appeared in the French language in 1884. According to the *Larousse Gastronomique,* it would come from the Russian word *bistro,* meaning quick. Apparently, the Cossacks wanted quick service as they were served drinks at the bar during the Russian occupation of Paris in 1815.

BUFFET A *buffet* is a table with foods and drinks for tired and hungry people. Travelers used to eat at café-restaurants in *la gare* (the train station), before taking their next train. Today, *buffets* provide food and refreshments on the trains. Nevertheless, there are still some famous *buffets de gare* (train station restaurants) in existence, such as in Lille, Avignon, and Paris. For instance, *Le Train Bleu* at the Gare de Lyon in Paris is a restaurant that serves quality food that attracts many travelers. It has been listed as an historic monument since 1972 because of its architecture and beautiful paintings. Marius Toudoire was the architect who decorated it, helped by thirty artists. Its Belle Epoque interior is still the way it was since its opening in 1901 complete with gold leaves, heavy curtains, beautiful chandeliers, and frescos showing areas of Paris, Marseille, Lyon, and views of the Alps, Algeria, Tunisia, and the Midi (south of France).

CABARET The *cabaret* was a type of nightclub that originated in France. Writers, artists, and wealthy people mingled and watched *avant-garde* and satirical literary works. One of the most famous cabarets was *Le Chat Noir*, which opened in Paris in 1881.

CAFÉ According to the *Larousse Gastronomique*, the first café in the world was opened in Constantinople in 1550. In 1672, an Armenian set up a stall selling cups of coffee at the Saint-Germain fair in Paris. The French enjoyed conversing and drinking coffee in public places, and *maisons de café* (coffee houses) began to open and be popular. Café de la Paix, opened in 1862, became an international *rendez-vous* place for artists; Zola, Maupassant, and Chagall, among others, were *habitués* of the Café de la Paix. Among others, Café Anglais, Café de Paris, Café de Madrid, Café d'Orsay are frequented by fashionable people.

NOUVELLE CUISINE It is a culinary movement that avoids traditional rich sauces and emphasizes fresh ingredients and attractive presentation, short cooking times, and small helpings. *Bons vivants* with a big appetite do not have the ghost of a clue what one serving means and they are probably *d'accord* with the statement that one unsatisfied customer is to have made after eating such a meal. "I can't believe I paid ninety dollars and I am still hungry!"

The movement began with Fernand Point (1897–1955), who is known as the father of *nouvelle cuisine*. His golden rule was simplicity, natural flavor, and healthy eating. The fashion for *nouvelle cuisine* spread beyond France in the 1970s and early 1980s.

HAUTE CUISINE *Haute cuisine* is considered an art, as opposed to *cuisine bourgeoise,* the simple, wholesome home cooking of the middle class citizens. In *haute cuisine,* the food is prepared in an elaborate and elegant manner and it is eaten in an opulent *décor* and stylish atmosphere. Whether one can afford it or not, *haute cuisine* has nevertheless more appeal to a *gourmet* than "Haute junk food," now served at Simon Kitchen and Bar, a "chic" eatery in Las Vegas Hard Rock Hotel. Where else? According to the pastry chef there, dessert addicts can now treat themselves with "faux Twinkies, SnoBalls, and Hostess chocolate cupcakes because they are good for you." Indeed, they are "lite" and "free of preservatives."[34] Napoléon Bonaparte once said *"Impossible, n'est pas Français!"*—a philosophy truly alive and well in America.

BE A SNOB

The short French phrases in this section contain one or more French word(s) and one or more loanwords selected from each vocabulary list in Chapter I. They are fun to learn and easy to remember.

For instance, *tout baba* is one example of such phrase in which *tout* (all) is a French word, and *baba* is a French loanword meaning light rum cake (see Desserts). The literal meaning of *tout baba* is therefore, total rum cake. However, when a Frenchman says, "I am *tout baba,*" he means, "I am completely stunned."

Anyone who wants to be Francophile, show off, or add *panache* to their daily conversations can use any of the French expressions below. Their literal meaning is in parentheses, followed by a short sentence illustrating how the expression is used in France.

DESSERTS

BRIOCHE (f) Round-shaped pastry made with flour, butter, eggs and yeast.
De la brioche (some pastry).
He has *de la brioche*; he has a beer belly, a paunch.

CHOU (m) Short for *chou à la crème*; cream puff; pastry filled with cream.
Bête comme un chou (stupid as a cream puff).
This is really *bête comme un chou*; it is really so simple to do.

COMPOTE (f) Fresh fruits stewed with water and sugar.
En compote (stewed fruits).
I am *en compote*; I am all bruised, in a pitiful state.

ÉCLAIR (m) Oblong pastry filled with a flavored custard or whipped cream.
COMME UN ÉCLAIR (like a custard pastry).
He went by *comme un éclair*; he flashed past.

GALETTE (f) A thin flat cake made with flour, butter, and eggs.
De la galette (flat cake).
He has *de la galette*; he has money, he has lots of dough.

GANACHE (f) Rich chocolate filling.
Vieille ganache (old chocolate filling).
He is a *vieille ganache*; he is an incompetent fool.

GÂTEAU (m) Cake.

Du gâteau (some cake).

C'est du gâteau; it's a piece of cake; it's really easy.

Ce n'est pas du gâteau; it's no picnic.

C'est son pupa gâteau; that's her sugar daddy.

LANGUE DE CHAT (f) *(langue)* A tongue of cat; a tongue-shaped biscuit.

Mauvaise langue (bad tongue).

She is a *mauvaise langue*; she is a malicious gossip.

Langue de vipère (viper tongue); wicked tongue.

TARTE (f) Pastry shell filled with cream or fruits.

Quelle tarte (What a pastry shell); What an idiot!

The French also say *Quelle cloche* (What a dumbbell).

Tarte is not be confused with *tart* in English (What a tart; what a strumpet, a prostitute).

FRUITS

CITRON (m) A yellow, thick-skinned fruit that resembles a lime or lemon.

Mal au citron (pain in the lemon).

I have *mal au citron*; I have a headache.

FRAISE (f) Strawberry.

Sucrer les fraises (to put sugar on strawberries).

Il/elle sucre les fraises; he/she is gaga.

NOIX DE GRENOBLE(f) *(noix)* Walnut from Grenoble.

Quelle noix (What a walnut); What an imbecile! What a dope!

Bonjour vieille noix (Good morning, old walnut); Hello, old pal.

Une noix de beurre (a walnut of butter); a pat of butter.

PRUNELLE (f) A small, yellow prune.

La prunelle de mes yeux (the small prune of my eyes).

She is *la prunelle* of my eyes; she is the apple of my eyes.

MEATS

ANDOUILLE (f) Sausage made with pork or veal intestines.

Andouille! Quelle andouille! (Sausage. What a sausage!); Stupid. What a stupid man (or woman)!

CANARD (m) Duck.

Froid de canard (Duck cold).

Il fait un froid de canard; it is very cold, bitterly cold.

LARD (m) Lard; bacon.

Gros lard (Big lard).

He is a *gros lard*; he is fat. *Gros lard!* Fatso!

Tête de lard (head of lard); What a *tête de lard*; what a meathead!

POULE AU POT (f) *(poule)* A boiled chicken in a pot.

Poule mouillée (wet chicken); What a *poule mouillée*; what a wimp!

SAUCE

BEURRE NOIR (m) *(noir)* Sauce *au beurre noir* is made with butter melted until it is brown.

Un petit noir (a little black).

I'll have *un petit noir*; I'll have a black coffee, an espresso.

SOUPS

SOUPE (f) *Soupe au lait* (milk soup).

He is *soupe au lait*; He is very impatient, hot-tempered.

Soupe à la grimace; a grimace soup.

She makes a *soupe à la grimace*; She is sulking.

Gros plein de soupe; (big, full of soup); fat man, fat slob.

VEGETABLES

HARICOT (m) A bean; a leguminous plant.

La fin des haricots (the end of the beans).

It's *la fin des haricots*; It's the end of everything, nothing else can be done.

MACÉDOINE (f) Salad of mixed fruits or vegetables cut in small pieces.

Quelle macédoine (what a fruit or vegetable salad); What a medley (a potpourri of things or people); what a strange (ill-assorted, or unusual) mixture.

PETITS POIS (m) Small, green peas.

Rond comme un petit pois (round as a small pea).

He is *rond comme un petit pois*; he is blind drunk.

POMME (f) Short for *pomme de terre*, (apple of the earth), potato; *pommes frites*.

Un sac de pommes de terre (a bag of potatoes).

She is a real *sac de pommes de terre*; she is fat and unattractive.

MISCELLANEOUS

ASSIETTE (f) *Assiette anglaise*: platter of assorted cold meats.

Dans mon assiette (in my plate).

I am not *dans mon assiette*; I am out of sorts, I am not feeling well.

Pique-assiette (from piquer, to steal, to take what is in the plate); What a *pique-assiette*, what a freeloader, what a sponger.

CORNICHON (m) A tiny, sour, pickled cucumber.

Cornichon (pickle).

Quel cornichon; what a nitwit.

CROÛTE (f) Crust as in bread crust.

Quelle croûte. (What a bread crust); What an imbecile.

Ma croûte (my crust).

I earn *ma croûte*; I earn a living.

Un casse-croûte (a break crust).

I am having *un casse-croûte*; I am having a snack.

CROÛTON (m) Crouton; pieces of toasted or fried bread served with soup or salad.

Vieux croûton (old crouton); old stick-in-the-mud.

DU JOUR (m) *(jour)* Of the day, as in *soupe du jour, plat du jour, mode du jour.*

Beau comme un jour (beautiful as a day).

He is *beau comme un jour*; he is very handsome.

WINES

BOUQUET (m) The perfume of wine; its smell; its taste.

C'est le bouquet (It is the aroma).

Alors là, c'est le bouquet. Alors là is added for emphasis. (Well, it's the aroma.)

C'est le bouquet mon ami; It takes the cake *mon ami.* That's the last straw.

VIN (m) Wine.

Entre deux vins (between two wines).

I am *entre deux vins;* I am tipsy.

The French also say I am pompette (tipsy), a funny expression to French ears.

CHEESE

FROMAGE (m) Cheese.

Tout un fromage (a whole cheese).

He makes *tout un fromage* of it; much ado about nothing; he makes a big deal out of nothing.

PETIT-SUISSE (m) *(Suisse)* A small, round, cream cheese.

En Suisse (Swiss style).

He eats or drinks *en Suisse,* he eats or drinks alone.

The antisocial who endorses such practice might keep in mind an Arab proverb that says, "He who eats alone, chokes alone."

CULINARY TERMS

A L'ANGLAISE (f) English style.

Filer à l'anglaise (to leave English style).

Il file à l'anglaise, he takes a French leave.

The expression *filer à l'anglaise* means to leave a room quickly without being noticed, without saying goodbye or thank you to your host, to be impolite.

In France, *filer à l'anglaise* refers to the behavior of their neighbors, the English that they accuse of being rude and *sans-gêne*, hence to leave a place *à l'anglaise*, English style.

Understandably, the English return the favor, claiming that the French have poor *étiquette*, and it shows in their mentality, particularly during the centuries of war between France and England. Therefore, they too, leave *à la française*, French style. *Du tac au tac.* A loanword meaning tit for tat.

A LA DIABLE (f) *(diable)* Deviled.
Au diable (to the devil).
She lives *au diable*; she lives far away, in the boondocks.
Va au diable. Go the devil!
Un bon diable (a good devil).
He is *un bon diable*; he is a good fellow.

DAUBE (f) *En daube,* as in beef *en daube*; stewed beef.
De la daube (stewed beef).
It's *de la daube*; its cheap stuff, bad quality.

FARCI Stuffed.
La tête farcie (stuffed head).
I have *la tête farcie*; my head is crammed, full.

FOURCHETTE (f) Fork.

Un bon coup de fourchette (a good stroke of the fork).

She has *un bon coup de fourchette*; she has a hearty appetite.

FRAPPÉ Partly frozen, iced, cooled.

Complètement frappé (completely frozen).

He/she is *complètement frappé(e)*; he/she is completely nuts; crazy.

MAIGRE Lean, low fat.

Maigre comme un clou (lean as a nail).

She is *maigre comme un clou*; she is skinny as a rail.

RÉCHAUFFÉ Reheated.

Du réchauffé (reheated).

It's *du réchauffé*; it's old hat.

PLACES

AUBERGE (f) Inn.

Sorti de l'auberge (out of the inn).

I am not *sorti de l'auberge*; I am not out the woods.

BUFFET (m) A service of food from a sideboard or counter.

Rien dans le buffet (nothing in the sideboard).

I have *rien dans le buffet*; I have nothing in my stomach; I am hungry.

CUISINE (f) Kitchen, cooking.

Quelle cuisine (What cooking!).

Quelle cuisine, my dear; what an intrigue, what a mess my dear.

Ma petite cuisine (my little cooking).

I am doing *ma petite cuisine*; I am doing my own thing.

SOUPE À L'OIGNON (f) *(oignon)* Onion soup.

Occupe-toi de tes oignons (Occupy yourself with your onions).

Occupe-toi de tes oignons; my dear friend, mind your own business.

PROVERBS

CERISE (f) A cherry; or cherry-red.

C'est la cerise sur le gâteau; it's the icing on the cake.

CHINOIS (m) A fine mesh conical strainer resembling an old Chinese hat.

C'est du chinois; It's Greek to me. (Allusion to the difficulty of learning a new language or something difficult).

MADELEINE (f) A small cake baked in a fluted mold.

Elle pleure comme une Madeleine; She cries her eyes out (like Mary Magdalene, the repentant sinner).

MOUSSE (f) A sweet dish made with whipped cream, egg whites, etc., and flavored as *mousse au chocolat.*

Pierre qui roule n'amasse pas mousse; a rolling stone gathers no moss.

CONCLUSION

Francophiles, hip "foodies," intellectual snobs, wine snobs, and naturally, sophisticated intellectually motivated English speakers (snobs or not) have hopefully enjoyed this chapter. One may wonder, however, if bad cooks did, because among other bad things, they have been condemned for having "delayed human development longest and impaired it most." So why blame them if they are not interested in reading about food, particularly when almost half of it is in a foreign tongue?

The above discriminatory remark is attributed to Friedrich Nietzsche (1844–1900), the famed German existentialist that somebody, probably a bad cook,[35] accused of being abnormal. Obviously, bad cooks are necessary to appreciate *cordons bleus*. It's like day and night; one must have one to value the other. But in the end, bad cooks or not, snobs or not, we all love to eat good food and should be able to agree that, "The joys of the table belong equally to all ages, conditions, countries, and times" and that "gourmandism is one of the main links uniting society" according to Jean Anthelme Brillat Savarin, French cook (1755–1826).

Chapter 2

ARTS

> "The art world, equally homogeneous,
> is quite different; every artist is a
> humbug, estrange to his family, never
> wears a top hat, and speaks a special
> language . . . Nevertheless, artists
> constantly produce masterpieces . . .
> they sleep all day, go out all night,
> work God knows when, and with
> their heads always flung back, their
> limp scarves fluttering in the wind,
> they perpetually roll cigarettes."

The above is *The portrait of an artist* [36] as seen by French novelist Marcel Proust in: *Social ambitions and Musical Taste of Bouvard and Péruchet*, a short story in *Pleasure and Days*, a collection of short stories published in 1896.

Those who need a structured life to be productive often perceive artists as Proust describes them. However, if they view artists as being unconventional, they can also recognize, as Camille Pissaro did, that they are able to see beauty where others do not. "Blessed are they those who see beautiful things in humble places where other people see nothing," wrote Camille Pissaro (1830–1903), the great French painter associated with the "Manet's gang," the name by which the young Impressionists were known in the 1870s. John Constable (1776–1837), the renowned English landscape artist, had a similar opinion. "I never saw an ugly thing in my life: for let the form of an object be what it may, light, shade and perspective will always make it beautiful."

INTRODUCTION

When the Norman conquered England in 1066, they initiated more than two hundred years of political and linguistic domination. French became the language of the élite in politics, religion, fashion, and in the arts. As they settled in England, Norman artists began to travel between the two countries. These *troubadours* [37] brought with them not only their creative skills, but also the French art terms describing their masterpieces in music, poetry, literature, and theatre among other art fields.

The word art derives from Latin *ars*, meaning "skill," a word that denotes the ability to perform a set of manual tasks dexterously to make useful products. The word "art" is now mostly used when referring to the fine arts, which naturally require manual dexterity—a special skill—but also creativity, imagination; and the ability to be intensely aware of the way things look, sound, smell, and feel in order to produce beautiful artwork.

But what is beautiful? As the saying goes, "Beauty is in the eye of the beholder," and one person's beauty may be another's ugliness! For this reason, "beauty" is not an easy word to define to everyone's satisfaction.

Apparently, the French came up with a sensible solution to this dilemma. They wisely established that if a creation labeled as work of art could provide an audience with an emotional, aesthetic, and intellectual experience, it was beautiful. It was beautiful if one responded with one's heart and head to what one saw, heard, and understood in the work of its creator. The French coined the expression *beaux-arts*, a concept that separated the beautiful arts produced by artists from the useful arts made by skilled *artisans*. The term *beaux-arts* is expressed in English as fine arts, which is defined as "the making or doing of things that have form and beauty" (*Webster's Dictionary*).

Beaux-arts include architecture, plastic and graphic arts (sculpture, engraving, and painting), sometimes music and dance, or any art form that gives pleasure to the eyes and to the soul. Aesthetic is not the only concern of architects, however. Their designs must be functional as well, since one of architecture's main purposes is to build sound and durable structures.

The French are passionately interested not just in *les beaux-arts*; they patronize *les arts libéraux* (the liberal arts) as well. Literature has always been and still is the foundation of French liberal education. France is the home to a great number of noteworthy literary masters. Emile Zola, Gustave Flaubert, Honoré de Balzac, Voltaire, and Marcel Proust are some famous figures among many more.

Madame de Pompadour is widely known as the patroness of the arts and literature. Among others, she protected two of the most famous French philosophers: Voltaire and Diderot. She was also the *maîtresse-en titre* (the official mistress) of Louis XV from 1745 to 1750. She loved the arts, architecture, and clothes, and the fashion she used was known as the "Pompadour Style," a style of dress that became *à la mode* in *le tout* Paris.

The work of all artists reflects the prevailing ideas and trends of their generation. Their work belongs to specific places and times because, as it has been said, art is the signature of a civilization. Today, computers make the execution of some types of arts faster and more precise, as in designing three-dimensional models of commercial products or sketching blueprints, for instance; however, computers cannot make art better. "Computers are useless. They can only give answers," said Pablo Picasso. People everywhere, artists or not, may share this great artist's opinion.

Most artists know and use many of the French art loanwords listed in *French for Le Snob* under Art terms, Music, Dance, Theatre, Painting, and Literature. The goal of most artists is to achieve perfection and if you are an artist, *French for Le Snob* can give you the means to describe or discuss your creations ingeniously by speaking the French art words of the English language *à la française*. And as you talk about *ombres chinoises, champlevé, chinoiseries, enluminures, nature morte,* and *objets trouvés,* you may appear literate to some and snobbish to others. It is your prerogative to be one or the other—or both.

ART TERMS

"Every child is an artist. The problem is how to remain a child once he grows up," said Picasso (1881–1973). Perhaps, if one stopped giving children too many things, they would continue to develop and use their innate creativity! Nevertheless, it is true that children of all times, including during the Norman era, did *collage, découpage, and assemblage* long before these terms were coined to describe such creations. Art terms, like any other words, are invented when they are needed to describe a style, an era, or a movement. Some French art words used in English are listed below.

FRENCH LOANWORDS

A DEUX CRAYONS With two crayons: this technique is a chalk drawing done in red and black or charcoal. A trois crayons is black, red, and white.

ARABESQUE (f) Interlaced lines with leaves, fruits, and flowers. First used by ancient Greeks and Romans.

ART BAROQUE (m) Style of European art and architecture dominant during the seventeenth century and characterized by bold forms and elaborate ornamentation.

ART BRUT (m) Primitive or pseudo-primitive art.

ART DÉCO (m) Decorative style popular in 1920s and 1930s, characterized with bold colors and curved lines.

ART NOUVEAU (m) Modern decorative art style with flowing lines and floral motifs. It was popular in the late nineteenth century, early twentieth century in Europe, particularly England. It became popular again in the 60s and 70s.

ART RUPESTRE (m) Mural art cave; from Latin, *rupes*, French, *roche* or *rocher*, (roc).

ART SACRÉ (m) Sacred art; a twentieth century attempt to re-establish religious art.

ASSEMBLAGE (m) Odds and ends elements such as metal, cloth, strings, and various *objets trouvés* glued or welded and assembled to create a three-dimensional work of art.

ATELIER (m) Studio or workshop where craftsmen, workers, or artists do their work.

AVANT-GARDE In the vanguard; innovator, claiming to be precursor, particularly in the arts.

BANDEROLE (f) Painted or sculpted ribbon bearing an inscription.

BAS-DE-PAGE (m) Literally, bottom of page: in a manuscript, the space under the text, framed by a border decoration and filled with figures and scenes.

BEAUX-ARTS (m.pl.) Fine arts.

BELLE ÉPOQUE (f) Expressed in *la douceur de vivre* (sweetness of living) that followed the end of the war. *La Belle époque:* late nineteenth century to First World War (1914–1918) in France.

BIBELOT (m) A small art object which is either rare or decorative; also a *miniature* book.

BRONZE (m) A work of art made of bronze: an alloy of copper and tin.

CARICATURE (f) A representation in which the subject's distinctive features are exaggerated; a cartoon.

CARTE-DE-VISITE (f) A calling card, but also one with a photographic portrait, especially in the nineteenth century. Cards of famous people or royalties are collectors' items.

CHAMPLEVÉ (m) The art of carving depressions through layers of a metal, leaving a *levé* (raised) *champ* (field) that forms the outline of the design; enamel is laid in the depressions and fused.

CHEF-D'OEUVRE (m) A masterpiece in art, in literature, music, etc.

CHINOISERIE (f) An art form associated with the Rococo movement; from *Chinois* (Chinese). A *chinoiserie* is a *bibelot* peculiar to Chinese; popular in Europe from about 1670.

CISELURE (f) Art of chasing metal; a *ciseleur* is a chaser; see Chapter IV under About Men.

CLOISONNÉ (m) Divided by *cloisons* (partitions); *cloisonné* enamel is a technique in which different ceramic colors are separated by thin lines of flattened metal.

COLLAGE (m) From French *coller* (to glue); a *collage* is a design created by gluing flat elements of contrasting texture and pattern such as newspapers, wallpaper, illustrations, photographs, cloth, strings, etc., to a flat surface.

CONTOUR (m) The edge or line that separates an area from another; the outline.

COQUILLAGE (m) Decorative motif resembling seashells; *un coquillage* is French for "seashell." *Une coquille* is a shell, as *une coquille d'oeuf* (eggshell) or *Coquille St. Jacques.* See Chapter I, Meats & Fish.

CRÈCHE ART *Crèche Art* was used to represent the Nativity scene using small profane or sacred puppet-like figures painted, sculpted, or drawn. *Crèche* is a French loanword meaning a manger, and also a nursery school.

CROQUIS (m) A sketch; a rough draft on paper used in architecture, sculpture, or painting to illustrate the concept of the work to be done; from one of meaning of *croquer*, (to draw). The French expression *mignon à croquer* means, "sweet enough that one wants to draw a *croquis*, a sketch;" said mostly about children.

DAMASSÉ In ceramics: a white ornamentation on a white background. Also a *damassé* fabric; see Chapter III under Fabric.

DÉCOUPAGE (m) The art of *découper* (cutting out) illustrations from paper, foil, and pasting them on a surface in a decorative arrangement, applying coats of varnish or lacquer to simulate painting.

DILETTANTE (m) In the eighteenth century, an admirer or lover of the arts; a connoisseur. Today, it indicates a person who dabbles in the arts, and it has a somewhat negative meaning.

ECORCHÉ (m) Literally, skinned: a technique that removes the skin of a figure, a sculpture that exhibits the muscular system.

ENLUMINURE (f) Illuminated design; decorations in manuscripts using natural pigments and ink applied to real parchment.

ENSEMBLER (m) A scene on stage in which the whole cast appears *ensemble* (together). *Un ensemble* is also a loanword for suit.
See Chapter III under Clothes.

FAÏENCE (f) Short for pots of *faïence*; a tin-glazed pottery or porcelain usually with elaborate and colorful painted decoration; from Faenza in Romagna, Italy.

FIGURINE (f) A small sculpted or molded figure; a *statuette*.

FIN DE SIÈCLE (m) Literally, end of the century: a term that connotes the idea of an art style or a movement on the decline, particularly the late nineteenth century.

FROTTAGE (m) The technique of putting a sheet of paper over a texture surface and rubbing with a pencil across the paper; the resulting image is also called a *frottage*. From *frotter* (to rub). Max Ernst, Surrealist German painter (1891–1976), was the first to introduce *frottage* in his works.

GOUACHE (f) Water-based paint made opaque by adding a white pigment. From the Italian *guazzo*, a place where water is; see this chapter under Paintings.

GRAVURE (f) Short for *photogravure*; engraving obtained by using plates made by a photographic process.

HACHURE (f) Shading effect obtained by tracing closely spaced parallel lines; the technique is used in cartography to indicate relief.

ILLUMINATION (f) Designs, tracings used to decorate and illustrate manuscripts and books (*Webster's*); Old French word used in English but now obsolete in France.

MAQUETTE (f) A small sculpture made as a model for a full-scale work.

MÉTIER (m) Craft; the forte of an artist.

MINIATURE (f) A small painting or illuminated letter in medieval manuscripts; type of detailed delicate painting; a reproduction *en miniature* is a replica.

MONTAGE (m) A composition made of pictures previously drawn, painted, or photographed; the term *photomontage* is used in motion pictures. From *monter* (to assemble, to mount).

MOTIF (m) A recurrent pattern or feature in a composition or a design.

MOULAGE (m) The technique of making a *moule* (a mold). Plaster of Paris is often used to make a cast from a natural object.

NATURE MORTE (f) Literally, dead nature: still life; Picasso and Cézanne were prolific still life artists.

OBJET D'ART (m) A work of art; usually a small sized object.

OBJET TROUVÉ Literally, found object: a word that applied in the twentieth century to odd *objets trouvés*, man-made or natural, used in *assemblage*. The Surrealists believed that an artist could make a work of art with any found object. Antoni Gaudí used broken pieces of ceramic to cover the roof of pavilions in the Park of Güell building (1900–1914) in Barcelona. *Le bureau des objets trouvés* (the Lost and found Office) in France.

OEIL-DE-PERDRIX (m) Literally, partridge's eye: a small round spot in a pattern; a dot. Frequently used on Sèvres porcelain.

OEUVRES (f.pl.) Works of art, music, or literature; the total body of work of an artist or writer.

OMBRÉ (m) Gradual shading of color going from light to dark. From *ombrer* (to shade); *une ombre* (shadow); *à l'ombre* (in the shade).

OMBRES CHINOISES (f.pl.) Chinese shadows: European version of Chinese shadow puppets used in courtly shows.

PAPIER COLLÉ (m) Pasted paper; a kind of *collage* incorporating various types of paper such as newspaper, wallpaper, bus or subway tickets. The technique was first used by Braque, French painter (1882–1963), and later by other Cubists such as Picasso and Gris, both Spanish painters.

PAPIER MÂCHÉ (m) Literally, paper chewed: a material made of paper pulp mixed with rosin oil that can be molded into various objects while moist.

PASTICHE (m) Literary, artistic, or musical compositions made up of bits from various sources; a potpourri; a hodgepodge; imitation of another artist's work.

PÂTE DE VERRE (f) Paste of glass: powdered glass that has been fired a second time.

PÂTE DURE (f) Hard clay.

PÂTE TENDRE (f) Soft clay.

PEAU D'ORANGE (f) Orange skin: a term used in ceramics to describe a surface that resembles the skin of an orange. In French, a *peau d'orange* is another word for cellulite: lumpy thighs, saddlebags, dimple *derrière*. Disaster! A lump-and-bump fix is a must!

PLEIN AIR (m) *En plein air* (in open air); the expression describes paintings that have been made outdoors.

POINTILLISME (m) Pointillism is a Neo-Impressionist style of painting of the nineteenth century in which little *points* (dots) of color are placed very close together to create various colorful shapes.

POMPIER (m) A term used to describe a work of art that is garish and pretentious. Art *pompier* painters: Adolphe William Bouguereau (1825–1905), Jean-Léon Gérôme, (1824–1904) among others; *Un pompier* is also French for "a fireman."

POTICHE (f) A vase of porcelain.

QUATRE-COULEUR (m) Said of an *objet d'art*: decorated with carved gold of different colors, especially four.

REPOUSSÉ (m) Embossed: a pattern of thin metal obtained by hammering the reverse of an object, as in the Statue of Liberty; from *repousser* (to push back).

ROCAILLE (f) Artistic representation of rockwork; a kind of rococo or scroll ornament; from *roche* (rock). In the sixteenth century, *Rocaille* was used in grotto decoration to imitate natural rock formation.

ROCOCO (m) From *rocaille*: art style in the eighteenth century, particularly in France, inspired from Italian Baroque style and the French *rocaille décor*. Rococo is characterized by asymmetry and shell-like watery forms.

ROSETTE (f) Literally, little rose: a painted, sculpted, or carved ornament resembling the petal of a rose.

SILHOUETTE (f) Outline drawing; outline of an object against the light, usually a profile portrait in black.

STATUETTE (f) A small statue.

VERNISSAGE (m) A private reception to view paintings before an exhibition.

VERRE ÉGLOMISÉ (m) Glass decorated with a layer of engraved gold.

VIE DE BOHÈME (f) Bohemian life: unconventional lifestyle of artists, writers, actors, and musicians.

VIGNETTE (f) Ornamental motif of wine leaves and grapes used as a border to illustrate a text in a book; from *vigne* (vine).

SHORT STORIES

ART BRUT The term that French artist and collector Jean Phillipe Arthur Dubuffet coined in 1945 to describe artwork produced by artists outside the common run. Jean Dubuffet (1901–1985), theoretician of *l'art brut*, got his inspiration mostly from mental patients and also from simple people and places, from children's drawings, and from graffiti on the walls. This rebel, anti-social, and isolated artist used gravel, mastic, and tar among other materials, to create his primitive raw artwork. His work was exhibited at the Pierre Matisse Gallery in New York City in 1947.

ASSEMBLAGE Jean Dubuffet first used the term in 1953 to describe his series of collaged butterfly wings he called *assemblages d'empreintes* (imprints, impressions). *Assemblage* is the three-dimensional equivalent to *collage*, and like it, is associated with Cubism where disparate *objets trouvés* are glued to create a *collage* or assembled in three-dimensional structures, called *assemblages*.

Before Dubuffet, Picasso, and French artist Marcel Duchamp (1887–1968), who became an American citizen, had both been using *objets trouvés* to create sculptures resembling (but not yet labeled) *assemblage*. Indeed, an *assemblage* is similar to a sculpture except that elements are put together (assembled) instead of being carved. In 1912, Picasso's *Glass of Absinthe* was a painted bronze on which he placed a wax piece of an absinthe glass and a silver absinthe spoon holding a sugar cube on which absinthe was poured before drinking it. Absinthe, *la Fée Verte* (the Green Fairy), has been used to cure jaundice, rheumatism, flatulence, and as a vermifuge. Members of the Foreign Legion drank it in combat and to fight malaria. This bitter potion was banned in many countries in the 1900s. In 1975, it was included on the list of unsafe herbs by the FDA in the United States because drinking this emerald-green, anise-flavored liquor distilled with oil of the wormwood plant was addictive. It caused delirium and hallucinations. Using it as *apéritif* was *en vogue* in the bohemian café culture of the nineteenth century France, however. Apparently, Henri de Toulouse Lautrec, Edouard Manet, Paul Gauguin, Ernest Hemingway, Van Gogh, and Pablo Picasso, among others, enjoyed it. Picasso's *Glass of Absinthe* is on display at the Museum of Modern Art in New York.

Louise Nevelson, a Russian born sculptor living in the United States made a more recent *assemblage* called *Royal Tide V*, (1960). With *objets trouvés*, she created large wooden relief-like *assemblages* that often covered an entire wall.

ATELIER An *atelier* used to be a place where seamstresses, carpenters, painters, and artists could create their products. It was a place where they shared their ideas and found inspiration and answers to their questions. Ateliers promoted research, support, and self-expression.

CHINOISERIE A *chinoiserie* is an *objet d'art* made in China, but the word is also used to describe Chinese influence on the arts and crafts of Europe, whether they are produced by Chinese or European artists. The term was *en vogue* in Europe in the late seventeenth and throughout the eighteenth centuries. The interest in *chinoiseries* roughly coincides with an increase in exports from China following the lifting of China's ban on foreign trade in 1684. The word *chinoiseries* (plural) is used in the French expression *chinoiseries administratives*, meaning "red tape."

CLOISONNÉ The art of making *cloisonné* was introduced in Europe, Japan, and Persia from China. *Cloisonné* is also called Blue of Jingtai because blue is the predominant color used for enameling and because the art became prevalent during the reign of Jingtai (1450–1456) during the Ming Dynasty. *Cloisonné* is a technique in which small metal strips forming *les cloisons* (the partitions), usually gold, are soldered to a metal background. When this is done, an enamel paste is fired inside the *cloisons* and semi-precious stones, such as garnets, are put in the compartments to produce ornaments of great beauty.

COLLAGE *Collage* is an art form introduced by Cubist artists in the early 1900s. A *collage* is a design created with *objets trouvés*, such as pieces of newspapers, illustrations, cloth, or strings that are *collés* (glued) to a flat surface, hence the word *collage*. A *collage* reflects the environment and is intended to deliver a message or a feeling. French painter Georges Braque (1182–19630) and Pablo Picasso (1881–1973) made *collages* in the early twentieth century.

The first Cubism *collage: Still Life with Chair Caning* was created in 1912 by Pablo Picasso, the Spaniard painter/sculptor from Malaga. Picasso glued a real piece of oilcloth printed with caning pattern onto the canvas and framed his creation with a rope. The *collage* is at Musée Picasso in Paris.

Caning originated in India in the second century A.D. Caning is a pattern formed by interlacing the flexible stems of reeds or rattan, a climbing palm of tropical Asia. Caning is a craft used to make the backs and seats of chairs. Chair caning was especially popular in France during the eighteenth century and the craft is still practiced on open street markets where French people love to stroll and look for bargains during the weekend.

DÉCOUPAGE The term *découpage* comes from French *découper* (to cut up). A *découpage* usually depicts a scene or tells a story. The art of *découpage* developed in Italy in the seventeenth century. Originally, skilled artisans were employed to hand-paint furniture but as it became too expensive they cut out colored pictures, glued them to plain furniture or boxes and other items, and applied coats of varnish or lacquer to make it look as if it had been painted. This process was called the *arte povero*, the poor man's art. It was also called japanning which was a European imitation of lacquered *papier mâché* objects made in Japan. *Découpage* emulated the work made in Japan and in China, where using paper for artwork existed long before it was used in Europe. *Découpage* became a hobby of the ladies of the court. Children everywhere are experts at it and can *découpe* (cut) anything in sight in the wink of an eye.

ENLUMINURE Until the late twelfth century, making books was the monopoly of the monks who used some of their time transcribing manuscripts. The first books were made of parchment. The name *parchemin* (parchment) comes from Pergamum, an ancient city in Asia Minor where it was made. Sheep, goat, and cow skins were used to produce it. Vellum was made of calfskin and young goat, lamb, or deerskin. Parchment predates paper, invented in China in the year 105, by at least 1,500 years.

Illuminators made the *enluminures* in the parchment manuscripts, adding their creative work to the tedious work of the scribes who copied the text by hand. Initial letters in manuscripts had both a decorative and functional purpose; not only were they beautiful because they were made with rich blue and red colors and real gold, they were also used to mark the beginning of a body of text and to separate paragraphs or chapters. The art of *enluminure* was brought to perfection in Europe during the Middle Ages. A book with *illuminations* was a sign of wealth and has always been appreciated as a work of art.

FAÏENCE The word *faïence* was used in France to describe tin-glazed earthenware in the late sixteenth century. However, earthenware pottery was first made by Islamic potters during the Middles Ages after they were inspired by the finely decorated Chinese Porcelain. Then from Persia, the Islamic whitetin glaze technique spread into Spain and was later introduced in Italy where Italian potters in Faenza used a technique called maiolica, a word derived from Majorca, a city in Spain from where they imported the tin-glazed ware.

The word Majolica is used in English and *faïence* in French (after the city of Faenza) to describe a maiolica tin-glazed ware.

FIN DE SIÈCLE The term refers to the decades of the 1880s and 1890s during which social and artistic values were on the decline. Toward the end of the nineteenth century, just before the First World War (1914–1918), decadence was *en vogue*. Homosexuality, nudity, drug addiction, and social behaviors intended to shock the *bourgeoisie* prevailed in the arts and literature.

ILLUMINATIONS The oldest-known *illuminations* are on Egyptian papyrus rolls. *The Book of the Dead*, 1240 B.C., is a recipe book designed to guide the deceased to a happy afterlife. The no longer living could look for answers to his quest in *The Chapter of not being boiled in the fire* and *The Chapter of not letting the head of a man be cut off from his body*, for instance. Useful tips! The Egyptian book is illustrated and written on papyrus and like almost anything else, the sacred texts are now sold on CD-ROM. *The Book of the Dead* is on display at the British Museum in London.

OMBRES CHINOISES The art has its roots in China. According to a legend, when Lady Li died, Emperor Wudi (156–87 B.C.) became very depressed. She was his favorite concubine. A compassionate oculist thought of something to cheer him up. He carved a wooden figure resembling Lady Li and projected its shadow against the curtains; the sad Emperor believed that he saw the spirit of his beloved departed and this consoled him a little. It may have been the beginning of the Chinese Shadows plays used today by many countries around the world.

In *ombres chinoises* plays, finely cutout figures are manipulated behind a screen; a bright light behind projects their animated shadows through the screen to entertain the audience sitting on the other side. When French missionaries returned from China, they took the idea back to France where it became popular with the opening of a shadow theatre in Versailles in 1774. Later, *Ombres chinoises* art was used at Le Chat Noir, a café in Montmartre in Paris where painters, musicians, and writers used the technique to present their satirical works. Coffeehouses were places where not only writers and artists, but politicians, scientists, and businessmen could get information, reliable or not, and hear the latest gossip. It is still true today. People gather with their laptops at Starbucks to check their e-mail, read the news, chat, spy and be spied on, while they savor their lattes.

PAPIER MÂCHÉ *Papier mâché* is one of the oldest art forms invented in China during the second century A.D. The Chinese, who also invented paper, used *papier mâché* to make helmets, of all things. From China it spread to Japan and Persia where they used it, among other things, to make masks for festivals and ceremonies. At the end of the tenth century A.D. *papier mâché* was used in Europe, particularly in Spain, France, and Germany. In the seventeenth century, it was the French who first realized its potential; they used it to make dolls, snuffboxes, little boxes of all sorts, and other objects they covered with several layers of lacquers to add strength and beauty. Puppeteers also used a type of *papier mâché* made from paper and sawdust. In the United States, The Litchfield Manufacturing Company in Connecticut was built in 1850 and specialized in making *papier mâché* alarm clock cases decorated with colored or golden ornaments. Schools use it for art projects and people use it in stage productions to make props that are easy to move between the acts of a play.

POINTILLISME Georges Seurat (1859–1891) was the inventor of the technique, characterized by tiny *points* (dots) of contrasting colors that appear mixed together in a process called optical mixing. One of his most famous paintings, *Un Dimanche d'été à la Grande Jatte* took him two years to complete (1884–1886). Not surprising, if one considers that more than three million little dots were made to achieve this work of art. *La Grande Jatte* is the name of an island in the River Seine, northwest of Paris. Pointillisme, also called Post-Impressionism, was an offshoot of Impressionism, and the precursor of Fauvism.

PLEIN AIR Schools of French Impressionist painters during the late 1860s in France engaged mainly in painting the effects of outdoor lights and atmospheres. English painters Richard Parks Binington (1802–1828) and John Constable (1776–1837) did *plein air* paintings, as did, naturally, the Barbizon School artists. Barbizon refers to a group of French painters from the early 1830s to the 1870s. The artists met in Barbizon, a small town near Paris, to paint landscapes and nature in the forest of Fontainebleau. *Plein air* became central to Impressionist painters Edouard Manet (1832–1883), Claude Monet (1840–1926), and Pierre-Auguste Renoir (1841–1919), to name some of the most famous.

REPOUSSÉ The Statue of Liberty, designed by French sculptor Auguste Bartholdi in 1856 and erected in the United States in 1886, is made of copper *repoussé* on a frame of steel. To do *repoussé*, copper is hammered into shape against a plaster mold, which becomes rigid, light, and easily disassembled and re-assembled. The copper shape is then bolted firmly on an iron armature.

The Statue of Liberty is located on Bedloe Island, renamed Liberty Island in 1956. The island was originally the property of Isaak Bedloe, who bought it in 1667. Immigrants coming to America can see the Statue from Ellis Island, designated as an immigration station, April 11, 1890 and declared part of the Statue of Liberty Monument in 1965. *La Statue de la Liberté* was a present from France to the United States and symbolizes the friendship between the two countries; it is the most universal symbol of political freedom and democracy. It was dedicated on October 28, 1886 and established as a National Monument on October 15, 1924.

SILHOUETTE The word comes from Etienne de Silhouette (1709–1767), French Minister of Finance in 1759. Cutting *silhouettes* was his hobby. One of the most prolific silhouettists was Augustin Amant Constant Fidel Edouart (1789–1861) who served under Napoléon and cut approximately 3,800 *silhouettes*.

THEATRE

> "The theatre world is barely distinct
> from the art world; there is no family
> life on any level; theatre people are
> eccentric and inexhaustibly generous,"
> said Marcel Proust.

The origin of theatre goes back to primitive societies. People performed religious dances—and still do—to obtain favors from the gods: a fertile soil, good weather, tribal success in hunting or in warfare; they also danced to expel bad spirits. Later on, legends about the gods or tribal heroes were enacted not only to entertain but also to educate people. These types of shows were the precursors of theatre performances as we enjoy them today when we go to a *matinée* and applaud the *dénouement* of an *opéra comique*.

FRENCH LOANWORDS

CLAQUE (f) A hired group of people paid to applaud during a performance; from *claquer* (to applaud). *Une claque* is also colloquial French for *une gifle* (a slap).

CLAQUEUR (m) A member of the claque.

COSTUMIER (m) A person who sells or rents theatrical costumes; a costumer.

COULISSE (f) The wings, the dressing rooms; the backstage.

DÉBUT (m) First appearance of a performer, actor, or musician before the public.

DÉBUTANT (m) A actor making a *début*, his first appearance.

DÉBUTANTE (f) An actress making her *début*.

DÉCOR (m) Stage set.

DÉNOUEMENT (m) The outcome, the unfolding of a plot in a drama; from *dénouer* (to untie).

FARCE (f) A comedy, a humorous play; a buffoonery. Also, a prank done by a *farceur*; *Quelle farce* (What a joke).

GRAND GUIGNOL Puppet show; Punch and Judy show.

INTERLUDE (m) Short entertainment between the acts of a play while the *décor* is changed.

JEU DE THÉÂTRE (m) Stage-trick.

JONGLEUR (m) Juggler; a wandering minstrel in medieval times who sang, recited poetry, played the fiddle, or did acrobatics.

LEVER DE RIDEAU (m) Raising of the curtain before a play.

LOGE (f) Compartment for spectators in a theatre.

MATINÉE (f) A morning reception, especially a performance as of a play held in daytime for the first time. *Le matin* (morning); *la matinée* (time between dawn until noon); *dans la matinée* (in the morning). *Le soir* (evening); *la soirée* (time between dusk and bedtime); *une robe de soirée* (a dress for the whole evening). *Le jour* (day); *la journée* (time between sunrise and sunset); *bonne journée* have (a good day).

MISE-EN-SCÈNE (f) The staging of a play.

MONTAGE (m) In theater, *montage* involves selecting and assembling material to be performed before an audience; from *monter* (to assemble), one of the meanings of *monter*. *Photomontage* is the term used in the film industry.

NOM DE THÉÂTRE (m) Stage name.

OPÉRA BOUFFE (m) *Opera buffa*: light or comic opera same as *opéra comique*.

OPÉRA COMIQUE (m) A type of opera, comic or not, but originally humorous, later romantic, characterized by spoken dialogue.

PANTOMIME (f) A mimic; a story told without words through expressive body and facial movements.

PARQUET (m) The term used in French for the main floor of a theatre is *orchestre*, also called "orchestra" in English. In both French and English *parquet* is "flooring, parquetry."

PARTERRE (m) On the ground: the part of a theatre beneath the balcony and behind the parquet; called orchestra circle.

PIERRETTE (f) A female member of a company of *pierrots*.

PIERROT (m) Little Pierre: a typical character in a French *pantomime*; a white-faced entertainer wearing a loose white costume with black spots.

PREMIÈRE (f) A first performance or showing of a play, of a film; also the leading lady in a play.

SOUBRETTE (f) A maidservant as a character in a play or opera; especially one of a coquettish character.

TRAGÉDIENNE (f) Actress of tragedy.

VAUDEVILLE (m) A stageshow consisting of mixed specialty acts including songs, dances, and skits.

VEDETTE (f) A leading star of stage or screen; a celebrity.

SHORT STORIES

CLAQUE Roman Emperor Nero, a despot who persecuted the Christians and threw them alive to hungry lions, was also dedicated to artistic and athletic excellence. During the Roman Empire, *claqueurs* were hired to applaud at private performances sponsored by wealthy patrons of the arts. Nero himself, who loved chariot races and fancied himself as Apollo in his four-horses-drawn chariot, also believed he was an athlete, a singer, and a poet. It is said that the prudent emperor would take with him an army of soldiers to applaud him in his concert tours, just in case. Apparently, his singing and his acting were neither bad nor good. In the sixteenth century, Jean Dorat, a French poet born in Limoges in 1508, introduced *la claque* in the French theatres and by 1830, *la claque* had become a regular institution.

FARCE Among many others, *Les Chaises* (1952), a one-act drama by Eugene Ionesco, is one example of a *farce tragique* intended to be funny. Ionesco (1909–1994) was a French writer of Romanian origin who denounced the absurd. Many others did the same, such as Samuel Beckett in *En attendant Godot* (*Waiting for Godot*), a hilarious, sadly realistic *comédie* in which Estragon and Vladimir wait for Godot, hoping desperately for something to happen that will make their wretched lives better. When a concerned or nosy Frenchman must know what a *compadre* who stares into space is waiting for, the reply he will get from a literate French person is often, "*J'attends Godot*," meaning, "I have no idea *mon cher*," or "None of your business," depending on who is asking the question, why, how, and when (before or after *pousse-café*). In *Les Chaises*, Ionesco has two very old people stranded in some small island, eagerly preparing for visitors that no one can see. The stage is filled with chairs to welcome them and of course, as in Beckett's play, they never show. In the end, the poor lonely souls commit suicide . . .

PANTOMIME The most ancient *pantomimes* were performed in China in 100 B.C. In the sixteenth and seventeenth centuries, comic drama acts called the *commedia dell'arte* were improvised in Italy to entertain audiences. The plots of the *pantomimes* were based on folk tales. French writer Charles Perrault (1628–1703) collected many stories in his book: *Mother Goose Fairy Tales*, published in 1697. Classic stories such as *Le Chat Botté* (*Puss in Boots*), *Cendrillon* (*Cinderella*), and *Le petit Chaperon Rouge* (*Little Red Riding*

Hood), although written for children, were in fact reminders of grown-ups' greed, dishonesty, and prejudice.

Pantomimes were traditionally acted in England at Christmas and as New Year entertainment. The most famous farcical characters were Harlequin, *Pierrot,* and Columbine. Harlequin, dressed in a diamond-patterned costume and wearing a mask, was the capricious lover of Columbine. He was very popular in England in the eighteenth century. *Pierrot* became popular in the nineteenth century.

PIERROT Originally, *Pierrot,* as well as *Pulcinella* (Punch) and *Arlechinno* (Harlequin) in his colored diamond-pattern outfit were characters of the *Commedia dell'Arte,* a form of improvised artistic comedy performed by Italian traveling troupes in the second half of the sixteenth century. The *Commedia dell'Arte* spread throughout Europe, particularly in France where *Pedrino* was popularized as *Pierrot* by Jean-Gaspard, *dit* (said, called) Jean-Baptiste Deburau, the French mime artist. Deburau was born in Kolin, Bohemia in 1796 and died in Paris in 1846.

The *Pierrot's* costume is white with black pom-poms and black spots. Do you know why? Or why there is a tear on *Pierrot's* cheek? The answers are all in a legend.

One day, Saint Pierre found a little naked boy on his doorstep. The poor child was covered with snow. Saint Peter, who has the keys to Heaven, blessed the freezing creature and, magically, the snow became a soft, clean, white garment. He named the little moppet *Pierrot, petit Pierre.* Saint Peter is good-hearted but apparently he is also strict; he has rules and like many rules, this particular one didn't make sense: he forbade the *gamin* [38] to play with human children outside of Heaven. How is a little boy supposed to do that? Naturally, *Pierrot* went to play with other children because, like the apple for Eve in the gardens of Eden, it had some appeal—it was forbidden. When he came back, Saint Peter didn't look happy at all and he put black marks on little Peter's outfit wherever children from the earth had touched him, and furthermore, he kicked the poor infant out of Heaven. This is why a poor *Pierrot* always looks melancholic in his black-spotted-white costume!

GRAND GUIGNOL The *Grand Guignol*, originally from Italy, was a well-known *marionnette* show introduced in Lyon, France at the end of the eighteenth century by Laurent Mourget (1769–1844). *Guignol* and his friend Gnafron were the symbols of rebellion and unconventional behavior. Later on, the show went to Paris and eventually, live actors performed plays dealing with the macabre, ghosts, and murderers at the Grand Guignol theatre. *Polichinelle* (Punchinello) was another comical figure in puppet shows, which are still popular today in many parts of the world. Punchinello was famous for his satires exposing the male domination over the *sexe faible* in the Victorian era. The French *Polichinelle* has two humps—one in front, one behind—and a crooked nose. The tasteless idiom *avoir un Polichinelle dans le tiroir*, literally, to have a *Polichinelle* in the drawer, is translated in English by an equally tasteless expression: to have a bun in the oven. Where have the poets gone?

VAUDEVILLE The word *vaudeville* comes from Vau de Vire; Vire is the name of a small river in Normandy. In the fifteenth century there was a man called Olivier Basselin who lived in a small town nearby. He composed satiric songs that he called *chanson du Vau de Vire* (song of the Vire valley). The word was shortened to *vaudevire* and later, people forgot all about the river and said *vaudeville*. The English borrowed the word in the early eighteenth century to refer to any light, popular, or satiric song, often accompanied with *pantomimes*. Later on, the English used the word *variété* instead of *vaudeville*, and today, people go to *variété* shows in England; and they watch *vaudevilles* in America.

PAINTINGS

Two young boys were playing in a field with their little dog. All of a sudden, the mischievous animal disappeared in a hole. They ran to rescue him and heard him bark down below. Bravely, they went to look for him and, lo and behold, there, in a cave, they found their little companion. But as they used matches to see where they were going, they discovered something else: the walls were covered with *art rupestre*, beautiful rock paintings and engravings. Thanks to their little pet, they had just found the caverns of Lascaux. It was the year 1940 in Montignac, a small town in the Dordogne region of southwest France.

Later on, it was assessed that the paintings and drawings of the animals—mammoths, horses, wolves, and others—were more than 15,000 years old. The Lascaux caverns were closed to the public in 1963 because a fungus, resulting from moisture and carbon dioxide emanating from hordes of curious visitors, was damaging the paintings.

Lascaux, among other cave art, shows that throughout the ages, people have expressed their creative talents in one form or another. Artists everywhere have painted the world around them: landscapes, animals, flowers, life; they have produced wonderful *aquarelles, paysages,* and *singeries,* and they probably will always do so.

Frank Auerbach is to have said, "It seems to me madness to wake up in the morning and do something other than paint, considering that one may not wake up the following morning," a statement that may sound morbid to those who do not understand obsession!

Apparently, Auerbach painted 365 days a year, seven days a week, and probably more than eight hours a day. He was born in Berlin and sent to England in 1939 never to see his parents again. On the other hand, René Magritte wrote, "Life obliges me to do something, so I paint." *Pourquoi pas!* (Why not)! But whatever drives artists to paint also allows them to create masterpieces to be enjoyed by all those who cannot paint, or have no interest in painting at all, other than their kitchen walls once in a blue moon.

Artists everywhere are familiar with French loanword art terms, some of which are listed below.

FRENCH LOANWORDS

AQUARELLE (f) Watercolor painting. From Latin *aqua*, water.

ARABESQUE (f) Complex painting of intertwined flowers, foliage, or geometric shapes.

BISTRE A yellowish-brown, transparent pigment.

CAMAÏEU (m) A monochromatic painting made with two or three tints of the same color; similar to a chiaroscuro painting in which light and shade, clear and dark, are used to achieve the effect of a third dimension. When done in various shades of gray it is called *grisaille*; see below.

CHAMPÊTRE (m) A painting representing a pastoral scene. From *champ* (field).

EBAUCHE (f) A rough sketch in oils, particularly of portraits.

FÊTE GALANTE (f) A landscape painting made popular by the French painter Antoine Watteau (1684–1721); it depicts outdoor gatherings of women and men dancing, talking, and flirting in fashionable and contemporary clothes. The French Academy coined the term in 1717. *Fête* also means a holiday. The French say *Bonne Fête* to celebrate a Saint's day, for instance Saint Geoffroy (Jeffrey) on November 8; Sainte Anne on July 26. If you are invited to celebrate a *fête*, it is expected that you will bring a card, a gift, flowers, or a bottle of wine. The hostess will prepare and serve a special meal.

FROTTIS (m) A watercolor painting technique using a dry brush to allow the texture of the paper to show. From *frotter* (to rub). Also called dry brush.

GOUACHE (f) A work of art produced by applying opaque watercolor to paper; the paint itself.

GRISAILLE (f) A style of painting in gray monochrome resembling bas-relief. From *gris* (gray).

GROTESQUE (m or f) A style of painting or sculpture representing distorted and monstrous figures. From *grotte* (cave).

LUNETTE (f) A semicircular painting placed over a window or a doorway. Also used in architecture.

NATURE MORTE (f) A still life; used as a descriptive term in French art since the eighteenth century.

NOCTURNE (f) *Tableau nocturne*: a painting of a night scene. From *nuit* (night); the opposite is *diurne* (daytime). *Di* is Latin for "day," hence the days of the week in French: *Lundi: lune* day (day of the moon), *Mardi* (Mars day), *Mercredi* (Mercury day), *Jeudi* (Jupiter day), *Vendredi* (Venus day), *Samedi* (day of the Sabbath), *Dimanche* (God's day).

PALETTE (f) A thin, oblong or oval tablet with a hole near one edge through which the thumb is inserted; used by artists for mixing pigments.

PASTEL (m) A picture made with pastel crayons. In French, a *pastel* is a plant whose leaves yield a bleu dye called *bleu pastel.*

PASTORAL (m) A type of painting which depicts the lives of shepherds and shepherdesses.

PAYSAGE (m) A representation of a rural scene or landscape.

POSE PLASTIQUE (f) A type of *tableau vivant,* usually featuring near-naked women.

SALON DES REFUSÉS (m) Exhibition of the rejected. *Le Salon des Refusés,* ordered by Napoléon III in 1863, was an exhibition of the works refused by Le Salon, which is the annual exhibition of paintings and sculptures, created by living artists in Paris. One of the main paintings at the *Salon des Refusés* exhibition was Manet's *Le Déjeuner sur l'herbe* and works by Cézanne and Pissaro, among others.

SINGERIE (f) A painting in which monkeys are dressed as humans and engaged in human activities. From *singe* (monkey). In the late seventeenth century, Jean Berain developed a style of elegant *singeries* that included graceful birds and exotic *chinoiseries.*

TABLEAU (m) A painting.

TABLEAU VIVANT (m) Literally, living painting: a scene presented by actors who remain silent and motionless on a stage, as if in a picture.

TRANCHE DE VIE (f) Literally, slice of life: a realistic representation of daily life, especially in literature and painting.

TROMPE-L'OEIL (m) Literally, trick the eye: a rendering of objects that have spatial and tactile qualities; optical technique intended to give an illusion of reality.

SHORT STORIES

ARABESQUE It was an art form prevalent in Islamic culture from the tenth to the fifteenth centuries. *Arabesque* became a word used in Europe in the sixteenth century when Renaissance artists used Islamic designs for book ornamentation and decorative bookbinding.

GOUACHE The term was coined in the eighteenth century in France but *gouache* was used long before to make *enluminures* in medieval manuscripts. It was used in the sixteenth century and afterward to do *miniature* paintings. Because *gouache* (also called body) is a type of water-soluble pigment that produces matte and even colors, it is often used today by designers, illustrators, and airbrush artists in commercial illustrations.

Gouache is a water-based paint, made opaque by adding a white pigment to a mixture of Gum Arabic, a water-soluble binder made from the hardened sap of acacia trees. Gum Arabic is also widely used in the food industry as an emulsifier or thickener, and in making glues and inks. One of the greatest water colorists of all times was English painter Joseph Mallord William Turner (J.M.W. Turner 1775–1851). He was known as "the painter of light." He used a watercolor gouache in *The Red Room*, a beautiful painting he did in 1827.

GROTESQUE The word derives from the Italian word *grottesco*, a type of ornament combining distorted human and animal figures and loosely connected motifs. *Grottesco* were discovered by archeologists on the walls and ceilings of Roman underground rooms known as *grotto, grotte* in French, hence the word *grotesque*, which has come to represent abnormal and disturbing images.

Spanish Surrealist Salvador Dali (1904–1989) painted the world of dreams in which objects, animals, or people are distorted, odd, and strange-looking. Dali was able to express the weird images of the unconscious called *grotesque* because they defy accepted aesthetic conventions.

TROMPE-L'OEIL It is a technique rooted in antiquity and used by still-life artists. It was part of the Greek and Roman Empire culture in the second century. A skilled artist is able to trick the eye and make the viewer believe that what he sees are real three-dimensional objects, just like a magician can create illusions and fool her audience and make people believe that they see little doves flying out of a hat. *Trompe-l'oeil* is the closest imitation of realism.

In the United States, *trompe-l'oeil* had its beginning in Philadelphia with Charles Wilson Peale (1741–1827). Another American, born in Ireland, William Michael Harnett (1848–1892) revived *trompe-l'oeil* painting in the late 1800s. *The Old Violin* that he painted in 1886 is in the National Gallery of Art in Washington D.C. Harnett is also renowned for his *trompe-l'oeil Five Dollar Note*, (1877) that symbolizes the American fascination for wealth. Many collectors value the artist's paintings.

LITERATURE

Many of the European literature trends originated in France where people are passionately interested in exploring ideas. Several French writers have received the Nobel Prize for literature: Albert Camus (1957), born in what was French Algeria until the end of the war for the independence of Algeria in 1962; François Mauriac (1952), Anatole France (1921), André Gide (1947), and Romain Rolland (1915) to name a few. Jean-Paul Sartre refused the prize in 1964. Apparently, Sartre, one of the most famous French existentialists, believed that human existence is characterized by nothingness as emphasized in his book *l'Etre et le Néant* (*Being and Nothingness*), published in 1943; he also claimed that one has the capacity to negate and rebel. He did both, explaining that accepting the Nobel Prize would compromise his integrity as a writer.

The earliest French written texts date from the eleventh century and the Norman invasion in England. It is during that period that narrative poems describing the exploits of famous heroes were written. They were called *chansons de geste*, and *La Chanson de Roland* is considered to be the first example of early French literature. This epic poem celebrated the heroic deeds of Roland, Charlemagne's nephew who fought bravely with his sword named Durandal before dying at Ronceveaux in the Pyrénées.

French literature is the source of famous stories that have become familiar to many people around the world through films and musicals: *Les Trois Mousquetaires* (*The Three Musketeers*) by Alexandre Dumas, *Cyrano de Bergerac* by Edmond Rostand, *Les Misérables* by Victor Hugo. Many children, and hopefully many adults, have read *Le Petit Prince* by Antoine de Saint Exupéry (1940–1944), the daring French aviator and novelist whose work contains poignant observations on human existence.

People everywhere love to read *ballades* and *vers-de société, romans à thèse* or *romans policiers*. Some of the French words used in English and found in literary works are listed below.

FRENCH LOANWORDS

AUBADE (f) A poem or a song about dawn such as *The Sun Rising* by John Donne. From *aube* (dawn).

BALLADE (f) A verse form in poetry that appeared in the fourteenth century. *La Ballade des Pendus* (*Ballade of the Hung*), by François Villon, Middles Ages French poet.

BELLES-LETTRES (f.pl.) Literally, beautiful letters: refers to literary masterpieces in poetry, drama, etc.

BOUTS-RIMÉS (m.pl.) Rhymed endings: poem in set rhymes.

BURLESQUE (m) A work caricaturing another work: ludicrous, farcical, odd.

CHANSON (f) A song.

CHANSON DE GESTE (f) A medieval lyric about heroic deeds.

CHANSONNETTE (f) A short song.

COMÉDIE HUMAINE (f) Human comedy: a literary portrait of human activities. *La Comédie Humaine* by Honoré de Balzac (1799–1850) is a study of society described in some of his novels such as *Eugénie Grandet, Le Père Goriot,* and *La Peau de Chagrin.*

COMÉDIE NOIRE (f) Black comedy: a macabre rendering of a tragic story.

CONTE (m) A short story, a tale.

CONTEUR (m) A composer of *contes*; or a storyteller.

DRAMATURGE (m) A dramatist; a playwright.

FABLIAU (m) Short comic or satirical tale written in verse such as Chaucer's *The Miller's Tale.*

NOM DE PLUME (m) Pen name: a writer's pseudonym.

NOUVELLE (f) A short, fictitious narrative; a short novel, dealing with only few characters.

PIÈCE À THÈSE (f) Thesis play: a play written to support a political or philosophical thesis.

PIÈCE DE CIRCONSTANCE (f) A literary composition with a theory arising out of a particular situation.

PIÈCE D'OCCASION (f) A literary or musical work written for a special occasion.

PIÈCE NOIRE (f) Black play: a play with a tragic theme; also *film noir.*

POÈTE MAUDIT (m) Cursed poet: a poet who is not appreciated by his contemporaries because of his controversial ideas.

POT-POURRI (m) Anthology.

RECUEIL (m) A literary compilation.

ROMAN À CLEF (m) Clef also spelled *clé*; novel in which actual people or events appear under fictitious names.

ROMAN À THÈSE (m) A novel with a thesis; philosophical novel.

ROMAN DE GESTE (m) Romance of heroic deeds: a *chanson de geste*, a romantic story of daring exploits often written in verse.

ROMAN-FLEUVE (m) Literally, river novel: a long novel featuring the lives and members of several generations of a family; a sequence of self-contained novels, a saga novel.

ROMAN NOIR (m) Black novel, a crime novel.

ROMANCE (f) A fictitious novel emphasizing love and adventure.

ROMAN POLICIER A detective story, whodunit.

RONDEAU (m) Short, lyrical poem.

TIRADE (f) A long, vehement speech on some subject; a declamation.

TRAGÉDIE LYRIQUE (f) Lyric tragedy: a type of serious French opera of the seventeenth and eighteenth centuries making use of tragic mythological or epic subjects, same as Opera Seria.

TRAGÉDIENNE (f) An actress of tragedy.

VERS DE SOCIÉTÉ (m) Light, witty, polished poetry.

VERS LIBRE (m) Free verse.

SHORT STORIES

POÈTE MAUDIT *Les Poètes maudits* (1884) was the title of a study of several such cursed poets by the French Symbolist poet Paul Verlaine (1844–1896) who lived with Rimbaud, another naughty poet who had left his wife to live with Verlaine—a very daring thing to do in those days! The study included short biographies of misfits who had interest in the morbid, the perverse, who were homosexuals and wanted freedom of morals and behavior in a society that condemned them without making an effort to understand them. Nothing much has changed!

The archetype of *poète maudit* was Charles Baudelaire, the bad boy known for *Les Fleurs du Mal* (*Flowers of Evil*), a sexually explicit poem and a threat to the ideas and lifestyle of the *bourgeoisie* that he despised. Baudelaire was a dandy, a *débauché,* an opium addict, and a great poet who died of syphilis in his mother's arms.

DANCE

> "Human beings, vegetables, or cosmic
> dust, we all dance to a mysterious
> tune intoned in the distance by an
> invisible player," said Albert Einstein.

Dancing is a universal and spontaneous self-expression; it is a celebration of life. In some cultures, dancing was and still is a ritual expressing religious and philosophical beliefs. The purpose of various dance forms was to become the spirit of the sun, of the moon, of an animal, of a plant because—consciously or not—man always seeks cosmic harmony and integration with his environment.

From the beginnings of recorded history, people have danced to express joy, sadness, hope; they have danced to pray, to worship the gods and obtain their favors; they have danced to find inner peace and to heal. Various dance forms have illustrated or imitated actions or events of people's lives: war, hunting, birth, and death, among other things.

Dancing is spiritual, intellectual, sensual, or sexual; it is graceful, artistic, or erotic. "Dance is the hidden language of the soul, of the body," said Martha Graham (1894–1994) an American dancer and choreographer. And according to a Hopi Indian,[39] "To watch us (the Hopi) dance is to hear our hearts speak."

The Academy of Dance was the first ballet school, founded in the 1600s by King Louis XIV; it was later named the *Paris Opéra Ballet*. The core of classical ballet vocabulary was established then and the French terminology is now used worldwide. Therefore let us do a *cabriole, la danse macabre, la danse du ventre, la pirouette, le pas de deux* and the French *cancan*!

FRENCH LOANWORDS

Selected words used in dancing are listed below. Among other sources, professional dancers can find a more complete list in the *Dictionary of Classical Ballet Terminology* by Rhonda Ryman.

ALLONGÉ (m) A movement with the arms *allongés* (extended) as far as possible.

ARABESQUE (f) A ballet position in which the weight of the dancer is on one leg while the other one is stretched behind.

ATTITUDE (f) A dancer's pose such as attitude *cambrée*; see *cambré* below.

BALANCÉ (m) A swaying step from one foot to the other. *Une balance* is French for "scale."

BAL COSTUMÉ (m) A dressed ball; a costumed dance.

BAL MASQUÉ (m) A masked ball.

BALLET (m) Dance that originated in Italy but was established as an art form in the French courts during the sixteenth century.

BALLET RUSSE (m) The Russian ballet.

BALLONNÉ (m) Bouncing step on one leg while the other does a *battement replié*.

BARRE (f) A waist-high handrail that dancers use to steady themselves.

BATTEMENT (m) A dancing step in which one leg is raised and brought back to the ground.

BOURRÉE (f) A lively French (or Spanish) dance similar to a *gavotte.*

CABRIOLE (f) A type of agile dance step; from Latin *capra,* a goat; French *cabrioler* (to caper about like a goat).

CAMBRÉ (m) Cambered, arched, curved position, especially forward or back.

CANCAN (m) A lively dance, a *quadrille,* that originated in France in the 1830s and involves high kicks performed by a line of women.

CHASSÉ (m) A sliding dance step in which one foot rapidly follows the other during the execution of a glide; one foot *chasse,* (chases), and tries to catch up with the other foot.

CHASSÉ-CROISÉ (m) A dance in which two dancers pass alternatively in front of each other, changing places. *Chasser* (to chase). *Croiser* (to pass somebody).

CISEAUX (m.pl.) Opening of the legs like the blade of *ciseaux* (scissors).

CONTREDANSE (f) A dance in which partners form two facing lines, a kind of country dance.

CORPS DE BALLET (m) A group of ballet dancers; the backbone of a ballet company that performs all of the ensemble work.

COTILLON (m) Brisk and lively country dance of the nineteenth century; music for such dance.

DANSE DU VENTRE (f) Belly dancing.

DANSE MACABRE (f) Dance of death; grim, gruesome.

DIVERTISSEMENTS (m.pl.) Dances, songs to entertain the audience between acts of a play or opera; *entr'acte* (see below). From *divertir* (to entertain).

DOS-À-DOS (m) Literally, back-to-back: in a squaredance figure before returning to original place.

EN DEDANS Inward movement; back to front in a circular motion.

EN DEHORS Outward motion; front to back in a circular movement in classical dance.

EN L'AIR In the air; a step done off the ground.

EN POINTE Standing on one's tiptoes in classical dancing.

ENTR'ACTE (m) Literally, between acts: the time between any two acts of a play or opera; a musical interlude, dance, etc., performed between acts.

ENTRECHAT (m) Jump in which one foot crosses in front of the other while in the air.

ETOILE (f) The *étoile* (the star) is the highest level a dancer can reach in the Opéra in Paris.

FARANDOLE (f) French dance from Provence.

FOUETTÉ (m) *Un fouetté*: a whip-like movement; from (*fouetter*), to whip. *Crème fouettée*, whipped cream. See Chapter I, under Desserts.

GAVOTTE (f) Alpine dance; a sixteenth century French dance. From Provençal *gavoto*.

GIGUE (f) A jig.

GLISSADE (f) Gliding step in any direction. From *glisser* (to glide).

GLISSÉ (m) As in pas *glissé*, a sliding step in which the flat of the foot is used.

JETÉ (m) A leap forward or to the side from one foot to land on the other.

MAÎTRE BALLET (m) Ballet Master; one who composes ballet and teaches the dancers.

PAS (m) A step in dancing.

PAS DE BASQUE (m) A dance step in three beats similar to a waltz step but a circular movement of the right leg on the second beat.

PAS DE BOURRÉE (m) A *bourrée* step.

PAS DE CHAT (m) Cat's step: a springing, catlike step in which each foot in turn is raised to the opposite knee.

PAS DE CHEVAL (m) A horse's step: a step in which a pawing movement is executed with one foot.

PAS DE CISEAUX (m) Scissors' step: a jump in which the legs are opened wide apart in the air.

PAS DE DEUX (m) A figure of dance for two people in classical ballet.

PAS DE QUATRE (m) A dance for four people; especially in classical ballet.

PAS DE TROIS (m) A dance for three people; especially in classical ballet.

PASSE (f) The transitional movement of the leg from one position to the next.

PASSE-PIED (m) Seventeenth-century French dance, similar to minuet.

PAS SEUL (m) A figure of dance for one person.

PAVANE (f) A stately dance performed in elaborate clothing and popular in the sixteenth century; a piece of music for this dance. French word deriving from Spanish *pavo*, peacock; French verb *se pavaner* (to strut about).

PENCHÉ (m) Especially of an arabesque performed while *penché* (leaning) forward.

PIROUETTE (f) A whirling on the toes of one foot.

PLIÉ (m) Bent at the knee; folded. From *plier* (to fold).

POINTES (f.pl.) A position of the body on *la pointe des pieds* (the tips of the toes).

POINTES (shoes)(f.pl.) Satin shoes without heels to enable dancers to dance on the tips of their toes.

POLONAISE (f) A stately processional Polish dance. *Les Polonaises* by Chopin.

POSÉ (m) A prolonged, held position.

POUSSETTE (f) Used in English only to describe a country dance figure in which couples join hands and swing around the floor. *Une poussette* in the Larousse or Petit Robert French dictionaries is a baby stroller (U.S.); a pushchair (G.B.). Not to confuse with *un pousse-pousse*, French for "rickshaw."

PREMIER DANSEUR (m) A leading male dancer in a ballet company.

PREMIÈRE DANSEUSE (f) A leading female dancer in a ballet company; a ballerina.

PROMENADE (f) A turning in place on one foot while maintaining a pose such as an arabesque; a march by a *danseur* around a *danseuse*.

QUADRILLE (f) A type of square dance; the music for it.

RÉVÉRENCE (f) A curtsy, a bow.

ROND DE JAMBE (m) A semicircular movement with one leg.

RONDE (f) Dance in which people move in a circle.

SARABANDE (f) A slow and stately Spanish dance; a piece of music for this dance.

SAUT (m) A leap; a *saut Basque* is one made while turning, holding one leg straight and the other at right angle to the body.

TAMBOURIN (m) Lively folk dance in Provence.

TEMPÊTE (f) A country dance popular in England in the late nineteenth century; a piece of music for this dance.

TEMPS (m) A movement in which there is no transfer of weight from one foot to the other.

TENDU (m) Stretched; held tautly.

TERRE À TERRE (m) A step in which the feet remain on or close to *la terre* (the ground).

TOUR DE FORCE (m) A feat such as a series of *pirouettes*, difficult jumps, etc.

TUTU (m) A skirt, short in classical ballet; below the calf in romantic ballet.

SHORT STORIES

DANSE DE SAINT GUY *La danse de Saint Guy,* Vitus's dance, is a nervous disease characterized by jerky movements and involuntary muscular contractions. Vitus's dance is the old name for Sydenham's chorea, after British physician George Sydenham (1624–1689) who identified the disease. In the Middle Ages, people that were afflicted with this nervous disorder prayed for a cure at St. Vitus shrine, after which the disease was renamed. St. Vitus became the patron saint of dancers, of dogs, and dog bites! Good to know when one sees a mad dog on the horizon!

DANSE MACABRE The word *macabre,* also spelled macaber, is an alteration of the French word *macchabée,* which means cadaver or corpse, and alludes to the Jewish martyrs of the Maccabees family who died while fighting Antiochus Epiphanes, a Syrian ruler between 175–163 B.C. Today, if the connection between *Danse Macabre* and the Jewish Maccabees family, or the Black Death, tends to be forgotten, the meaning of such a dance is still one that has to do with death.

The term describes a type of dance that is macabre, ghastly, and gruesome. *Danse Macabre* is a medieval allegorical concept about death, expressed in the arts and literature. The *Danse Macabre* has its origins in the late thirteenth century as a result of people's obsession with death due to a plague epidemic that killed millions of people in Europe between 1347 and 1351. The plague originated in China and Inner Asia and came to Europe when dead bodies infested with the disease were thrown in seaports on the Mediterranean cost. The plague, known as Black Death, was transmitted by rats' fleas and caused the death of more than 25 million people in Europe.

People became frightened and obsessed with dying, and the church played an important role in making them aware that death spares no one because indeed, your time comes whether you like it or not, whether you are a King or a poor beggar, young or old. As Isaac Asimov[40] expressed it well, "Life is pleasant, Death is peaceful, it's the transition that's troublesome." And as somebody else who didn't want to take *le grand voyage* (the big trip) said it simply, "I am not afraid of dying, I just don't want to be there when it happens." In any case, one way to communicate this eternal and universal truth was to preach, or to use an art form that illiterate could understand. In the *Danse Macabre*, Death was personified as a grinning skeleton that grabbed its victims and dragged them away.

DANSE DU VENTRE Its Arabic name is *Racks Sharki* or Dance of the Orient but it is hard to know the real truth about the origins of belly dancing because history of past practices was not always recorded.

Belly dancing is a dance designed for the woman's body and characterized by flowing sensual movements. Belly dancing was often an expression of worship or a ritual. While some people understand it as a celebration of the woman's body giving birth, others view it as erotic and sexual.

The dance would have originated in southern Egypt where it is traditional to hire a belly dancer at a wedding as a symbol of fertility. *La danse du ventre* was introduced in the United States in 1893 during the World's Columbian Exposition that celebrated the 400th anniversary of Christopher Columbus's discovery of the New World. Unfortunately, the purpose was to attract people, not to express the cultural meaning of belly dancing as it is understood in the Middle East. Belly dancing became known as hoochy-koochy, implying a type of sexy and seductive dancing, a perception that many people have about it today.

MUSIC

The history of a people is revealed not only in its dances and its cooking, it is fortunately always expressed in its music. "A nation creates music. A composer only arranges it," said Russian composer Mikhail Glinka Ivanovich (1804–1857). It goes without saying that every society, or group within a society, expresses its own identity through its music.

Music has the power to excite, to calm, to soothe, and to inspire; it expresses joy, sadness, or anger. Robert Schumann, German composer and pianist (1810–1856) said it well, "Music is the perfect expression of the soul." And Igor Stravinsky (1882–1971) is to have stated, "I have not understood a bar of music but I have felt it."

Composers everywhere hear the sounds of life around them and translate them into beautiful music that gives satisfaction to the player and to the listener. Without music, *the aubade, the berceuse, the pastorale*, life would be as sad and desolate as a barren land without trees and flowers.

FRENCH LOANWORDS

AUBADE (f) Music about dawn; from *aube* (morning).

BAGATELLE (f) A short, light piece of music, usually for piano. Loanword for triviality, a trifle.

BALLADE (f) A romantic or sentimental story told in a song; *Les Ballades* by Chopin.

BÂTON (m) Staff used by a conductor to direct musicians or singers during a musical performance. In French, the staff of the orchestra conductor is called *la baguette du chef d'orchestre*; in French a *bâton* is a stick, as *le bâton du berger* (the shepherd's stick).

BERCEUSE (f) A lullaby; a cradle-song; from *bercer* (to lull); *un berceau de bébé* (a cradle). *La Berceuse* by Schumann.

BOUFFE (f) Opéra bouffe, comic opera; *un bouffon* is French for "jester."

CAPRICE (m) A vocal or instrumental lively piece of music; from Italian, *capriccio*. *Caprice*, a loanword for whim.

CHALUMEAU (m) A musical pipe of reed or straw with six to eight holes; the forerunner of the clarinet; a little *flûte*; *le chalumeau du berger* (the shepherd's *chalumeau*).

CHEF D'ORCHESTRE (m) Conductor of an orchestra.

CLAVIER (m) Clavichord.

CONSERVATOIRE (m) Conservatory; a school for musicians.

COR ANGLAIS (m) English horn similar to the oboe; basset horn.

COR DE CHASSE (m) Hunting horn.

COR D'HARMONIE (m) French horn.

CORNEMUSE (f) Type of bagpipe used in Brittany: *cornemuse bretonne*.

CORNET À PISTONS (m) A cornet with pistons; the cornet, smallest of brass-wind instruments; similar to a trumpet.

DÉTACHÉ (m) A light breaking between notes; detached but not staccato; detached.

EMBOUCHURE (f) Position of the lips to the mouthpiece of an instrument; mouthpiece itself.

ENCORE (m) Again; an audience's demand for an item to be performed again.

ETUDE (f) A piece of music to demonstrate a particular aspect of a musician's technique (used in *Chopin's Etudes* for piano).

GALANT (m) Country music of the eighteenth century.

GAMME (f) Musical scale.

IDÉE FIXE (f) A musical phrase, a melody repeated several times in a symphony. Loanword for fixed idea, obsession.

IMPROMPTU (m) Short musical piece, often for piano; from Latin *in promptu*, promptly.

INTERLUDE (f) Music played on the organ between the verses of a choral. Also, a short instrumental piece of music played between the acts of a play.

MORCEAU (m) A short composition as *un morceau de piano* (a piano piece).

MUSETTE (f) A kind of small bagpipe of the eighteenth century with a soft tone; a soft pastoral air imitating sound of the *musette*; a dance performed to such music.

MUSIQUE CONCRÈTE (f) Electronic music constructed by the rearrangement of recorded real sounds in nature; first created in France in the late 1940s by Pierre Schaeffer.

NOCTURNE (f) A piano piece appropriate for night time; *Les Nocturnes* by Chopin. From Latin *nox, nuit* (night); *la vie nocturne* (the nightlife).

PASTORAL (m) Also spelled *pastorale (f)* : musical composition suggesting rural scenes and shepherds; *La Pastorale* is the beautiful Beethoven's 6th *Symphony*.

POT-POURRI (m) A medley of tunes.

REFRAIN (m) A phrase or verse repeated at intervals at the end of each verse in a song or a poem.

RÉPERTOIRE (m) A repertory.

RONDEAU (m) A rondo; often the last movement of a sonata.

SÉRÉNADE (f) A piece of music played outdoors at night; especially by a lover under a window to his sweetheart; a melody. *Sérénade* derives from Italian *serenata*.

SOURDINE (f) Originally, musical instruments with a soft tone. A device used on various musical instruments to muffle or soften the sound, as in *une trompette bouchée* (a muted trumpet); the soft pedal of a piano. *Sourd* means "deaf" in French; (Latin, *surdus*); Play the radio *en sourdine* (quietly) so that I do not become *sourd (m) sourde (f)*.

TAMBOUR (m) A bass drum.

TAMBOURIN (m) *Un tambourin provençal*: a high and narrow drum that one beats with one stick only while the other hand is used to play a wind instrument.

TIMBRE (m) The characteristic quality of sound that distinguishes one voice or musical instrument from another. Also the tone of what is spoken or written as in, "I like the *timbre* of your message."

TREMBLEMENT A thrill, a shake of a musical note. *Un tremblement de terre* is French for "earthquake."

SHORT STORIES

IDÉE FIXE French composer Hector Berlioz (1803–1869) used the *idée fixe* technique in his *Symphonie Fantastique* that he composed between 1820 and 1830 when he was twenty-seven years old. The symphony is the tale of a young artist (Berlioz himself) who falls in love with a young actress who ignores him at the beginning because she is successful and he is not. The *idée fixe* is the theme that celebrates with obsession the loved one who does not reciprocate his feelings; the theme is repeated in each of the five movements of his famous *Symphony Fantastique*.

His fixation finally paid off because the recalcitrant *belle* finally marries him and they have a son. She becomes ill and depressed and starts drinking. He divorces her to marry another woman who later dies of a heart attack; his son dies from yellow fever and he himself dies in Paris in 1869. Death had become an *idée fixe* in this great musician's life!

IMPROMPTU The word *Impromptu* was coined by Jan Vaclav Vorisek (1791–1825), a Bohemian composer in 1822, in *Impromptu Op. 7*. *Impromptu* is an instrumental music composition, and not necessarily an improvisation as literally implied. Vorisek was born in Bohemia in 1791, the same year Mozart died. He was friends with Austrian composer Shubert and introduced him to *Impromptu* music. Schubert's most famous

Impromptus were those for solo piano. Chopin also wrote *Impromptus*, his most famous being the *Fantaisie Impromptu*. Vorisek died of tuberculosis when he was thirty-four years old. He was buried in the Wahring Cemetery in Vienna where Schubert and Beethoven would also be buried.

NOCTURNE John Field (1782–1837), Irish composer and one of the greatest pianists of his time, created the *nocturne*. Son of a violinist, John Field studied in Dublin, and moved to London with his family in 1793; he then went to France, Germany, and Russia where he settled and died in 1837.

BE A SNOB

The short French phrases in this section contain one or more French word(s) and one or more loanwords selected from the vocabulary lists in Chapter II.

For instance, *tête de papier mâché* is one example of such a phrase in which *papier mâché* is a loanword and *tête* is French for "head." The literal meaning of *tête de papier mâché* is head of paper *mâché*. In France, you don't look very healthy if you have *une tête de papier mâché* because it means that you are ghostly pale with a pasty face and you look awful.

The literal meanings of the French phrases listed below are in parentheses and each phrase is included in a short sentence to illustrate how it is used in a French conversation.

ART TERMS

FAÏENCE (f) Tin-glazed pottery.
En chien de faïence (dogs of faïence).
They look at each other *en chiens de faïence*; they look daggers at each other.

GRAVURE (f) Engraving.

Gravure de mode (fashion engraving).

She looks like *une gravure de mode*; she is very stylish, (as if she came out of a fashion magazine).

PÂTE (f) Paste.

Une bonne pâte (a good paste).

C'est une bonne pâte; she or he is good natured, easygoing.

POTICHE (f) A vase.

Quelle potiche (what a vase).

Quelle potiche! What a wallflower!

THEATRE

DÉCOR (m) Stage set.

Dans le décor (in the stage set).

She drove *dans le décor*; she drove off the road, in the scenery!

GRAND GUIGNOL (m) *(guignol)* Puppet show; Punch and Judy show.

Du guignol (of the guignol).

C'est du guignol; it's farcical.

MATINÉE (f) A morning reception.

La grasse matinée (fat morning reception).

I did *la grasse matinée*; I slept in.

PAINTINGS

TABLEAU (m) A painting.

Vieux tableau! (old painting).

Quel vieux tableau!; What an old frump!

LITERATURE

CHANSON DE GESTE (f) *(chanson)* A medieval lyric; a song of heroic deeds.

La même chanson (the same song).

It's always *la même chanson*; it's always the same story.

The French also say, "It's always *la même histoire*, the same story."

COMÉDIE (f) Comedy.

De la comédie (comedy).

C'est de la comédie!; It's just an act!

CONTE (m) A tale.

Conte à dormir debout (tale to sleep standing)

It's a *conte à dormir debout*; it's a cock-and-bull story.

Des contes de bonnes femmes (tales of good ladies).

Des contes de bonnes femmes ma chère!; Old wives tales *ma chère!*

ROMAN-À-CLÉ (m) *(roman)* Novel in which actual people or events appear under fictitious names.

Tout un roman (a total novel). It's *tout un roman*; it's a long complicated story, a real saga.

DANCE

BALANCÉ A swaying step in which the weight of the dancer is on one leg while the other is stretched behind.

Bien balancé (well-swayed step).

She is *bien balancée*; she is well built, a nice bit of stuff (G.B.), a nice piece (U.S.).

BARRE (f) A handrail for dancers to hold on.

Un coup de barre (a handrail stroke).

I have *un coup de barre*; I feel drained all of a sudden, I am exhausted.

CANCAN (m) A lively dance that originated in France in the 1830s.

Des cancans (lively dances).

She does *des cancans*; she is gossiping.

DOS-À-DOS (dos) Back-to-back, before returning to the original place.

Bon dos (good back).

She has *bon dos*; she is saddled with the blame.

I have *bon dos*; it's always me! I always get blamed.

ETOILE (f) Star.

A la belle étoile (at the beautiful star).

I slept *à la belle étoile*; I slept out in the open (under the stars).

GIGUE (f) Jig.

Quelle grande gigue (what a big jig).

Quelle grande gigue!; what a beanpole (of a tall skinny girl).

ROND DE JAMBE (m) (rond) A semicircular movement with one leg.

Un rond (a circle).

I do not have *un rond*; I am broke; I do not have a penny.

Rond is French slang for "money."

Pas un radis, pas un sou; not one radish, not one penny; I am broke.

SAUT (m) A leap.

Faire le saut (to do the leap).

He made le saut; he took the plunge.

Le grand saut (the great leap).

She did *le grand saut*; she went west, she died.

MUSIC

BAGATELLE (f) Short piano piece.

Une petite bagatelle (a small piano piece).

I bought you *une petite bagatelle*; I bought you a little something.

MUSIQUE (f) Music.

Je connais la musique (I know the music).

You don't fool me, *je connais la musique*; I know the score!

TREMBLEMENT (m) A thrill, shake of a sound or musical note.

Tout le tremblement (the whole thrill).

He brought his chair, food, and *tout le tremblement*; the whole kit and caboodle.

The French also use tout le tralala, *tout le bazar, tout le bataclan*
(the whole works).

PROVERBS

ART NOUVEAU (nouveau) *Tout nouveau, tout beau!*
A new broom sweeps clean! The novelty will wear off.

CHANSON DE GESTE (chanson) *Tout fini par des chansons.*
There is a always a happy ending.
Oeuvre A l'oeuvre on connaît l'ouvrier.
We judge a man by his work.
Tempête—Qui sème le vent, récolte la tempête.
He who sows the wind, reaps a whirlwind.

Temps—Le temps perdu ne se rattrape jamais!
You cannot make up for lost time!

CONCLUSION

"Have you ever been to France, M. Martin?" asked Candide.[41]

"Yes," said Martin. "I have traversed several provinces. In some half, the inhabitants are crazy, in others they are too artful, in some they are usually quite gentle and stupid, and in others they are very clever. In all of them, the chief occupation is making love; the second, scandal mongering; and the third, talking nonsense!"

This depicts the French pretty well, although most Frenchmen may believe it, or accept it, only because Voltaire said it. By now, however, you probably identify with some of this witty French author's philosophy. And most likely some of your jealous peers who are not as motivated as you are to learn and improve their English vocabularies will accuse you of talking nonsense, of being a snob! But as Euripides (484–406 B.C.) noticed it wisely, "Talk sense to a fool and he calls you foolish." Either way, it is a lost cause, so, keep on talking nonsense, because *entre nous*, you'll have the *dernier mot!*

Chapter 3

FASHION & STYLE

~❧~

"I find that in France the
capriciousness of fashion is amazing.
They have forgotten how they were
dressed this summer; still less do they
know how they will dress this winter.
But the hardest thing of all to believe
is how much it costs for a husband to
keep his wife in fashion."

—*Persian Letters, Letter 99: The caprices of fashion,*
by French author Montesquieu [42]

In a follow-up letter, *Letter 100: French authority over fashion,* Montesquieu
says, "I was telling you the other day how extraordinarily capricious French
are about fashion. Yet it is incredible how obsessed they are with it; they
relate everything to it; it is the standard by which they judge everything
that happens in other countries; they always think that anything foreign

is absurd. I admit that I find hard to see how this infatuation with their clothes fits in with the inconstant way in which they alter them every day."

So was it three hundred years ago, according to Montesquieu, who ought to know since he was French, and so it is today. The French have indeed the reputation for being the world's biggest fashion snobs. Today, in the twenty-first century, they still dare say that Paris is *la capitale de la mode*, although they evidently share the title with other main hubs worldwide. But, snobbism is universal and the French have every right to be fashion snobs! After all, Paris *chic* is undeniable and recognized everywhere; even French little dirty fluffy *toutous* [43] (pronounced "tootoo," as some people say "tutu") wear designers' elegant sweaters with frills, *pompons*, and little pockets to put doggies' treats, warm quilted jackets, and other fancy *ensembles!* [44]

INTRODUCTION

The Bayeux Tapestry is a pictorial story of the Battle of Hastings and of the events that lead up to it. This seventy-meters-long embroidered *chef-d'oeuvre* is the oldest source illustrating the clothing of the everyday man at the time of the Norman invasion of England in the eleventh century. Men wore tight-fitting leggings and knee-length tunics pulled in at the waist by a belt. In the winter, they put on large cloaks over the garments. Women did not show their legs then, they wore long dresses and cloaks fastened with brooches. Fabrics made from natural fibers were hand-woven by peasant women.

The Norman did not invent fashion, of course, but they brought their flair for fine fabrics and style to England, where they settled after William the Conqueror, Duke of Normandy won the Battle of Hastings. Indeed, the

French have always been known for setting clothing trends, and for a very long time Paris enjoyed a world-famous reputation in the fashion industry.

However, due to industrialization, new technology, and globalization, *la ville lumière* is no longer the traditional main hub for fashion. Paris now shares the spotlight with other centers throughout the world, namely Milan, Rome, and London in Europe, and New York in the United States.

Fashions have come and gone; the hemline has fluctuated many times. Micro, mini, midi, and maxi have all been in and out. *Corsets* have been *en vogue* and *démodés*, and *à la mode* again! During the feminine liberation movement women got rid of them, shaved their legs, and burned their bras to protest the Miss America beauty pageant, which was held for the first time in Atlantic City, New Jersey, in 1921. Predictably, *corsets, corselets*, and *brassières* came back in style later on. The fashionable *silhouette* has varied from straight, to high-waist, low-waist, no-waist, and whatever! Some may declare that nothing is ever new under the sun and that what we perceive as a new fashion is only an interpretation of yesterday's style. However, retro fashion is never quite the same, although it may appear so. Indeed, if things seem to be the same, they change nevertheless because lifestyles change. It's like going back to your hometown twenty years later—it is still home, yet you don't quite feel home anymore.

Oscar Wilde (1854–1900)[45] had a rational explanation for all this. "Fashion is a form of ugliness so intolerable that we have to alter it every six months," he concluded. Even if this is sometimes true, there is no doubt that fashion is influenced by the changes happening in technology, by economical conditions, and geographical location. It is affected by the type of leisure people enjoy or the work they do at a given time and by cultural and moral values, among other factors. Fashion is a means of self-expression and it has always been used to communicate social status although today, the clothes people wear tend to reflect more a lifestyle than a social class.

"A fashion is nothing but an induced epidemic," remarked George Bernard Shaw (1856–1950). It is true that the public is influenced by the image projected by actors and artists, by famous athletes, and other celebrities. Among them, some can afford to wear the custom-made clothes designed by famous *haute couture* designers; their collections are shown twice a year in Paris and Rome during an élite showcase, but they are only for a few privileged. The majority will don the *prêt-à-porter* collections that hit the catwalks twice a year in London, Paris, New York, and Milan. And again, only the well-off will be able to purchase the ready-to-wear *en vogue* outfits sold *en masse* everywhere; as it has always been the case throughout history, the penniless will wear whatever they can find to stay cool or warm, *à la mode* or not.

The fashion industry is a big business. It is also an art form that involves the skills of fashion designers, fabric experts, colors specialists, dressmakers, advertising agencies, and *branché* (French loanword meaning *au courant*, up-to-date) magazines. Each and every one contributes to create the new style *la mode du jour* and has a role to play to ensure the making of stylish garments that will ultimately be financially successful products.

Any born shopaholic can find a good alibi to go on a frantic spree. "I am depressed and I have to get a new dress, a hat, a bracelet, anything. Besides, I'll wear it all the time or I'll return it tomorrow!"

Nevertheless, all those who must shop because they enjoy it will find long lists of French loanwords in this chapter to purchase the *à la mode* cargo pants, the *magnifique cotton piqué* polo shirt, the little vest sprinkled with *diamantés* or floral *appliqués*, or the not so *à bon marché* shirt made of sheer *chiffon!* The experience can be all the more enjoyable when employing the perfect smug French accent!

CLOTHES

If fashions change, some styles live on. *La petite robe noire* (the little black dress) for instance, is one such example. The signature "little black dress" was created by Coco Chanel in 1926 and has remained the epitome of timeless fashion ever since. People put it on at funerals; they wear it at cocktail parties. Audrey Hepburn donned it in *Breakfast at Tiffany's* and *Sabrina,* and Elizabeth Taylor and the Princess of Monaco, among other celebrities, have purchased garments designed by this worldwide renowned designer, whose life began rather sadly.

Jeanne Gabrielle "Coco" Chanel was born August 19, 1883, in Saumur, a picturesque small French town in the Loire Valley, renown for its delicious sparkling white wines as well as its beautiful castles. Coco was six years old when her mother died; her loving father vanished and she was raised in a Catholic orphanage. Later on, she worked as a singer at la Rotonde, a *café-concert* in Paris. It is said that Coco, her nickname and designer's name, comes from the only songs she knew: *Ko Ko Ri Ko* (*Cocorico, cock-a-doodle-do*), and *Qui a vu Coco dans le Trocadéro* (*Who's seen Coco in the Trocadéro*), a song about a little dog named Coco, lost in an area called Place du Trocadéro in Paris where the *Palais* (Palace) of Chaillot was built in 1937.

Coco Chanel never married and never had children. She had *une liaison* with a Nazi officer, among other men, and had to exile for fifteen years in Switzerland because of it. She created the worldwide famous Chanel #5, the first perfume to bear a designer's name. She died in 1971 at age 88, in the private quarters she kept at the Ritz Hotel in Paris. Of fashion she said, "Fashion is like architecture, it is a matter of proportions." And about women, she declared, "A woman has the age she deserves." Here you go old wrinkled faces, don't whine—it's all your fault! Coco was a hard-working self-made *maîtresse femme*[46] who called a spade a spade, who called *un chat, un chat*, as the French say, "to call a cat, a cat!"

The Coco Chanel shop is still located at 31 rue Cambon in Paris, and *le salon* has been kept pretty much as it was when she was alive.

FRENCH LOANWORDS

BASQUE (f) A tight-fitting bodice with a flared waist. In the mid-seventeenth century *basques* were short, pleated tabs sewn on the bodice of a dress or jacket.

BASQUINE (f) An elaborate petticoat with pagoda sleeves worn by Basque women for special occasions; also worn in Spain provinces adjacent to the Basque region.

BIKINI (m) Registered trademark for a very brief two-piece bathing suit worn by women, except in Saint Tropez beaches and nudist camps. In 1946 two Frenchmen, Jacques Heim and Louis Reard, designed a skimpy two-piece bathing suit. They were inspired to call their creation *bikini* because the atoll Bikini in the Marshall Islands was in the news at the time. Indeed, atomic bomb tests were carried out by the United States in the Bikini islet in July 1946. Morbid connection!

BLOUSON (m) A casual, hip-length jacket, tight at the waist and made of leather or suede. In France, from 1955 until approximately 1965, the *blousons noirs* (black jackets) were gangs of young delinquents wearing black leather *blousons*.

BRASSIÈRE (f) In France, a baby's shirt or vest; also a woman's sports-bra; See Accessories.

BURNOUS (m) A Moorish cloak; outer sleeveless garment with a hood usually made of one piece; in France, it is also a sleeveless bathrobe with a hood for babies.

BUSTIER (m) A strapless bra that extends to the waist to enhance the bust. Singer Madonna made the conical *bra-bustier* popular again by wearing it in the 1990s. Jean-Paul Gaultier, the French designer, is apparently her dresser.

CAMISOLE (f) Or *cami*, a diminutive for *chemise*; a woman's undershirt with shoulder straps, often embroidered. Originally a *camisole* was a *gilet*, a kind of jacket for men. It was also a petticoat bodice worn under blouses or sweaters, or between the *corset* and a dress; or a short, loose jacket worn by a woman on top of a *négligée*. *La camisole de force* is French for straitjacket.

CANEZOU (m) A sleeveless blouse made of lace; also a shawl made of lace or *mousseline*.

CAPOTE (f) Great-coat; (often worn by soldiers). A type of hat. See Hats.

CARACO (m) Originally, a wide straight smock worn by country women. Today, a feminine undergarment with straps covering the bust and often worn with matching panties, similar to cami-knickers: cami, short for *camisole* and knickers, bloomer-like undergarment for women. In her publication *The Lily*, Amelia Bloomer (1818–1894) promoted the idea of women getting rid of their petticoats to wear a type of trousers, later known as bloomers.

CEINTURE (f) *Corset* covering the bust and held by shoulder straps; a cincture, a girdle *ceinture* is French for "belt."

CHASUBLE (f) A hooded, sleeveless garment with no waist worn by the

---

clergy. A woman's robe *chasuble*, similar to the above. Also a tunic and a pinafore dress, sleeveless sponge-like garment.

CHEMISE (f) A loose-fitting undergarment or dress hanging straight from the shoulders (U.S.). In France, a woman used to wear a *chemise* (undershirt for cold days); today, a *chemise* is a long-sleeve shirt for men; also a loose blouse that women wear over pants; *une chemise américaine* also called *un tee-shirt* (both words are used in France). *Une chemise de nuit* is French for "nightgown."

CHEMISE À JABOT Blouse closing in the back with attached *jabot*. See *jabot* under Accessories.

CHEMISE-CULOTTES Cami-knickers in English; in France, the word *caraco* is used instead of *chemise-culottes*.

CHEMISETTE (f) Literally, little chemise: short sleeved bodice worn as undergarment by women; a detachable shirt front, worn to fill in the neckline of a dress; a *guimpe* (U.S.). In France a *chemisette* is a short-sleeved shirt for men or a short-sleeved blouse for women or children.

CORSAGE (m) A bodice; a fitted blouse covering the bust; also a bouquet (U.S.).

CORSELET (m) A woman's lightweight, tight-fitting costume, laced up in front and worn over a blouse; Swiss belt.

CORSET (m) A back-lacing and front-fastening garment with stays, such as whalebone, designed to define the waist and flatten the stomach; it often has garters to attach the stockings.

COSTUME (m) Dress in general, including accessories as in a riding costume. A style of dress typical of a country, region, or worn by theatrical performers, for instance. Also a man's suit: trousers and coat made of the same material.

COTILLON (m) Cotillion; petticoat; *jupon*.

COTTE (f) Dungarees, overalls; see *salopettes* at the end of this list.

CRINOLINE (f) Stiff petticoat made of *crinoline* (see *crinoline* under Fabrics) worn under a skirt to make it bulge out widely from the waist.

CULOTTES (f) Knee-length trousers made full in the legs to resemble a skirt, what the French call *une jupe-culotte*: *une jupe* (skirt) and *une culotte* (pants, trousers); *culottes* is also French for feminine underwear (panties). However, most French women say *slip (panties)* instead of *culottes*.

DÉSHABILLÉ (m) A garment made of light fabric; a morning wrapper. Also spelled *dishabillé* in English (*Webster's Dictionary*).

ENSEMBLE (m) A suit; a costume of matching parts.

FAUX CUL (m) Literally, fake arse: bustle; also called *tournure*.

FOURREAU (m) Sheath dress; a very narrow fitted dress or skirt.

FUSEAU (m) As in *fuseau* pants: stirrup pants; *fuseau de ski* (ski pants).

GABARDINE (f) Long, loose overcoat or raincoat. In medieval times people wore a *gabardine*. The old French word was *gaverdine* in 1482.

GILET (m) Waistcoat (G.B.); short, sleeveless garment for men worn under a jacket (U.S.).

GUÊPIÈRE (f) A narrow girdle; a body-shaper with garters (U.S.) or suspenders (G.B.). From *guêpe* (wasp).

GUIMPE (f) A *chemisette*: high-neck sleeveless blouse; false shirt front, a dickey; a wimple for a nun.

HABIT (m) Costume; dress, outfit for a particular situation, as in a riding habit.

HOUPPELANDE (f) A long and wide heavy overcoat with ample sleeves; a greatcoat.

JUPE (f) A skirt; *Webster's* defines a *jupe* as being the same as a *jupon* (see below). In France, *le jupon* is the slip a woman wears under a *jupe*.

JUPON (m) Petticoat; under-skirt, a slip.

JUSTAUCORPS (m) Literally, close to the body, also spelled *just-au-corps*: a close-fitting garment for men and women, going back to the Middle Ages; what is called a *léotard* in the U.S.

LÉOTARD (m) Body stocking worn by dancers and acrobats. In France the word *collant*, from *colle* (glue) is used instead of leotard.

LIMOUSINE (f) A heavy cape with a hood, a *pélerine* worn by shepherds in *Le Limousin*.

LINGERIE (f) A woman's undergarments formerly made of *lin* (linen).

MAILLOT (m) *Maillot de corps*; *corps* (body); undergarment, a vest (G.B.), a jersey.

MANTEAU (m) A woman's cloak or mantle, an overcoat.

MANTEAU DE ZIBELINE (m) A sable coat; a *zibeline* resembles the sable or the marten.

MANTELET (m) Literally, small *manteau*: a short woman's cape or cloak that covers the shoulders and the arms.

MAROCAIN (m) A long garment with long sleeves and a hood worn by men and women in *Maroc* (Morocco), usually made from a *crêpe* fabric of silk or wool or both. *Maroquin* (Morocco leather) is a kidskin or a goatskin used in bookbinding, among other things.

MATINÉE Woman's *déshabillé* worn *in la matinée* (in the morning); a tea jacket worn in the early twentieth century.

NÉGLIGÉ (m) A woman's loosely-fitting dressing gown made of flimsy semi-transparent fabric trimmed with ruffles, lace, etc. In French, *négligé* also means sloppy, neglected, as in *une femme négligée* (a neglected wife) *un travail négligé* (sloppy work).

PALETOT (m) Loose-fitting short overcoat, great coat (heavy overcoat) to keep warm.

PANIERS (m) Underskirt stretched over metal hoops to puff out a skirt at the hips; a *crinoline*; also spelled pannier in English; French for "basket."

PARACHUTE (pants) Shaped as a parachute, a trend made famous by Norma Kamali, a New York designer who made fashion affordable.

PARDESSUS (m) A man's overcoat, a garment to wear *pardessus* (on top) other clothes.

PEIGNOIR (m) A dressing gown or robe, long or short, often with a matching robe made with heavy spongy fabric; women put it on after the shower to comb their hair and put on their makeup. From *peigner* (to comb). *Un peignoir de bain* is French for a bathrobe.

PÉLERINE (f) A sort of hooded shawl; a cape with long ends coming down in front as the *pélerins* (pilgrims) used to wear.

PELISSE (f) A long cloak or wrap lined with fur; fur lined-coat; a *pelisse robe* was a dress that buttoned down the front to the hem; from Latin *pellis*, *peau* (skin).

POURPOINT (m) A stuffed and quilted close-fitting body garment, so named because of the needlework on it; a *justaucorps*, dates back to the Middle Ages.

REDINGOTE (f) Altered from English riding-coat; a frock coat for a man; a fitted, long, unlined, double-breasted lightweight coat; also a woman's fitted coat.

ROBE (f) A loose-flowing garment; a woman's dress.

ROBE À FOURREAU (f) A sheath dress (or skirt).

ROBE À L'ANGLAISE (f) Dress with a fitted back called *en fourreau*.

ROBE BUSTIER (f) Strapless dress.

ROBE CHASUBLE (f) Pinafore dress; jumper.

ROBE CHEMISE (f) A straight-cut dress with no waistline introduced in 1957 by French designer Hubert de Givenchy.

ROBE DE CHAMBRE (f) A dressing gown; a robe, also called *un peignoir* in France (see above).

ROBE DU SOIR (f) Evening gown.

ROBE SAC (f) Sack dress also called Watteau dress because the French painter Antoine Watteau (1684–1721) featured the sack dress in his paintings.

SALOPETTES (f.pl.) French overalls to protect body from dirt worn by mechanics, for instance; dungarees; long pants with sleeveless bib-top and shoulder straps used for sports activities such as skiing. From French *saloper* (to stain with dirt); a *Marie Salope* or a *salope* is French for "a tart," "a nasty woman."

SOUTANE (f) A cassock or tunic worn by Roman Catholic priests.

SURTOUT (m) A man's long overcoat that resembles a frock coat.

TABLIER (m) A part of a woman's dress resembling a *tablier*, French for "apron."

TAILLEUR (m) A woman's tailor-made suit; also the French word for "tailor."

TOQUE (f) A long cape made of wool; also a type of hat. See under Hats.

TUTU (m) A skirt worn by ballet dancers.

SHORT STORIES

BRASSIÈRE Mary Phelps Jacob (also known as Caresse Crosby), from Mamaroneck county of Westchester, in the State of New York, filed a patent for what she named a Backless *Brassière* in November 1914. With the help of Marie, her French maid, she had resourcefully designed a prototype with two *mouchoirs* tied in the back so that she could wear it under her gown at a fashionable *soirée*. Later on, the ingenious lady opened the Caresse Crosby, a store where women could purchase this new invention. However, she closed it a while after and sold the rights to her patent to the Warner Brothers Corset Company.

Naturally, other people before Jacob had designed and patented similar contraptions under other names such as the breast supporter, what the French sensibly call *le soutien-gorge* since the device *soutient la gorge* (supports the bosom), not *le bras*, French for arms! If French women wear a *soutien-gorge*, not a *brassière*, infants do however! A *brassière* in France is a baby's vest; it is also now a woman's sports bra.

CORSET *"Il n'est point agréable de voir une femme coupée en deux comme une guêpe,"* (It is not pleasing to see a woman cut in two like a wasp), remarked

French philosopher Jean Jacques Rousseau in *Emile on Education*. Of course, he was referring to the *guêpière* (waspie), a type of *corset* engineered by perverts and masochists.

The term straight-laced had a real meaning when women had to wear this barbaric undergarment, which at one time in the history of the *corset*, had a front busk made of wood, whalebone, or even metal! If a woman was a *cocotte* (a tart, not the pastry kind), the tightly-laced corset would not make her *comme il faut* but it had to keep her body straight. Any woman wearing this devilish bone-crushing, organ-squeezing garment had to feel squashed, stifled, repressed, and probably depressed, but nevertheless, she put it on, in the name of fashion and because she was vain, or because, as always, she wanted to please her selfish man.

The idea of wrapping the body in some sort of device is not new. Originally, dancers, acrobats, and circus people wore tight narrow bands around their waists to support their busts while they jumped up and down, swung from ropes, or did stunts on the trapeze. Today dockers, movers, and truck drivers still don a sort of girdle to avoid breaking backs and bones.

As always, somebody got the idea that a utilitarian item could be transformed to sell fashion and torment people, particularly women. It is said that some poor corseted creatures could barely breathe and sometimes fainted, or even suffocated and died! Even young girls were made to wear *corsets* so that they would stand straight and grow up with good posture. This was still the case in the mid-1950s in France. It is as perplexing as wearing small shoes to keep the feet from growing. Strange customs! But again, at a time where women let it all hang out, one may wonder if some would not benefit from wearing a device that helps contain it all to hide unsightly bulges, which is in the realm of possibilities since the corset is making a comeback.

CRINOLINE If modern fashion tends to reveal bulges and other bodily flaws, the *crinoline* had the advantage of covering unsightly physical defects. Men could imagine and dream! The cumbersome garment was often ridiculed by cartoonists because women in this kind of attire would get caught in the doorways or even catch on fire. According to Adrian Bailey in *Passion for Fashion*, the *crinoline* "could be hoisted by means of cords run through a shirr along the hem and up through the waistband." In the United States this device was known as the elevator! This curious invention would raise the hoops of women's skirts in emergency situations. Apparently, Eugénie, wife of Napoléon III, upgraded her title from Empress of France to Queen of Crinoline. She made it fashionable, if not comfortable, to wear in trendy *soirées*.

PANIER À SALADE: BLACK MARIA Black Maria is a slang word used in England for a police patrol wagon. Apparently, it took its name after Maria Lee, who owned a black lodging house in Boston and would help the constables when they took drunks and prisoners to their cells. It was also used to refer to a horse-drawn funeral hearse. The first paddy named Black Maria was acquired in 1898 after the Spanish-American War.

FAUX CULS They were as fake as faux Renoir. *Faux culs*, literally, false arse or bottom, were also called *les culs de Paris* (the arses of Paris) in the 1870s when it was in style to place an armature or cushion under the skirt just above the *derrière*.

FOURREAU French designer Paul Poiret, known as the "evil genius of high fashion," introduced the *fourreau* dress, sheath-like skirt. Women who could hardly breath because of the tight *corsets* they were compelled to wear, could now hardly walk with their very tight skirts for, "Fashion is a tyrant from which there is no deliverance; all must conform to its whimsical" (French proverb). And to paraphrase French philosopher Jean-Jacques Rousseau, we are born free but everywhere we are in chains!

GUÊPIÈRE This savage contraption was designed by Marcel Roches in 1946 so that a woman would have the stylish *taille de guêpe* (the wasp waist), apparently obtained by surgically removing some lower ribs, a barbaric procedure just as frightening as liposuction. The *guêpière* was also used by French designer Christian Dior (1905–1957) to create the Dior New Look characterized by a tight waist, rounded shoulders, and a flowing skirt.

HABIT *Le grand habit* was a close-fitting bodice with short sleeves and a petticoat with a long train worn at the king's court festivities. Your *habits du dimanche* are your Sunday best.

LÉOTARD This garment took its named from famous French trapeze acrobat, Jules Léotard, (1842–1870) who wore a one-piece, sleeveless, tight-fitting garment. In France the word *collant* from *colle* (glue) is sensibly used instead of *léotard*.

MAILLOT The name comes from Monsieur Maillot, a French costume and hosiery designer for the Paris Opéra. A *maillot de bain* is a one-piece bathing suit; *bain* is French for "bath," as in *la salle de bain*, (the bathroom). *Le maillot jaune* (yellow maillot), as anyone who watches *Le Tour de France* knows, is worn by the victor at the end of each *étape* (stage) of the Tour.

TUTU The word *tutu* is a euphemism for *cucu*, familiar for *cul* (*derrière*) and refers, therefore, to what the garment was designed to cover. The classic *tutu*, made up of layers of stiffened frills, is a skirt that stands out from the dancer's legs; the romantic *tutu* extends to mid-calf. Marie Taglioni introduced the Romantic *tutu* in the ballet *La Sylphide*.

HATS

Never leave home without your *chapeau!* You must wear it to shield your fair skin from damaging sunrays, to protect your curly hair from spring raindrops and autumn downpours, from playful whirlwinds or nasty north winds, and from fluffy snowflakes, so lovely on Christmas morning. Make sure you cover your head with a pretty *bonnet* to stay warm and cozy on cold, wintry days.

And, before you shut the door behind you to face the world, reach for a *petit bibi* to feel pretty, a *gibus* to attend a *soirée*, a *canotier* to stroll lazily on a warm sandy beach, your *béret basque* to look *française*; and pick a *fichu*, a *foulard*, a *capeline*, or any other *chapeau* to flaunt your status and express your individuality!

In France, some women would rather wear a *chapeau cloche* or any other *couvre-chef* than *coiffer la Sainte Catherine* (to coif Sainte Catherine), patroness of old maids. Sainte Catherine, November 25, is the traditional celebration of the *catherinettes*, young unmarried *ouvrières de la mode* also called *cousettes*, (factory girls in the fashion industry). If these unfortunate are still single by the time they reach the old age of twenty-five, they *coiffent la Sainte Catherine* and must wear a special yellow and green *chapeau* to celebrate the occasion, yellow to symbolize that they have joined the *vieilles filles* (old maids) club, and green for hope. This custom seems to be fading away, however. Apparently in recent years, an old tradition seems to be coming back. Happy bachelors who have not yet found their soul mates by the time they are thirty years old can make it public by wearing hats with similar colors. Why are they allowed five years more than *bachelorettes* who may have chosen to postpone family obligations until they are older? In a land whose motto is *Liberté, Egalité Fraternité,* this state of affairs needs to be fought one day!

FRENCH LOANWORDS

BAVOLET (m) Plain cap with a floating flap in the back that used to be worn by French peasant women.

BÉBÉ BONNET (m) Small outdoor hat trimmed with ribbons and flowers with a brim turned up, worn in the late 1870s as *bébés* (babies) would wear.

BÉGUIN (m) A close-fitting *bonnet* attached under the chin originally worn by the Béguines, an order of lay sisterhoods founded in the twelfth century. In France, *un bonnet d'enfant* (a child's or new born *bonnet*) is also called un *béguin* and it is often made of lace and tied under the chin.

BÉRET (m) A flat round wool or felt cap.

BÉRET BASQUE *Béret* worn in the Basque Country.

BIBI (m) Woman's small hat first made in the 1830s; any small fanciful hat with sides flaring upward and forward around the face and tied with a ribbon; it became known as a *bibi* in Paris in late nineteenth century. *Un chapeau à la bibi* (a *bibi* style hat or bonnet); *un bibi à plumes* (a feathered *bibi*).

BICORNE (m) A man's hat in the late eighteenth, early nineteenth centuries; it was the signature hat of Napoléon Bonaparte.

BONNET (m) Brimless hat with a chin ribbon worn by women and children; a flat woolen cap worn by men and boys in Scotland. Originally called *chapeau* or *capote*.

BONNET BABET (m) Evening hat made of tulle and covering the ears, worn in the 1830s; also called *Babet bonnet*.

BONNET DE NUIT (m) Nightcap.

BONNET ROUGE (m) Red cap during the French Revolution, worn as a symbol of liberty.

BOUDOIR BONNET Soft, lace-trimmed cap with ruffled edge worn in the *boudoir*, woman's private sitting room, worn to apply makeup.

CABRIOLET BONNET (m) Or *chapeau cabriolet*: a *bonnet* with a brim looking like a carriage top; worn in the 1820s through 1850s.

CALOTTE (f) A small, round skullcap worn in the 1940s and 1950s.

CANOTIER (m) A straw sailor hat. From *canot* (rowboat).

CAPELINE (f) A woman's hat with a wide floppy brim, in style in the 1930s and again in the 1970s, to protect the face from sun rays.

CAPOTE (f) Used to be a woman's hat tied under the chin; also a long, hooded cloak; soldiers in the infantry wore a *capote* kaki. (*La capote anglaise* is slang for condom).

CAPUCHE (f) Long, pointed hood worn by the Capuchin monks; a hood.

CAPUCHON (m) Cowl; a sort of cape with a hood. In France a *capuchon* is also a rain garment of similar shape.

CASQUE (m) A helmet.

CHAPEAU (m) A hat with a crown and a brim.

CHAPEAU BRETON Round-crowned hat with a turned-up brim resembling the French sailor hat. Also *coiffe de Bretonne*; in the past, *une coiffe* was a cloth headdress worn by country women; today a regional *coiffe* is worn during traditional folk celebrations.

CHAPEAU CLAQUE An opera hat; similar to a *gibus*.

CHAPEAU CLOCHE (m) Brimless, bell-shaped hat popular between 1915 and the 1930s. *Cloche* is French for bell, as in *la cloche à fromage*, (a cheese dish cover).

CHAPERON (m) A pointed, hooded cape worn by the Knights of the Garters in medieval times. *Le Petit Chaperon Rouge,* (the Little Red Riding Hood) wore such a cape.

CHARLOTTE (f) A big hat named after Queen Charlotte of England; hat with tightly gathered crown and flounced covered brim; a mobcap, also called mob.

CHOU (m) A soft hat with crushed crown. See *chou* under Accessories.

COUVRE-CHEF (m) Literally, cover head: *couvre* (covers) the *chef* (the head); any hat that covers the head.

GIBUS (m) Gibus hat; a collapsible opera hat; named after the French inventor Monsieur Gibus who patented it in 1837.

GONDOLIER (m) Hat with a wide brim and a shallow crown worn by boatmen in Venice.

KÉPI (m) A flat-topped oval crown with a brim in the front; hat worn by *La Légion Etrangère* (The Foreign Legion).

LIMOUSINE (f) A hood, a *pélerine* worn by the shepherds in Limousin, the Limoges region in France. Limoges, 374 kilometers south of Paris is famed for its porcelain.

MARMOTTE (f) A type of headdress made with a scarf around the head, tied above the forehead; worn in the eighteenth century.

THÉRÈSE (m) A calash; chapeau Thérèse; late sixteenth century large hood made of gauze over a frame of wire or whalebone.

TOQUE (f) A small, close-fitting hat with a very small brim, or brimless. *Une toque de cuisinier* (cook's hat).

TRICORNE (m) Literally, three horns: a man's hat of the eighteenth century with wide brims folded to form three horn-like points.

TUQUE (f) A winter cap; a Canadian stocking cap.

TURBAN (m) A headwear of Moslem origin consisting of a cap with a scarf wound round it.

SHORT STORIES

BÉRET God ordered *Noé* (Noah) to embark two of all living creatures with him in the Ark he had built with his sons to survive the great Deluge. Is this a myth, a legend, fiction, or a true story? As far as the origin of the *béret* is concerned, it happened. The legend tells that after Noah sheared the two sheep he had taken along, for obvious reasons, he disposed of the fresh wool at the bottom of the boat to make a comfortable bedding for his animals. A futon of some sort! When the water finally receded, forty days after the deluge had begun, the felted wool was used to make *bérets*. The legend forgets to tell who made them and how. Since it is a legend, it can say whatever it wants but what it reveals is that the *béret* is not a Coco Chanel nor a Christian Dior creation—it goes back a long way.

Anyone interested in the history of the *béret* can visit *Le Musée du Béret* and read the above legend, worded differently, since legends are dreams and can be told in myriad of ways. *Le Musée du Béret* is located in Nay, a small French town 20 kilometers from Pau in the Pyrénées. A visitor will also learn there that the word *béret* comes from *berret*, a *béarnais* (from Bearn) term meaning a type *of couvre-chef* worn by Béarnais, Gascons, and Basques people. *Bérets* are still made in Béarn today. In fact, it is the only place in France where they are still produced, according to the Museum.

A *béret* is a symbol of manhood and in the past this little flat wool cap was given to every little schoolboy between the ages of eight and twelve to keep their heads warm in winter months but mostly as an initiation ritual. From regional identity, *le béret* became a national emblem. Indeed, a man wearing a *béret basque* holding a French *baguette* and a bottle of *vin rouge* is the caricature *par excellence* of a typical Frenchman. The *béret* is also a symbol of French patriotism in wartime. A green *béret* is part of the *Légionaires'* uniform and a red *béret* is worn by the *paras*, short for *parachutistes* (the paratroopers).

Bérets were *en vogue* during the 1960s and 1970s; Greta Garbo wore one in the early 1900s and actress Faye Dunaway sported it in the movie *Bonnie and Clyde* in 1967. Many people own one today. It is a versatile little *toque* and people put it on to stay warm, to look French, snob or *mondain*.

The curious may wonder why there is a little spike on top of the *béret*, also called *bounet* or *capet*, (two Béarn words) in Les Landes, a region in southwest France. The explanation, obtained viva-voce, is that "the little tail on top of the *béret* is called *cabillou*, a Béarn word for *cheville de bois*,

French for wood dowel." Of course, the *cabillou* was made of wool, not wood. Indeed, a long time ago, *bérets* were hand-knitted with four wood knitting needles and the little tail on top of the *béret* was simply the knitting starting point. It has been kept there ever since because without it, snobs or Francophiles cannot look French since they do not own the real thing, the authentic *béret basque*.

CANOTIER This straw hat was the trademark of French singer Maurice Chevalier (1888–1972). Buster Keaton and Harold Lloyd Boater, two famous American comedians, wore a similar type of hat called a boater.

ACCESSORIES

The *Webster's Dictionary* defines accessories, as follows: "Any article of clothing worn to complete one's outfit, as purse, gloves, stockings, etc." An accessory is to an *ensemble* what a sauce is to a meal—it can make it or break it.

Bagologists have to be the most creative people on the planet! Bags *à la mode* today, and like the wind, gone tomorrow, and they—the bag designers—had better come up with something new for all the *belles dames* out there.

From the beginning of time, *le sexe faible* (the weaker sex) had to adorn their hair with all sorts of gadgets, *bandeau, barrette, fichu, foulard, papillote,* and various devices; they also had to deal with countless bad hair days! Imagine having to sleep upright with your hair covered with a bag to prevent mice from nesting in the enormous hair mop you had to endure because it was fashionable. Funny, but creepy!

French maniacs say that, "*Il faut souffrir pour être belle,*" literally, "It is necessary to suffer in order to be pretty." You would expect sensible people to preach that, "*Il faut être bête pour souffrir*." But so it goes in the name of beauty and fashion.

FRENCH LOANWORDS

AIGRETTE (f) Tuft made of egret, osprey feathers, or diamonds to adorn *le chignon*; a *panache*. *Un casque à aigrette* (a plumed helmet).

BABOUCHE (f) A leather slipper with pointed toes and no heel, used as shoes in Eastern countries; a kind of mule.

BANDEAU (m) A diadem; a narrow band or fillet worn around the head to confine the hair.

BARRETTE (f) A bar-shaped clasp to hold the hair in place.

BIJOU (m) A jewel, a trinket.

BOTTINE (f) Ankle boot; a riding boot in the sixteenth century.

BOURSE (f) Large bag in the mid-fifteenth through mid-eighteenth centuries. Now, a small bag to put coins; see *porte-monnaie* below.

BOUTONNIÈRE (f) A flower or small *bouquet* or flower worn by men in the *boutonnière* (the buttonhole), on the lapel of a jacket.

BRACELET (m) Ornamental band or chain for the wrist. From *bras* (arm).

BRASSIÈRE (f) A bra: undergarment worn by women to support the breasts; called a *soutien-gorge* in France; word used in the 1930s to refer to a boned strapless *brassière*.

BRELOQUE (f) Seal or locket worn on a watch chain or necklace; a charm.

CABAS (m) A lady's handbag, a workbasket made of straw or cloth; a fruit or shopping bag.

CABOCHON (m) Precious stone; cabochon de *rubis* (ruby).

CACHE-NEZ (m) Literally, hide-nose: a muffler; scarf. The French also call it *cache-col*; a *col* (collar) covers *le cou* (the neck).

CHANDELIER (m) As in chandelier earrings; long, dangling, oversized earrings popular in the 1960s.

CHÂTELAINE (f) Ornamental chain clasped at the waist of the *châtelaine* (the lady of a *château* in the fourteenth century) and holding keys, scissors, and a thimble.

CHAUSSURE (f) Shoe.

CHEVRON (m) A galloon, worsted braid, or ribbon shaped as an inverted V on the sleeve of garment, particularly military; *à chevrons* or *en zigzag*: said of a V-patterns fabric.

CHIFFONS (m.pl) Ribbons, laces. See under Fabrics; *un chiffon* is also a rag in France.

CHINOISERIES (f) *Objets de luxe*, as expensive bracelets, rings, etc. See Chapter II under Art Terms.

CHOU (m) Also called *bouffette* in French: a *chou* is a cabbage bow, a *rosette* resembling a *chou* (cabbage) made with lace or ribbon and used as an ornamentation on hats in the late nineteenth century.

COL EN V (m) V-neckline.

COL RABATTU(m) A soft lace-edge collar.

COQUE (f) A small loop or bow of ribbon or hair puffed out in shape of the *coque* (shell).

CORSAGE (m) In the U.S., a small *bouquet* worn at the shoulder or waist; a bodice, the waist of a woman's dress. In France, a *corsage* is a woman's blouse, a bodice. Women do not wear bouquets at the shoulder or wrist. If they wear a rose or another flower this is what they call it, not a *corsage*; men wear a *boutonnière*, see above.

EPAULETTE (f) A shoulder pad; a shoulder's ornament for military uniforms. From *épaule* (shoulder).

ESPADRILLE (f) Rope-soled shoe (Provençal origin).

ETOILE (f) A figure or decoration shaped as a star, used in embroidery.

ETUI (m) A small case or box for carrying implements for needlework and *trousse de toilette* (toilet accessories). *Un étui à revolver* (a holster); *un étui à lunettes* (glasses case).

FICHU (m) Three-cornered lace or *mousseline* cape; small lace scarf or shawl wrapped around the shoulders and fastened with a brooch.

FILET (m) A hairnet; also called a *réticule*.

FOULARD (m) Scarf, headscarf; silk handkerchief. A type of material. See under Fabric.

GALOCHE (f) A galosh; clog, or wooden shoe; a special sandal worn on rainy days by *courtiers* of the French King Louis XIV.

JABOT (m) Kind of ruffle or frill used as an ornament for the front of a woman's bodice. See *chemise à jabot* above under Clothes.

LAVALLIÈRE (f) Wide piece of soft fabric tied around the neck and forming two *coques* in the front top of a shirt; a loosely tied cravat.

LORGNETTE (f) Eyeglasses mounted on a handle; opera glass. From *lorgner* (to eye up, to stare).

LORGNON (m) A monocle; same as *pince-nez* (see below).

MACRAMÉ Ornamental trimming or coarsely knotted thread from Arabia; a craft that has enjoyed a comeback in recent times in the U.S.

MANCHETTE (f) Wrist ruffle made of lace worn in the 1830s through 1850s; from *manche* (sleeve).

MARQUISE (f) A finger-ring set with a pointed oval gem or cluster of gems; a marquise ring.

MARTINGALE (f) A half-belt of cloth or leather to contain the extra material in the back of a garment; usually placed above or below the normal waistline.

MENTONNIÈRE (f) Lace ruffle sewn to bonnet strings tied under the *menton* (chin) to hold the *bonnet*; a protective chinstrap worn in tournaments.

MINAUDIÈRE (f) A small handbag without a handle; a clutch-bag. *Une minaudière* in France is also a simpering, affected woman; *un minaudier* is a simperer (man); see also *minauderie* under Loanwords listed alphabetically, Chapter IV. From *minauder* (to be affected, to simper).

MOUCHE (f) A small patch of black plaster worn on the face as ornament or to conceal a blemish; a beauty spot; a *mouche* is French for a "fly."

MULE (f) A lounging sleeper that does not cover the heel. *La mule du Pape* (the Pope white slipper) with a gold cross.

PAILLETTE (f) Literally, little *paille* (straw): small shiny ornament or spangle, as a metal disk sewn on fabrics for decoration; same as sequin, or spangle (U.S.).

PANACHE (m) A plume; a cluster of feathers on a hat.

PANTOUFLES (f) Slippers.

PAPILLOTE (f) Same as *paillette* above. Also, curlpaper used for curling hair. *En papillote*: cooked wrapped in foil paper: see Chapter I under Culinary Expressions.

PARURE (f) Finery; a set of jewels intended to be worn together. *La Parure* (*The Necklace*) is the title of a short story by Guy de Maupasssant (1850–1893). Maupassant is considered one of the greatest French short-story tellers. He tried to commit suicide and died in an asylum near Paris in 1893.

PEAU D'ESPAGNE (f) Literally, skin of Spain: a perfumed leather; a scent suggestive of the aroma of leather.

PÉLERINE (f) A woman's fur cape, tapering to long points in the front.

PENDELOQUE (f) A gem, especially a diamond cut in the shape of a drop (on earrings or bracelets).

PERRUQUE (f) A peruke; a wig, a periwig.

PETIT POINT (m) Type of purse used for more than a hundred years in France, Austria, and Hungary.

PINCE-NEZ (m) Literally, nose pincher: a type of eyeglasses kept in place on the nose by means of a spring.

PLASTRON (m) A starched shirt front; *faux* dickey, a man's detachable shirt front; a *faux* shirt front; used to be called a stomacher.

POCHETTE (f) A handbag shaped like an envelope; a *pochette* bag, a clutch bag, a pouch for papers, money, etc.; a small pocket. In France, *une pochette* is also a fine handkerchief worn in the small pocket on the lapel of a suit.

POMPADOUR (m) A hairstyle.

POMPADOUR (m) Drawstring handbag made of velvet or lace made popular by Madame de Pompadour.

POMPON (m) Ornamental tuft of silk, wool, or feathers worn on a hat on shoes (or on a soldier shako); a cylindrical military dress hat with a flat top.

PORTE-MONNAIE (m) Literally, a carry-money: a purse, small leather or fabric bag to put coins.

POUF (m) *Un pouf*: similar to a *faux cul* and used to puff up the back of the skirt; also called a *tournure*.

POULAINE (f) Long, pointed toe of a shoe worn at the end of the Middle Ages.

RÉTICULE (m) A woman's small drawstring handbag originally made of satin, mesh, or red morocco leather; a *réticule* is also a loanword for a little net, in France it is a hairnet.

REVERS (m) A part of a garment turned back to show the reverse lining, the wrong side.

RIVIÈRE (f) A necklace of diamonds or other gems (also French for "river").

SABOT (m) A shoe made of a single piece of wood originally worn by peasants in Europe.

SACHET (m) Small bag filled with perfumed powder.

SAUTOIR (m) A long necklace consisting of a fine gold chain usually set with jewels.

SEQUIN (m) A small, shiny ornament sewn on fabric for decoration; same as *paillette* (see above) and popular in the 1940s and again in the 1960s; sequin also refers to a piece of ancient gold money from Italy.

SIGNATURE (f) A purse or silk scarf *en vogue* in Paris in the 1960s; a designer scarf with the name of the *couturier* printed in one corner.

SOLITAIRE (m) A ring with a diamond or another gem set by itself.

TIGNON (m) A handkerchief worn as a *turban*, especially in Louisiana by Creole women; also in the 1720s a few short pieces of hair kept and curled in the back of the head after a haircut; a word no longer used in France.

SHORT STORIES

Boutonnière The fashion of wearing of a *boutonnière* was initiated by rich *boulevardiers* who wore flowers on the lapels of their coats in formal gatherings. *Un boulevardier* is a man about town who frequents the boulevards, particularly the Grands Boulevards in Paris.

Pompadour Madame de Pompadour (1721–1764) *née* Jeanne-Antoinette Poisson, was married to Charles Le Normant d'Etioles. When she became Marquise de Pompadour, she also became Louis XV's mistress and later, his second wife. She played a political and cultural role, protecting artists and writers, for whom she is the patron. In the *pompadour* hairstyle for men the hair was combed back from the forehead without a parting, *à la* Elvis or Little Richard's style. For women, the hair was turned back off the forehead in a roll.

FABRIC

Fabric is the foundation of the fashion industry as bricks are to a house, milk to cheese, or oxygen to air. Originally, most fabrics were made with natural fibers such as silk, cotton, and wool produced by plants or animals. Some of the major producers of cotton are China, the United States, and India; one of its main uses is the production of denim. This fabric was first made in Nîmes, a city in France, and was called *serge de Nîmes*. The word was later shortened to denim. Synthetic fibers that were developed later on include polyester, nylon, spandex, and acrylic.

Avant-garde companies are always developing new fabrics to be used in tomorrow's fashions. Two years ago, a small team of researchers at Infineon Technologies began to talk about "smart textiles," fabrics in which microchips will be integrated and used to design and fabricate Smart Clothes or Wearable Electronic. They call it "intelligent solutions for tomorrow's fashions!"[47] Yet, if such clothes sound groovy and far-out, as they said in the 1960s, the concept is not at all surprising, since fashion, like everything else, is affected and influenced by technological progress.

FRENCH LOANWORDS

BARÈGE (f) A silk or cotton-worsted gauzy fabric. Named after Barèges, a French region in the Hautes-Pyrénées in France.

BATISTE (f) A medium-weight plain weave fabric made of cotton or cotton blends used for blouses and dresses. Named after its first maker, Baptiste de Cambrai (Cambrai is a city in the north of France).

BEIGE (f) A fabric of soft, unbleached wool. Originally made in Poitou, a region in western France.

BOUCLÉ (m) Fabric made with a type of yarn with a knotted (*bouclé*) rough texture; used for sweaters and jackets, sportswear; from *boucle*, (curl, loop).

BROCATELLE (f) A silk fabric similar to *brocart* (brocade); a *brocart* has a raised pattern of silver and gold threads, it is used mainly for upholstery. See *jacquard* under Miscellaneous later in this chapter.

BROCHÉ (m) Said of a fabric with pattern resembling brocade. *Un tissu broché* (a *broché* fabric); ornamentally woven; brocaded.

CAMOUFLAGE (m) A type of fabric with colors similar to the environment. From *camoufler* (to cover up, to conceal). *Camouflage* was worn by soldiers during the First and Second World Wars so that they would blend in with the surroundings.

CHARMEUSE (f) Originally a trade name for manmade, washable silk and silk-like fabric; a soft, lightweight satin-like cloth. *Charmeuse* is not used with the above meaning in France where *une charmeuse* is defined as being a seductress, a charming woman; *un charmeur* is a charming man. From *charmer* (to charm, to seduce, to be engaging) as in *charmeur de serpents* (snake charmer). *Les charmeuses* is French for *moustaches; moustache à la Charlot* (Charlie Chaplin style).

CHENILLE (f) Velvety *passementerie* shaped as a caterpillar; used to knit or make trimmings, fringes, etc. A French fabric dating from the seventeenth century made of silk, cotton, wool, or other yarn with a fuzzy feel similar to that of *une chenille*, (a caterpillar).

CHIFFON (m) A plain, lightweight sheer silk material used to make women's blouses and dresses.

CLOQUÉ (m) A puckered fabric resembling a *matelassé*; similar to a seersucker fabric which is a light crinkled fabric of linen or cotton, usually with a striped pattern.

COUTIL (m) Twilled cotton fabric used to make corsets, mattresses, and working clothes.

CRÊPE (m) A variety of thin natural or synthetic fabric with a crinkled texture; crape (not *crêpe Suzette*).

CRÊPE DE CHINE (m) Grosgrain silk *crêpe* for woman's blouse or eveningwear; China *crêpe (m)* .

CRÊPE GEORGETTE Sheer fabric made of silk, or silk and cotton, silk and rayon, almost transparent and used for women's blouses and dresses.

CRÉPON (m) Generic name for a heavy crinkle wool fabric resembling *crêpe.*

CRETONNE (f) Heavy, unglazed cotton or linen cloth with patterns printed in colors on one or both sides and used to make curtains or draperies. From Creton, a village in Normandy.

CRINOLINE (f) A fabric in which threads of horsehair and linen are interwoven. Today, a cloth of cotton, silk, or linen used as a lining for stiffening garments. From *crin* (horsehair) and *lin* (linen).

DAMASSÉ (e) (m or f) A fabric similar to a *damas* (damask) fabric, a rich patterned fabric of cotton, linen, silk, or wool woven with figures or flowers. *Damas* takes its name from the city of Damascus in Syria. *Un tissu damassé; une étoffe damassée* (*tissu* and *étoffe*, French for "fabric").

DRAP (m) Thin twilled woolen fabric; *Drap* is French for "bedsheet."

EPONGE (f) Soft, spongy weave of uneven knobby yarn used for beachwear since the 1930s. *Eponge* is also French for "sponge."

ETAMINE (f) Lightweight, loosely woven cotton, similar to bunting or voile, used to sift flour.

FAILLE (f) A ribbed, soft fabric, with a light luster made of silk or cotton and used to make suits, coats, and dresses. *Faille* is French for "fault," as in Saint Andrea Fault in California.

FOULARD (m) Lightweight, printed silk or cotton, used to make ties or dresses; *un foulard* is a also a loanword meaning "scarf." Originally imported from India.

FRISÉ (m) *Velours frisé*: a type of upholstery fabric with fine tight uncut loops; *frisé* means curly; a pile fabric with cut and uncut loops forming a pattern.

GABARDINE (f) A registered trade name for a closely woven serge-like cloth, twilled on one side only; used for suits and sport-wear, uniforms, rain-coats. Also an overcoat. See under Clothes.

GRISETTE (f) An inexpensive *gris* (grey) dress fabric, formerly worn by young *coquettes*, French working girls called *grisettes* because they wore clothes made of *grisette*, an inferior fabric worn by women of the poorer classes.

GROS (m) A heavy silk-fabric. A silk fabric originally associated with a specified city: *un gros de Londres, un gros de Lyon, un gros de Naples.*

GROS-GRAIN (m) A heavy ribbed fabric, especially silk or rayon; grosgrain; a ribbon made of this fabric; a grosgrain; ribbon made of this material.

GUIPURE (f) Lace without a mesh, but with a distinct pattern held in place by connecting threads.

LAINE (f) *De laine* (of wool); lightweight wool fabric.

LAMÉ (e) (m or f) Said of a fabric made of metal threads, especially gold and silver, sometimes interwoven with silk, wool, or cotton; heavy material that is lustrous and rich. *Une robe de lamé* (a *lamé* dress).

LIMOUSINE (f) Hairy, woolen fabric used to make the cape worn by shep-herds in the Limousin region in France.

LISIÈRE (f) A jacquard fabric made of colored, warped threads, usually with a taffeta or a *faille* ground; selvage edge of a piece of cloth so woven as not to unravel, needing no hem.

MARCELINE (f) A thin fabric of silk used for lining women's garments.

MARQUISETTE (f) A sheer, lightweight, open-mesh fabric; originally made from silk, and later on from cotton or rayon; used to make curtains, dresses, and mosquito nets.

MATELASSÉ (m) Puckered silk or wool fabric with a padded look, a surface that appears quilted. A *manteau matelassé* that the French also call a *doudoune,* or *anorak.*

MESSALINE (f) Soft, lightweight, and lustrous silk or rayon fabric.

MIGNONNETTE (f) Lustrous striped rayon cloth often used as lining for men' garments, particularly the sleeves of a jacket.

MOIRE (f) A silk fabric with a watered, wavy pattern.

MOIRÉ (e) (m or f) *Un tissu moiré, une étoffe moirée* (*moiré* fabric); watered or frosted appearance of the *moire* fabric; a watered pattern pressed into cloth.

MOQUETTE (f) Kind of carpet or upholstery fabric with a thick, soft, napped surface.

MOUSSELINE DE LAINE (f) A lightweight woolen cloth, often printed, used for dresses. French muslin was made in the 1820s in France and in 1840 in America.

MOUSSELINE DE SOIE (f) A gauzelike transparent silk or rayon cloth, a *chiffon* fabric, with a plain weave used for blouses.

PANNE (f) A soft silk, rayon, or wool fabric resembling velvet but with long, loose hairs; *panne de velours* (velvet); *panne de laine,* (wool) *panne de soie* (silk).

PAPIER (m) A paper fabric en vogue very briefly in the 1960s used to make inexpensive disposable paper suits or panties; *mouchoirs en papier* (Kleenex).

PEAU DE SOIE (f) Skin-of-silk: a close-woven, heavy, satin silk.

PERCALE (f) Closely woven cotton fabric; used to make sheets, tablecloths, etc. *Percale glacée* (glazed): chintz. Originally imported from India in the seventeenth and eighteenth centuries.

PERCALINE (f) A fine cotton fabric with a glazed finish used for linings.

PIQUÉ (m) Firmly woven cotton fabric with a small V-pattern or honeycomb texture, or other geometrical shapes.

POMPADOUR (m) A crimson color fabric with small *bouquets* and flowers.

RATINE (f) A coarse wool fabric with a knotty frizzed surface; used for lining furniture covers, coats; *un manteau de ratine* (a *ratine* coat).

SATIN (m) A silk, rayon, or nylon cloth having a smooth finish, glossy on the face, dull on the back; *satin de coton* (satinized cotton). Originated in China.

SATINETTE (f) Sateen; cotton or silk fabric resembling satin; used to make trousers and aprons.

SERGE (f) A twilled worsted cloth used for making suits or linings; a brushed wool fabric with a soft texture. *Serge de Nîmes*, known as denim, short for *de Nîmes*.

TOILE (f) A variety of sheer linen cloth with a plain weave used to make home furniture and clothing; a variety of fine *cretonne*. *Naviguer la Toile*, literally, to navigate the *toile*, is French for "to surf the web." The purists and the Acamédie française advocate saying *naviguer la Toile* to avoid using "web," but most French people say, "surfer le web," " *naviguer* (to navigate) le web," or "*surfer sur l'Internet*." They also say, "*faire du surf*": literally to do surf, to surf the waves. The French tend to be undisciplined. You will not see French people stand quietly in line at a bus stop or in the subway. An immigrant or a visitor landing in Canada or America from France is *tout baba* (completely flabbergasted) when he sees for the first time how people enter the bus, one by one without struggling and pushing to get in. To ask the French who get easily irritated and contrary to use the expression: *naviguer la Toile* is the best way to make them say, "Surfer le web!" In snob circles, *c'est cool* anyway!

TRICOT (m) A fine warp knitted fabric made of a natural or manmade fiber. From *tricoter* (to knit).

TULLE (m) A fine, soft silk used for women's dresses. From Tulle, a town in southwest France where the fabric was originally made.

VELOURS (m) Plush fabric similar to velvet used for hats, garments, upholstery, draperies; *velours côtelé* (ribbed corduroy).

VOILE (f) Thin sheer fabric of cotton, silk, rayon, or wool used to make blouses or dresses; made of *voile*. Not to confuse with *le voile* (the veil) or *la voile* (the sail); *un bateau à voile* is French for "sailboat."

ZIBELINE (f) A thick, soft, woolen, fur-like or mohair fabric with a lustrous pile made from zibeline, an animal resembling the sable. See: *manteau de zibeline* under Clothes.

MISCELLANEOUS

A *pot-pourri* of French loanwords is listed below for fashion magazine editors so that they can keep their readers *au courant* of what is *à la mode* or *démodé*. Fashion designers can also use it to sound *très distingués* as they introduce *le prêt-à-porter* collection, describing with flair *la mode du jour, le décolletage* of a stunning *toilette de soirée*, made of silky *chiffon, parsemé* with beads, and *le très chic ensemble* that gorgeous models parade like swanky zombies. Of course, they too, must show-off their French, and not just their perfect features as they *pirouette* on the runway, for they must remember that beauty is ephemeral and that, at the end of the day, it is meaningless and futile anyway! So, claim ugly people! Therefore, the list below is for them. It is also for *avant-garde couturiers, boutiques,* and *maisons de couture,* and for the myriad of incurable shopaholics everywhere.

FRENCH LOANWORDS

A LA MODE (f) Fashionable.

ACCOUTREMENT (m) Way of wearing clothes; garb. In France the word also implies bizarre or ridiculous clothes. *Quel accoutrement!* (What a ridiculous get-up!)

APPLIQUÉ (m) Fabric decorations or trimmings sewn to another fabric, as in floral *appliqués.* In France, the word used for the above is *applique* (without the accent on the 'e'); *une applique* is a design cut-out and *appliqué* (applied), sewn to a fabric.

BATEAU (m) As in *bateau* neckline: boat neckline; a wide, straight neckline that goes from one shoulder bone to the other. The word *bateau,* meaning flat-bottomed river boat, is commonly used in Louisiana.

BOUFFANT (m) As in *robe bouffante;* puffed out dress, gathered with ruffles.

BOUILLONNÉ (m) Crinkled texture; parallel rows of short stitches gathering a band of fabric; shirred fabric that can be used to make *appliqués.*

BOUTIQUE (f) Small shop devoted to specialized merchandise. *La Boutique de la Maison Couture* was opened in Paris in 1929 by Lucien Lelong.

BRANCHÉ (m) *Au courant* of the latest, *à la mode,* trendy as in a club *branché* in France where one can order a whisky and soda. The French say: to have *le look branché* (an informed air, *au courant*).

BRILLANTINE (f) Oily preparation to make the hair *brilliant* (shiny, glossy) and smooth.

CACHE-CHIGNON (m) Literally, hide-*chignon*: a hairnet; also a bow attached to hold loose ends of hair in place in the 1840s and 1850s.

CAPITONNÉ (m) Padded.

CHIGNON (m) A knot or coil of hair at the back of the head; a bun. A hairstyle *en vogue* from the nineteenth century until late 1920s, and again in the 1960s and 1970s.

CHINÉ (m) Dyed or woven Chinese style of several colors, as in *laine chinée* (mottled wool); *tissu chiné* (chiné fabric).

CIRÉ (m) A trademark name for a shiny fabric used to give the wet look popular during the twentieth century up to 1969. Waxed; a *toile cirée* (oilskin). Also, a waterproof garment as in *un ciré de marin* (a sailor's raincoat).

CISELÉ (m) As in velvet *ciselé*: ornamental motifs cut in fabric with *ciseaux* (scissors); see *ciselure* Chapter II under Art Terms.

CLOQUÉ (m) Embossed or puckered fabric; *une cloque* is French for "blister"; *du cloqué* is cloqué fabric, seersucker.

CORSAGE (m) A bodice; the waist of a woman's dress; also the *bouquet* worn at the waist or wrist, but not in France where *un corsage* is a woman's blouse only.

COUTURE (f) Sewing.

COUTURIER (m) Man dressmaker; designer; a woman dressmaker is *une couturière*.

DÉCOLLETAGE (m) The neckline of a woman's garment.

DÉCOLLETÉ (e) *(m or f)* A *décolleté* shows the neck and part of the bosom or back and can be low or not. *Une robe décolletée en V* (a V-neck dress); *un grand décolleté,* means low-cut, low cleavage, *très décolleté.*

DÉFILÉ (m) A parade; a march; a procession: *un défilé de mode* (a fashion show).

DÉMODÉ (e) (m or f) *Un chapeau démodé; une robe démodée;* old-fashioned, out of style.

DÉPASSÉ (m) Outdated; outmoded.

DIAMANTÉ (m) Ornamented with small false *diamants* (diamonds), with glittering particles; very popular throughout the twentieth century for evening dress.

DRAPÉ (m) Draped; *le drapé d'une robe* (folds in the fabric of a dress).

DU JOUR (m) Of the day, as in item *du jour;* something or somebody *en vogue* now as in: *le couple du jour, l'homme du jour, la soupe du jour, le plat du jour.*

ENSEMBLE (m) A whole costume; an outfit.

ENTRELAC (m) Scrollwork: a knitting pattern of interlacing lines.

FAÇONNÉ (m) *Façonné* cloth, as in a *façonné* velvet: with patterns scattered woven into the cloth, similar to a *damassé* and a *broché* fabric.

FALBALA (m) Frill, flounces, pleats used as ornament at the hem of a dress; *robe à falbalas.*

FROU-FROU (m) Or *froufrou;* rustling sound made by a fabric such as silk. The mini-skirt is *la bête noire* of the *frou-frou* lover; a *robe à froufrous* (a *froufrou* dress, with frills and elaborate trimmings). See Chapter IV under French Loanwords Alphabetically.

GARÇONNE (f) As in *garçonne silhouette* (a boyish look), short hair, little or no makeup; a mannish independent girl. *La Garçonne* is the title of a very *risqué* (at the time) novel by Victor Marguerite published in 1922, describing the sexual mores of a Sorbonne student who has an illegal child.

GIGOT (f) As in *gigot* sleeves: a long sleeve that is tight fitting from the wrist to the elbow and very wide from the elbow to the shoulder. Not to confuse with *gigot de mouton* (leg of lamb); see Chapter I under Meats and Fish.

HAUTE COUTURE (f) High fashion; one-of-a-kind garment created by fashion designers; a custom-made original garment that nobody wears because they cannot afford them or because they are simply so bizarre that only Aunt Charlotte put them on to go to church a century ago. *Haute Couture* dates back to Charles Frederic Worth, who founded the first *Maison de Haute Couture* in 1858 at 7 rue de la Paix in Paris with the purpose of designing original models for individual clients.

JACQUARD (m) Patterns made by the loom invented by Joseph Marie Jacquard (1752–1834) in Lyon, France. The loom produces a variety of decorative designs; some of these patterns are brocade, damask, or tapestry; a jacquard weave is a weave with figures produced by a Jacquard loom; to wear *un pull jacquard*, a jacquard sweater.

LINGERIE (f) Formerly articles of linen; Today *lingerie* refers to women's underwear made of *lin* (linen), silk, or rayon.

MAISON DE COUTURE (f) A fashion house.

MANNEQUIN (m) In both French and English a *mannequin* is a model of a human being used by tailors; a dummy in a store window. In France, *un mannequin* is also a fashion model; during a fashion show one sees the *défilé des mannequins* (the models parade).

MAQUILLAGE (m) Makeup application of cosmetics; a word meaning "stain" in Old French.

MAQUILLÉ (e) (m or f) A man or woman wearing cosmetics; made-up.

MERVEILLEUX (m) *Merveilleuse* (feminine); a fashionably dressed man or woman, a fop, a dandy; name given during French Directory era, late 1700s; dressed with eccentric elegance.

MIDI (m) As in midi-skirt, a calf-length skirt worn with knee high boots in the late 1960s; longer than the mini that came well above the knees. *Midi* is also French for "midday"; *il est midi* (it is twelve noon). *Midi* is French for "South," as *Le Midi* (the South of France), *the Côte d'Azur* (the Riviera).

MIDINETTE (f) French seamstress or salesperson in a *boutique*. Also French for "bimbo," scatterbrained young girl.

PARSEMÉ (e) (m or f) Sprinkled over a background; decorated with embroidered *motifs*, beads, etc.

PASSEMENTERIE (f) Trimming made of gimp cord, beads, braids, etc.

PERRUQUIER (m) A wig maker.

PETIT POINT (m) Literally, little stitch: embroidery on canvas using small stitches; tent-stitch.

PICOT (m) Decorative edging on a ribbon or lace made by small, repetitive loops.

PLISSÉ (e) (m or f) Pleated: a piece of fabric gathered into narrow folds; also used for a crinkled, puckered fabric.

POINT (m) A stitch; *point de* (stitch from) indicates the real or supposed place of manufacturing; as *point d'Alençon, point de Paris, point de Venise*, etc.

POMPADOUR (m) A style of dress with a square, low-cut neck.

POUF (m) Any part of a dress gathered into a puff; in the 1870s a metallic frame put under the fabric would inflate the skirt from behind; similar to a *faux cul* or a *tournure*.

PRÊT-À-PORTER (m) Literally, ready to wear: term used to refer to mass produced quality clothes; *Boutique de prêt-à-porter*.

PRINCESSE (f) Close-fitting garment with the skirt and waist in one; unbroken at the waistline; a *princesse* gown; *Princesse*-line dress.

ROULEAU (m) Padded *rouleau* (roll) of fabric used as trimming.

SILHOUETTE (f) Overall outline of an outfit; as in *silhouette coquetier* (eggcup *silhouette*).

TAILLE (f) Waist of a dress; also waistline as in, "She has *une taille fine*" (She is slim; she has a small waist).

TAMBOUR (m) Embroidery frame made of two hoops fitting closely to hold the fabric stretched between them to embroider.

TOILETTE DE SOIRÉE (f) Evening dress.

TORSADE (f) Twisted braid, ribbon, etc., used as trimming. Popular in France when the *guêpière* was in style.

TOUPET (m) Toupee; small wig to cover a bald spot.

TRÈS CHIC (m) Very stylish, elegant.

TROUSSEAU (m) A bride's personal possessions: household items, clothes, linen, etc.

TROU-TROU (m) *Un trou* is French for a hole; a *trou-trou* is a little hole, (not two holes); eyelet in embroidery.

VOLANT (m) A flounce in a skirt or curtain.

ZAZOU (m) Eccentric dress style adopted by unconventional jazz lovers during the Second World War; a French version of the zoot suit worn in the U.S. in the 1940s; a *zazou ensemble* consisted of a very tight skirt, a jacket, and very high heels.

COLORS

> It was the Rainbow that gave thee birth,
> And left thee all her lovely hues.
>
> —*The Kingfisher*, W. H. Davies (1870–1940)

Colors are either masculine or feminine depending on the noun they qualify.

FRENCH LOANWORDS

AUBERGINE Dark purple color of the *aubergine* (eggplant).

AZUR Light blue; *La Côte d'Azur* (the Riviera).

BEIGE A grayish-tan.

BLANC DE PERLE Pearl-white.

BLEU CIEL Sky blue; pale blue color.

BLOND (e) Flaxen; light golden-brown.

BOIS DE ROSE Rosewood, a soft, rosy-pink color fashionable in the 1920s and 1930s.

BRONZE A reddish-brown color.

BRUYÈRE Pinkish-purple color of *bruyère* (heather).

CAFÉ Coffee color.

CAFÉ AU LAIT Coffee with milk: a brownish-beige color.

CENDRÉ (e) Pale ash-gray; ashen; *cendre* is French for "ash"; *Cendrillon* is Cinderella.

CERISE Cherry-red.

CHAMOIS Fawn-colored; a chamois is a goat-like antelope.

CHARTREUSE Pale yellowish-green; color of the Chartreuse liquor.

CITRON Lemon yellow.

CLAIR DE LUNE A soft white or pale blue-grey color; a Chinese porcelain glaze of this color; not a common name in France. *Clair de Lune (Moonlight)* is the title of one of Achille-Claude Debussy's (1862–1918) best known compositions for piano.

COQUELICOT Color of the corn poppy, a mixture of orange and scarlet; also corn poppy.

CORBEAU Crow, raven; in the drapery trade, a dark green color verging on black.

ECRU (e) Beige; light tan; color of unbleached linen.

FEUILLE-MORTE Dead leaf: reddish brown color.

FRAMBOISE *Couleur framboise*: raspberry color; a shade of pink.

JONQUILLE *Jaune jonquille*: light yellow color; a *jonquille* resembles a daffodil.

MARRON Reddish-brown as a chestnut or horse-chestnut color.

MAUVE Lilac color; delicate purple.

MORDORÉ (e) Golden brown; copper color.

NACARAT A pale red color tinged with mother-of-pearl glints. Proust used it in *"une soirie nacarat"* (a silky *nacarat*).

NACRÉ (e) Having the iridescent effect of *nacre*.

NOIR (e) Black.

PAILLE Pale yellow, color of straw.

PASTEL A soft pale color, as in bleu pastel; *pastel* (*provençal* word) is the name of a plant whose leaves yield a blue dye; also called woad, a cruciferous plant cultivated extensively in Great Britain.

PELURE D'OIGNON Onion peel: a tawny color characteristic of some pale *rosé* wines.

PERVENCHE Light blue resembling the color of the *pervenche* (periwinkle); *bleu pervenche*.

POMPADOUR A shade of crimson or pink.

ROSE From Latin *rosa*, pink.

ROSE BONBON Candy pink; pastel pink color.

ROUGE Red; reddish powder, chiefly ferric oxide used to polish metal or glass; red or reddish cosmetics.

SANGUINE Color of blood (*sang* is French for "blood"); said of complexion (ruddy).

TAUPE A brownish shade of gray; color of moleskin.

TILLEUL A *tilleul* is a lime or linden tree; a pale yellowish-green color; a *vert tilleul* (lime green).

VERMEIL Bright red color; crimson-red to orange-red garnet; said of complexion: un *teint vermeil*, of wine: *un bourguignon vermeil*, etc.

VERMILLION Bright yellowish red; vermilion.

VERT (e) Green.

VIEUX ROSE Old-fashioned pink; a deep pink color.

BE A SNOB

The short French phrases in this section contain one or more French word(s) and one or more loanwords selected from each vocabulary list in Chapter III.

For instance, *courir le cotillon* is one example of such phrase in which *courir* (to run) is a French word, and *le cotillon* is a French loanword meaning "petticoat." The literal meaning of *courir le cotillon* is "to run after the petticoat." When a French woman gossips about *le petit cochon* (the little pig; the pervert) next door, she says that *il court le cotillon*, "He is a womanizer."

Anyone can use any of the French expressions below to be snob or appear to be intellectual. Their literal meaning is in parentheses, followed by a short sentence illustrating how the expression is used in France.

CLOTHES
MANTEAU (m) A woman's cloak or mantle.
Sous le manteau (under the coat).
A book published *sous le manteau*; a book published or sold underground *clandestinement* (illegally).

ROBE DE CHAMBRE A dressing gown; a robe.

Pommes de terre en robe de chambre (Potatoes in their dressing gown).

I eat *des pommes de terre en robe de chambre*; I eat potatoes in their jacket; cooked with the skin.

TABLIER (m) A part of a woman's dress resembling a *tablier*, French for apron.

Rendre son tablier (to return part of one's dress).

Je rends mon tablier; I resign, I quit; I give my notice.

HATS

BÉGUIN (m) A close-fitting bonnet.

Avoir le béguin (to have the bonnet).

J'ai le béguin; for him or for her; I have a crush on him, or on her.

Son béguin (her or his bonnet).

It is *son béguin*; it is her/his darling, his/her love.

You are *mon béguin*; you are my love.

BIBI (m) Woman's small hat; *bibi* is also colloquial French or child language for *moi*: I.

Pour bibi (for bibi hat).

It's *pour bibi*; it's for me (pour moi).

C'est bibi (it's bibi hat).

Coucou, c'est bibi; pikeboo, it is I (*c'est moi*).

BONNET DE NUIT (m) Nightcap.

Quel bonnet de nuit! (What a nightcap).

Quel bonnet de nuit this man is!; what a bore this man is!

CHAPEAU Hat.

Travailler du chapeau (to work of the hat).

He or she *travaille du chapeau*; he/she is a bit cracked; he (she) is bats.

Chapeau bas! (hat down); Hats off! Well done! Congratulations! Bravo!

CHOU (m) A soft hat with crushed crown.

Très chou (very soft hat).

C'est très chou; It's darling; it is adorable, very cute (usually talking about clothes).

CLOCHE (f) A woman's close-fitting, bell-shaped hat.

Quelle cloche! (What a bell-shaped hat).

Quelle cloche!; what a nincompoop! what a dumbbell! (Can be said about men or women.)

ACCESSORIES

BRELOQUE (f) A locket, a charm.

Battre la breloque (to beat the locket).

Il/elle bat la breloque; he/she is a bit batty.

He/she is *zinzin* (a bit cracked), as the French often say.

CHAUSSURE (f) Shoe.

Chaussure à mon pied (Shoe for my foot).

I have found *chaussure à mon pied*; I have found my soulmate.

CHOU (m) Cabbage-bow.

Un petit bout de chou (a little piece of cabbage-bow).

He/she is *un petit bout de chou*; he/she is a little darling. (Used when talking about children.)

PANACHE (m) A plume; a cluster of feathers on a hat; also brilliance, *éclat*.

Son panache (his cluster of feathers).

He/she has *son panache*; he/she is tipsy.

PANTOUFLES (f.pl.) Slippers.

Comme une pantoufle (like a slipper).

He/she reasons *comme une pantoufle*; he/she talks nonsense.

POMPON (m) Ornamental tuft of silk; pompon.

C'est le pompon! (It is the pompon).

C'est le pompon mon cher!; that takes the cake mon cher!

Avoir le pompon (to have the pompon).

He/she has *le pompon*; he/she won the prize, came first.

Avoir son pompon (to have one's pompon).

Il/elle a son pompon; he/she is tipsy, a little drunk.

I have *mon pompon*; I am plastered.

SABOT A shoe made of a single piece of wood.

Comme un sabot (like a wooden shoe).

He/she works *comme un sabot*; he/she works very poorly; he/she is sloppy.

He/she sleeps *comme un sabot*; he/she sleeps deeply, like a log.

Dans le même sabot (in the same shoe).

He/she has both feet *dans le même sabot*; he/she is inefficient.

FABRIC

DRAP (m) Thin, twilled, woolen fabric; French for bedsheet.

Dans de beaux draps (in beautiful wool fabric).

I am *dans de beaux draps*; I am in a fine mess.

EPONGE (f) Soft, spongy weave of uneven, knobby yarn.

Comme une éponge (like a sponge).

He/she drinks *comme une éponge*; he/she drinks like a fish.

MOQUETTE (f) Kind of carpet or upholstery fabric with a thick, soft, napped surface.

Fumer la moquette (to smoke the carpet, the *moquette*).

He/she *fume la moquette*; he/she is delirious, off the rocker, in the clouds.

In France, it is an expression that makes some French smile or laugh. Indeed, you have to be totally off your rocker to smoke your *moquette*! In some circles, the expression *fumer la moquette* refers to drug addiction where an individual may become so desperate that he is ready to do whatever it takes, including smoke his own carpet!

PEAU DE SOIE (f) *(peau)* Skin of silk: a close-woven heavy satin silk.

Dans la peau (in the skin).

I have him or her *dans la peau*; I am infatuated with him/her; I am passionately in love with him or her.

Peau de vache! (Cow's hide)!

He is a *peau de vache!*; he is a bastard!

Vieille peau! (Old skin)!

What a *vieille peau*; what an old hag!

La peau des fesses (the skin of the *derrière*, of the buttocks).

It costs *la peau des fesses*; it costs an arm and a leg!

The French also say, "It costs *les yeux de la tête*" (the eyes on your face).

VELOURS (m) Plush fabric similar to velvet.

Du velours (some velvet).

This sauce is *du velours*; this sauce is delicious.

MISCELLANEOUS LOANWORDS

MIDINETTE (f) French seamstress.

Une petite midinette (a little French seamstress).

C'est une petite midinette; she is a feather-brained girl, a bimbo.

Un roman pour midinettes (a novel for French seamstresses).

C'est un roman pour midinettes; it is a sentimental novel.

The French also say, *un roman à l'eau de rose* (rose water).

PRINCESSE (f) Princess-line dress.

Aux frais de la princesse (at the expense of the princess).

They live *aux frais de la princesse*; at the tax payers' expense.

TOUPET (m) Toupee.

Quel toupet! (What a toupee!); What a cheek!

Du toupet (some toupee).

She/she has *du toupet*; he/she has lots of nerve!

COLORS

BLEU Blue.

Une peur bleue (a blue scare).

I have *une peur bleue*; I am scared stiff.

BLEU-CIEL Sky (sky-blue).

(*ciel*) *Tomber du ciel* (to fall from the sky, heavens).

He/she *tombe du ciel*; he/she arrives without warning, out of the blue.

BOIS DE ROSE Rosewood, a soft rosy pink color fashionable in the 1920s and 1930s.

(*bois*) *La gueule de bois* (mouth of wood).

I have *la gueule de bois*; I have a hangover.

COQUELICOT Color of the corn poppy.

Rouge comme un coquelicot (red as a poppy).

She/he is rouge *comme un coquelicot*; she/he is as red as a beetroot, as a beet.

NOIR Black.

Tout en noir (all in black).

He/she sees *tout en noir*; he/she sees the black side of things. A pessimist.

Des idées noires (black ideas). *Noire* is feminine for *noir*.

I have *des idées noires*; I am in the dumps.

La misère noire (black misery).

C'est la misère noire; it is dire poverty.

PAILLE Straw (color).

Sur la paille (on the straw).

Je suis (I am) *sur la paille*; I am penniless; I am broke.

ROSE Pink.

La vie en rose (a song by French singer Edith Piaf in the 1950s).

I see *la vie en rose*; I see life in pink, through rose-colored glasses.

PROVERBS

CLOCHE *Qui n'entend qu'une cloche, n'entend qu'un son.*

He who hears only one bell, hears only one sound; one should hear both sides of the story.

HABIT Costume; dress, outfit for a particular situation.

L'habit ne fait pas le moine.

You can't judge a book by its cover; appearances can be deceptive.

REVERS (m) The wrong side of a garment.

Toute médaille a son revers or (*Il n'y a pas de rose sans épines*).

There is no rose without a thorn.

RIVIÈRE (f) A necklace of diamonds or other gems (*rivière* is also a river).

Les petits ruisseaux font les grandes rivières.

Great oaks from little acorns grow.

Many a little makes a mickle (much, a lot).

CONCLUSION

L'habit ne fait pas le moine, literally, the outfit does not make the monk! In other words, one cannot judge a book by its cover. This may be true, but consciously or not, we are often influenced by the way people dress because clothes always do and always will reveal taste, lifestyle, and status. As Mark Twain sums it up, "Clothes make the man. Naked people have little or no influence on society."

Of course, this may be the case in our materialistic neck of the woods, but there are naked men out there who have status and a mighty power over their fearful and admiring tribes.

Chapter 4

POTPOURRI
OF FRENCH
LOANWORDS AND
EXPRESSIONS

INTRODUCTION

One could learn French by speaking English well, and vice-versa. A *cliché* that is almost true, therefore, why not *faire d'une pierre deux coups* (kill two birds with one stone)!

A better knowledge of the English language will empower the reader in many ways, including giving him the flexibility to be a diversified snob. As for those who continue to look down on him because he acts like a *fanfaron* or a vain fool who speaks a foreign tongue, be reassured if need be they are just as snobbish as he is or appears to be! The mere fact they are pretentious enough to feel above the heap makes them reverse snobs. Snobs nevertheless!

Snobs and snob hopefuls may find a plethora of words and expressions that can be used to spice up daily conversation grouped under: French Loanwords by Categories that include: Brouhaha, The Great Outdoors, Up-to-Date or Not, About Men, About Women, and About Children; Potpourri of French Loanwords and Expressions such as: *à bas, d'accord, au contraire, sans chichi, tout le monde, etc.*; and French Loanwords Alphabetically.

FRENCH LOANWORDS BY CATEGORIES

French loanwords that any sophisticated English speaker must know to add culture and *verve* to his daily interactions are listed below under: Brouhaha, The Great Outdoors, Up-to-Date or Not, About Men, About Women, and About Children.

BROUHAHA

Brouhaha is an onomatopoeia that was apparently used in medieval theatre in France in the early sixteenth century. According to several sources, it would have been "the cry of the devil disguised as a priest."

Whether it is true or not, only the Devil knows! It makes some sense, however. When people heard these diabolical sounds coming out of the mouth of a demon-priest, we can imagine a pandemonium and people screaming and running in all directions to escape! And *voilà*, the word *brouhaha* has meant "commotion" ever since in France and for *faute de mieux*, English speakers adopted it in their vocabulary.

Many expressions below are used with what: *quel* (masculine) or *quelle* (feminine). The word is used as an exclamation to express surprise, admiration, indignation, or compassion as in: *Quel fanfaron* (what a *fanfaron*); or *Quelle surprise* (what a surprise)! The pronunciation of *quel* or *quelle* is the same.

BROUHAHA (m) Hubbub; hoopla; commotion; a noisy stir or wrangle. *Quel brouhaha!* (What a noise! What a hoopla!); not to confuse with *houp-là,* French for "upsi-daisy" *(Harrap French-English Dictionary).*

CHARIVARI (m) A racket; discordant sounds; a vacarm. *Quel charivari!* (What a racket!)

COHUE (f) An unruly and noisy crowd. *Quelle cohue!* (What an unruly crowd, What a scramble!)

FLIC FLAC (m) Onomatopoeia; the lapping of something; a splish-splash; for instance (French) raindrops go *flic flac* (splish-splash). (Spelled *flic-flac,* with a hyphen, when used as a noun; for example: the *flic-flac* of the rain).[48]

MÊLÉE (f) A confused mass of people; a scramble, also a skirmish. *Quelle mêlée!* (What a *cohue,* what a mess!)

PÊLE-MÊLE (m) Pell-mell, disorderly crowd (another French word for it is *méli-mélo*). *Quel pêle-mêle!* (What a jumble!)

RATAPLAN (m) A drumming sound.

THE GREAT OUTDOORS

Rangers at the Bridger Wilderness station in the Teton National Forest collect strange comments from weird hikers. Here are a few made in 1996 by fanatic rugged outdoors fans! Their bizarre requests below leave you *bouche-bée* (agape). *En passant, un téton* is familiar French for "tit."

"Please, avoid building trails that go up hills!" Well, go *à cheval!*

"Please, pave the trails so they can be plowed of snow during the winter!" Probably from some *mondain* in *le tout* New York!

"The coyotes made too much noise last night and kept me awake. Please eradicate these annoying animals." *Assassin! Canaille!*

"Escalators would be helpful on steep up-hills!" What a *blagueur!*

"Too many rocks in the mountains." Where is this one coming from? Probably *un homme d'esprit!*

"A small deer came into my camp and stole my jar of pickles. Is there a way I can get reimbursed? Please call: —,—,—!" What a *froufrou* for a jar of *cornichons!*

"A McDonald's would be nice at the trailhead!" *Vive* America!

A CHEVAL (m) On horseback.

A LA BELLE ÉTOILE (f) Under the stars; in the open air.

A L'ABRI (m) Under shelter, protected.

A LA CAMPAGNE (f) In the country.

A PIED (m) On foot.

APRÈS-SKI (m) When ski is over; after skiing.

DEHORS Out of doors; outside.

EN PLEN AIR (m) In the open air; especially with reference to the working methods of the French Impressionist painters, as compared with their academic *confrères* who worked in studios and from posed models.

FÊTE CHAMPÊTRE (f) A rural festival; *champêtre* derived from *champ* (field) as in *Les Champs Elysées*.

MAISON DE CAMPAGNE (f) A country home.

UP-TO-DATE OR NOT

The French expression for *passé* is *passé de mode* when referring to outdated clothes, philosophy, opinions, etc. Nostalgic French often reminisce about *le passé* (the past) and swear that all that *c'est du passé* (it's all in the past). Today, when they talk about an old man or woman who is no longer *au courant*, they say: *c'est un has been* (He/she is a has-been), a poor lost soul behind the times! They also use the word *passé* when they lament about the faded color of an old dress that has seen better days.

Antole France used the word *passé*, referring exclusively to a *cantaloup* (a cantaloupe *melon*) in the expression, *"Un cantaloup vert ou déjà passé"* (a green or already very matured, ripe cantaloupe *melon*) (*Le Petit Robert, Dictionnaire de la Langue Française*). The word was also used in France to talk about other fruits (besides *melon*), or food that had passed their use-by-date, but today the French say that a fruit or a food is *périmé*, in other words, hazardous to your health!

A LA MODE (f) Fashionable. Today, many French people say: *in*, as she is *très in*; or she is *dans le vent*, literally, in the wind; both expressions mean: (trendy), *à la mode, à la page, en vogue, dernier cri* (see below).

A LA PAGE (f) Up-to-date; *très à la page, très in* (very stylish).

CHIC (m) Smartly dressed; elegant; a flair for style and fashion; *très chic*.

DÉMODÉ (m or f) As in *un chapeau démodé* (m); out of fashion; or *démodée* (f) as in *une robe démodée* (a dress out of style).

DÉPASSÉ (m or f) Outdated; outmoded.

DERNIER CRI (m) Literally, the last cry: the very latest fashion.

EN VOGUE (f) Fashionable; trendy.

PASSÉ (m) Outdated; the French expression is *passé de mode* as in, "This dress is *passée de mode*."

VIEUX JEU (m) Literally, old game: old-fashioned, outmoded, *très has-been* as the French now say. *Il (elle) est vieux jeu, un has been* (he/she is old-fashioned, behind times).

ABOUT MEN

> "A man is a collection of chemicals
> with delusion of grandeur."

Not very kind, even if it is true. But, on the positive side, any man can manipulate his collection to his advantage and enjoy himself as a *bon vivant*, a *bon diable*, a *coiffeur*, or a *chocolatier* and wear other titles that he can choose from a long list below. Of course, he can take solace in the fact that some of the uncharitable qualifications apply to women as well.

All the words below are masculine.

See Chapter I under People for a definition of the following loanwords:

Chef; chocolatier; Cordon bleu; garçon; gastronome; gourmand; gourmet; Maître d'hôtel; négociant; pâtissier; patron; plongeur; restaurateur; rôtisseur; saucier; sommelier; sous-chef; traiteur; vendangeur; vigneron.

The above words are not included in the list below.

ABONNÉ Subscriber.

ACCOUCHEUR Medical practitioner who attends to women in childbirth; *Accouchement*, the act of childbirth (*Webster's*); from *accoucher* (to give birth).

AGENT PROVOVATEUR A person who provokes a disturbance; an agitator.

AIDE-DE-CAMP Field helper: an officer in the army, navy, etc., acting as an assistant to a superior officer; plural: *aides-de-camp*.

AMATEUR One who pursues a study or art without doing it professionally.

ARRIVISTE Social climber; reckless, unprincipled individual.

ARTISAN Skilled manual worker.

ASSASSIN A murderer.

ATTACHÉ A person assigned to a diplomatic post; from *attacher* (to attach).

AUTEUR Creator of literary or artistic work; a film director can be the *auteur* of his own movies.

BADINEUR A banterer; one who indulges in badinage, nonsense, or playful talking. From *badiner* (to banter). Also *badin* in French.

BARON A member of the lowest rank of British nobility.

BARONNET Diminutive for *baron*: rank next below a *baron*, and above a knight.

BEAU A gallant; a sweetheart. Term used in the late seventeenth to mid-nineteenth centuries for a man fastidious about his clothes and accessories; a dandy, a fop.

BEAU GARÇON Beautiful boy: a good looking man. *Quel beau garçon!* (What a handsome guy!)

BEL ESPRIT Beautiful spirit: a cultivated person; *beau, bel*: see end note.

BÊTE NOIRE Black beast: a bugbear; somebody's nightmare.

BIEN-PENSANT Literally, well-thinking: a conformist. It is a derogatory implication of mindless compliance with current intellectual or moral fashion.

BLAGUEUR A joker; one who tells *blagues*.

BLASÉ Bored, satiated by excess of anything.

BON DIABLE Literally, good devil: a good-natured fellow; a decent sort. *Un grand diable* (a beanpole); *un pauvre diable* (a poor devil).

BON ENFANT A good-natured individual. In France, Americans are often called *bons enfants* because they are generally perceived as being relaxed and fun-loving, big kids.

BON VIVANT One who indulges a taste for good things of *la vie* (life); jovial, fun-loving. From *vivre* (to live). Not a *bon à rien* (a good for nothing).

BON VIVEUR Party animal; one who enjoys having fun.

BORNÉ Narrow-minded; limited intellectually.

BOULEVARDIER A man about town; from *boulevard*. One who frequents *les Grands Boulevards de Paris*.

BOURGEOIS Middle class; a conventional, commonplace, respectable individual.

BRICOLEUR A handyman; from *bricoler* (to do odd jobs). In France Bric-orama are stores similar to Home Depot in the U.S.

BRIGADIER One who commands a troop, a unit of soldiers, a *brigade*.

BRIGAND A lawless individual; a bandit, a crook.

BRUNET Boy or man with dark brown hair.

CAMOUFLEUR One employed or skilled in *camouflage*.

CANAILLE Scoundrel; *la canaille*: the riff-raff; the rabble.

CARILLONNEUR A *carillon* player.

CAVALIER A courtly gentleman; a knight; a horseman. Not to confuse with adjective *cavalier*, meaning free and easy; supercilious; as in a *cavalier* manner.

CHANSONNIER A cabaret performer; from *chanson* (song).

CHANTEUR A singer; from *chanter* (to sing).

CHARGÉ D'AFFAIRES Literally, in charge of affairs; a person entrusted with business; a government official who temporarily takes the place of a minister, ambassador, or other diplomat.

CHARLATAN A quack; an impostor; one who makes false pretenses.

CHASSEUR A hunter; huntsman; from *chasser* (to hunt).

CHAUFFEUR Individual who drives an automobile for someone else.

CHER MAÎTRE A flattering form of address to a famous person, or to somebody perceived as important by some: a lawyer for instance.

CHEVALIER A gallant.

CISELEUR One who does *ciselure*; a chaser; see Chapter II under Art Terms.

CLAIRVOYANT Literally, clear-seeing: one who has the ability of knowing things that are not perceived by normal human senses; also used as an adjective as in a *clairvoyant* person.

CLAQUEUR Member of the *claque*: people hired to applaud after a play, or show; see Chapter II under Theatre.

COIFFEUR Hairdresser; from *coiffer* (to do somebody's hair); one who coifs the hair.

COLPORTEUR A colporter; a peddler; a door-to-door salesman. From *colporter* (to spread the news, to peddle).

COMPAGNON DE VOYAGE A traveling companion.

COMPÈRE An accomplice; a partner; a buddy (U.S.), a mate (G.B.).

CONCIERGE A door keeper (man or woman); the warden of a house.

CONFÉRENCIER A lecturer; a public speaker.

CONFIDENT A friend to whom secrets are confided; also spelled *confidant* in *Webster's*. From *confier* (to entrust something to somebody); *se confier* is French for "to confide oneself."

CONFRÈRE A fellow member of the same profession: doctors, lawyers, etc.; associate; plural *confrères; un frère:* French for "brother." *Un collègue* (a colleague is a partner or associate in the same office or establishment). *Consoeur* (female colleague); *soeur* is French for "sister."

CONNAISSEUR Connoisseur, from Old French *connoistre* (to know). Modern French is *connaître,* hence a *connaisseur,* a person with a thorough knowledge of a subject: arts, food, wines.

CONTEUR One who tells *contes,* stories.

COQUET A flirt; a *beau* who struts like a little cock. *Coquet* used as an adjective means well-kept, cute in French as in: *un appartement coquet* (a nice, pleasant apartment).

COSTUMIER One who makes costumes.

COURRIER A messenger; a dispatch rider as in a diplomatic courier. Spelled "courier" in *Webster's Dictionary:* from Old French courier, deriving from *courir* (to run). In France the word also means mail, letters; Courrier électronique is French for "electronic mail, e-mail."

CRÈME DE LA CRÈME The cream of the crop; the best of the best.

CRÉTIN Idiot; feebleminded; dunce.

CROUPIER One who collects and pays the money at a gaming table; a casino *croupier.*

DANSEUR A dancer; from *danser* (to dance).

DÉBONNAIRE Carefree, courteous; having an affable manner.

DÉBUTANT A male person making his social or acting *début;* from *débuter* (to begin).

DÉCLASSÉ Fallen in social class, status, or rank.

DÉGAGÉ Unconstrained; free of manners; unconventional.

DÉLÉGUÉ Delegated; responsible for.

DÉRACINÉ Uprooted; from *racine* (root).

DÉTENU A political prisoner; from *détenir* (to detain).

DIABLE Devil.

DISTINGUÉ Distinguished; having an air of distinction.

DIVORCÉ A divorced man.

DOUANIER An officer of the French customs, *douane.*

DROIT DU SEIGNEUR The lord's right: a custom whereby a medieval feudal lord might have sexual intercourse with a vassal's bride on the latter's wedding night.

ÉMIGRÉ An immigrant.

ENFANT TERRIBLE Literally, child terrible: a troublesome, unconventional person, usually within a group: artists, writers, thinkers, as in: *c'est l'enfant terrible du groupe* (he is the unconventional *enfant terrible* of the group). *Les*

Enfants Terribles is the title of a novel (1929) and movie (1952) by French writer and film director Jean Cocteau (1889–1963) about a teenaged brother and sister and their incestuous obsession.

ENTREPRENEUR One who organizes and directs a business undertaking assuming the risk for the sake of profit.

FAINÉANT Idler; literally, a do-nothing.

FANFARON A blusterer, a boaster. A *zigoto*, as they also say in France; a word with a funny, amusing ring to the French ear when they talk about somebody who tries to impress somebody; *un drôle de zigoto* (a funny guy, a queer customer, one that plays the fool to be noticed).

FARCEUR A joker; a writer or actor of *farces. Quel farceur!* (What a joker!)

FIANCÉ The man to whom a woman is engaged to be married.

FINANCIER One who is skilled in important financial matters.

FLÂNEUR One who idly saunters without a destination; one who has a certain aloofness; a stroller. Manet was apparently the perfect Parisian *flâneur* who enjoyed *flânerie;* from *flâner* (to stroll leisurely, to loaf).

FONCTIONNAIRE Civil servant; government official; also called *un rond-de-cuir.*

FRÈRE Brother.

FRIPON A knave, a scamp.

GALANT Courteous, gentlemanly, gallant.

GARDE DU CORPS Guard of the body, a bodyguard.

GENDARME Armed police in France and Belgium; a constable; a policeman.

GENTILHOMME A gentleman; from *gentil* (gentle) and *homme* (man). Feminine for *gentil* is *gentille*, as in *elle est gentille* (she is nice, gentle).

GIGOLO A man paid to escort a woman; a man kept by a woman older than he is; From *gigue*: colloquial French for *jambe* (leg); *une grande gigue* (a girl with long legs). *Une gigolette*, is a *femme facile*, (streetwise; loose woman), the *gigolo's* lover. Not as commonly heard or used in France as *gigolo*. A *gigolette* is likely to be kept by an older man.

GONDOLIER A man who rows or poles a gondola.

HABITUÉ One who has the habit of frequenting a place.

HOMME D'AFFAIRES Businessman.

HOMME DE BIEN Altruistic man; benevolent, one who shares his *biens* (possessions) with others less fortunate. To own *du bien* (sing.) or *des biens* (pl.) is to own properties, to be wealthy. *Bien* as an adverb means "well," as in *je vais bien* (I am well); *très bien* (very well).

HOMME DE LETTRES Literally, a man of letters, a literary man, a writer.

HOMME DE ROBE Magistrate; lawyer (also, *homme de loi* in French).

HOMME D'ESPRIT A man of wit.

HOMME D'ÉTAT A statesman.

IMBÉCILE Stupid; deficient intellect (applies to women also).

ESPÈCE D'IMBÉCILE!, (Silly fool!); *Imbécile heureux*, literally, happy imbecile, simpleton.

INCONNU Unknown; as in *la tombe du Soldat Inconnu*, the grave of the Unknown Soldier.

INSOUCIANT Carefree; unconcerned, one with *pas de soucis* (no worries).

INTRIGANT A man involved in a plot or scheme, *intrigue.*

JONGLEUR A juggler; a wandering minstrel in Medieval times.

LOUP-GAROU Werewolf.

MAÎTRE Title or way to address a French lawyer.

MARAUD A villain; a rascal; a rogue; a tramp. From *marauder* (to rove in search of something to steal).

MARQUIS Title of a nobleman, next in rank below a duke.

MASSEUR A man that provides professional massages.

MAUVAIS SUJET A bad guy; unsavory specimen.

MÉCHANT A wicked, nasty individual.

MON AMI My (man) friend; Plural *mes amis* (my friends).

MON CHER My dear fellow.

MON VIEUX An affectionate form of address; my old man; my old friend.

MONDAIN Worldly man; man who frequents *le haut monde.*

MONSIEUR Mister or Sir; abbreviation is M.; plural is *Messieurs.*

MOUCHARD A squealer; a sneak; a police spy.

MOUSQUETAIRE Musketeer; seventeenth, eighteenth century French Royal bodyguards. *Les Trois Mousquetaires* (*The Three Musketeers*) by Alexandre Dumas.

NAÏF Naïve, simplistic.

NONCHALANT Calm, casual, lacking enthusiasm; unconcerned.

NOUVEAU RICHE A person who has acquired wealth and displays it ostentatiously or vulgarly; a *parvenu*; plural: *nouveaux riches.*

PAPA Daddy; child's talk corresponding to *maman* for mother. To do something *à la papa, papa* style (without haste or risk). *Maman*; (Mom, Mommy). The French say *Papy* or *papi* instead of *grandpa*; (*pépé* or *pépère* are obsolete in most parts of France). A *pépère* (a quiet, old fellow); *une vie de pépère* (a cushy, comfortable life). The French also say: *Mami, mamy* or *mammy* instead of *grandma* (*mémé* is *démodé* in some circles).

PARTISAN One that strongly supports a side, a party.

PARVENU A man who has suddenly acquired wealth and does not have the *savoir-vivre* and manners required of his new position; the *parvenus*, the *nouveaux riches*.

PENSIONNAIRE (m or f) Man or woman who boards in a French lodging house or institution, or with a French family.

PÈRE Father; often used after a surname as in *Dumas père*; also, title of some priests.

PERSIFLEUR A person who indulges in pleasantry, see *persiflage* in French Loanwords Alphabetially under "P."

PETIT-BOURGEOIS Lower middle class, the least well-off of the bourgeois class, traditionally reputed for being conformist and narrow-minded: *préjugés petits-bourgeois* (*petit-bourgeois* prejudices). *Les Bourgeois de Calais* are the six bourgeois who gave their lives to save Calais during the War of Hundred-Years between France and England.

POSEUR One who affects an attitude to impress people; a poser. From *poser* (to pose, attitudinize).

PROTÉGÉ One under the patronage, care, or protection of an influential person. From *protéger* (to protect).

RACONTEUR One skilled in the narration of anecdotes and stories. From French *raconter* (to tell stories).

RAFFINÉ Of refined taste and manners.

RAILLEUR A jester; a mocker; from *railler* (to laugh at, to mock).

RANGÉ Of a man's lifestyle, orderly, settled.

RÂTÉ A failure.

RAVISSANT Delightful; ravishing.

RAYONNANT Beaming, radiant. A *rayon* (ray) as *un rayon de soleil* (sun ray); *un rayon de lune* (moonbeam).

RÉGISSEUR Stage manager in theatre; from *régir* (to govern).

RENTIER One who has a fixed income as from lands or other sources.

REVENANT A person who has supposedly come back from the dead; a ghost. From *revenir* (to come back).

RÊVEUR A dreamer; from *rêver* (to dream); one who indulges in rêverie. See French Loanwords Alphabetically under "R."

ROI FAINÉANT Sluggard king: anyone with merely nominal power who does nothing; *fait* (does) *néant* (nothingness).

ROI SOLEIL Sun King: a preeminent person, name for Louis the XIV. See end note.

ROND-DE-CUIR Literally, circle of leather, round leather, (cushion on office chairs). Refers to *bureaucrates* (bureaucrats), a word used with contempt in France.

ROTURIER A commoner; not of noble rank.

ROUÉ A debauchee; a rake; cunning.

ROUTIER A vagabond; a freebooter, brigand; one who takes *la route*, the road. In France a *routier* is also a truck driver.

SABOTEUR One who engages in *sabotage*.

SAVANT A learned man; from *savoir* (to know). In French, to know is translated by *savoir* or *connaître*: *Savoir quelque chose* (to know something) as in: *je sais son nom* (I know his or her name). *Connaître quelqu'un* (to know somebody, or a place), as in *je connais Paul et Paris*.

SIFFLEUR A person who entertains professionally by whistling; from *siffler* (to whistle).

SOIGNÉ Meticulously dressed; well-groomed.

SOLITAIRE One who lives in solitude.

SOUPIRANT An admirer; a suitor; from *soupirer* (to sigh, to yearn); *un soupir* (a sigh).

SOUTENEUR A pimp; a procurer; from *soutenir* (to support, to help).

SPORTIF A man active in athletics.

SUAVE Sweet; pleasant; from Latin *suavis*, sweet, polite, polished, urbane.

VAGABOND A wanderer with no fixed abode.

VALET A servant; attendant; a hotel employee who performs a variety of services.

VAURIEN Literally, worth nothing: *un bon à rien* (a good for nothing).

VOLTIGEUR A leaper; vaulter; tumbler. From *voltiger* (to flutter: fly here and there) as in *un papillon voltige* (a butterfly flutters) but *un avion vole*, thank God! (a plane flies) and also *un voleur vole* (a thief steals).

VOYAGEUR A traveler; a voyager. From *voyager* (to travel); *bon voyage* (have a good trip).

VOYANT A clairvoyant.

VOYEUR One given to voyeurism; a Peeping Tom; from *voir* (to see).

VOYOU Lout; hoodlum; rascal; hooligan.

ABOUT WOMEN

> "No matter how old a woman
> becomes, no matter how many years
> pass, she has yet more; a flirtage,
> more stages, and more first times
> awaiting her."

> —*Women Who Run with the Wolves*,
> by Clarissa Pinkola Estés

Special privilege! A woman can pick and choose whoever and whatever she wants to be from the list below and enjoy life in one form or another. So beware, unwise men, because it is a well known fact that, "*Souvent femme varie, bien fol est qui s'y fie;*" literally, "Often a woman changes her mind and you're a fool if you trust her." In other words, "Woman is fickle." But, so is man!

It was François Ier, King of France (1515–1547), who made this wise observation about women, probably from experience. Like most men, he had *sans doute* accepted the fact that, "Women and cats do as they please, and men and dogs should relax and get used to the idea!" (Robert A. Heinlen, American author.)

ACCOUCHEUSE A midwife; Also called *une sage-femme* (a wise woman) in France.

BAS-BLEU Bluestocking: a scholar, learned lady. In France, it is an outdated term referring to a pedantic person, claiming to be a scholar.

BONNE A maid, a servant.

BONNE AMIE Good lady friend.

BOURGEOISE Middle class, traditional, respectable lady.

BRUNETTE Woman with dark brown hair.

CHANTEUSE A singer.

CHÈRE AMIE Dear (female) friend.

CONCIERGE Caretaker in a building. *C'est une vraie concierge* (She is a real gossip). The compliment applies to a man concierge as well: *un vrai concierge* (a nosy body).

CONCUBINE A lady who lives with a man or a lady without being married.

CONFIDANTE A lady to whom you confide your secrets.

COQUETTE One given to flirting or coquetry; a flirt. *Quelle coquette* (What a flirt). *Coquette* also means "cute," particularly about her appearance.

DAME School mistress; a lady, as in *Notre-Dame* de Paris; *une grande Dame.* The French say: *ma petite dame* or *ma bonne dame:* my dear.

DAME DE COMPAGNIE A paid female companion.

DAME D'HONNEUR Matron of honor; a maid of honor; a lady-in-waiting.

DANSEUSE A woman dancer.

DÉBUTANTE A young girl making her social or acting *début.*

DÉCLASSÉE Having lost class and status in society.

DEMOISELLE Unmarried; a damsel; a spinster. *A demoiselle d'honneur* is French for "bridesmaid, maid of honor."

DISEUSE A lady speaker; an entertainer who performs dramatic impersonations. From *dire* (to tell, to say). In France, *une diseuse d'aventures* is a fortune-teller.

DISTINGUÉE Distinguished; having an air of distinction.

DIVORCÉE A divorcee.

ELÉGANTE Fashionable.

ENTREPRENEUR A woman who organizes and directs a business undertaking.

FEMME DE CHAMBRE A chambermaid.

FEMME DE MÉNAGE A domestic's help. *Faire le ménage* means "to do housework." *Je fais le ménage* (I am cleaning the house).

FEMME DU MONDE A woman of the world; sophisticated.

FEMME FATALE An irresistibly and dangerously attractive woman.

FEMME INCOMPRISE Unappreciated, misunderstood woman.

FEMME SAVANTE A learned woman; usually with an implied derogatory allusion to Molière's play *Les Femmes Savantes* (*The Learned Ladies*), 1672.

FIANCÉE The woman to whom a man is engaged to be married.

FILLE DE JOIE Literally, girl of joy: a lady prostitute.

FILLE D'HONNEUR Also *demoiselle d'honneur*; a maid of honor.

GRANDE DAME Literally, a great lady: a woman of high rank and dignified bearing.

GRISETTE A young, working class French woman; See *grisette* Chapter III under Fabric.

HABITUÉE One who has the habit of frequenting a place.

INCONNUE Unknown, stranger.

INGÉNUE Artless innocent young woman, especially as a stage role; inexperienced unworldly young woman. *L'Ingénu*, a man in this case, is the title of a novel by Voltaire.

INSOUCIANTE Carefree.

INTRIGANTE One involved in an intrigue or scheme.

JEUNE FILLE Young girl.

JOLIE LAIDE A fascinatingly ugly woman!

MA CHÈRE My dear (lady).

MADAME Equivalent to Mrs.; abbreviation *Mme.*; Plural is *Mesdames*.

MADEMOISELLE Unmarried woman, Miss; abbreviation is *Mlle.* In France, a nurse or governess is addressed as *Mademoiselle*. Plural is *Mesdemoiselles*.

MAÎTRESSE Mistress; lover; *C'est sa maîtresse* (She is his mistress).

MAÎTRESSE FEMME A domineering woman; a strong-willed, high-powered woman.

MARQUISE The wife of a *marquis*; or a woman with a rank equal to a *marquis*.

MASSEUSE One that provides massage professionally.

MA VIEILLE An affectionate form of address; my old (lady) friend.

MÉCHANTE Bad girl; mean woman.

MIDINETTE A Parisian shop-girl, especially a milliner's assistant; a frivolous girl.

MINAUDIÈRE A coquettish, affected woman; a simperer.

MODISTE A woman who makes fashionable clothes and hats, etc.; a milliner.

MON AMIE My (lady) friend; Plural *mes amies*.

MONDAINE A worldly woman who frequents *le beau monde*.

NAÏVE Simplistic.

NÉE Born: used mostly in genealogy to refer to a woman maiden's name; as in Madame Clicquot, *née* Nicole-Barbe Ponsardier. See Chapter I under Wines. From *naître* (to be born).

PARISIENNE A lady native of, or living in Paris.

PETITE With a small, trim figure.

PETITE-BOURGEOISE Lower middle-class lady.

PETITE AMIE A young mistress.

RACONTEUSE Storyteller. In France the word also implies a person who tells lies, or exaggerate facts.

RAFFINÉE Of refined taste and manners.

RAILLEUSE A mocker; from *railler* (to tease, to mock).

RAYONNANTE Beaming, radiant.

SERVANTE A maidservant employed to perform services.

SOIGNÉE Meticulously dressed; well-groomed.

SOUBRETTE A lady's maid; flirtatious, frivolous young woman, especially one involved in *intrigue*.

SPORTIVE A woman active in athletics.

TRAGÉDIENNE Actress of tragedy.

VENDEUSE A saleswoman specifically employed in a fashion house; from *vendre* (to sell).

VEUVE A widow, as in Veuve Clicquot Champagne.

ABOUT CHILDREN

> "Children today are tyrants. They
> contradict their parents, gobble their
> food, and tyrannize their teachers."
> —Socrates (470–399 B.C.)

Some things never change, yet on the other hand, we cannot live without these little *choux* for, "There is only one pretty child in the world and every parent has it" (proverb).

CHOU Darling; *Mon petit chou*, literally my little cabbage or my little cream puff, (my little darling). *Le chouchou* or *la chouchoute* does not mean two *choux*, it is French for "teacher's pet."

ELÈVE (m or f) Pupil: boy or girl.

ENFANT GÂTÉ Spoiled child.

ENFANT PERDU Lost child; also a military term referring to troops in dangerous positions; lost sentry.

ENFANT TERRIBLE (m or f) An unmanageable, mischievous child (*Webster's*) a difficult child, *mal élevé*, rude.

ETOURDI (e) Thoughtless, irresponsible boy or girl; scatterbrained.

QUEL OR QUELLE ÉTOURDI (e) (What a birdbrain) (boy or girl).

FILLETTE A little *fille*, a little girl.

FILS Younger son, the junior; as in *Dumas fils*.

GAMIN A street urchin; a streetwise or impudent child; also a mischievous little boy.

GAMINE A female *gamin*; a small, mischievous, or elfish young child.

MIGNON A pretty little boy; delicate, cute; dainty. *Bonjour mon mignon!* (Hello my sweet little darling!) In French *mignons* also means "minions" as in *les mignons d'Henri III*, (the favorite, the servile effeminate followers), term of contempt.

MIGNONNE A pretty little girl; delicate. *Bonjour ma mignonne!* (Good morning my darling!)

POLISSON Naughty boy, little rascal; scamp. *Propos polissons* (smutty talk).

POLISSONNE Naughty girl, little rascal; scamp.

FOR FRANCOPHILES ONLY

The words or expressions below are not French loanwords; they are French words for the Francophile, those who talk to children. Below, they will find a list of French names they can call their little ones, or bigger ones if they wish. When appropriate, a literal translation in parentheses is given, followed by the English translation.

(m) abbreviation for *masculin* when talking to a boy or a man; (f) abbreviation for *feminin* when addressing a little girl or a woman.

French Words	English Translation
Mon petit chat	My little cat; my little darling, talking to a boy or girl.
Ma chérie (f)	My darling.
Mon chéri (m)	My darling.
	French also use these words between husband and wife or loved ones.
Mon amour	My love.
Mon petit lapin	My little rabbit; my little bunny, my pet (to a girl or boy).
Mon poulet (m)	My pet; honey (U.S.); term of affection.
Ma poulette (f)	My pet; honey (U.S.) (*poulette* is a little *poule*, a little hen).
Ma poule (f)	My darling, my pet; a term of affection between husband and wife or lovers.
	In France, to have *une poule* (pejorative) is to have a mistress.
	Poule de luxe is French for "a classy prostitute."
	Poupoule is as also used as familiar term of affection as above or can be colloquial for a woman *facile*, with loose morals.
Mon petit poussin	My little chick; my little poppet (G.B.), honey-bunch (U.S.).
Petit cochon	Little piggy (boy or girl).

Petit démon	Little imp (boy or girl).
Petit diable	Little devil (boy or girl).
Petit drôle	Little rascal, little scamp.
Petit coquin (m)	Little rascal, little monkey.
Petite coquine (f)	Little rascal, little monkey.
Ma petite puce	My little flea; my little pet, honey; usually to a little girl.
Ma biche, ma bibiche, ma bichette (f)	My doe, my little doe; my pet, honey (U.S.); my poppet (G.B.).
Mon loulou, mon petit loulou	My little pet, honey (girl or boy); A *loulou* is an apartment dog, a little dog from Poméranie.
Petit mioche (m)	Little kid; little gamin.
Petit lardon (m)	Little brat; used particularly in the South of France. (Not to confuse with *gros lardon*, fatso.)
Mon coeur, Mon petit cœur	My heart, my little heart (girl or boy)
Mon trésor	My treasure (girl or boy).
Mon ange	My angel (girl or boy).
Mon chérubin	My cherub (girl or boy).
Ma cocotte (f)	Honey; *cocotte* (child talk for hen).
Mon coco (m)	My darling, my pet.

Foufou; Fofolle	Silly boy; silly girl. Also used when talking to or about grown-ups.
Dodo	Beddy-bye; bedtime.
Doudou (f)	Child talk for security blanket: *ma doudou*.
Bisou (m)	A kiss in child-talk; *gros bisous* (big kisses).

Note:

Coco is (or used to be) child-talk for egg. Today, the trend in France, as it is in other countries, is to avoid babytalk when addressing young children: words such as: *lolo* (milk); *bobo* (a booboo), are no longer used in some circles.

Adults say: *bisous,* or *gros bisous* rather than say *au revoir* to friends and family members; they also say *Salut!* (See *bonjour* under 'B', Loanwords Alphabetically).

They also use the word *dodo,* for instance, to the question, "How is it going? How are you doing?" They reply, particularly in Paris: *Métro, boulot, dodo,* literally, metro, work, beddy-bye, meaning, "More of the same, the daily grind!" *Boulot* is familiar for *travail* (work).

POTPOURRI OF FRENCH LOANWORDS AND EXPRESSIONS

Most words used in previous chapters: Food, Arts, and Fashion are not usually included in the lists below; there are only a few mentioned again.

When the gender (m) for masculine or (f) for feminine is not indicated it is because the word is neutral, as in the expression *ainsi va la vie* or various interjections such as *allons*!

EPRESSIONS WITH À

A BAS Down with; *à bas les mouchards*.

A BIENTÔT Until later; see you soon.

A BON DROIT With good reason, legitimately; a synonymous French expression is *à juste titre* (quite rightly). It is considered *à bon droit* that it is the perfect way to do it.

A BON MARCHÉ Inexpensive; cheap. One of the first department stores in Paris was *Le Bon Marché* in the 1850s.

A BRAS OUVERTS With open arms; I was greeted *à bras ouverts*.

A CONTRECOEUR Against the heart: reluctantly, in spite of oneself; I did it *à contreceour*.

A CORPS PERDU With breakneck speed; recklessly; with enthusiasm, with passion. I drove *à corps perdu*, at breakneck speed; I embarked on this adventure *à corps perdu*, with enthusiasm.

A COUP SÛR With certainty; surely. He is *à coup sûr* (the instigator) of this fight.

A COUVERT Under cover; protected; *à couvert* of the enemy.

A DEMI Half; as in, to do things *à demi*, half-way done see *à moitié* below.

A DEUX As in, *la vie à deux* (life as a couple).

A DISCRÉTION At discretion; as much as one wishes. Wine *à discrétion*, all you can drink!

A DROITE To the right; *Tournez à droite* (turn to the right).

A FOND Thoroughly; completely; totally; I cleaned my room *à fond*.

A GAUCHE To the left; *Tournez à gauche* (turn to the left).

A GENOUX On one's knees; I ask you *à genoux* (I am begging you). *Faire du genou*, literally, to do some knee, (to play footsie).

A GOGO In abundance; as in wine *à gogo*.

A GRAND FRAIS With great expense; it is *à grand frais* that he repaired it.

A HAUTE VOIX In a high voice; aloud; she spoke *à haute voix*.

A HUIS CLOS In law, hearing *à huis clos*, closed hearing; held in camera; figuratively, behind doors, secretly.

A JAMAIS Forever, as in *c'est fini à jamais*, (it is over) forever.

A LA BONNE HEURE! Well done; that's the spirit; right on; good for you. You brought it with you! *A la bonne heure!*

A LA CARTE *Menu à la carte*: by the bill of fare meaning various items and various prices to choose from the menu as opposed to *table d' hôte* (fixed time and prices).

A LA DÉROBÉE Secretly; on the sly; stealthily; He looked at her *à la dérobée*. A synonymous French expression *is en cachette*, literally, in hiding; *cacher* (to hide) See cache under 'C,' Loanwords Alphabetically.

A LA LETTRE To the letter; the literal sense of a word; seriously; the French also say, *au pied de la lettre*, literally, to the foot of the letter; he takes things *à la lettre*.

A L'ÉPOQUE At the time; *à l'époque*, I was teaching in a small town.

A L'IMPROVISTE Unexpectedly; without warning; she arrived *à l'improviste*.

A LOISIR At leisure; taking one's time; on vacations, I read *à loisir*.

A MERVEILLE Marvelously, wonderfully as in this dress fits you *à merveille*.

A MOI! Help me; help!

A MOITIÉ Half; as in he is *à moitié* crazy.

A MON AVIS In my opinion.

A PEU PRÈS Nearly; practically; almost; it costs *à peu près* one Euro; the street is *à peu près* empty.

A POINT Perfectly on time as you arrive *à point*. Also, just right as a steak *à point*. See Chapter I, Culinary Expressions.

A PROPOS Apropos; by the way; relevant; as in *à propos* remarks.

A PROPOS DE RIEN About nothing in particular, apropos of nothing, without a good reason; you get mad *à propos de rien*.

A QUOI BON? What's the good of it?

A RAVIR Charmingly; ravishingly as *cela vous va à ravir*, this suits you *à ravir*, like a charm.

A REBOURS Against the grain, the wrong way as in to take everything *à rebours*, to misconstrue everything that is said or to take a one-way street *à rebours*; to go the wrong way.

A TORT ET À TRAVERS At random; as in: She speaks *à tort et à travers* (She talks nonsense).

A TOUTE FORCE At all cost, whatever the cost, same as *à tout prix* (below).

A TOUT HASARD Whatever happens, just in case, at all hazards; I'll take my umbrella, *à tout hasard*.

A TOUT PRIX At all costs; at any price; I have to have chocolate *à tout prix*.

A TRAVERS Across; through; as I walk *à travers* the fields.

A VOL D'OISEAU As the crow flies.

A VOTRE SANTÉ Formal expression for "To your health! Cheers!" *A ta santé* is used between friends. See Introduction.

EXPRESSIONS WITH AU

AU CONTRAIRE To the contrary.

AU COURANT Fully acquainted with matters; abreast of the latest developments; as in "I am *au courant*."

AU DÉSESPOIR In despair.

AU FAIT By the way; incidentally.

AU FOND Fundamentally, when it comes down to it, as in: *au fond*, you are right. Also: at the bottom of, as in: *au fond* of the sea, or in the back of, as in: *au fond* of the room.

AU FROMAGE With cheese; as in a *soufflé au fromage*.

AU JOUR LE JOUR From day to day; from hand to mouth; I live *au jour le jour*.

AU MIEUX At best; he will win by two votes *au mieux*; To be *au mieux* with somebody is to have a good relationship; to be on the best of terms with somebody; I am *au mieux* with her.

AU NATUREL In the natural state.

AU PAIR International student is a student *au pair* when working as helper in a family in exchange for room and board to learn the language and the culture of a country.

AU PIED DE LA LETTRE To the foot of the letter; down to the last detail; see *à la lettre* above.

AU PREMIER On the first (floor).

AU RESTE As for the rest; besides.

AU REVOIR To see you again; until we meet again; good-bye. *Ce n'est qu'un au revoir* (It's only a good-bye): title of a New's Year day song. A familiar way of greeting friends in France is *Salut, ça va?*, literally, Hey, how goes it? How are you? Instead of saying *bonjour*. The French also say *Salut*, meaning *au revoir* (See you later, *salut*)!

AU SECOND On the second (floor).

AU SECOURS A call for help; help!

AU SÉRIEUX Seriously; She takes herself *au sérieux*.

EXPRESSIONS WITH C'EST

C'EST-À-DIRE That is to say.

C'EST AUTRE CHOSE It's another (thing) matter.

C'EST LA GUERRE It's war; a conflict, hostility between people. The French say: *à la guerre comme à la guerre*, literally, in war as in war, meaning that one must accept things as they are, war justifies the means.

C'EST LA VIE It's life, a fatalistic expression spoken with a resigned sigh or a helpless shrug as in *c'est la vie mon ami!*, an expression that *Jacques* or *Can-*

dide related to or identified with (*Jacques Le Fatalist* by French philosopher Diderot, and *Candide* by French author Voltaire.)

C'EST MAGNIFIQUE It's magnificent.

C'EST SELON That is as may be; *selon vous* (according to you).

EXPRESSIONS WITH COUP

COUP D'ÉTAT A sudden, decisive blow in politics.

COUP DE GRÂCE A finishing stroke.

COUP DE MAIN A helping hand.

COUP DE PIED A kick as in *un coup de pied* in the *derrière*.

COUP DE SOLEIL A sunstroke; a sunburn.

COUP DE THÉÂTRE A theatrical hit; sudden dramatic turn of events.

COUP D' OEIL A rapid glance; a general view. *Un clin d'oeil* (a wink), as in, to make a *clin d'oeil* (to wink at somebody); or to do something in *un clin d'oeil* (to do something in a flash, in the wink of an eye).

EXPRESSIONS WITH DE

DE BONNE GRÂCE With good grace; willingly.

DE HAUT EN BAS From top to bottom.

DE LUXE Of a superior kind; luxurious.

DE MAL EN PIS From bad to worse; my life goes *de mal en pis*.

DE PIS EN PIS Worse and worse; My cold is getting *de pis en pis*.

DE RÈGLE According to the rule; A hat was *de règle*, in keeping with the norms.

DE RETOUR To be back, as I will be *de retour* soon.

DE RIGUEUR Required by good form; socially and/or culturally obligatory, according to *étiquette*; fashionable; a tuxedo is *de rigueur*; attendance is *de rigueur*.

DE TROP Too much; superfluous as in to be *de trop*, to be in the way, unwanted in some circles.

EXPRESSIONS WITH EN

EN AMI As a friend.

EN ARRIÈRE In the back.

EN ATTENDANT In the meantime.

EN AVANT Forward; off we go!

EN BLOC As a whole; collectively; performed *en bloc*.

EN BROSSE Of haircut: cut short and bristly as a brush.

EN DÉSHABILLÉ In a *négligé*.

EN ÉCHELON Arranged hierarchically; from *échelle* (a ladder). *Monter d'un échelon* (to go up the ladder, to have a promotion).

EN EFFET In effect; indeed.

EN ÉVIDENCE In (at) the forefront; conspicuously.

EN FACE In front of.

EN FAMILLE With one's family; all together, without ceremony, as in a diner *en famille*.

EN FÊTE In a festive mood as in the whole city is *en fête*.

EN GRANDE TENUE In full dress.

EN GROS In general, in broad terms.

EN MASSE All together; as a group, as in produced *en masse.*

EN NOIR In black, as in, she is dressed *en noir*; or she sees life *en noir*: its black side, in the worst light.

EN PASSANT In passing; by the way; incidentally.

EN PENSION In a boarding school.

EN PERMANENCE Permanently.

EN PLACE In place.

EN PLEIN AIR In the open air.

EN PLEIN JOUR In broad day.

EN PRINCE In a princely manner.

EN PRINCIPE In principle.

EN QUEUE Standing one behind another; what the French never do in the subway or anywhere else!

EN RAPPORT In harmony: as a work *en rapport avec* my qualifications, a work in harmony with my qualifications. Also, in touch: as to put people *en rapport* with one another.

EN RÈGLE In order; in due order; everything is *en règle.*

EN RETOUR In return, as in, "I am doing it *en retour* for your help."

EN REVANCHE In return, in compensation, on the other hand.

EN ROUTE To set out; to start on one's way as in: *Allez, en route*, let's go.

EN TOUT CAS In any case.

EN VÉRITÉ In truth; in all honesty.

EN VILLE In town, as in, I am going *en ville* (I am going to town). I am going *au centre ville* (I am going downtown).

EXPRESSIONS WITH MAL

MAL À PROPOS Unsuitably; inappropriate manner.

MAL DE MER Seasickness. *J'ai le mal de mer* (I am seasick).

MAL DE TÊTE Headache. *J'ai mal à la tête* or *j'ai un mal de tête* (I have a headache).

MAL DU PAYS Homesickness. *J'ai le mal du pays* (I am homesick).

MAL DU SIÈCLE World's weariness; deep melancholy because of the condition of the world.

MAL ÉLEVÉ (e) (m or f) Bad-mannered; ill-bred; a boy *mal élevé* or a girl *mal élevée*.

MALENTENDU Misunderstanding; It is simply *un malentendu*.

MAL VU Looked down on; held in low esteem; I am *mal vu* (m) mal vue (f) at the office. Not to confuse with *ni vu ni connu*, literally, not seen, not known, meaning (nobody will ever know).

EXPRESSIONS WITH PAR

PAR ACCIDENT By accident or chance.

PAR AVION By airplane; French label for Air Mail.

PAR-CI PAR-LÀ Here and there.

PAR DÉPIT Out of spite.

PAR EXCELLENCE Supremely above all; the best of the best; snob *par excellence*.

PAR EXEMPLE For example.

PAR FAVEUR As a favor; as to obtain something *par faveur.*

PAR FORCE By force: using force as a recourse; as he did it *par force.*

PAR HASARD By chance; I met him *par hasard,* unexpectedly. *Tout à fait par hasard,* (loanwords) quite by chance.

PAR RAPPORT Compared with, as in he is tall *par rapport* to his wife.

EXPRESSIONS WITH SANS

SANS Without.

SANS BLAGUE Without joking: no kidding!

SANS CÉRÉMONIE Without formality, no ceremony.

SANS-CULOTTE Without trousers; a shabbily dressed person; a ragamuffin. *Ragamofin* was a ragged demon in mystery plays. A lower-class Parisian republican in the French Revolution who wore knee-breeches, *culottes.*

SANS DOUTE Without doubt; *sans aucun doute* (without any doubt).

SANS-FAÇON Without ceremony; without the customary formality as in a diner *sans façon.* (No hyphen between sans & façon.) Without manners, same as rude, *sans-gêne* below: he is *sans-façon.* (With the hyphen between sans & façon.)

SANS-GÊNE Without embarrassment: lots of nerve; to disregard the ordinary forms of civility; rude. He is *sans-gêne,* he is rude. The French also say, "She has *du toupet* (not the toupee on a bald head)."

SANS PAREIL Not having its like; unique, unequalled.

SANS PEUR Fearless.

SANS RECOURS Without recourse.

SANS REPROCHE Without reproach; blameless. Lord of Bayard, the hero of a legend (1475–1524) is known as *Le Chevalier sans peur et sans reproche* (the Knight without fear and reproach).

SANS SÉRIF A letterform without serifs (cross-stroke).

SANS SOUCI Without worry as in: I am *sans souci*.

SANS TACHE Spotless.

EXPRESSIONS WITH TOUT

TOUT À FAIT Entirely; completely; quite, as *tout à fait vrai*, (quite true, absolutely true).

TOUT À L'HEURE In a moment; in a little while; I will do it *tout à l'heure*. A *tout à l'heure* (see you later), same as *à bientôt*.

TOUT AU CONTRAIRE Quite the contrary.

TOUT À VOUS Wholly yours; all yours.

TOUT COURT Without preface; simply said; briefly (no need for additional information).

TOUT DE MÊME All the same; as in: it is *tout de même* very strange.

TOUT DE SUITE Right away; immediately; I will do it *tout de suite*.

TOUT LE MONDE Everyone; as *tout le monde* is coming.

TOUT PARIS As in *le tout Paris*, the fashionable people in Paris.

FRENCH LOANWORDS ALPHABETICALLY

Under each letter, a short easy phrase composed of French loanwords will give any snob a chance to show off his English.

A

ADIEU MON AMI!

ABRÉGÉ (m) An abridgement.

ACCOLADE (f) An embrace; a ceremony used to confer knighthood; an approving, a praising.

ACCORD (m) A settlement of points at issue between nations; an agreement.

ACTE GRATUIT (m) Gratuitous, inconsequent action, *acte gratuit* is a concept explored in *Les Caves du Vatican* by French novelist and essayist André Gide (1869–1951).

ADIEU Farewell! (interjection); Literally to God (I commend you). Also used as a masculine noun: a farewell: *un adieu*; I say *mes adieux* (I say my goodbyes).

ADROIT (m) Dexterous, clever, skillful, as in an *adroit* mechanic.

AFFAIRE (f) That which is to be done, as in: *c'est mon affaire* (it is my business); *Ce n'est pas votre affaire* (it does not concern you); *Quelle affaire!* (What a scandal!); *Les affaires sont les affaires* (business is business); *Homme d'affaire*; *voyage d'affaires* (business trip); *une affaire de famille* (a family affair). In English, to have an *affaire* means to have an amorous relationship between two lovers, often a brief one; also to have a *liaison*. In France, only the word *liaison* is used to talk about a romantic intrigue, what is defined or perceived as being an illicit relationship by some. A Frenchman has *une liaison* or *une aventure*, not *une affaire*, when he sleeps with his secretary and generally, people will simply say that: *il couche avec la secrétaire* (he sleeps with the secretary). Many of us have heard the song: *Voulez-vous coucher avec moi, ce soir?*

AFFAIRE D'AMOUR (f) A love affair, defined as being an *amour* honorable or dishonorable. The expression *affaire d'amour* is not used in France but people say *une histoire d'amour* (a love story).

AFFAIRE DE COEUR (f) An affair of the heart.

AFFAIRE D'HONNEUR (f) An affair of honor.

AGILE (m or f) Nimble, alert, as in an agile manner.

AIDE-MÉMOIRE (m) Help-memory: memorandum of a discussion.

AIGUILLE (f) Needle; a sharp-pointed pinnacle of rock as in *l'Aiguille du Midi* in the French Alps.

AINSI VA LA VIE So goes life.

ALLEZ-VOUS EN Go away; get out.

ALLIANCE (f) Agreement to cooperate, particularly between nations. *Une alliance* is also French for "wedding ring."

ALLONS! Let's go; or, come on, cut that nonsense!

ALLUMETTE (f) A match; also a type of pastry. See Chapter I under Desserts.

ALLURE (f) Bearing; mien; air: as in Elvis's *allure*.

AMBIANCE (f) Atmosphere; ambience.

AMOUR (m) *Webster's* and the *Oxford of Foreign Words & Phrases* dictionaries define *amour* as: to have an affair, especially a secret one. In France: the word *amour* by itself means love, affection, tender feelings and in some instances physical attraction. *Faire l'amour* (to make love); *mon amour* (my love); *un amour d'enfant* (adorable child); *un amour de lampe* (a darling beautiful lamp); *une belle histoire d'amour* (a beautiful love story); *beau comme un amour* (very handsome).

AMOUR COURTOIS (m) Courtly love.

AMOUR-PROPRE (m) Self-love; self-esteem.

ANECDOTE (f) A short account of some happening: personal or biographical.

ANIMÉ (m) Animated; *un dessin animé*, literally, a drawing animated, (a cartoon).

APERÇU (m) Quick impression or insight; from *apercevoir* (to perceive).

APÉRITIF (m) Alcoholic drink taken before a meal to stimulate the appetite.

APRÈS-COUP Afterthought; after the event.

ARGOT (m) Jargon; as in argot of criminals; Parisians' *argot*.

ARRÊT (m) Judgment of a tribunal.

ARRIÈRE-PENSÉE (f) Literally, back-thought: ulterior motive or mental reservation.

ARROGANCE (f) Unwarranted self-importance.

AUSSITÔT DIT AUSSITÔT FAIT No sooner said than done.

AUTREFOIS In the past.

AVALANCHE (f) A large mass of snow, ice, rock, or other material in swift motion down a mountainside.

AVANT-GARDE Vanguard; advanced; as in *avant-garde* ideas, techniques.

AVEC PLAISIR With pleasure.

AVEC VOTRE PERMISSION With your permission.

"APRÈS NOUS LE DÉLUGE" After us the deluge: a remark attributed to Madame de Pompadour, the favorite of Louis XV *le Bien-Aimé* (the beloved), who saw the signs of the approaching Revolution. *Après moi le déluge* (after me the deluge) is attributed to Louis XV himself, a *cliché* meaning, "We don't care what happens because the trouble will come after we die! Therefore, we do not worry about tomorrow!"

B
BONJOUR MON CHER

BADINAGE (m) Light or playful discourse; banter.

BAGATELLE (f) A trifle; a thing of no importance; *Quelle bagatelle!* (What a trifle!)

BANAL Commonplace; trite.

BARAGOUIN (m) Gibberish; unintelligible jargon; gobbledygook. *Charabia* is another word used in France for *baragouin*.

BATEAU (m) A lightweight flat-bottomed river boat used mainly in Canada and Louisiana. *Un bateau-mouche* is French for "pleasure boat" on the river Seine to visit Paris.

BAVARDAGE (m) Chattering; *un bavard* is French for "a talkative person," "a chatterbox."

BEAU GESTE (m) Literally, beautiful gesture: generous, magnanimous act.

BEAU IDÉAL (m) Ideal beauty; standard of excellence, the perfect thing. In *Jane Eyre*, " . . . nothing, in short, was wanting to complete the *beau-idéal* of domestic comfort."

BEAU MONDE (m) Fashionable society; the French also say *le grand monde*; or *la haute* (people of upper crust, the *haute société*). *Le petit monde* (the world of children).

BEAUTÉ DU DIABLE (f) Literally, beauty of the devil: beauty and bloom of youth, usually in a woman not otherwise beautiful.

BELLE ÉPOQUE (f) An era of cultural and social refinement at the end of the nineteenth Century in France. The Renaissance was the *belle époque*.

BÊTISE (f) Folly, stupidity; from *bête* (stupid). *Une bête* (animal); *pauvre bête* (poor animal), as the French say when their dog is sick. *Une bêtise* is also the name given to a mint-flavored candy, manufactured since 1850. It is a specialty of Cambrai, a city in northern France.

BÉVUE (f) A blunder, a slip, an error.

BIBELOT (m) A small curio or artistic trinket; a knick-knack, ornamental object.

BIEN ENTENDU Literally, well heard: of course, that goes without saying.

BIEN-ÊTRE (m) Well-being.

BIENSÉANCE (f) Decorum; good manners; *savoir-vivre*; as in *bienséance* is *de rigueur*.

BIENVENUE (f) Welcome.

BIJOU (m) A jewel; a trinket.

BIJOUTERIE (f) Jewelry store.

BILLET DOUX (m) Sweet note: a love note; a love letter.

BIZARRE (m or f) Strange; odd in manner or appearance; peculiar.

BLAGUE (f) A joke; a humbug; a joke made by a *blagueur*.

BOÎTE DE NUIT (f) Literally, a box of night: a night club.

BON (m) Good; used in loanword expressions such as *bon ton, bonjour, bon mot,* etc.

BON APPÉTIT! Good appetite; enjoy your food.

BON GRÉ, MAL GRÉ Willing or unwilling; willy-nilly.

BON MARCHÉ (m) Inexpensive, a good bargain, cheap as in this dress is *bon marché.*

BON MOT (m) *Bons mots* (plural) witty, a clever word(s) or saying.

BON TON (m) Good breeding, as in *c'est de bon ton* (it is good form, proper behavior).

BON VOYAGE (m) Pleasant journey; have a good trip.

BONBON (m) Candy.

BONBONNIÈRE (f) Candy dish, candy box.

BONJOUR (m) Good day; good morning.

BONNE CHANCE (f) Good luck.

BONSOIR (m) Good evening.

BORDEL (m) Vulgar for house of prostitution; a bordello, a brothel. *Quel bordel!* A commonly heard inelegant French expression meaning, "What a mess!"

BOUDERIE (f) Pouting; sulking; from *bouder* (to sulk).

BOUGIE (f) Wax candle, originally made in Bougie, Algeria.

BOULEVERSEMENT (m) An upheaval; a turmoil.

BOUQUET (m) A nosegay; clump of trees; a bunch of flowers; the perfume of wine and cheese.

BOURG (m) A large village, often under the shadow of a castle, where markets are held.

BOURGADE (f) A small village.

BOURGEOISIE (f) The middle class: between the very wealthy and the working class.

BOUTADE (f) A whim; a sudden outburst.

BOUTIQUE (f) Small retail shop since the thirteenth century. Today's *boutiques* are small shops that sell fashionable, expensive clothes.

BOUTONNIÈRE (f) A flower or a small bouquet that a man wears in *la boutonnière* (the buttonhole) on a lapel.

BRAILLE (m) A method of printing and writing for the blind developed in the French army by Louis Braille. Combined raised words on paper or cardboard that could be decoded in the dark by sentries on duties, avoiding light that could endanger the soldiers.

BRIC-À-BRAC (m) Miscellaneous ornaments, usually old, knick-knacks, small trinkets, sold in antique store; a *bric-à-brac* shop (G.B.). In France, *un bric-à-brac*, is a pile of scattered used objects to be resold by *un marchand de bric-à-brac*, also called *un brocanteur* (a used objects trader); things are disorganized, hence, *Quel bric-à-brac!* (What a mess!)

BRICOLAGE (m) The action of *bricoler* (to tinker with); the work itself done by a *bricoleur*.

BROCHURE (f) A pamphlet; publicity booklet.

BRUIT (m) Noise: a rumor.

BRUSQUE (m or f) Blunt; abrupt.

BRUT (m) Of wine: unsweetened, dry: *un vin brut*.

BULLETIN (m) Official report of public news.

BUREAU DE CHANGE (m) An office where currency can be exchanged.

BURLESQUE Farcical, ludicrous as of a play, a film, or an idea.

C

CARTE BLANCHE, MONSIEUR!

CABRIOLET (m) A two-wheeled, one-horse carriage.

CACHE (f) A hiding place; from *cacher* (to hide). In Québec, French province of Canada and other cold places, hunters hide their lunch from animals in a *cache* (a box set on a post). In France, children play *à cache-cache* (hide-and-seek). *Une cachette* (a small hiding place); *en cachette* (secretly), as to do something *en cachette*, on the sly.

CACHE-POT (m) A casing or ornamental design to hide an ordinary flower-pot; flowerpot holder.

CACHET (m) Originally a stamp or a seal on an official letter. Also, a mark by which quality or authenticity can be distinguished: *chic* stylish, distinctive; She has *du cachet* (she has style).

CADEAU (m) Gift; present; *un cadeau de Noël* (a Christmas present).

ÇA ET LÀ Here and there, to and from.

CAHIER (m) A notebook.

CAILLE (f) A quail.

CAMARADERIE (f) Mutual trust between comrades; good fellowship.

CANARD (m) False report; a hoax; culinary: a duck.

CANCAN (m) Gossips; also a French dance.

CAPRICE (m) A whim as in *les caprices de la mode* (caprices of fashion).

CARILLON (m) A chime of bells; a melody played on such bells.

CARNAGE (m) Slaughter.

CARTE BLANCHE (f) *Cliché* used figuratively to mean: full discretionary power granted. Originally, it was mostly political.

CARTE-DE-VISITE (f) A small photographic portrait mounted on a card.

CARTE D'IDENTITÉ (f) An identity card.

CARTE DU PAYS (f) Map of the country.

CASSE-TÊTE (m) Literally, break-head: a bludgeon; a club; a *casse-tête* also means a puzzle; from *casser* (to break).

CATALOGUE (m) Enumeration of names, articles, titles in alphabetical order; a catalog.

CAUSE CÉLÈBRE (f) A notorious legal case; generally a controversy or scandal that attracts attention: *l'Affaire Dreyfus* is one good example.

CAUSERIE (f) Informal talk, chat; as in *une causerie littéraire, scientifique,* etc. (a speech). From *causer* (to chat, to converse).

CELA VA SANS DIRE Needless to say, that goes without saying.

CHACUN SON GOÛT The proper French expressions are either: *Chacun son goût,* or *A Chacun son goût* (to every man his own taste).

CHACUN À SON GOÛT is a literal translation of: each (person) to his/her own taste.

CHAGRIN (m) Sorrow; melancholy; also disappointment. *La Peau de Chagrin* (1831) is a famous novel by Honoré de Balzac in which life shrinks away, like a *peau de chagrin,* name given to the leather skin from goats or sheep used in book-binding.

CHANTAGE (m) Blackmail.

CHARADE (f) A riddle; a guessing game in which a word is acted in *pantomime*.

CHARME (m) Charm; power to please.

CHAUSSURE (f) Shoe.

CHEMIN DE FER (m) Literally a trail of iron: a railway.

CHERCHEZ LA FEMME *Cliché* meaning, "Look for the woman;" used often facetiously to imply that a woman is the cause of trouble. Originally, a French witty remark made by Dumas *père* in *Les Mohicans de Paris*, 1864.

CHEVELURE (f) Hair on the head; *les cheveux* is French for hair (on head). *Le poil* is hair on the arms or legs. *Il a un poil dans la main*, literally, he has one hair in his hand; means, "He is lazy." French soldiers from the First World War (1914–1918) were called *Les Poilus* (the hairy ones), a slang alluding to unkempt appearance because they were living in such horrible conditions in trenches.

CHICHI (m) Showiness; affectation; lack of simplicity. *Quel chichi!* (What a fuss! What a *froufrou!*)

CHEZ At (the house of) as in *chez moi*, at my house; *Chez Maxime*, restaurant in Paris.

CHOSE (f) Thing; *quelque chose* (something).

CI-GÎT Here lies, written on a gravestone. *Ci*: short for *ici* (here); *gît*: from *gésir* (to be lying down).

CLICHÉ (m) A stereotyped expression; a hackneyed phrase or opinion. From French *clicher* (to stereotype). In printing, to prepare a *cliché* is to make an electrotype or stereotype plate that can be used repeatedly; hence a *cliché* is used like a rubber stamp in a conversation or in writing to state a stereotype expression or idea figuratively, rather than precisely. Examples of *clichés: Bête noire, cause célèbre, cela va sans dire, coup de grâce* are some of many French borrowings used in English.

CLIENTÈLE (f) Customers; a customers base; clients collectively.

CLIQUE (f) Exclusive, clannish circle of people, such as snobs.

CLOCHE (f) A bell-shaped glass jar used to cover delicate plants *(Webster's)*.

CLOCHER (m) A bell tower. *Un esprit de clocher* (a small town mentality).

COIFFURE (f) A headdress, a coif or a hairstyle.

COMME CI COMME ÇA Literally, like this, like that; so-so. How are you feeling? *Oh! Comme ci comme ça.*

COMME IF FAUT As it should be; properly; prim and proper. She behaves *comme il faut*; She is *très comme il faut* (She is very proper).

COMMUNIQUÉ (m) An official statement reporting on a meeting; an official communication. From *communiquer* (communicate).

CONCIERGERIE (f) A doorkeeper's lodge. Also, *La Conciergerie* is the name of an ancient prison in Paris.

CONDUIT (m) A channel allowing communication either between things or people as in, he was a *conduit* between you and your father.

CONFÉRENCE (f) A lecture: informative literary, or scientific presentation; or a meeting, a discussion to exchange opinions. In English the word *lecture*, meaning "reading," is now obsolete. In French, *lecture* means "the act of reading a book, a letter, a newspaper, etc."

CONSEIL D'ÉTAT (m) Council of state.

CONTRETEMPS (m) Embarrassing situation; inopportune happening causing confusion.

CONVERSATION (f) Verbal exchange of ideas or information.

COQUILLAGE (m) Shellfish; a decoration in the form of shells, especially on furniture.

CORDAGE (m) Ropes or cords; *le cordage*: ropes of a ship.

CORDON (m) A ribbon or cord worn as a badge of an order, or as a decoration.

CORPS (m) A tactical division of an army; a body of people engaged in a particular activity.

CORPS À CORPS Literally, body to body: in close bodily contact.

CORPS DE BALLET (m) A troop or company of ballet dancers.

CORPS DE GARDE (m) A small body of soldiers set as a guard.

CORSAGE (m) A small bouquet for a woman to wear at the waist or shoulder; also a bodice. In French *un corsage* is a blouse, a bodice; what is called a *corsage* (bouquet) in English is a *boutonnière* that a Frenchman wears with a formal attire at weddings, etc.; a woman will wear a rose or another flower, not a *corsage*.

CORTÈGE (m) A ceremonial procession, as in *funéral cortège* (funeral procession).

COULÉE (f) A coulee.

COULEUR (f) Color; as in *couleur de rose*: (rose color), something presented in a way that exaggerates attractiveness.

COULOIR (m) A deep mountain ravine or gorge.

COUPÉ (m) A four-wheeled carriage with a seat for two inside and an outside seat for the driver; an enclosed, two-door (without pillars) motor car.

COUPE-COUPE (m) A machete; from *couper* (to cut).

COURAGE (m) Bravery; fortitude.

COÛTE QUE COÛTE Cost what it may; at all cost.

CROIX DE GUERRE (f) Literally, cross of war: French military decoration awarded for bravery.

CUL-DE-SAC (m) Literally, bottom of bag: a passage with only one outlet; a blind alley.

D

D'ACCORD, MON CHER CONFRÈRE

D'ACCORD Agreed; *je suis d'accord avec vous* (I agree with you), or simply, *d'accord!*

DÉBÂCLE (f) A sudden disaster; a break-up; an overthrow; a collapse.

DÉBOUCHÉ (m) A commercial outlet for goods; a market.

DÉBRIS (m. pl.) Fragments; pieces of wreckage; scraps, remains.

DÉCOR (m) Decoration and furnishings of a room, building, etc.; scenery.

DÉJÀ-VU Literally, already seen: the feeling of having already experienced the present moment or situation; as "I have a sense of *déjà-vu.*"

DÉLUGE (m) Downpour of rain; a flood. The French saying: *Cela remonte au déluge* (It is as old as the hills).

DÉMARCHE (f) A step, measure, particularly a diplomatic *démarche.*

DEMI-JOUR (m) Half-day: twilight; subdued light.

DÉPÊCHE (f) A dispatch; a message. *Se dépêcher* (to hurry); *dépêche-toi,* friendly form and *dépêchez-vous,* formal (Hurry up!).

DÉRAILLEUR (m) A variable bicycle gear; from *dérailler* (to derail); as *un train déraille* (a train derails).

DERNIER MOT (m) The last word.

DERNIER RESSORT (m) The last resource.

DERRIÈRE (m) The behind (noun); or behind (neutral gender) as: I am *derrière vous* (I am behind you).

DÉSORIENTÉ (e) (m or f) Having lost one's way; not knowing where to turn; bewildered.

DÉTENTE (f) The easing of strained relations, especially between States or countries.

DÉTOUR (m) A deviation from one's route.

DEVOIR (m) Duty; *c'est mon devoir* (it is my duty); *le devoir avant tout* (duty comes first).

DIEU AVEC VOUS God (be) with you! Or *Dieu avec nous,* God (be) with us; *Mon Dieu* (my God).

"DIEU ET MON DROIT," "God and my right," the motto of British Royalty.

DISCOTHÈQUE (f) A club to listen to music or to dance.

DOSSIER (m) A set of documents recording information about some person or matter.

DOUANE Customs; *bureau de douane* (customs house) in France.

DOUCEUR DE VIVRE (f) Sweetness of living.

DRESSAGE (m) From *dresser* (to train) as for instance *le dressage* of a horse.

E

EDITION DE LUXE, CHÈRE MADAME!

EAU DE COLOGNE (f) A lightly scented perfume made mainly from alcohol and essential oils. Originally produced in Cologne, Germany.

EAU DE JAVELLE (f) A solution of sodium or potassium hypochlorite used as bleach; called Javelle water; Javel is a village outside of Paris where the solution was first used.

EAU-DE-TOILETTE (f) A diluted form of perfume.

ÉCLAIR (m) Lightning; or a pastry.

ECLAIRCISSEMENT (m) A clearing up, as of a dispute; a clarification, an explanation.

ECLAT (m) Distinction, showy splendor; brilliant success of performance or achievement, as she acted with *éclat. Avec éclat*: dramatically, with great pomp. *Sans éclat*, dull as in *un regard sans éclat* (a dull look), without expression. *Faux éclat* (false glamour; tawdriness). *Éclat* meaning scandal is used in France but more rarely in English. To leave *sans éclat*: to leave quietly, without any scandal.

ECOLE (f) A school.

EDITION DE LUXE (f) An expensive and splendid edition of a book.

EGALITÉ (f) Equality.

EGAREMENT (m) Bewilderment; mental confusion; from *égarer* (to lead astray).

EGLANTINE (f) Sweet brier; hip tree; wild rose: the *églantine* has pretty pink flowers and a prickly stem.

ELAN (m) Enthusiasm; passion, warmth as to speak with *élan*.

ELITE (f) The best of society, of a group; exclusive.

ELOGE (m) A funeral oration; a panegyric; a compliment.

EMBARRAS (m) Embarrassment.

EMBARRAS DU CHOIX (m) Spoiled for choice.

EMEUTE (f) Popular rising or uproar.

ENCEINTE (f) Pregnant.

ENCLAVE (f) Foreign territory surrounded by a specified country as in, "East Prussia was an enclave of Poland"; from *enclaver* (to enclose).

ENFANTILLAGE (m) Childish action; a prank as from *un enfant* (little boy), or *une enfant* (little girl).

ENFIN! At last; finally.

ENGAGEMENT (m) A commitment.

ENNUI (m) Boredom.

ENSEMBLE Together; the French also say *tous ensemble* (all of us) (pronounce the final 's' in *tous*). Other meanings for *ensemble*: Chapter II, Music & Chapter III, Clothes.

ENSUITE Next.

ENTENTE (f) Understanding between two nations.

ENTENTE CORDIALE (f) Cordial understanding, especially between two governments.

ENTOURAGE (m) A group of associates; family circle, as in: the King and his *entourage*. From *entourer* (to surround).

ENTR'ACTE (m) An interval, *entre* (between) the acts of a play. The final 'e' of *entre* is eliminated because the next word *acte* begins with 'a,' another vowel; this makes it easier to pronounce.

ENTRAIN (m) Liveliness of spirit; he has *beaucoup d'entrain* (he is full of life, very lively).

ENTRE DEUX VINS Literally, between two wines; half-drunk.

ENTRE NOUS Between us; between you and me.

ENTREPÔT (m) Warehouse; a place to store goods.

ENTREZ! Come in!

EPATANT! Wonderful, marvelous! *C'est épatant* (it's wonderful).

EQUIPE (f) A team in motor racing and other sports; *une équipe de football* (football team).

ESPIONNAGE (m) Spying; from *espionner,* to spy; *un espion* (a spy).

ESPRIT DE CORPS (m) Solidarity; team spirit.

ESPRIT D'ESCALIER, ESPRIT DE L'ESCALIER (m) To think of the perfect retort too late.

ETAGE (m) Floor story as *le premier étage* (first floor).

ETALAGE (m) A display in a store window.

ETAPE (f) Halting-place; stage (of journey); lap; word used in France in *une étape du Tour de France.*

ETIQUETTE (f) Conventional rules of personal behavior in polite society. *Etiquette* is also French (and less frequently in English) for "label."

EXPERTISE (f) The skill, knowledge, and experience of an expert.

EXPOSÉ (m) An orderly statement of facts.

EXTRAORDINAIRE Remarkable; outstanding.

F

FAÇON DE PARLER MON AMI!

FAÇADE (f) *Façade* is used figuratively as to put on a *façade*, a false front.

FACILE Easy; as in *c'est facile* (it's easy); *une vie facile* (an easy life); *une femme facile* (a loose woman).

FAÇON DE PARLER (f) Manner of speaking.

FAGOT (m) A bunch of wood sticks and small branches (also spelled faggot in English).

FAIT-ACCOMPLI (m) Accomplished fact; a situation with no return. *Mission accomplie* (mission accomplished).

FAITES VOS JEUX Used in gambling: place your stakes.

FAITS DIVERS (m.pl) Sundry facts; short news items, usually trivial in character.

FALBALA (m) Furbelow, frills; showiness. *Quel falbala!* (What a fuss!)

FATIGUE (f) Tiredness; to be fatigued. *Je suis fatigué (e)* (I am tired).

FAUBOURG (m) Suburb

FAUTE DE MIEUX For want of something *mieux* (better), as in: *faute de mieux* (I'll wear my pink *cravate*).

FAUVETTE (f) A warbler.

FAUX AMIS (m.pl) Literally, false friends: pairs of words of two different languages—especially French & English—that appear identical but have entirely different meanings. For instance: In France, *entrée* is served after soup or after *hors-d'oeuvres*, it is a dish served before *le plat principal*; in the U.S., the *entrée* is *la pièce de résistance*, the main course of the meal. In French, a *légume* is a vegetable; in English, a legume is a leguminous, as of the pea family. In French *large* means "wide, broad," as in *une rue large* (a broad street); in English, large means "big," as in a *large* family, a big family.

FAUX PAS (m) Literally, false step: a social blunder, tactless remark, a breach of good manners.

FÊTE (f) A festival; a fair; a saint's day, celebrated in France. See *fête galante* Chapter II under Paintings.

FÊTE CHAMPÊTRE (f) A rural festival.

FEU D'ARTIFICE (m) Fireworks show.

FEU DE JOIE (m) Bonfire; a celebration.

FEU FOLLET (m) A will-o'-the-wisp; frolicsome fire; *follet* from *fol* or *fou* (crazy).[49] *Tout-fou* (completely crazy) as the French say and also, *foufou*, *fofolle* (scatterbrained, crazy boy or girl).

FILM NOIR (m) A genre of cinematographic film of a pessimistic and somber character popular in the late 1940s and early 1950s, such as *Force of Evil*, *Gun for Hire*, and more recently, films dubbed *néo-noir* such as *Chinatown* and *Body Heat*.

FIN DE SIÈCLE (m) End the century (nineteenth), characterized by weariness, decadence, and despair.

FINESSE (f) Refinement; adroitness of performance.

FLACON (m) A scent-bottle as *un flacon de parfum* (a bottle of perfume).

FLAMBEAU (m) A burning torch; a big ornamented candlestick; *le flambeau Olympique* (Olympic Torch).

FLÂNERIE (f) Idle walking; loafing.

FLEUR-DE-LYS (f) Flower of the lily, also spelled *lis:* the flower of any various plants of the iris family. The Fleur-de-lys was used as a device of the former Royal arms of France and of Québec.

FOLIE (f) Madness; *C'est de la folie!* (It's madness!) *Quelle folie!* (How foolish!)

FOLIE DE GRANDEUR (f) Delusion of *grandeur* or importance; seeking power as was Napoléon and other dictators.

FORTUNE (f) Success; prosperity.

FOU RIRE (m) Uncontrollable laughter; a fit of giggles.

FOYER (m) A center of activity; a large room in a theater, concert hall; also hearth; a home.

FRACAS (m) In French: a noisy disturbance; a crash; an uproar; as to launch a product with big *fracas,* as, in a blaze of publicity, some fear that the *fracas* may drive customers away. To leave a place *avec fracas:* mad, enraged, or speak *avec fracas:* to speak forcefully in order to be noticed; from *fracasser* (to break in pieces, destroy). In English: *fracas* is used in the sense of disturbance, tumult, quarrel, a brawl *(Webster's).*

FRAÎCHEUR (f) Freshness; coolness.

FRISETTE (f) Little curls: curly hair; also spelled *frizette.*

FRISSON (m) A shiver of excitement, fever, desire, fear.

FRISURE (f) A curling and frizzing of the hair.

FROUFROU (m) Excessive affected elegance. *Quel froufrou!* (What a *frou-*

frou!); an expression used in English; the French use the word *chichi* in that sense but they say *le froufrou* of a dress, (the swishing sound) made by some fabrics; *une robe à froufrous* (a frilly dress).

FUREUR (f) Extravagant admiration, to be all the rage as in *ce sport fait fureur* (this sport is very popular); also means "fury, rage," as in *une crise de fureur* (a fit of rage).

FUSELAGE (m) The elongated body section of an aircraft in which the crew, passengers, and cargo are carried.

G

GAUCHERIE, À MON AVIS!

GABELLE (f) A tax on salt, levied in France before the 1879 Revolution.

GAFFE (f) A blunder; a faux pas; *Quelle gaffe!* (What a mistake! What a blunder!)

GAGE D'AMOUR (m) A pledge of love; a love token; see *amour* under Loanwords Alphabetically.

GALA (m) A festive occasion; from Old French *gale* meaning enjoyment, pleasure.

GALANTERIE (f) Courtesy, especially to women.

GALIMATIAS (m) Nonsense; confused speech; farrago. *Quel galimatias* (What nonsense).

GAMIN (m) *gamine (f)* Childlike; as *un air gamin, une gaieté gamine* (childlike air, a *gamine* gaiety).

GAMINERIE (f) Childish behavior of a *gamin* or *gamine*.

GAMME (f) Musical scale.

GARAGE (m) From *garer*, (to park cars, boats, etc.).

GASCONNADE (f) Extravagant boasting. The Gascons, people from *Gascogne* (Gascony) in France have the reputation for being the biggest *fanfarons*.

GAUCHE Clumsy; socially awkward, boorish.

GAUCHERIE (f) Faux pas; tactlessness.

GAZON (m) Turf; sod.

GENTILLESSE (f) The quality of being gentle; kindness.

GOGO, À GOGO Plentiful; in abundance; galore.

GOÛT (m) Taste: the faculty to appreciate food, arts, etc.; *bon goût* (good taste).

GOUTTE (f) Drop (of water, etc.); *goutte à goutte* (drop by drop).

GRAND (m) The word is used in expressions such as: *grand merci* (many thanks); *grand cru* wine and others listed below.

GRAND MAL (m) An epileptic seizure characterized by severe convulsions, followed by coma.

GRAND MONDE (m) Fashionable society; same as *le beau monde*.

GRAND PRIX (m) The highest prize awarded in competition or exhibition. An international horse race that takes place annually in June at the hippodrome of Longchamp, near Paris.

GRAND SIÈCLE (m) A classical or golden age; especially in the reign of Louis XIV (1643–1715).

GRANDEUR (f) The quality of being *grand* (noble, great); greatness; dignity.

GRANDIOSE (m or f) Imposing; magnificent style; splendid; *un art grandiose* or *une oeuvre grandiose*.

GRATIN (m) The upper crust (familiar) as in *le gratin de la société* (the upper crust of society).

GRATITUDE (f) Thankfulness; appreciation.

GRIMACE (f) Distortion of the face.

GRIPPE (f) Influenza.

GRIS-GRIS (m) African charm, amulet, fetish, (*fétiche* in French). Also spelled *gri-gri*.

GUILLOTINE (f) From Joseph Ignace Guillotin (1738–1814) who proposed its use during the French Revolution to behead people. The *guillotine* was invented by a German mechanic named Tobias Schmidt under the direction of Dr. Antoine Louis, a French surgeon.

H

HORS-DE QUESTION, MADEMOISELLE!

HABITANT (m) A person of French descent living in Canada and Louisiana.

HAUTE (f) High; the word is used in expressions listed below. It is also used today in fashion magazines as in: *haute* buzz; *haute* tips; *haute* stuff. (*Marie Claire*, August 2004).

HAUTE BOURGEOISIE (f) The upper middle class.

HAUTE COUTURE (f) High fashion; the leading dressmakers and fashion houses.

HAUTE CUISINE (f) High-class cooking.

HAUTEUR (f) Haughtiness.

HAUT MONDE (m) High society people (*Webster's, Oxford Dictionary of*

Foreign Words & Phrases). The French, however, do not use the word *haut monde* to refer to high society people, they say *le beau monde, le grand monde, les gens* (people) *du monde, les gens de la haute* (people of *la haute*).

HAUT TON (m) People of high fashion (*Oxford Dictionary of Foreign Words & Phrases*). The French do not use that expression. French snobs say, "People are in!" meaning, "They are *à la mode, dernier cri*," (high fashion, stylish).

HÉRITAGE (m) Inheritance.

HOMME (m) Man; see under All About Men for expressions using *homme*.

HORS DE COMBAT Out of combat: unable to fight.

HORS DE QUESTION Out of the question.

HORS DE SAISON Out of season.

HORS LA LOI Outlawed (no hyphens); but the *hors-la-loi* (a noun) the outlawed, the *desperados*.

HORS SÉRIE Excluded from a series as a *hors série automobile*.

HÔTEL DE VILLE (m) A town hall; municipal building.

I

ICI ON PARLE FRANÇAIS, MON AMI!

ICI ON PARLE FRANÇAIS French is spoken here (*Webster's*).

IDÉE FIXE (f) An obsession; a fixed idea.

IGNOBLE (m or f) Worthless; dishonorable; disgusting, as in, "What he did is *ignoble*."

IMMORTELLE (f) Everlasting flower; from *mort* (death): a flower that does not die.

IMPASSE (f) A blind alley; a situation with no solution and no escape.

IMPOSSIBLE Not possible; *"Impossible n'est pas français,"* attributed to Napoléon.

IMPRÉVU (m or f) Unforeseen; unexpected; as in *un plaisir imprévu (m), une visite imprévue (f)* (unexpected pleasure or visit).

IMPUDENCE (f) Insolence; boldness.

INCAPABLE Unable.

INÉDIT (m) Unpublished work.

INFERNAL(m) Hellish, diabolical; from *enfer* (hell).

INSOLENCE (f) Impudence; arrogance; impertinence.

INSOLENT (m) Impertinent, rude.

INSOUCIANCE (f) Heedlessness; lighthearted unconcern.

INTRIGUE (f) Underhanded plotting by *un intrigant* or *une intrigante*. See under About Men, About Women.

J

JE NE SAIS QUOI, MA CHÈRE

JE NE SAIS QUOI Literally, I know not what: a *cliché* to talk about something one has difficulty to explain clearly.

JET D'EAU (m) Jet of water rising from a fountain or pipe.

JEU DE MOTS (m) A play on words, a pun; a clever turn of phrase.

JEU D'ESPRIT (m) Literally, game of the mind: a humorous literary trifle.

JEUNESSE DORÉE (f) The rich, fashionable youth. In France, the fashionable set of the reactionary party in 1794.

JEUX (m.pl.) Games; *les jeux sont faits*, or *faites vos jeux*, the die is cast: expressions used in gambling.

JEUX DE SOCIÉTÉ (m.pl.) Party games, charades, etc.

JOIE DE VIVRE (f) Literally, joy of living: zestful enjoyment of life.

JOUR (m) Day; as in *bonjour*.

JOUR DE FÊTE (m) A festive day.

JOURNAL (m) A diary. *Le journal* is also French for newspaper; *canard* (rag) is the colloquial term.

JUSTE-MILIEU (m) The golden mean; happy medium, especially in politics as defined by Louis-Philippe, King of France (1773–1950).

K

KILOMÈTRE À PIED
KILOGRAMME Kilogram.

KILOMÈTRE Kilometer; the above expression is part of a French song: *Un kilomètre à pied, ça use les souliers.* One kilometer on foot is wearing out your shoes: a song to motivate children to walk happily at camp.

L

LAISSEZ-FAIRE, S'IL-VOUS PLAÎT!
LAISSER-ALLER (m) To let, to go; *laisser-aller* is a noun meaning "a lack of constraint in manners, attitudes, or behavior;" to have *du laisser-aller* (to

be careless or carefree); scruffiness in way of wearing clothes; sloppiness in doing work.

LAISSER-FAIRE (m) To let, to do; *laisser-faire* is a noun meaning "non-interference; an attitude that consists in letting people do as they please." See *Laissez-faire* meaning "let it be" (imperative) under Short Stories.

LAISSEZ-PASSER (m) A permit to travel or to enter a particular place; a pass.

LARD (m) Hog's fat.

LARGESSE (f) Liberality, generosity of spirit or attitude, in giving money or gifts. To give *avec largesse* (generously).

L'AVENIR (m) The future.

LAYETTE (f) Clothes, bedding for a newborn baby.

LE MONDE SAVANT (m) The learned world.

LE POINT DU JOUR (m) Daybreak.

LÈSE-MAJESTÉ (f) Treason; offense against the sovereign power.

LEVANT (m) The East, where the sun rises.

LIAISON (f) A relation or connection, as to be *en liaison* (in contact) with another group, or as in Air France assures *la liaison* between New York and Paris. Also a culinary expression as in, to make *une liaison*, to thicken a sauce. In both French and English, a *liaison* is a love affair considered naughty, as in he has *une liaison* with his wife's best friend; from *lier* (to bind, to join).

LIBERTÉ, EGALITÉ, FRATERNITÉ Motto of France since the French Revolution of 1789.

LIEU (m) As in *lieu* of; instead of.

LINGERIE (f) Woman's underwear and night clothes. Originally, *lin* (linen) articles in a woman's wardrobe or *trousseau*.

LIQUEUR (f) Syrupy alcoholic liquors variously flavored.

LIVRE DE CHEVET (m) A bedside book, a favorite book.

LIVRE DE POCHE (m) Pocket book; a paperback book.

LOUCHE (f) A ladle.

LOUP (m) A mask or half-mask worn by masqueraders.

LOUP-GAROU (m) A werewolf.

LOUIS D'OR (m) Gold coin, first struck in 1640 in the reign of Louis XIII and superseded in 1795.

LYCÉE (m) A public secondary school in France.

M

MA FOI, CHÈRE AMIE!

MACABRE (m or f) Grim, gruesome; as in *un air macabre* (a somber look) or une *danse macabre* (grisly dance).

MAISON (f) House. *Maison d'édition* (a publishing house); *La Maison Blanche* (The White House).

MAISON DE CAMPAGNE (f) A country home.

MAISON DE COUTURE (f) A fashion house; from *coudre* (to sew).

MAISON DE PASSE (f) A brothel.

MAISON DE SANTÉ (f) A home to treat mental illness.

MAISON DE VILLE (f) A townhouse.

MAISONNETTE (f) A small house.

MA FOI! Upon my faith!

MALADE IMAGINAIRE (m) A person with an imaginary illness. *Le Malade Imaginaire*, title of a play by Molière (1673).

MALADRESSE (f) Lack of tact, or dexterity; awkwardness.

MALAISE (m) Uneasiness; vague discomfort; from *mal* (badly), *aise* (ease).

MALENTENDU (m) Misunderstanding.

MALGRÉ ELLE In spite of herself; *malgré moi* (in spite one myself); *malgré tout* (in spite of everything).

MALGRÉ LUI In spite of himself as in *Le Médecin Malgré Lui* (*The Doctor in Spite of Himself*), a comedy by Molière.

MAL VU Literally, poorly seen: looked down on; held in low esteem.

MANÈGE (m) Enclosed area where horses are trained. In France it is also a merry-go-round; also a trick as in: I know your *manège*. (I know what you are up to).

MANOEUVRE (f) Word used mostly in Great Britain; from Latin *manu operari*, work with *la main* (the hand); a skill, a maneuver (U.S.).

MANQUÉ (m) Fallen short of one's ambitions, as in a pianist *manqué* (mediocre). From one of the meaning of *manquer* (to fail). *Un garçon manqué* is French for tomboy!

MAQUIS (m) The dense shrub characteristic of certain Mediterranean coastal regions, especially in Corsica; a member of the French *résistance* movement during the German occupation (1940–1945).

MARDI GRAS (m) Shrove or Fat Tuesday.

MARGUERITE (f) A daisy.

MARIAGE DE CONVENANCE (m) A marriage of convenience for practical reasons.

MARIONNETTE (f) A puppet moved by strings.

MARIVAUDAGE (m) Sentimental or affected style, characteristic of Marivaux (1688–1763), French novelist and dramatist.

MAROTTE (f) A fool's bauble (a short stick with a fool's head).

MARTINET (m) A very strict military disciplinarian; a whip.

MASSAGE (m) Massage.

MASSIF (m) Bulky, heavy; a large mountain; in horticulture a mass or clump of flowers.

MATÉRIEL (m) Tools, equipment necessary to perform work.

MAUVAIS GOÛT (m) Bad taste as in ways of dressing, decorating, etc.

MÉFIANCE (f) Mistrust.

MÉLANGE (m) A mixture; a medley. Not to confuse with *mêlée*; See under Brouhaha.

MÉNAGE (m) A household.

MÉNAGE À TROIS (m) A living arrangement often but not necessarily sexual, between a couple and a third person; a love triangle.

MERCI BEAUCOUP Thank you very much. Replies to *merci*, or *merci beaucoup*, are: *Je t'en prie* (familiar) or *je vous en prie* (formal), literally, I pray you, I beg you; or the more casual answer: *pas de quoi* (don't mention it) or *de rien*.

MERDE! Interjection expressing annoyance; See Short Stories below. Merd, dung: English word now obsolete.

MÉSALLIANCE (f) Unsuitable union; a marriage with one of inferior social position.

MÉTIER (m) Trade; profession; occupation that one is suited for, a calling.

MÉTIS (m) A person with one White and one American Indian parent.

MÉTRO (m) Urbane railway system.

MILIEU (m) Environment; social surroundings; a group of people with a shared cultural outlook.

MINAUDERIE (f) Affected mannerisms.

MISE-AU-POINT (f) Clarification of an obscure subject or problem.

MISE-EN-PAGE (f) Page-setting: layout of text and illustrations.

MISTRAL (m) A strong, cold northwest wind which blows through the Rhône Valley and southern France in winter.

MODE (f) Fashion. *C'est la mode* (it is the style) but *c'est une mode* (it is a trend).

MOI! I; pretentious reference to oneself since the late 1970s.

MONDE (m) The World. *Monde* means society as in *beau monde* and people as in *beaucoup de monde ici* (lots of people here).

MON DIEU! My God! Often used as an interjection.

MONTAGE (m) Setting-up (pictures, music, etc.).

MONTAGNARD (m) A native or inhabitant of a *montagne* (a mountain); a highlander.

MONTAGNE RUSSE (f) A roller coaster.

MONT-DE-PIÉTÉ (m) A pawn shop authorized and controlled by the government for lending money to the poor at a low rate of interest.

MORCEAU (m) A morsel; a bit; a fragment; *je mange un morceau* (I am having a snack). Also a musical composition, poetry, etc. See Chapter II.

MORGUE (f) A mortuary. *The Murders in the Rue Morgue*, by Edgar Allan Poe (1841).

MOT JUSTE (m) The precisely appropriate word.

MOTS D'USAGE (m) Words in common use.

MOUCHOIR (m) A handkerchief; from *moucher* (to wipe the nose).

MOUE (f) A pouting grimace.

MOULIN (m) Mill stone; a mill; *Le Moulin Rouge* in Paris.

MOULIN À CAFÉ (coffee grinder); *moulin à vent* (windmill), *moulin à paroles* (chatterbox).

MOUSTACHE (f) Mustache.

N

N'IMPORTE, MON CHER!

NACELLE (f) A little boat; the car of a balloon, airship, etc.; originally the cockpit of an airplane.

NAÏF (m) Simple; gullible; credulous.

NAÏVETÉ (f) Artlessness; naivety; candor.

NAVETTE (f) A railway truck designed to shuttle cars; *faire la navette* (to commute, to travel back and forth) between Paris and Grenoble.

NÉ; NÉE (m or f) Born; a word placed before the name by which a person is originally known: Mary Smith, *née* Jones.

NÉCESSAIRE (m) A small case for pencils, scissors, tweezers, etc. *Nécessaire de couture* (sewing kit); *nécessaire de toilette* (toiletries).

N'EST-CE PAS? Is it not?

NÉVÉ (m) The crystalline or granular snow on the upper part of a glacier which has not been yet been compressed into ice.

NICHE (f) A specialized but profitable segment of a commercial market. Also an *alcôve*, Architecture term.

NICOTINE (f) A poisonous alkaloid found in tobacco leaves. From Jacques Nicot, French ambassador at Lisbon who first introduced tobacco in France (1560).

NI L'UN NI L'AUTRE Neither one nor the other.

N'IMPORTE! It does not matter.

NOBLESSE (f) Nobility: a class of people of noble rank.

NOBLESSE OBLIGE (f) "Nobility obliges," meaning that noble ancestry entails responsibility and people of high rank or birth should behave nobly toward others.

NOËL (m) Christmas; *joyeux Noël* (Merry Christmas).

NOM DE GUERRE (m) War name under which a person fights or engages in some action.

NOM DE PLUME (m) Literally, pen-name: the assumed name of a writer.

NOM DE THÉÂRE (m) An assumed name under which a person performs on stage.

NONCHALANCE (f) Lack of interest, of enthusiasm; indifference; unconcern.

NON PAREIL Having no equal; unrivalled or unique person or thing; same as *sans pareil.*

NOTRE-DAME (f) Our Lady: as in *Notre-Dame de Chartres* or *Notre-Dame de Paris.*

NOUVEAUTÉ (f) A novelty. Well! *C'est une nouveauté!* (That's a new one!)

NOUVELLES (f. pl.) The news. The French listen to *les nouvelles* or *les informations à la télévision,* or *à la radio.*

NOUVELLE VAGUE (f) New wave; *La Nouvelle Vague*: a new movement or trend, specifically in filmmaking originating in France in the late 1950s. The *Nouvelle Vague* guru was Jean-Luc Goddard.

NUANCE (f) Slight or subtle variation in or shade of meaning, expression, or color in artwork, fabric, etc.

NUISANCE (f) A person or thing that annoys, vexes, or does harm; from *nuire* (to harm).

NUIT BLANCHE (f) Literally, white night: sleepless night.

O

OBJET D'ART SANS PAREIL

OBJET D'ART (m) Small objects of artistic value.

OEILLADE (f) A flirting glance; an ogle; from *oeil* (eye); plural is *yeux* (eyes).

OEUVRE (f) A work of art or literature; a masterpiece, a *chef-d'oeuvre.*

ORDURES Refuse; garbage; filth. *Espèce d'ordure!* (Filthy bastard!)

OSIER (m) Willow; wicker as *une chaise en osier* (a wicker chair).

OUBLIETTE (f) A dungeon with a trap door, formerly used for persons condemned to perpetual imprisonment to perish secretly; from *oublier* (to forget).

OUÏ-DIRE (m) Hearsay; *par ouï-dire* (by hearsay). From *ouïe* (hearing); I am *tout ouïe* (I am all ears); I have *l'ouïe fin* (I have good hearing).

OUTRANCE (f) *A outrance*, with excess; to the utmost limit; as in a combat *à outrance*, a desperate fight.

OUTRÉ (e) (m or f) Exaggerated; eccentric; outraged; as in *un air outré* (an outraged look).

P

PAS DU TOUT, CHÉRE MADAME!

PANACHE (m) Spirited self-confidence; flamboyance; dashing elegance of manner; *verve*; as in adding *panache* to your daily conversations. Also a tuft of feathers on a helmet or a hat.

PAPERASSERIE (f) Excessive paper work; bureaucracy.

PAPETERIE (f) Stationer's shop.

PARDON (m) Forgiveness. From *pardonner* (to pardon); *pardonne-moi,* (familiar), *pardonnez-moi* (formal); pardon-me, excuse-me.

PARFAITEMENT BIEN Perfectly well.

PARFUMERIE (f) A shop that sells perfume; a perfume factory.

PARI MUTUEL (m) System of betting on horses races; PMU: *Pari Mutuel Urbain.*

PARLOIR (m) A conversation room in a monastery or convent; a parlor; from *parler* (to speak).

PAROLE D'HONNEUR (f) Word of honor.

PARTERRE (m) An ornamental garden area in which the flowerbeds form a pattern.

PARTIE (f) A match in a game; a game; *une partie de tennis* (a tennis match).

PARTI PRIS (m) A preconceived opinion; a bias.

PARTOUT Everywhere.

PAS DE No + (another word) as in *pas de* sweat (no sweat). Expression often used in *Bright Lights, Big City*, a novel Jay McInerney.

PAS DE TACT (tactless); *pas de chance* (no luck); *pas de cadeau* (no gift).

PAS DU TOUT Not at all; by no means; as in answer to, "Do I disturb you?" *Non, pas du tout!*

PASSADE (f) A passing romance; a transitory love affair; it's only a *passade!*

PASSE-PARTOUT (m) Literally, pass-everywhere: as a master key.

PATOIS (m) A dialect; jargon.

PATTE (f) A paw.

PATTE DE VELOURS (f) Velours's paw: ruthlessness hidden beneath apparent softness. A cat's paw with the claws retracted; *le chat fait patte de velours*, (the cat draws in its claws) and then scratches you.

PELOTON (m) The main group or pack of cyclists in a race.

PELOUSE (f) A lawn.

PELURE (f) A very thin paper; *pelure*-paper. *La pelure de pomme* (apple skin) *la pelure de pomme de terre* (potato skin).

PENCHANT (m) An inclination; a leaning for; a strong liking as in a *penchant* for instant wealth. From *pencher* (to lean).

PENSÉE (f) A thought, an idea. *Pensées, extraits* (excerpts) by Blaise Pascal, French philosopher and writer (1623–1662).

PENSION (f) Boarding school.

PERMIS DE SÉJOUR (m) Permission to stay in a country; a residence permit.

PERSIFLAGE (m) Frivolous or flippant manner of speaking or writing; see *persifleur* under About Men.

PERSONNEL (m) The body of people employed in an organization.

PÉTARD (m) An explosive device; word used in the expression "hoist with one's own *petard*[50]": to undo by ensnaring in his own machinations. From *péter* (to break wind); less elegantly, to fart; *un pet* (a fart). *Un pet-de-nonne,* literally, a nun's fart, is a *beignet soufflé* (a *soufflé* friter)! See *beignet* Chapter I, under dessert.

PÉTILLANT (m) Lively, sparkling; *un vin pétillant.*

PETIT (m) Little, small.

PETITE (f) Of small stature; a petite size in woman's clothing.

PETIT MAL (m) Mild epilepsy with only momentary loss of consciousness (see *grand mal*).

PEU À PEU Little by little.

PEU DE CHOSE A trifle; a thing of slight importance; I have done *si peu de chose* (so little).

PIED-À-TERRE (m) Literally, foot on the ground: a place to rest or to live especially for a short time; a lodging; a home base.

PIED-NOIR (m) Black foot: a person of European origin who settled in North Africa, particularly in Algeria during French rule. See Pieds-Noirs, under Short Stories.

PIROGUE (f) A canoe made by hollowing out a large log; any boat resembling a canoe.

PIS-ALLER (m) The lesser evil; it was *un pis-aller*, it was a solution one used as the last resort, something we did *faute de mieux*.

PISSOIR (f) A public urinal, especially in France. From *pisser*, to piss (vulgar).

PIVOT (m) Something on which a part rotates or on which an important matter hinges.

PLATEAU (m) A period when there is neither an increase or decrease in something; also, a stretch of elevated, level land.

POIGNANT (m) Sharply painful; poignant; heart-rending as *un souvenir poignant*.

POINT D'APPUI (m) Point of support: a strategic point.

POINT DE DÉPART (m) A point of departure.

POINT DE REPÈRE (m) A point of reference.

POLITESSE (f) Politeness; civility.

PORTAIL (m) A door or gateway.

PORTE-BONHEUR (m) Literally, a carry happiness: a charm carried for luck.

PORTE-BOUQUET (m) A device for holding a bouquet.

PORTEFEUILLE (m) Portfolio; as to have *le portefeuille de la Défense*, to have the defense portfolio; also French for "wallet."

POTABLE (m or f) Drinkable; fit to drink, as in: *une eau potable* (drinking water).

POTAGER (m) A vegetable garden used to make potage (soup).

POT DE CHAMBRE (m) Chamber pot; also called poetically by the French *un vase de nuit* (a *vase* for the night).

POT-POURRI (m) Literally, rotten pot: a mixture of dried flowers; the vase or jar that holds the mixture; anthology; a potpourri.

POURPARLER (m) An informal discussion or conference preliminary to actual negotiation.

POUR RIRE Literally, for laughing: not seriously, as in *c'est pour rire* (it's a joke).

POUR-SOI For oneself; philosophy of Jean Paul Sartre.

PRÉCIS (m) A summary or abstract of a text or speech.

PREMIÈRE (f) A first performance; masculine form is: *premier* as in *Premier Ministre du Canada*.

PRESTIGE (m) Renown; power to command admiration.

PRIX FIXE (m) Fixed price: in some restaurants, a set price for a meal.

PROCÉDÉ (m) Manner of proceeding; a method, a procedure.

PROFESSION (f) A vocation or occupation requiring special training: engineering, teaching, architecture, etc.

PROMENADE (f) A relaxing walk; a public place for walking; a dance.

Q

QUI-VIVE!

QUADRILLÉ (m) Having a pattern of small squares; *papier quadrillé* for technical people, engineers and architects, among others (*Webster's*).

QUARTIER (m) A district or area; *Le Quartier Latin,* (the Latin Quarter) in Paris on the left bank of the Seine where students and artists work and live.

QUELQUE CHOSE Something.

QUEUE (f) A pigtail; a line of people; *faire la queue* (to line up).

QUI VA LÀ? Who goes there?: a sentry's challenge.

QUINZAINE (f) A fortnight.

QUI-VIVE! A sentry's challenge: *Halte-là, qui-vive:* (Stop there, who goes there?). Also to be on the *qui-vive;* to be on the alert, on the lookout.

R

RÉPONDEZ S'IL VOUS PLAÎT, CHER AMI!

RADEAU (m) A raft.

RAISON D'ÉTAT (f) A reason having to do with the security or interests of a State.

RAISON D'ÊTRE (f) Reason for being: the reason for existing; as: you are my *raison d'être.*

RAMPANT (m) Growing luxuriantly; as *rampant* plants; widespread, insidious as in poverty is *rampant;* from *ramper* (to crawl).

RAPPEL (m) A recall; a descent by a mountain climber.

RAPPORT (m) Agreement; harmony; relationship; connection with people as to have a good *rapport* (not to confuse report) with other people or nations.

RAPPROCHEMENT (m) Reconciliation; restoration of cordial relations; *se rapprocher* (to come closer).

RAVAGE (m) Destruction; desolation; devastation; as in *les ravages du temps* (the ravages of time); from *ravager* (to destroy, to wreak havoc).

RÉCHAUFFÉ (m) Reheated: stale news; rehashed.

RECHERCHÉ (e) (m or f) Much sought out; exotic; refined; select.

RÉCIT (m) Narrative, a story; from *réciter* (to recit).

RÉCLAME (f) An advertisement; publicity; as a *réclame* for Chanel perfumes.

RÉDUIT (m) Cubbyhole; usually poor: as he lives in *un réduit sombre et pauvre* (a small room dark and poor).

REFLET (m) Reflection; brightness or iridescence of a surface.

REFUGE (f) A refuge; shelter; a place of safety.

RÉGIME (m) A political system; a method of rule of government.

REGRET (m) Remorse; grief.

RELIGIEUSE (f) A nun; (adjective: pious); also a type of pastry. See Desserts, Chapter I.

RELIGIEUX (m) A monk; (adjective: pious; religious).

RENCONTRE (f) An encounter; a casual meeting.

RENDEZ-VOUS (m) Also spelled rendezvous in English, the word is used to mean a prearranged meeting, or meeting place. "This generation of Americans has a *rendez-vous* with destiny" (F. D. Roosevelt). In France you make a *rendez-vous* (appointment) at the doctor's office; you also have a *rendez-vous galant*, or a *rendez-vous* social. To miss a *rendez-vous galant* is *poser un lapin* in French, literally to set up a rabbit, (to stand somebody up).

RENTRÉE (f) A return, especially after a holiday: *La rentrée des classes* (back to school).

RÉPLIQUE (f) A reply.

RÉPONDEZ S'IL VOUS PLAÎT RSVP: reply *s'il vous plaît*.

REPORTAGE (m) The act of reporting as for a publication.

RÉPUDIATION (f) The act of repudiating.

RÉSEAU (m) A spy or intelligence network; a network.

RÉSUMÉ (m) A summary; an epitome; a curriculum vitae.

RETROUSSÉ (m) Turned up at the tip; often used as in *un nez retroussé* (a snub nose).

RÉVEILLON (m) A night time celebration, originally a meal after midnight on Christmas Day.

RÊVERIE (f) The condition of being lost in thought; daydreaming; from *rêver* (to dream).

RICOCHET (m) Rebounds, skips made by an object over a flat surface; like a pebble over water; a *richochet* action.

RIDEAU (m) A small mound of earth. It is also French for curtain; used in theatre as *lever de rideau* Chapter II, Arts.

RIEN NE VA PLUS Nothing goes, no more bets; *in roulette*, the call made by the *croupier*.

RIPOSTE (f) A swift, sharp reply; from *riposter* (to retort).

RISQUÉ (e) (m or f) Liable to shock; daring; almost indecent; licentious, overly provocative, as in a *risquée* anecdote.

RITE DE PASSAGE (m) Any formal practice or custom; as in, "Dissecting the appearance of public figures seems to have become a political 'rite of (de) passage.'"[54]

ROUGE-ET-NOIR A gambling game in which stakes are placed on a table marked with red and black diamonds on which bets are placed. *Le Rouge* *et le Noir* (1830), title of a book by French writer Henri (Beyle) Stendhal (1783–1842).

ROULETTE (f) A little wheel: a gambling game; from *roue* (wheel). Russian *roulette*: a deadly game using a revolver.

ROUTINE (f) Rut; habit; routine; a customary way (of life).

RUSE (f) A stratagem; a trick.

RUSE DE GUERRE (f) Ruse of war: a stratagem intended to deceive the enemy in war; a trick. The Trojan horse is one example.

S

SAUVE-QUI-PEUT MON VIEUX!

SABOT (m) A shoe made of a single piece of wood, worn by peasants in Europe.

SABOTAGE (m) Deliberate damage to, or destruction of property done by a *saboteur*. From *saboter* (to botch, to damage).

SAIN-ET-SAUF Safe and sound.

SALLE À MANGER (f) Literally, room to eat: the dining room.

SALLE D'ATTENTE (f) Literally, room to wait: a waiting-room; especially *à la gare* (in a train station).

SALLE DE JEUX (f) A gambling house.

SALLE DES PAS PERDUS (f) Room of the lost footsteps; a waiting-hall at a. court of law, station. In Paris, *Gare Saint Lazarre La Salle des Pas Perdus* is so called because millions of passengers go back and forth, waiting, leaving.

SALON (m) Drawing room; a lounge; saloon. French phrases using *salon*: *le salon de l'automobile, de thé, de coiffure, de beauté.*

SANG-FROID (m) Literally, cold blood: coolness, self-possession especially in the face of danger.

SANGLIER (m) Wild boar.

SANS Without; as *sans tattoo* or *sans-gêne* (see expressions with sans).

SAUTOIR (m) A long necklace.

SAUVE-QUI-PEUT Literally, save himself who can: to run away, to be off; expression used during a disorganized retreat; a stampede.

SAVATE (f) Old shoe or slipper. In France, *traîner la savate* (familiar) means to do nothing, to go slipshod, be careless. *A traîne-savate* (an idler), one who does not get much done, and indigent as a result; from *traîner*, (to drag one's feet). *C'est une vraie savate*, (he/she is really clumsy, slipshod).

SAVOIR-FAIRE (m) To know how to do (something): the ability to act suitably in any situation; tact.

SAVOIR-VIVRE (m) To know how to live: knowledge of the world and the ways of society; worldly wisdom; sophistication; good breeding.

SCULPTURE (f) The art of carving wood, chiseling stone, etc.

SÉANCE (f) A meeting, a session; a meeting of spiritualists during which they try to communicate with the spirits of the dead.

SECRET DE POLICHINELLE Punchinello's secret; an apparent secret which is generally known. Punchinello is a buffoon, a clown, a prototype of Punch, the puppet that constantly fights with his wife, Judy (Punch-and-Judy, marionette show).

SERIN (m) A small, yellow European finch; related to the canary.

SERMON (m) A discourse delivered in public. *Le Sermon sur la Montagne (Sermon on the Mount).*

SERPETTE (f) A pruning knife.

SERVIETTE (f) A table napkin. In France, *une serviette* is also a briefcase; and *une serviette de toilette* (a bath towel).

SERVITUDE (f) Slavery; bondage; from *servir* (to serve).

SIÈCLE (m) A century.

SIÈCLE D'OR (m) Golden age; said of the reign of Louis XIV.

S'IL VOUS PLAÎT If you please (polite form); please; *s'il te plaît* is the friendly form.

SOBRIQUET (m) A nickname.

SOI-DISANT Of a person: would-be: a *soi-disant entrepreneur*. Of a thing: so-called: a *soi-disant* miracle.

SOIRÉE (f) An elegant evening party. From *soir* (evening).

SOIRÉE DANSANTE (f) An evening party with dancing.

SOIRÉE MUSICALE (f) An evening party with music.

SOIT! Agreed! *D'accord!*; *ainsi soit-il* (so be it), *amen*. *Soit* by itself means "either . . . or," as in, "I will visit *soit* Paris, *soit* New York (either Paris or New York)."

SON ET LUMIÈRE (m) Literally, sound and light, an expression used to describe a type of entertainment with sound and lighting effects, presented at night at a historic building or place as, for instance, at the Shakespeare Festival in Ashland, Oregon every summer.

SONDAGE (m) Opinion poll; from *sonder* (to poll, to survey).

SOTTISE (f) A foolish remark or action; *un sot* or *une sotte* (a foolish man or girl).

SOU (m) A French coin; *sans le sou* (penniless).

SOUPÇON (m) A trace; a very small quantity; also means suspicion in French.

SOUS-ENTENDU (m) Implied, understood but not expressed.

SOUTERRAIN (m) Underground.

SOUVENIR (m) A token of remembrance; a memento.

SUÈDE (m) Leather, originally kidskin; as in *gants de suède* (gloves of Sweden made of kidskin).

SVELTE (m or f) Slender; lithe.

T

DU TAC AU TAC MON AMI!

TABLE D'HÔTE (f) Table of the host: common table for guests at a restaurant; complete meal with courses as specified on the menu.

TAC AU TAC (m) Term used in fencing: *Riposter du tac au tac* (to parry with the riposte). Tit for tat as in to answer *du tac au tac*, to snap back; *du tac au tac mon cher.*

TANT MIEUX So much the better.

TANT PIS So much the worse; too bad.

TAPIS (m) Carpet; tapestry used as a curtain or to put on furniture.
The expression to be *sur le tapis* (to be on the *tapis),* means "to be under consideration;" as in, "My candidature is *sur le tapis."*

TERRAIN (m) Soil; ground; a portion of land; *la terre* (earth).

TERRASSE (f) A terrace; paved area where people sit to eat or take refreshments.

TÊTE-À-TÊTE (f) Face-to-face; confidential as a *tête-à-tête* conversation.

TÊTE-BÊCHE (f) Head-to-tail: printed so that one is inverted in relation to the other; side of a pair of postage stamps.

TÊTE-DE-PONT (f) A bridgehead.

TÊTE FOLLE (f) Literally, crazy head: scatterbrain.

TIC (m) Involuntary spasmodic muscle contraction.

TIC DOULOUREUX (m) Painful tic: spasms of pain accompanied by twitching of the facial muscles.

TIERS MONDE (m) The Third World; the developing nations.

TIMBRE (m) Tone, the way things that are said or written sound, as in, "I like *le timbre* of your message." Term also used in music; see Chapter II. *Un timbre* or *timbre-poste* (a postal stamp). *Il est timbré* or *elle est timbrée* (he or she is loony).

TIRADE (f) A long vehement speech; a harangue.

TON (m) The prevailing fashion; to set *le ton de la mode*. *De bon ton* (tasteful), as it is *de bon ton* to wear black.

TONNE (f) A ton.

TONNEAU (m) Enclosed rear compartment for passengers in early type of automobile.

TORCHON (m) As dish cloth; a duster.

TOUCHÉ! Term originally used in fencing, equivalent to "You got me"; **TOUCHE-TOUCHE** (to be on top of each other) (no accent on the 'e' is French for bumper-to-bumper traffic).

TOUPET (m) A patch of false hair or a small wig to cover a bald spot; toupee.

TOUR (m) A turn; a long trip as in *Tour de France.*

TOURBILLON (m) Whirlwind; a firework that rises with a spiral motion, a whirl.

TOUR DE FORCE (m) A feat of strength; an impressive achievement or performance.

TOURNIQUET (m) A device for stopping or slowing the flow of blood through the artery.

TOUT All; see under Expressions with *tout.*

TRAVAIL (m) Labor pains; toil; very hard work.

TRENTE ET QUARANTE Literally, thirty and forty; a gambling game; also called *rouge-et-noir.*

TRÈS Very; as in *très sportif; très chic; très à la mode,* etc.

TRIAGE (m) The action of sorting out samples of a commodity; from *trier* (to select, sort out).

TRISTE (m or f) Sad, sorrowful; *un visage triste* (a sad face); *une triste affaire* (a sad story).

TRISTESSE (f) Sadness; melancholy.

TROTTOIR (m) Sidewalk; from *trotter* (to trot). *Faire le trottoir* (to walk the street, to be a hooker).

TROU NORMAND (m) Literally, the Normand hole: a drink of *calvados.* See Liquors & Aperitifs, Chapter I.

TROUPE (f) A troop: dancers, actors, entertainers, soldiers.

TROUSSEAU (m) Small bundle; a bride's outfit of clothes, linen, jewelry, etc.

TURPITUDE (f) Baseness; depravity; shameful wickedness.

U

UNIQUE, MA CHÈRE MADAME!

UNIQUE One and only, as *un fils unique; une fille unique* (the only son or daughter).

URINOIR Public urinal from *uriner* (to urinate).

USAGE (m) Use.

V

VIVE LA BAGATELLE, MADEMOISELLE!

VALISE (f) Traveling case or portmanteau usually made of leather.

VALSE (f) A waltz.

VENGEANCE (f) Revenge.

VERDURE (f) Greenness; green vegetation; from *vert;* see Chapter III under Colors.

VERVE (f) Enthusiasm in expressing ideas; animation, *élan.*

VIE DE BOHÈME (f) A Bohemian way of life; see: *Vie de Bohème* under Short Stories below.

VIE DE CHÂTEAU (f) Aristocratic social life.

VIE EN ROSE (f) A life seen though rose-colored glasses. The phrase was made popular by French singer Edith Piaf (1915–1963), one of whose songs was called *La vie en rose* (*Life in pink*).

VIGNETTE (f) A small, decorative design or illustration on a blank space in a book, especially at the beginning or end of a chapter or on the title page; diminutive of *vigne* (vine).

VILLE LUMIÈRE (f) City of lights: an exciting modern city, specifically Paris.

VISAGE (m) The face.

VIS-À-VIS Face-to-face: a light horse-drawn carriage for two people sitting face-to-face; same as *tête-à-tête*. Also, with regard to; as in, my feelings *vis-à-vis* this particular subject.

VIVE! Long life! *Vive la France! Vive le roi!* From *vivre* (to live).

VIVE LA BAGATELLE! Expressing a carefree attitude to life as in success to frivolity, to nonsense!

VIVE LA DIFFÉRENCE! Expressing approval of the differences between the sexes, cultures, etc.

VIVE LE ROI! Long life to the king!

VOILÀ! There it is!

VOILÀ TOUT! That's all; there is nothing more to say.

VOIR DIRE (m) To speak true: term used in law; an oath requiring a person to make true answers; the questions themselves.

VOISINAGE (m) Neighborhood; *un voisin, une voisine*, (neighbor).

VOITURE (f) A carriage or wagon.

VOITURETTE (f) A small carriage.

VOIX CÉLESTE (f) Heavenly voice.

VOLAGE (m or f) Giddy; fickle; flighty.

VOLTE-FACE (f) A complete change of attitude, opinion, or position in an argument.

VOLUBLE (m or f) Fluent; speaking with ease; talkative.

VOYAGE (m) A trip; from *voyager,* (to travel). *Le Grand Voyage:* Literally, the Big Trip, the last one, (death).

VUE D'ENSEMBLE (f) An overview; a general view of matters.

W

WAGON-LIT (m) A sleeping car on a train in Continental Europe.

WAGON-RESTAURANT (m) A dining car on a train in Continental Europe.

Y

YÉ-YÉ A fashionable, sophisticated style of music, songs, dress of the 1960s (*Webster's*). Un yé-yé: a person with a yé-yé style. The word and style are understandably becoming obsolete.

Z

ZOUAVE (m) – Infantry soldiers in the French army, originally formed of Kabyles. From *zwâwa:* a Kabyle tribe in Algeria, former French colony. Papal, or Pontifical Zouave were a corps of French soldiers formed to protect the Pope in Rome between 1860 and 1871. *Faire le Zouave,* literally to do the Zouave means to play the fool (G.B.) to clown around (U.S.).

ZUT! Expressing impatience *Zut alors!* Darn! *Alors* acts as an intensifier.

SHORT STORIES

CHARIVARI *Punch* or the *London Charivari* is an illustrated weekly comic paper, first published in London on July 17, 1841. It ceased publication in the 1990s and was revived in 1996 with limited success. *Punch and Judy* is a puppet show in which Punch strangles his child, beats his wife Judy to death, and attacks policemen, among other horrible things. *Quel charivari!* The show was very popular in England during Queen Ann's reign and is still well-liked by children in England.

BEAU The word *beau* was used in the late seventeenth to mid-nineteenth centuries to describe a man who was fastidious about his clothes and accessories, similar but not as effeminate as a fop. Beau Brummel, English dandy (1778–1840), was the leader of the *beaux*; he exiled to France where he died in 1840, penniless and apparently incoherent.

ROI FAINÉANT A do-nothing king; a sluggard king. Any person with merely nominal power; originally, the term applied to the Merovingian Kings of France whose power was merely nominal.

FEMME FATALE Mata Hari, *née* Margaretha Geertruida Zelle, born August 7, 1876, in Leenwarden, the Netherlands, went down in history as *la femme fatale par excellence*. Mata Hari is the stage name she had created; it meant "Eye of the Morning" or "Child of European Dawn." Her spy code was H21. Apparently H was the code assigned to German spies before the First World War started. In France, where she had become a well-known nude dancer, the French Secret Service asked her to spy on the Germans. She agreed, but also received money from the Germans to spy on the French. The French became suspicious. They arrested her, interrogated her, found her guilty and responsible for the death of tens of thousands of French soldiers. The red-haired spy was shot by a firing squad in 1917. Apparently, she refused to be blindfolded and blew a kiss to the firing squad. Nobody came to claim her body.

CAUSE CÉLÈBRE: THE AFFAIR DREYFUS Alfred Dreyfus (1894–1906) was a French captain of Jewish origin. In December 1894, he was wrongly condemned for espionage and sent to jail at *l'Isle du Diable* (Devil's Island) in French Guyana. On January 13, 1898, French novelist Emile Zola (1840–1902) sent his famous letter *J'Accuse* to *L'Aurore*, a Paris literary newspaper and to French President Faure to denounce the French military establishment for wrongly condemning Dreyfus. In 1906, Dreyfus was freed. A graphologist had been able to show during the trial that Dreyfus's signature had been forged on the sensitive documents given to the Germans.

LAISSEZ-FAIRE The expression originated with the Physiocrats, a group of eighteenth-century French economists whose maxim was, "*laissez-faire et laissez passer*," an imperative statement that told people to let it happen and to let it be, to leave things as they were. This doctrine was popularized by the economist Adam Smith in his treatise, *The Wealth of Nations. Laissez-faire* (imperative) or *le laisser-faire* (noun) is the policy, whether economic or political, of letting things go their own course without official intervention from the State or the Government.

MERDE "*Mot de Cambronne*," was the reputed reply of General Pierre Cambronne (1770–1842) when called upon to surrender at the battle of Waterloo. The official version of what he said, "*La garde meurt mais ne se rend pas* (the Guard dies but does not surrender)," seems to have been a creative journalistic invention since the general himself denies saying the four letter word!

Pieds-noirs Europeans who settled in North Africa, particularly in Algeria, around 1870, were called *pieds-noirs*, literally black feet. They played an important role during the war for the Independence of Algeria (1954–1962), at the end of which France lost a colony where she had been since 1830. One plausible explanation for the appellation *pied-noir* is that the troops that supported the settlers wore the colonial uniform: white helmet, white jacket and trousers, and black ankle boots, hence the name *pieds-noirs*.

Salon des Refusés It was an Exhibition ordered by Napoléon III in 1863 to display paintings that were refused by Le Salon; Le Salon is the annual exhibition of paintings and sculpture by living artists in Paris. Le Salon was particularly hostile to Impressionists.

Vie de Bohème The expression *une vie de Bohème* means an easy-going, unconventional lifestyle characteristic of artists and dilettantes. Published in 1848, *Scènes de la vie de Bohème* by French author and writer Henri Murger (1822–1861), is a stage play that depicts aspects of Bohemian lifestyle.

Why is *vie de Bohème* synonymous with non-conformism and vagabondage?

Un bohémien, une bohémienne, French for "bohemian" (man and woman), is an inhabitant of *La Bohême* (Bohemia), a province of Czechoslovakia where a fair number of Roma people settled. *Rom*, meaning "man" or "husband" is singular for Roma; it is English for a gypsy man or boy.

Originally, the Roma came from India and wherever they migrated in

Europe, they took the name of Tsiganes, also spelled Tziganes. Tziganes coming to France from *La Bohême* took of the name of *bohémiens*.

There were many tribes of Roma. Some went to live in a region called Small Egypt and they became known as Egyptians, later shortened to Gyptians and finally to gipsy also spelled *gypsy*. *Egitanos* is Spanish for Egyptians, hence the word Gitanos in English and *gitans* in French, meaning "gyspy." The *gitans* live mostly in the South of France.

The word *bohémien* is therefore synonymous with Tsiganes, Gipsy, *Gitan*, and Romanichel, another Roma tribe. The roaming lifestyle of the Roma, whose language is Romany, is associated with their vagabondage and carefree, unconventional philosophy, hence the French phrase and loanword *la vie de Bohème* to describe the manner of living of bohemians who live in France and, by extension, of anyone who enjoys a freespirited, nonconforming lifestyle.

BE A SNOB

This section contains short phrases composed of French loanwords only. *Très à la mode ma chère* is one example of such a phrase created with three French loanwords: *très* (very), *à la mode* (stylish), and *ma chère* (my dear).

A versatile English speaker can now proudly say to her best friend while shopping at the Bon Marché, "*Très à la mode ma chère!*" instead of, "Very stylish, my dear!"

Both phrases are English but the man in the street is sure that she is showing off her French. She is a snob who craves attention. On the other hand, her friend knows that it is time to make some improvements. She is a little envious and she is determined to add *panache* to her conversations and a *je ne sais quoi* to her life. Beginning today, tonight, after watching *Desperate Housewives,* she is going to spend hours, days, months, whatever it takes to learn sophisticated English with *French for Le Snob* so that she can compete with her best friend.

French loanwords from Chapter IV are listed below in two sections: *French Loanwords About People* such as *mon ami, mon cher, cher Monsieur,* etc. and *English phrases à la française* such as *à bientôt mon cher, bien entendu mon ami, c'est la guerre Monsieur,* etc.

English phrases à la française are formed by adding one loanword from *French Loanwords About People* to one of the French loanwords and expressions listed in alphabetical order, such *à bientôt, bonjour, c'est magnifique, d'accord,* etc. Each *English phrase à la française* is followed by another English version, as a refresher. For instance, *à bientôt mon cher* (see you soon my dear) and *bien entendu mon ami* (of course, my friend).

Although examples of *English phrases à la française* are given below, creative English speakers can pick and choose to arrange loanwords together as they see fit.

FRENCH LOANWORDS ABOUT PEOPLE

(m) abbreviation for masculine; (f) abbreviation for feminine

Mon ami (m)	My friend
Mon amie (f)	My friend
Mon cher (m)	My dear (man)
Ma chère (f)	My dear (lady)
Mon vieux (m)	Old chap! Old pal!

Ma vieille (f)	My old woman (old friend)
Chère amie (f)	Dear (lady) friend
Monsieur (m)	Sir
Mon cher Monsieur (m)	My dear Sir
Madame (f)	Mrs.
Ma chère Madame (f)	Dear lady
Mademoiselle (chère Mademoiselle) (f)	Miss, (dear Miss)
Mon chou or mon petit chou	My darling (a man, woman, or usually *mon petit chou* to a child)
Canaille! (m)	Scoundrel!
Confrère (m)	Fellow member; associate
Distingué (e) (m or f)	Distinguished (man or woman)
Fainéant! (m)	Lazy-bones!
Méchant! (m)	Wicked man! Mean bully!
Méchante (f)	Bad girl, mean woman!
Vaurien! (m)	Good for nothing!
Beau garçon (m)	Good looking man
Femme du monde (f)	Woman of the world
Mignonne (f)	Cute, gentle
Polisson (m)	Rascal; scamp
Polissonne (f)	Naughty girl

ENGLISH PHRASES À LA FRANÇAISE

This section is made of two parts: *French Loanwords or Expressions listed alphabetically*, and a word from *French Loanwords About People*, followed by its other English version.

Loanwords alphabetically	Loanwords about People	English version
A		
A bientôt	*mon cher*	Until later, see you soon, my dear.
Adieu	*mon cher ami*	Farewell, my dear friend.
Ainsi va la vie	*mon amie*	So goes life, my friend.
Allez-vous en	*vaurien*	Go away, good for nothing.
Allons!	*Mademoiselle*	Come on, Miss (Cut that nonsense).
A la bonne heure	*mon ami*	Right on, my friend.
A moi	*mon cher*	Help, my dear!
A mon avis	*ma chère*	In my opinion, my dear.
A propos	*Mademoiselle*	By the way, Miss.
A quoi bon	*méchant*	What's the good of it, bad boy!
A tout prix	*ma chère amie*	At all cost, my dear (lady) friend.

Loanwords alphabetically	Loanwords about People	English version
Au contraire	mon cher ami	On the contrary, my dear fellow.
Au fait,	ma chère Madame	Incidentally (by the way), my dear lady.
Au revoir	polisson	Good-bye, naughty boy.
Au secours	cher confrère	Help! Dear fellow (associate).
Avec votre permission	ma chère	With your permission, my dear.

B

Bien entendu	vaurien	Of course, good for nothing.
Bienvenue	fainéant	Welcome, lazy-bones!
Bon appétit	ma chère Madame	Bon appétit, my dear Madam.
Bon gré, mal gré	mon frère	Willing or not, brother.
Bonjour	méchante	Good morning, bad girl.
Bonne chance	mon cher ami	Good luck, my dear friend.
Bonsoir	polissonne	Good-night, naughty girl.
Bon voyage	mes amis	Bon voyage, my friends.

Loanwords alphabetically	Loanwords about People	English version
C		
Cela va sans dire	*canaille*	That goes without saying, scoundrel!
Chacun son goût	*mes amis*	To each their own taste, my friends.
Chez moi	*chez mon ami*	At my house, dear friend.
Comme ci comme ça	*mon chou*	So-so, my darling.
Comme il faut	*cher Monsieur*	As it should be, dear Sir.
Coûte que coûte	*ma chère amie*	Whatever it takes, my dear friend.
C'est-à-dire	*mon vieux*	That is to say, old chap.
C'est la guerre	*mon cher*	It's war, my dear.
C'est la vie	*chère Madame*	It's life, dear Madam!
C'est magnifique	*mes amis*	It's wonderful, my friends.
D		
D'accord	*mon cher ami*	Agreed, my dear friend.
Déjà-vu	*mon cher confrère*	Déjà-vu, my dear fellow.
De mal en pis	*ma chère*	From bad to worse, my dear.
Du tac au tac	*mon cher*	Tit for tat, my dear.

Loanwords alphabetically	Loanwords about People	English version
E		
En avant	mes amis	Off we go, my friends!
En effet	ma mignonne	Indeed, my darling.
En passant,	cher confrère	In passing, by the way, dear colleague.
En tout cas	mes amis	In any case, my friends.
Encore	s'il vous plaît mon ami	Once more, please, my friend.
Enfin	chère amie	At last, dear friend.
Ensuite,	Monsieur	Next, Sir.
Entre nous	chère amie	Between you and me, dear friend.
Entrez	S'il vous plaît, Monsieur	Enter, If you please, Sir.
Epatant	mon chou	Wonderful, my darling!
Extraordinaire	mes amis	Outstanding, my friends!
F		
Façon de parler	cher Monsieur	Manner of speaking, dear Sir.
Faute de mieux	Mademoiselle	For lack of something better, Miss.

Loanwords alphabetically	Loanwords about People	English version
Faux pas	*ma chère amie*	Social blunder, my dear friend.

H-I-J-L-M-N-P-R

Hors de question	*mon ami*	Out of the question, my friend.
Ici on parle français	*mon cher*	French is spoken here, my dear.
Je ne sais quoi	*ma chère amie*	A *je ne sais quoi*, my dear friend.
Joie de vivre	*cher Monsieur*	Zest for life, my dear Sir.
Laissez-faire	*chère Madame*	Let it be, dear Madam.
Ma foi!	*mes amis*	Upon my faith, my friends!
Merci beaucoup	*canaille*	Thank you very much, scoundrel.
Mon Dieu	*mon cher ami*	My God! my dear friend.
N'est-ce pas	*mon cher*	Isn't it, my dear?
Ni l'un ni l'autre	*mon ami*	Neither one, nor the other, my friend.
N'importe	*mon vieux*	It does not matter, old pal.

Loanwords alphabetically	Loanwords about People	English version
Noblesse oblige	*cher Monsieur*	Nobility obliges, dear Sir.
Pardon	*mon petit chou*	Excuse me, my little darling, sweet thing.
Pas du tout	*chère Madame*	Not at all, dear Madam.
Répondez SVP	*ma chère amie*	Answer please, my dear friend.

S

Sans arrière-pensée	*ma chère*	Without ulterior motive, my dear.
Sans blague	*mon cher*	No kidding, my dear.
Sans cérémonie	*mes amis*	Without formality, my friends.
Sans chichi	*mon vieux*	Without *chichi* (*frou-frou*), old chap.
Sans doute	*Mademoiselle*	Without doubt, Miss.
Sans façon	*ma chère amie*	Without ceremony, my dear friend.
Sans-gêne	*Madame!*	Lots of nerve, Madam!

The French will also call such person: *Madame sans-gêne, Monsieur sans-gêne,* etc., as if it were her last name.

Sans panache	*ma mignonne*	Without *panache*, my darling.

Loanwords alphabetically	Loanwords about People	English version
T-V		
Tant mieux	*mes amis*	So much the better, my friends.
Tant pis	*mon frère*	Too bad, brother.
Touché	*mon ami*	Touché, my friend.
Tout à fait	*femme du monde*	Entirely a woman of the world.
Tout à vous	*ma mignonne*	All yours, my darling.
Tout de même	*mes amis*	All the same, my friends!
Tout de suite	*beau garçon*	Right away, good looking.
Tout le monde	*ma chère*	Everybody, my dear.
Très	*distingué cher ami*	Very distinguished, dear friend.
Vive la différence	*mes amis*	*Vive la différence,* my friends.
Voilà	*mon cher*	There it is, my dear.
Voilà tout	*mes chers amis*	Nothing more to say, my dear friends.

CONCLUSION

"A conclusion is simply the place where you got tired of thinking," said Mark Twain. Without any doubt, this great American author had an enduring thinking capacity combined with common sense since, obviously, all things have an end.

Yet, one fact is certain: If *French for Le Snob* must end, French loanwords and expressions will keep on entering the English speech, just as English will keep on enriching the French vocabulary in spite of the French Academy's efforts to prevent such a disgrace! Indeed, new trends in technology, international business, and cultural exchanges will continue to impact communications and interactions globally; the Internet will also continue to affect the way people access or exchange information. Like love, a language has—and will have—no borders.

Evidently, there are more English speakers worldwide than there are French. Nevertheless, English and French are both spoken worldwide. They are both official languages at the United Nations, UNESCO, NATO, at the International Red Cross and Olympic Committee, and in the airlines industry, among other organizations.

If in principle, the Académie française wants to keep English out of the French language, many French people, particularly the young generation, apparently have no problem using English loanwords in their daily activities, *au contraire*, because *c'est très cool*!

French snobs meet on select sidewalk cafés on the splendid Champs-Elysées or the colorful Boulevard Saint Michel. Clad in their bikini *dernier cri*, they saunter along the *très* touristic beaches of La Baule, Deauville, and Saint Tropez and they busily swarm campuses everywhere, proudly showing off their English skills. *C'est super* and *très in*.

While sipping *un Coke*, they discuss *le casting* of *Running Scared*, *un thriller* movie. They exchange views about *un gangster, un western,* or *un cowboy* movie. They talk about *la belle pin-up, les baby-boomers* and *le papy-boom; le pick-up* in *le ranch, le self-serving, le briefing,* and *les body bags, "le deal shit, le shérif of Notthingham* and *la big band de* (of) Duke Ellington." [52] And here you go, Elvis. They are great fans *du rock* over there and not only do they love you and your music, they swoon over Johnny Hallyday, *un rocker formidable. Il est si cool!*[53] *Un sex-symbol, un play-boy!* They shrink from *le spleen* or *le stress* and they love *les talk-shows* that discuss *le lifting* and *le peeling* that can take ten years off your face. *C'est nickel-chrome!* And after *le meeting* on Friday, they wish one another a very *bon weekend*. All that with a charming funny French accent!

We can no longer doubt, if we ever did, that the French are learning English in spite of themselves! Therefore, why not improve one's mother tongue, be bi-literate in the process, be proud of it on both sides of the Atlantic, and be happy to enjoy a hamburger with *pommes frites,* among other things! It seems that the French have acquired a taste for this unhealthy combination anyway. And it shows. Not only are they getting taller, they are a little fatter. Recent studies have established that "although only 11 percent of *la population française est obèse*," the Français are gradually getting bigger all the same and naturally, they blame America and *les Fast Food* restaurants, as they call them. Here and there in France, you can hear hungry people in a hurry say, "Let's go to *le Quick*," a restaurant that serves unhealthy greasy food. They also eat *le lunch* at McDonald's, one of several that has found a home in the land of *gourmets* eaters. What would they say, those "who before us were!"[54] English loanwords and now American food—what's next?

The above expression *c'est nickel-chrome*, whatever that means, is one of today's hip expressions in France, replacing *c'est super*, or *c'est génial*, as they used to say in the old days (last year)! All the misfits who resist innovation because they are stuck in their ways or the space cadets who are not yet quite aware of it, are still using yesterday's words, until they eventually wake up, at which time, the expression may have become obsolete! The expression *c'est nickel* is used in French to mean: it is spotless, very clean. Chrome is a white metal, so what does *c'est nickel-chrome* have to do with its *génial*? Who knows. The French don't know, but this is a good example of how new words become integrated in everyday speech to express a lifestyle, a fad, a generation, or an era. In a decade or so it will appear in French dictionaries because by then it will have acquired a meaning that nobody will question, except perhaps some Frenchman who has been anywhere but France for the last twenty years. Whether we like it not, our language will change and evolve, so we may as well do our best to be *au courant* and fit in. This is not snobbery—or can it be?

"Real knowledge is to know the extent of one's ignorance," declared Confucius. There is no doubt that the more we learn, the more we are likely to realize that we know very little. But it is also true that we always move one step further toward being less ignorant when we learn something new. Therefore, the knowledge acquired with *French for Le Snob* can allow the reader to speak his own language well and to be a more sophisticated snob in the process. Indeed, the book gives him the ammunition to impress his friends, guests, or audiences at the restaurant, parties, art galleries, at the shopping mall, and fashion shows. Some may not appreciate nor care to listen to her bilingual mumble-jumble; on the other hand, most will admire and envy her distinguished Parisian accent when, in a calculated matter-of-fact manner, she uses the French loanwords of the English language they wish they knew and could speak as well as she does.

Those who persist in insisting that snobbism cannot be one of their problems will hopefully recognize some day that the very fact they have the need to belong to a specific group, superior to those they call snobs, qualifies them as perfect snobs as well. Indeed, we may as well accept that we can all be snobs! What varies is to what extent we realize it.

Snobs have common patterns of behavior and instinctively respond alike: they feel and act superior about something they value. Naturally, people's standards and codes of ethics are different. Therefore, snobs of various *cliques*, and diverse groups within each *clique*, tend to be incompatible and may even have contempt for one another. But *ainsi va la vie!* In a way, those who look down on snobs, the other kind, are like Salvador Dali, the famous Spanish painter notorious for his extravagant remarks about himself and who is to have said, "The only difference between me and a mad man is that I am not mad!"

Snob or not, however, we can all agree that, "English is the richest of the world's languages because it has borrowed freely from virtually every other language spoken on the face of the earth."[55] It is true of American English.

Indeed, *Pluribus Unum*—from many, one! We are one society created out of immigrants from everywhere who brought not only their culture but also their language wherever they settled in America. French is one among many.

Ultimately, the purpose of *French for Le Snob* is to make English speakers more aware of the richness of the English language and to allow a better command of its many French loanwords. Evidently, information and knowledge can be used in many ways—to be snobby for instance, where, when, and how it suits one's fancy or purpose. After all, if snobbism is not a laudable quality, it is not a mortal sin either and in the end, the only person it may affect is the snob himself. Indeed, a fanatic snob is by definition a clannish, cliquish, clubby individual. His dream, American or otherwise, is to be part of a S.N.O.B. Club, be it the Snazzy [56]-Nifty [57]-Obnoxiously-Balderdashy [58] type or the Snappy [59]-Nippy [60]-Obnoxiously-Brainy [61] kind, among others. In his eagerness or desperation to be different, or to be included, a snob may have to say *adieu* to uniqueness and *au revoir* to individuality; but everything has a price and what are we to do? We all need to belong! *C'est la vie mes amis!*

BIBLIOGRAPHY

A History of the English Language, fifth edition, Albert C. Baugh & Thomas Cable; Prentice Hall (2002)

Architecture and Art Thesaurus on Line Dictionary, created by J. Paul Getty Trust

Artists and Illustrators Encyclopedia, John Quick; McGraw-Hill, (1969)

Dictionnaire des Difficultés de la Langue Française, Adolphe V. Thomas; Librairie Larousse, Paris (1968)

Dictionary of Classical Ballet Terminology, Rhonda Ryman; Toronto Dance Books Press (June 1, 1998)

Dictionary of Foreign Terms, C. O. Sylvester Mawson, second edition, updated and revised by Charles Berlitz; Thomas Y. Crowell Company, Inc. (1975)

Encyclopedia of Word & Phrase Origins, revised & expanded edition, Robert Hendrickson; New York (1997)

Fairchild's Dictionary of Fashion, Dr. Charlotte Mankey Calasibette; New York Publications (1988)

Grove Dictionary of Art (1996)

Harrap's New Shorter French and English Dictionary (1967)

Le Larousse Gastronomique, Crown, reprint edition (1988)

Le Petit Larousse, Paris (2002)

Le Nouveau Petit Robert Dictionnaire de la Langue Française, Maury Imprimeur, Paris (2004)

Morris Dictionary of Word & Phrase Origins, William and Mary Morris; Harper & Row, New York, NY (1971)

Sturgis Illustrated Dictionary of Architecture and Building, Russell Sturgies et al., Dover Publications, Inc., New York (1989)

The American Heritage Dictionary of the English Language, fourth edition; Houghton Mifflin, Boston; Bartleby.com, New York (2000)

The American Century Dictionary, Warner Books (1995)

The Chambers Dictionary, New Edition, published by Chambers Harrap Publishers Ltd. (1993)

The Concise Oxford Dictionary of English Etymology, Oxford University Press (1996)

The Harper Collins Dictionary of Art Terms & Techniques, second edition, Ralph Mayer (1969)

The Origin & Development of the English Language, third edition, Thomas Pyle, John Algeo; International Thomson Publishing (1982)

The Oxford Dictionary of Foreign Words & Phrases, Edited by Jennifer Speake; Oxford University Press (June 1, 1998)

The Oxford Essential Dictionary of Difficult Words, American Edition, Oxford University Press (2001)

The Oxford Hachette French/English Dictionary, second edition, Oxford University Press (1997)

The Story of the English Language, Dr. Mario Pei; J. B. Lippincott Company, New York (1967)

Webster's New Universal Unabridged Dictionary, second edition

END NOTES

INTRODUCTION

1 Without embarrassment; a disregard of the ordinary forms of civility; See Chapter IV under Expressions with *sans*.

2 Babel is the Hebrew name for Babylon, (the gate of the gods) city, capital of ancient kingdom of Babylonia in Mesopotamia, an ancient country in Western Asia lying between the rivers Euphrates and Tigris.

3 See Chapter IV, *Vie de Bohème* under Short Stories.

4 Denis Diderot, French philosopher (1713–1784) claimed in his novel *Jacques le Fataliste et son maître (Jacques le Fatalist and his Master)* that the human destinies are ALL written up there on *le grand rouleau*, (the big scroll).

5 *The Origins and Development of the English Language* by Thomas Pyles.

CHAPTER I

6 Molière, French author and playwright was the *nom de théâtre* for Jean-Baptiste Poquelin (1622–1673).

7 *Assiette anglaise:* French loanword. See Chapter I under Miscellaneous Words.

8 Loanword meaning in passing. See Chapter IV under Expressions with *en*.

9 *Degustation*, word used in English; from Latin degustary, to taste; a tasting (*Webster's*).

10 *La Dégustation des Vins, un art de vivre en Loire* by French author Jean-Michel Monnier, oenologue.

11   Michel Eyquem de Montaigne (1533–1592), French writer. There is a castle with his name in the town of Saint-Michel-de-Montaigne, in the Dordogne, thirty miles east of Bordeaux, in Southwest France where Montaigne was born.

12   A chacun son goût, French loanword meaning to each his own.

13   Chichi, French loanword meaning affectation, snobbism.

14   Source: The Anthropology Department of California Academy of Sciences, at Golden Gate Park in San Francisco.

15   Marcel Proust (1871–1922), French writer, born in Auteuil, a Paris suburb.

16   Jeanne d'Arc (Joan of Arc), dite La Pucelle d'Orléans (called the Maid of Orléans), heard voices telling her to deliver Orleans, besieged by the English; pucelle is French for virgin.

17   Jim Davis was born in Marion, Indiana in 1945.

18   Jean-Jacques Rousseau, French philosopher, born in Geneva, Switzerland, June 28, 1712. He contended that man was essentially good, "a noble savage," but that an artificial and corrupt society made him bad and unhappy. In 1776, he was run over by a dog, fainted, recovered but died July 2, 1778. His ashes were transferred to the Panthéon in 1794. Le Panthéon is located in the heart of the Latin Quarter in Paris and was built as a church between 1764 and 1790. It was turned into a memorial during the French Revolution (1789). The Panthéon houses the remains of Pierre and Marie Curie, the physicists who discovered radio-activity, as well as Voltaire, and Victor Hugo, among others.

19   Le Roi Soleil (Sun King) is a nickname that Louis XIV inherited because he wanted to shine everywhere by imposing the French presence and power to other countries.

20   Daily newspaper in France; others well-known are Le Monde and Le Canard Enchaîné (the chained duck "The Duck"), a very entertaining satirical, mostly political, newspaper.

21   Runner's World, August 2004.

22   O. Henry, pseudonym for William Sydney Porter, a prolific American short-story writer.

23   Montesquieu, né Charles-Louis de Secondat in 1689 at La Brède, near Bordeaux, became Baron de La Brède and later de Montesquieu. He cultivated 76 acres of wines and wrote his most important work, L'Esprit des Lois, (The Spirit of the Laws), published in 1748; this political and social study attacking despotism in favor of democratic institutions later inspired the Founding Fathers of the United States.

24   Hachis, French loanword meaning hash, Chambers 20th Century Dictionary, Cambridge University Press.

25   Coffee Cantata is also the name of a coffee shop on Meridian Avenue, in Willow Glen, a suburb of San Jose, California, in the Bay Area. The Coffee shop opened in 1996 and people can enjoy Bach's music—on request—as they drink a delicious cup of coffee.

26 Oenology, from *oinos*, Greek for wine, and *logy*, study, knowledge.

27 Source of information *Versailles que j'aime*, by Pierre Gaxotte, de l'Académie française, Jacques Perret, Roger Nimier, and Robert Descharnes, *Editions Sun* in Paris.

28 *Baguette* is French for stick; *ficelle* is French for string; both loanwords are bread names; a *baguette* is long, crusty, thin bread, and a *ficelle* is like a baguette but much thinner.

29 *Le fromage* is very coveted in *Le Corbeau et le Renard* (*The Crow and the Fox*) one of the many fables by Jean de La Fontaine (1621–1695).

30 From *Le Petit Nicolas* by Sempé/Goscinny.

31 *Le Petit Prince* by Antoine de Saint-Exupéry, (1900–1944) French writer and aviator. This French novelist lived a daring life as a military and airmail pilot in Africa and South America. In 1940, he escaped to the United States where he continued to write while organizing the French *résistance* to the German occupation. He disappeared during a mission in 1944. *The Little Prince* is a wonderful story loved by children and grown-ups alike.

32 *Un plateau à fromage* is a cheese tray; *un plateau de fromage* is a tray filled with various cheeses.

33 Source of information about forks, spoons, knives, chopsticks: The Anthropology Department at the California Academy of Sciences, located at the Golden Gate Park in San Francisco.

34 Robin Tunnicliff Reid in *The Columbus Dispatch: USA WEEKEND*, July 16–18, 2004.

35 A bad cook is called a *gâte-sauce* (a sauce spoiler) in France; from *gâter*, (to spoil); *un enfant gâté* is a spoiled child.

CHAPTER II

36 Lyric poets and musician-poets who lived in Provence, Catalonia, Northern Italy in the eleventh, twelfth, and thirteenth centuries.

37 *A Portrait of the Artist as a Young Man* (1916), title of a novel by Irish writer, James Joyce (1882–1941).

38 *Gamin* is used in English to refer to a homeless, neglected, and abandoned child.

39 Southwest Indian tribe living in Central and North-East Arizona.

40 Isaac Asimov, prolific writer, was born in 1920 in Petrovichi in the Soviet Union, moved to New York in 1923, met his wife on a blind date on Valentine's Day in 1942, and divorced her in 1973, but remarried later on. He was afraid of flying and flew only twice in his lifetime. He died in 1992.

---

41 Play by Voltaire (1694–1778) in which Candide the optimist claims, in spite of all his mis-
    fortunes, that *"Tout est pour le mieux dans le meilleur des mondes"* (All is for the best in the best
    of possible worlds). François Marie Arnouet (*nom de plume:* Voltaire) was born November
    21, 1694 in Paris. He was educated at the Jesuit College Louis Le Grand in Paris. He was
    imprisoned for more than one year at La Bastille for writing a satire of the French govern-
    ment. He died in Paris in 1778, at age 83.

CHAPTER III

42 *Persian Letters* were published in 1721 by Charles Louis de Secondat, Baron de Montesquieu
    (1689–1755). He is also the author of *L'Esprit des Lois*.

43 *Un toutou*, child-talk for doggy; it is to be noted that French parents today avoid talking
    baby-talk and prefer to call things by their names and say *un petit chien* (a little dog), rather
    than a *toutou*.

44 French loanword meaning a suit; a costume of matching parts; see Chapter III under
    Clothes.

45 Irish playwright who supported the Rational Dress Movement founded in 1881 to protest
    against the idea that you had to suffer and wear corsets to be beautiful, which in his opinion
    was a lack of common sense.

46 French loanwords meaning a strong-willed, high-powered woman. See Chapter IV under
    About Women.

47 *Digital Insight*, an Infineon Technologies AG publications, Volume 2/2002.

CHAPTER IV

48 Tic tac, (no hyphen) onomatopoeia meaning tick tock, as the clock goes tic tac but a loud
    tic-tac (hyphen).

49 *Fol* is used before a masculine noun beginning with a vowel as in *un fol enfant* (a foolish
    child); *fou* is used with a masculine noun, as in *il est fou* (he is crazy); *un homme fou* (a crazy
    man); *c'est un fou*, (he is a nutcase); *Folle* is used with a feminine noun as in: *elle est folle* (she
    is crazy); *Quelle folle!* (What a nutcase).

50 According to the BBC, the word *pétard* came from Act 3 of *Hamlet*: "For 'tis the sport to have
    the engineer hoist his own petar." Source: Donald A. DePalma, in *Spectrum*, May 2004.

51 *The Columbus Dispatch*, Lifestyle, July 25, 2004.

CONCLUSION

52 From an article in *Le Nouvel Observateur: TéléCiné Obs*; April 23, 2004.

53 *Il est si cool* (he is so cool); the word *si* in French means "so," (adverb: so much) and it also means: *oui* (yes). *Si*, instead of *oui*, is used to answer an interro-negative question, such as: didn't you do it? *Si*, (yes) I did it. Or, didn't you do it? *Si*, I did it.

54 "Where are they, those who before us were"; John Milton (1608–1674).

55 William and Mary Morris, authors of *Morris Dictionary of Word and Phrase Origins*.

56 Snazzy, is French for *tape-à-l'oeil*, literally hit the eye, meaning loud, garish, flashy, stylish.

57 Nifty, is French for *pimpant, coquet, chouette* meaning stylish, smartly dressed. *Une chouette* is French for an owl; the expression *c'est chouette* means it is nice, cool and also nice, as in *elle est vraiment chouette*, she is really nice; however, *une vieille chouette*, literally an old owl, means a disagreeable, wicked woman, an old harridan, a shrew (pej.).

58 Balderdashy, is French for *balivernes, idioties* meaning idiotic, senseless talks.

59 Snappy, is French for *chic, dernier cri*; it is also translated as *vif, plein de sel*, literally, full of salt, meaning witty as *une conversation pleine de sel*, a witty conversation. Indeed, according to French author Anatole France in *La Rôtisserie de la Reine Pédauque*, the offering of salt was a sign of hospitality and it was also considered by ancient people an essential seasoning needed to add taste to food and in metaphor, an ingredient that added wit and spice to conversations.

60 *Nippy*, is French for *alerte, vif, plein de vivacité* (full of vivacity), as in *un esprit alerte* meaning sharp, biting, sarcastic, witty.

61 *Brainy*, is French for intelligent.

PRONUNCIATION GLOSSARY

～∾⌒∾～

GLOSSARY OF FRENCH LOANWORDS

The IPA (International Phonetic Alphabet) is featured to illustrate the standard French pronunciation of the French Loanwords used in *French for Le Snob*.

English speakers who wish to pronounce the French loanwords of the English vocabulary *à la française* need to learn the sound of the phonetic symbols listed in the chart below, just as a French speaker must learn how the phonetic signs of the English language sound if he wants to speak the English loanwords of the French vocabulary *à l'anglaise*. Learning phonetic sounds is acquired through repetition, and like any skill one wants to master, it becomes easier and easier with practice.

Some French sounds do not exist in English, which explains why English speakers have difficulty pronouncing some French sounds, as for instance the 'u' in loanwords such as *déjà-vu, cul-de-sac,* or the 'ui' sound as in *cuisine* etc. See *How to pronounce French 'u.'*

In the chart below, the IPA symbols are listed in the first column and used in the fourth column in some well-known French loanwords that most English speakers can pronounce *à la française*. When possible, the English sound and a few English words in columns two and three illustrate as accurately as possible how these phonetic symbols sound in English.

IPA symbols	English sound	English words	Loanwords
FRENCH VOWELS			
i	Ee	s<u>ee</u>, b<u>ee</u>, w<u>ee</u>d	*prix f<u>i</u>xe, après sk<u>i</u>, apér<u>i</u>t<u>i</u>f*
e	á	f<u>a</u>te, d<u>a</u>te, c<u>a</u>pe	*ch<u>e</u>z, caf<u>é</u>, déjeun<u>e</u>r, <u>é</u>lite*
ɛ	ay	b<u>ay</u>, p<u>ay</u>, h<u>ey</u>, p<u>e</u>t	*f<u>ê</u>te, m<u>e</u>rci, p<u>è</u>re, café, au l<u>ai</u>t*
a	ah (short 'a' sound) see note: long & short 'a'	c<u>a</u>lm, c<u>a</u>r	*Champ<u>a</u>gne, <u>a</u>mi, aub<u>a</u>de*
ɑ	ah (long 'a' sound)	l<u>au</u>gh,	*p<u>â</u>té, ch<u>â</u>teau, mac<u>a</u>bre*
ɔ	aw	b<u>o</u>rn, l<u>aw</u>n, s<u>aw</u>	*B<u>o</u>rdeaux, cons<u>o</u>le*
o	ō	d<u>ou</u>gh, b<u>o</u>ne	*plat<u>eau</u>, chap<u>eau</u>, b<u>eau</u>, f<u>aux</u> pas*
u	oo	c<u>oo</u>k, t<u>oo</u>l	*p<u>ou</u>f, cr<u>oû</u>te, fr<u>ou</u>fr<u>ou</u>*
y	ü (as in German üder) Note: How to pronounce French 'u'		*coiff<u>u</u>re, déjà-v<u>u</u>*

IPA symbols	English sound	English words	Loanwords
ø	ö		_jeu, pas de deux_
œ		b<u>ur</u>n, l<u>ear</u>n, b<u>ir</u>d	_chauffeur, hors-d'oeuvre_
ə		th<u>e</u>	_premier, meringue, cerise, chenille_ (the final 'e' is silent)
ɛ̃	ăn (n)		_vin, gratin, terrain_
ɑ̃	än (n)		_sans, blanc, enfantillage_
ɔ̃	ŏn (n) (n) do not pronounce the final 'n'		_bonbon, pompon Pompadour, garçon_
œ̃		l<u>un</u>ch, l<u>un</u>g	_chacun son gout_
SEMI-CONSONANTS			
j		<u>y</u>et, mi<u>lli</u>on, <u>y</u>es	_fille, pied-à-terre_
w		<u>w</u>e, <u>w</u>ash	_oui, fille de joie, voilà, coiffure, flamboyant_
ɥ	[y + i] (French 'u' + ee sound: ui)		_cuisine, étui, tout de suite_
CONSONANTS			
p		<u>p</u>o<u>p</u>e	_père_
t		<u>t</u>ab	_très, theater_
k		<u>c</u>ot, <u>k</u>iss, <u>ch</u>ord	_corsage, képi_ See: How to pronounce 'c' + vowels
b		<u>b</u>i<u>b</u>	_baguette_

IPA symbols	English sound	English words	Loanwords
d		<u>d</u>og	<u>d</u>écor
g		<u>g</u>o	<u>g</u>ourmet, ba<u>g</u>uette
f		<u>f</u>ool	<u>f</u>arceur
s		<u>s</u>it, ri<u>c</u>e	mer<u>c</u>i, comme <u>ç</u>a, ta<u>ss</u>e See: how to pronounce c & ç + vowels
ʃ		<u>sh</u>ip, <u>s</u>ugar	<u>ch</u>aussure, <u>ch</u>ef, <u>ch</u>ic, <u>ch</u>i<u>ch</u>i
z		bu<u>zz</u>	ro<u>s</u>e, mai<u>s</u>on (one 's' between 2 vowels sounds 'z')
l		sa<u>l</u>e	<u>l</u>amé, so<u>l</u>
m		ra<u>m</u>, ru<u>m</u>	<u>m</u>aison, pantо<u>m</u>i<u>m</u>e
n		<u>n</u>ut, <u>n</u>o	<u>n</u>oix, <u>n</u>égligé
ʒ		mea<u>s</u>ure, vi<u>s</u>ion	<u>g</u>ilet, je ne sais quoi, <u>j</u>abot, <u>g</u>igue
v		ri<u>v</u>er	c'est la <u>v</u>ie
ʀ		<u>r</u>un	<u>r</u>obe
ɲ		can<u>y</u>on	filet mi<u>gn</u>on, ma<u>gn</u>ifique
'	See note: under Liaison		

NOTES

HOW TO PRONOUNCE THE FRENCH 'U' Place the tip of the tongue behind your lower teeth; pout as if you were to kiss somebody and utter the perfect French 'u' sound.

LIAISON When the symbol ['] precedes the phonetic signs, it indicates that there is no liaison between two words, as for instance: / le 'ero / *les héros*, but / lezabi / *les habits* (the 'h' of habits is silent and one 's' between vowels '/a/' & /i/ sounds 'z')

LONG & SHORT 'A' SOUND The long 'a' in *pâté* and the short 'a' in *pas de deux* are respectively represented by the phonetic symbols [ɑ] and [a], although some French speakers do not make a real distinction between the two. However, when a French word can be pronounced with either 'a' sound, it is indicated as follows: *à bas* / abạ, abɑ / or, / abạ(ɑ) /

PHONETIC SOUND (ə) IN PARENTHESES: ALTERNATIVE PRONUNCIATION When a word can be pronounced in two different manners it is indicated as follows:

A *cheval* / aʃəval, aʃ(ə)val /; the two pronunciations are separated by a comma and in the second option, the phonetic sound (ə) in parentheses indicate that the 'e' of *cheval* is not pronounced and that the 'ch': / ʃ / sound (as in s͟hoe) is directly linked to 'val': (ch-val)

CONSONANTS IN PARENTHESES: PRONUNCIATION When the same consonant is repeated between parentheses as in:

/ pɑt(t)ãdʀ / (*patte tendre*) or / puʀ(ʀ)ir / (*pour rire*) it indicates that this consonant is sounded twice as for instance: / puʀ-ʀiʀ /. If the phonetic were to be shown as / puʀiʀ /, (with only one / ʀ /), the French word would be "pourir," which means to rot.

HOW TO PRONOUNCE 'C' & 'Ç' FOLLOWED BY VOWELS c + a, o, u: ca, co, cu is pronounced: ka, ko, ku, as in *café, coquillage, culotte.*

c + e, i, y: is pronounced: se, si, sy, as in *cela, ici, cygne* (swan).

ç + a, o, u, ça ço çu is pronounced: sa, so, su, as in ça (sa) va bien, *garçon, aperçu.*

HOW TO PRONOUNCE PHONETIC SYMBOL / ɛ / When a phonetic word ends by / ɛ /, it is pronounced 'ay' as in b<u>ay</u>, p<u>ay</u>. For instance / bal<u>ɛ</u> / is pronounced as bal<u>ay</u> (ballet) but when the symbol / ɛ / is followed by a consonant, one must pronounce the final consonant, for example: / f<u>ɛ</u>t/ (*féte*), / fuʀʃɛt / (*fourchette*), as in the word p<u>ɛ</u>t in English. The same applies to other phonetic symbols as in for instance:

gourmand (masculin) / guʀmã / in which the final 'd' *gourmand* is not pronounced but *gourmande* (feminin)/gurmãd/ in which the final consonant (d) is pronounced, or in *blanc* / blã /, in which the final 'c' of *blanc* is not pronounced.

EXTRA "E" IN PARENTHESES When a word is followed by (e) as in *divorcé (e)*, it indicates masculine and feminine, and the pronunciation is the same.

"F" IN CHEF Pronounce the "f" in *chef d'orchestre*, as in *chef de restaurant*. Do not pronounce the "f" in *Chef-d'oeuvre*.

A

A bas	aba, abɑ	A l'époque	alepɔk
A bientôt	abjẽto	A l'improviste	alẽpʀɔvist
A bon droit	abɔ̃dʀwa	A l'indienne	alẽdjen
A bon marché	abɔ̃maʀʃe	A la belle étoile	alabeletwal
A bras ouverts	abʀazuvɛʀ	A la bonne femme	alabɔnfam
A cheval	aʃəval, aʃ(ə)val	A la bonne heure	alabɔnœʀ
A contrecœur	akɔ̃tʀʀəkœʀ	A la bordelaise	alabɔʀdəlez
A corps perdu	akɔʀpeʀdy	A la boulangère	alabulɑ̃ʒɛʀ
A coup sûr	akusyʀ	A la bourgeoise	alabuʀʒwaz
A couvert	akuvɛʀ	A la bourguignonne	alabuʀɡiɲɔn
A demi	adəmi, ad(ə)mi	A la bretonne	alabʀətɔn
A deux	adø	A la broche	alabʀɔʃ
A deux crayons	adøkʀɛjɔ̃	A la brochette	alabʀɔʃet
A discrétion	adiskʀesjɔ̃	A la campagne	alakɑ̃paɲ
A droite	adʀwat	A la carte	alakaʀt(ə)
A fond	afɔ̃	A la crapaudine	alakʀapodin
A gauche	aɡoʃ	A la créole	alakʀeɔl
A genoux	aʒənu, aʒ(ə)nu	A la dérobée	aladeʀɔbe
A gogo	aɡoɡo	A la diable	aladjabl
A grand frais	aɡʀɑ̃fʀɛ	A la Florentine	alaflɔʀɑ̃tin
A haute voix	a'otvwa	A la fourchette	alafuʀʃet
A huis clos	aɥiklo	A la française	ulafʀɑ̃sez
A jamais	aʒame	A la grand-mère	alaɡʀɑ̃mɛʀ
A l'abri	alabʀi	A la grecque	alaɡʀek
A l'alsacienne	alalzasjen	A la hollandaise	ala'ɔlɑ̃dez
A l'américaine	alameriken	A la japonaise	alaʒapɔnez
A l'ancienne	alɑ̃sjen	A la jardinière	alaʒaʀdinjeʀ
A l'anglaise	alɑ̃ɡlez	A la julienne	alaʒyljen
		A la letter	alaletʀ(ə)

A la limousine	ɑlalimuzin	A toute force	ɑtutfɔʀs(ə)
A la lorraine	ɑlalɔʀɛn	A travers	ɑtʀavɛʀ
A la lyonnaise	ɑlaliɔnez	A vol d'oiseau	ɑvɔldwazo
A la madrilène	ɑlamadʀilɛn	A votre santé	ɑvɔtʀ(ə)sɑ̃te
A la maître d'hôtel	ɑlamɛtʀ(ə)dɔtɛl	Abat-jour	abaʒuʀ
A la marinière	ɑlamaʀinjɛʀ	Abonné	abɔne
A la milanaise	ɑlamilanez	Abrégé	abʀeʒe
A la mode	ɑlamɔd	Accolade	akɔlad
A la mode de Caen	ɑlamɔd(d)əkɑ̃	Accord	akɔʀ
A la niçoise	ɑlaniswaz	Accoucheur	akuʃœʀ
A la page	ɑlapaʒ	Accoucheuse	akuʃøz
A la provençale	ɑlapʀɔvɑ̃sal	Accoutrement	akutʀəmɑ̃
A la reine	ɑlaʀɛn	Acte gratuit	akt(ə)gʀatɥi
A loisir	ɑlwaziʀ	Adieu	adjø
A merveille	ɑmɛʀvej	Adroit	adʀwa
A moi	ɑmwa	Affaire	afɛʀ
A moitié	ɑmwatje	Affaire d'amour	afɛʀdamuʀ
A mon avis	ɑmɔ̃avi	Affaire d'honneur	afɛʀdɔnœʀ
A peu près	ɑpøpʀɛ	Affaire de coeur	afɛʀdəkœʀ
A pied	ɑpje	Agent provovateur	aʒɑ̃pʀɔvɔkatœʀ
A point	ɑpwɛ̃	Agile	aʒil
A propos	ɑpʀɔpo	Aide-de-camp	ɛd(d)əkɑ̃
A propos de rien	ɑpʀɔpod(ə)ʀjɛ̃	Aide-mémoire	ɛdmemwaʀ
A quoi bon	ɑkwabɔ̃	Aigrette	ɛgʀɛt
A ravir	ɑʀaviʀ	Aiguille	egɥij
A rebours	ɑʀ(ə)buʀ	Ainsi va la vie	ɛ̃sivalavi
A tort et à travers	ɑtɔʀeatʀavɛʀ	Alcôve	alkov
A tout hasard	ɑtu'azaʀ	Allée	ale
A tout prix	ɑtupʀi	Allez-vous en	alevuzɑ̃

Alliance	aljɑ̃s	Argot	aʀgo
Allongé	alɔ̃ʒe	Armature	aʀmatyʀ
Allons	alɔ̃	Armoire	aʀmwaʀ
Allumette	alymɛt	Arrêt	aʀɛ
Allure	alyʀ	Arrière-pensée	aʀjɛʀpɑ̃se
Alsace	alzas	Arrière-voussure	aʀjɛʀvusyʀ
Amateur	amatœʀ	Arriviste	aʀivist(ə)
Ambiance	ɑ̃bjɑ̃s	Arrogance	aʀɔgɑ̃s
Amour	amuʀ	Art baroque	aʀbaʀɔk
Amour courtois	amuʀkuʀtwa	Art brut	aʀbʀyt
Amour-propre	amuʀpʀɔpʀ(ə)	Art déco	aʀdeko
Amuse-geule	amyzgœl	Art nouveau	aʀnuvo
Ananas	anana(s)	Art rupestre	aʀ(ʀ)ypɛstʀ
Andouille	ɑ̃duj	Art sacré	aʀsakʀe
Andouillette	ɑ̃dujɛt	Artisan	aʀtizɑ̃
Anecdote	anɛkdɔt	Assassin	asasɛ̃
Animé	anime	Assemblage	asɑ̃blaʒ
Aperçu	apɛʀsy	Assiette	asjɛt
Apéritif	apeʀitif	Atelier	atəlje
Applique, appliqué	aplik, aplike	Attaché	ataʃe
Après nous le déluge	apʀɛnul(ə)delyʒ	Attitude	atityd
Après-coup	apʀɛku	Au bleu	oblø
Après-ski	apʀɛski	Au contraire	okɔ̃tʀɛʀ
Aquarelle	akwaʀɛl	Au courant	okuʀɑ̃
Arabesque	aʀabɛsk(ə)	Au désespoir	odezɛspwaʀ
Arc brisé	aʀkbʀize	Au fait	ofɛ, ofɛt
Arcade	aʀkad	Au fond	ofɔ̃
Arc-boutant	aʀkbutɑ̃	Au fromage	ofʀɔmaʒ
Architrave	aʀʃitrav	Au gratin	ogʀatɛ̃

Au jour le jour	oʒuRləʒuR	Badinage	badinaʒ
Au jus	oʒy	Badineur	badinœR
Au lait	olɛ	Bagatelle	bagatɛl
Au mieux	omjø	Bague	bag
Au naturel	onatyRɛl	Baguette	bagɛt
Au pair	opɛR	Bahut	bay
Au pied de la lettre	opjed(ə)laletR(ə)	Bal costumé	balkɔstyme
Au premier	opRəmje	Bal masqué	balmaske
Au reste	oRɛst(ə)	Balancé	balɑ̃se
Au revoir	oR(ə)vwaR	Balcon	balkɔ̃
Au second	osəgɔ̃, os(ə)gɔ̃	Ballade	balad
Au secours	osəkuR	Ballet	balɛ
Au sérieux	oseRjø	Ballet russe	balɛRys
Aubade	obad	Ballonné	balɔne
Auberge	obɛRʒ	Balustrade	balystRad
Aubergine	obɛRʒin	Banal	banal
Aussitôt dit aussitôt fait	ositodiositofɛ	Bandeau	bɑ̃do
Auteur	otœR	Bandelette	bɑ̃dlɛt
Autrefois	otRəfwa	Banderole	bɑ̃d(ə)Rɔl
Avalanche	avalɑ̃ʃ	Banquet	bɑ̃kɛ
Avant-garde	avɑ̃gaRd(ə)	Banquette	bɑ̃kɛt
Avec plaisir	avɛkpleziR	Banquette de croisée	bɑ̃kɛtdəkRwaze
Avec votre permission	avɛkvɔtRəpɛRmisjɔ̃	Baragouin	baRagwɛ̃
Avenue	avəny, av(ə)ny	Barège	baRɛʒ
Azure	azyR	Baron	baRɔ̃
		Baronnet	ba(ɑ)Rɔnɛ
B		Barrage	ba(ɑ)Raʒ
Baba au rhum	babaoRɔm	Barre	ba(ɑ)R
Babouche	babuʃ	Barrette	baRɛt

Bas-bleu	bablø	Belle époque	belepɔk
Bascule	baskyl	Belles-lettres	bel(l)etr(ə)
Bas-de-page	bad(ə)paʒ	Belvédère	belvedɛʀ
Basque	bask(ə)	Bénédictine	benediktin
Basquine	baskin	Bénitier	benitje
Bas-relief	baʀəljɛf	Berceuse	bɛʀsøz
Bateau	bato	Béret	bɛʀɛ
Batiste	batist(ə)	Béret basque	beʀebask(ə)
Bâton	batɔ̃	Bergère	bɛʀʒɛʀ
Battement	batmɑ̃	Bête noire	betnwaʀ
Bavardage	bavaʀdaʒ	Bêtise	betiz
Bavaroise	bavaʀwaz	Béton	betɔ̃
Bavolet	bavɔlɛ	Beurre noir	bœʀnwaʀ
Béarnaise	beaʀnɛz	Bévue	bevy
Beau	bo	Bibelot	biblo
Beau garçon	bogaʀsɔ̃	Bibi	bibi
Beau geste	boʒɛst(ə)	Bibliothèque	bibliɔtek
Beau idéal	boideal	Bicorne	bikɔʀn(ə)
Beau monde	bomɔ̃d	Bidet	bidɛ
Beaujolais	boʒɔlɛ	Bien entendu	bjɛ̃nɑ̃tɑ̃dy
Beaujolais	boʒɔlenuvo	Bien-être	bjɛ̃netʀ(ə)
Beauté du diable	botedydjabl(ə)	Bien-pensant	bjɛ̃pɑ̃sɑ̃
Beaux-arts	bozaʀ	Bienséance	bjɛ̃seɑ̃s
Bébé bonnet	bebebɔnɛ	Bienvenue	bjɛ̃vəny
Béchamel	beʃamɛl	Bigarreau	bigaro
Béguin	begɛ̃	Bijou	biʒu
Beige	bɛʒ	Bijouterie	biʒutʀi
Beignet	bɛɲɛ	Bikini	bikini
Bel esprit	belɛspʀi	Billet doux	bijedu

Bisque	bisk	*Bon vivant*	bõvivã
Bistre	bistʀ(ə)	*Bon viveur*	bõvivœʀ
Bistro	bistʀo	*Bon voyage*	bõvwajaʒ(ə)
Bizarre	bizaʀ	*Bonbon*	bõbõ
Blague	blag	*Bonbonnière*	bõbɔnjɛʀ
Blagueur	blagœʀ	*Bonheur-du-jour*	bɔnœʀdyʒuʀ
Blanc de blancs	blãdəblã	*Bonjour*	bõʒuʀ
Blanc de perle	blãd(ə)pɛʀl(ə)	*Bonne*	bɔn
Blanquette	blãkɛt	*Bonne amie*	bɔnami
Blasé	blaze	*Bonne chance*	bɔnʃãs
Bleu ciel	bløsjɛl	*Bonnet*	bɔnɛ
Blocage	blɔkaʒ	*Bonnet babet*	bɔnɛbabɛt
Blond	blõ	*Bonnet de nuit*	bɔnɛdnɥi
Blouson	bluzõ	*Bonnet rouge*	bɔnɛʀuʒ
Boeuf bourguignon	bœfbuʀgiɲõ	*Bonnetière*	bɔn(ə)tjɛʀ
Bois de rose	bwa(ɑ)d(ə)ʀoz	*Bonsoir*	bõswaʀ
Boiserie	bwa(ɑ)zʀi	*Bordeaux*	bɔʀdo
Boîte	bwat	*Bordel*	bɔʀdɛl
Boîte de nuit	bwatdənɥi	*Borné*	bɔʀne
Bombe	bõb	*Bossage*	bɔsaʒ
Bombé	bõbe	*Bottine*	bɔtin
Bon	bõ	*Bouchée*	buʃe
Bon appétit	bɔnapeti	*Bouclé*	bukle
Bon diable	bõdjabl(ə)	*Bouderie*	budʀi
Bon enfant	bɔnãfã	*Boudeuse*	budøz
Bon gré, mal gré	bõgʀe malgʀe	*Boudoir*	budwaʀ
Bon marché	bõmaʀʃe	*Bouffant*	bufã
Bon mot	bõmo	*Bouffe*	buf
Bon ton	bõtõ	*Bougie*	buʒi

Bouillabaisse	bujabɛs	Brie	bʀi
Bouillon	bujɔ̃	Brigadier	bʀigadje
Bouillon cube	bujɔ̃kyb	Brigand	bʀigɑ̃
Bouillonné	bujɔne	Brillantine	bʀijɑ̃tin
Boulevard	bulvaʀ	Brioche	bʀijɔʃ
Boulevardier	bulvaʀdje	Briquette	bʀikɛt
Bouleversement	bulvɛʀsəmɑ̃	Brise-soleil	bʀizsɔlej
Bouquet	bukɛ	Brocatelle	bʀɔkatɛl
Bouquet garni	bukɛgaʀni	Broché	bʀɔʃe
Bourg	buʀ	Brochette	bʀɔʃɛt
Bourgade	buʀgad	Brochure	bʀɔʃyʀ
Bourgeois	buʀʒwa	Bronze	bʀɔ̃z
Bourgeoise	buʀʒwaz	Brouhaha	bʀuaa
Bourgeoisie	buʀʒwasi	Bruit	bʀɥi
Bourrée	buʀe	Brunet	bʀynɛ
Bourse	buʀs(ə)	Brunette	bʀynet
Boutade	butad	Brusque	bʀysk
Boutique	butik	Brut	bʀyt
Boutonnière	butɔnjɛʀ	Bruyère	bʀyjɛʀ
Bouts-rimés	burime	Bûche de Noël	byʃdənɔel
Bracelet	bʀaslɛ	Buffet	byfɛ
Braille	bʀɑj	Bulletin	byltɛ̃
Braisé	bʀɛze	Bureau	byʀo
Branché	bʀɑ̃ʃe	Bureau de change	byʀod(ə)ʃɑ̃ʒ
Brassière	bʀasjɛʀ	Burlesque	byʀlesk
Breloque	bʀəlɔk	Burnous	byʀnu
Bric-à-brac	bʀikabʀak	Bustier	bystje
Bricolage	bʀikɔlaʒ		
Bricoleur	bʀikɔlœʀ		

C

C'est-à-dire	sɛtadiʀ	Caille	kaj
C'est autre chose	sɛtotʀəʃoz	Caisson	kɛsɔ̃
C'est la guerre	sɛlagɛʀ	Calotte	kalɔt
C'est la vie	sɛlavi	Calvados	kalvados
C'est magnifique	səmaɲifik	Camaïeu	kamajø
C'est selon	sɛsəlɔ̃, sɛs(ə)lɔ̃	Camaraderie	kamaʀadri
Ça et là	saela	Cambré	kɑ̃bre
Cabaret	kabaʀɛ	Camembert	kamɑ̃bɛʀ
Cabaret service	kabaʀɛsɛʀvis	Camisole	kamizɔl
Cabas	kabɑ	Camouflage	kamuflaʒ
Cabinet	kabinɛ	Camoufleur	kamuflœʀ
Cabochon	kabɔʃɔ̃	Canaille	kanaj
Cabriole	kabʀijɔl	Canapé	kanape
Cabriolet	kabrijɔlɛ	Canard	kanaʀ
Cabriolet bonnet	kabrijɔlebɔnɛ	Cancan	kɑ̃kɑ̃
Cache	kaʃ	Canezou	kan(ə)zu
Cache-chignon	kaʃ(ʃ)iɲɔ̃	Cannelure	kan(ə)lyʀ
Cache-nez	kaʃne	Canotier	kanɔtje
Cache-pot	kaʃpo	Capeline	kaplin
Cachet	kaʃɛ	Capitonné	kapitɔne
Cadeau	kado	Capote	kapɔt
Café	kafe	Caprice	kapʀis
Café au lait	kafeolɛ	Capuche	kapyʃ
Café crème	kafekʀɛm	Capuchon	kapyʃɔ̃
Café liégeois	kafeljeʒwa	Capucin	kapysɛ̃
Café noir	kafenwaʀ	Caqueteuse	kaktøz
Cafetière	kaftjɛʀ	Caraco	kaʀako
Cahier	kaje	Carafe	kaʀaf
		Caricature	kaʀikatyʀ

Carillon	kaʀijɔ̃	Châlet	ʃalɛ
Carillonneur	kaʀijɔnœʀ	Chalumeau	ʃalymo
Carnage	kaʀnaʒ	Chambranle	ʃɑ̃bʀɑ̃l
Carrefour	kaʀfuʀ	Chambré	ʃɑ̃bʀe
Carrelage	kaʀlaʒ	Chamois	ʃamwa
Carte blanche	kaʀtəblɑ̃ʃ	Champagne	ʃɑ̃paɲ
Carte d'identité	kaʀtididɑ̃tite	Champêtre	ʃɑ̃pɛtʀ
Carte des vins	kaʀtdevɛ̃	Champignon	ʃɑ̃piɲɔ̃
Carte du pays	kaʀtədypei	Champlevé	ʃɑ̃ləve
Carte-de-visite	kaʀtəvizit	Chandelier	ʃɑ̃dəlje
Carton-pierre	kaʀtɔ̃pjeʀ	Chanson	ʃɑ̃sɔ̃
Cartouche	kaʀtuʃ	Chanson de geste	ʃɑ̃sɔ̃d(ə)ʒɛst
Casque	kask	Chansonnette	ʃɑ̃sɔnet
Casse-tête	kastɛt	Chansonnier	ʃɑ̃sɔnje
Cassis	kasis	Chantage	ʃɑ̃taʒ
Catalogue	katalɔg	Chanterelle	ʃɑ̃tʀel
Cause célèbre	kozselɛbʀ	Chanteur	ʃɑ̃tœʀ
Causerie	kozʀi	Chanteuse	ʃɑ̃tøz
Causeuse	kozøz	Chantier	ʃɑ̃tje
Cavalier	kavalje	Chapeau	ʃapo
Ceinture	sɛ̃tyʀ	Chapeau breton	ʃapobʀətɔ̃
Cela va sans dire	səlavasɑ̃diʀ	Chapeau claque	ʃapoklak
Cendré	sɑ̃dʀe	Chapeau cloche	ʃapoklɔʃ
Cerise	səʀiz, s(ə)ʀiz	Chaperon	ʃap(ə)ʀɔ̃
Chablis	ʃabli	Charade	ʃaʀad
Chacun son goût	ʃakœ̃sɔ̃gu	Charcuterie	ʃaʀkytʀi
Chagrin	ʃagʀɛ̃	Chargé d'affaires	ʃaʀʒedafɛʀ
Chaise longue	ʃɛzlɔ̃g	Charivari	ʃaʀivaʀi
Chaise percée	ʃɛzpɛʀse	Charlatan	ʃaʀlatɑ̃

Charlotte	ʃaʀlɔt	Cherchez la femme	ʃɛʀʃelafam
Charlotte russe	ʃaʀlɔtʀys	Chère amie	ʃɛʀami
Charme	ʃaʀm	Chevalier	ʃəvalje, ʃ(ə)valje
Charmeuse	ʃaʀmøz	Chevelure	ʃəv(ə)lyʀ
Chartreuse	ʃaʀtʀøz	Chèvres	ʃevʀ
Chassé	ʃase	Chevron	ʃəvʀɔ̃
Chassé-croisé	ʃasekʀwaze	Chez	ʃe
Chasselas	ʃasla	Chic	ʃik
Chasseur	ʃasœʀ	Chichi	ʃiʃi
Chasuble	ʃazybl(ə)	Chiffon	ʃifɔ̃
Château	ʃato	Chiffonnade	ʃifɔnad
Château d'eau	ʃatodo	Chiffonnier	ʃifɔnje
Chateaubriand	ʃatobʀijɑ̃	Chiffons	ʃifɔ̃
Châteauneuf-du-Pape	ʃatonœfdypap	Chignon	ʃiɲɔ̃
Châtelaine	ʃat(ə)lɛn	Chiné	ʃine
Chaud-froid	ʃofʀwa	Chinois	ʃinwa
Chauffeur	ʃofœʀ	Chinoiserie	ʃinwazʀi
Chauffeuse	ʃoføz	Chocolatier	ʃɔkɔlatje
Chaussure	ʃosyʀ	Chose	ʃoz
Chef	ʃef	Chou	ʃu
Chef d'orchestre	ʃefdɔʀkɛstʀ	Choucroute	ʃukʀut
Chef-d'oeuvre	ʃedœvʀ	Ci-gît	siʒi
Chemin de fer	ʃ(ə)mɛ̃d(ə)fɛʀ	Ciré	siʀe
Chemise	ʃəmiz, ʃ(ə)miz	Ciseaux	sizo
Chemise à jabot	ʃ(ə)mizaʒabo	Ciselé	siz(ə)le
Chemise-culottes	ʃ(ə)mizkylɔt	Ciseleur	siz(ə)lœʀ
Chemisette	ʃ(ə)mizɛt	Ciselure	siz(ə)lyʀ
Chenille	ʃənij, ʃ(ə)nij	Citron	sitʀɔ̃
Cher maître	ʃɛʀmɛtʀ	Civet	sivɛ

Clair de lune	klɛʀdəlyn	Comédie noire	kɔmedinwaʀ
Clairvoyant	klɛʀvwajɑ̃	Comme ci comme ça	kɔmsikɔmsa
Claque	klak	Comme if faut	kɔmilfo
Claqueur	klakœʀ	Commode	kɔmɔd
Clavier	klavje	Communiqué	kɔmynike
Cliché	kliʃe	Compagnon de voyage	kɔ̃paɲɔ̃d(ə)vwaja3
Clientèle	klijɑ̃tɛl	Compère	kɔ̃pɛʀ
Clique	klik	Compote	kɔ̃pɔt
Cloche	klɔʃ	Compotier	kɔ̃pɔtje
Clocher	klɔʃe	Concierge	kɔ̃sjɛʀ3
Cloisonné	klwazɔne	Conciergerie	kɔ̃sjɛʀ3əʀi
Cloqué	klɔke	Concubine	kɔ̃kybin
Clos-Vougeot	klovu3o	Conduit	kɔ̃dɥi
Cocotte	kɔkɔt	Conférence	kɔ̃feʀɑ̃s
Coffre	kɔfʀ	Conférencier	kɔ̃feʀɑ̃sje
Coffret	kɔfʀɛ	Confident	kɔ̃fidɑ̃
Cognac	kɔɲak	Confidente	kɔ̃fidɑ̃t
Cohue	kɔy	Confiture	kɔ̃fityʀ
Coiffeur	kwafœʀ	Confiturier	kɔ̃fityʀje
Coiffeuse	kwaføz	Confrère	kɔ̃fʀɛʀ
Coiffure	kwafyʀ	Connaisseur	kɔnesœʀ
Cointreau	kwɛ̃tʀo	Conseil d'état	kɔ̃sejdeta
Col en V	kɔlɑ̃ve	Conservatoire	kɔ̃sɛʀvatwar
Col rabattu	kɔlʀabaty	Console	kɔ̃sɔl
Collage	kɔla3	Consommé	kɔ̃sɔme
Colombier	kɔlɔ̃bje	Conte	kɔ̃t
Colonnade	kɔlɔnad	Conteur	kɔ̃tœʀ
Colporteur	kɔlpɔʀtœʀ	Contour	kɔ̃tuʀ
Comédie humaine	kɔmediymɛn	Contredanse	kɔ̃tʀədɑ̃s

Contretemps	kɔ̃tʀətɑ̃	Costume	kɔstym
Conversation	kɔ̃vɛʀsasjɔ̃	Costumier	kɔstymje
Coq au vin	kɔkovɛ̃	Côtes du Rhône	kotdyʀon
Coque	kɔk	Cotillon	kɔtijɔ̃
Coquelicot	kɔkliko	Cotte	kɔt
Coquet	kɔkɛ	Coulée	kule
Coquette	kɔkɛt	Couleur	kulœʀ
Coquillage	kɔkijaʒ	Coulisse	kulis
Coquille St. Jacques	kɔkijsɛ̃ʒak	Couloir	kulwaʀ
Cor anglais	kɔʀɑ̃glɛ	Coup d'état	kudeta
Cor d'harmonie	kɔʀdaʀmɔni	Coup d'oeil	kudœj
Cor de chasse	kɔʀdəʃas	Coup de grâce	kud(ə)gʀas
Corbeau	kɔʀbo	Coup de main	kud(ə)mɛ̃
Corbeille	kɔʀbɛj	Coup de pied	kud(ə)pje
Cordage	kɔʀdaʒ	Coup de soleil	kud(ə)sɔlej
Cordon	kɔʀdɔ̃	Coup de théâtre	kud(ə)teɑtr
Cordon bleu	kɔʀdɔ̃blø	Coupé	kupe
Cornemuse	kɔʀnəmyz	Coupe-coupe	kupkup
Cornet à pistons	kɔʀnɛɑpistɔ̃	Cour d'honneur	kuʀdɔnœʀ
Cornichon	kɔʀniʃɔ̃	Courage	kuʀaʒ
Corps	kɔʀ	Courrier	kuʀje
Corps à corps	kɔʀakɔʀ	Court-bouillon	kuʀbujɔ̃
Corps de ballet	kɔʀdəbalɛ	Coussinet	kusinɛ
Corps de garde	kɔʀdəgard	Coûte que coûte	kutkəkut
Corridor	kɔʀidɔʀ	Coutil	kuti
Corsage	kɔʀsaʒ	Couture	kutyʀ
Corselet	kɔʀsəlɛ	Couturier	kutyʀje
Corset	kɔʀsɛ	Couvre-chef	kuvʀəʃɛf
Cortège	kɔʀtɛʒ	Crapaud	kʀapo

Crapaudine	kʀapodin	Crottin	kʀɔtẽ
Crèche d'art	kʀɛʃdaʀ	Croupier	kʀupje
Crédence	kʀedɑ̃s	Croustade	kʀustad
Crème anglaise	kʀɛmɑ̃glɛz	Croûte	kʀut
Crème au caramel	kʀɛmokaʀamɛl	Croûton	kʀutɔ̃
Crème brûlée	kʀɛmbʀyle	Crudités	kʀydite
Crème Chantilly	kʀɛmʃɑ̃tiji	Cuisine	kɥizin
Crème de cacao	kʀɛmdəkakao	Cul-de-four	kyd(ə)fuʀ
Crème de la crème	kʀɛmdəlakʀɛm	Cul-de-lampe	kyd(ə)lɑ̃p
Crème de menthe	kʀɛmdəmɑ̃t	Cul-de-sac	kyd(ə)sak
Crème de noyau	kʀɛmdənwajo	Culottes	kylɔt
Crème fraîche	kʀɛmfʀɛʃ		
Crème glacée	kʀɛmglase	**D**	
Crème pâtissière	kʀɛmpɑtisjɛʀ	D'accord	dakɔʀ
Crème pralinée	kʀɛmpʀaline	Damassé	damase
Crème renversée	kʀɛmʀɑ̃vɛʀse	Dame	dam
Crêpe	kʀɛp	Dame d'honneur	damdɔnœʀ
Crêpe de Chine	kʀɛpdəʃin	Dame de compagnie	damdəkɔ̃paɲi
Crêpe georgette	kʀɛpʒɔʀʒɛt	Danse du ventre	dɑ̃sdyvɑ̃tʀ
Crêpe suzette	kʀɛpsyzɛt	Danse macabre	dɑ̃smakɑbʀ
Crépon	kʀɛpɔ̃	Danseur	dɑ̃sœʀ
Crétin	kʀetẽ	Danseuse	dɑ̃søz
Cretonne	kʀətɔn	Daube	dob
Crinoline	kʀinɔlin	De bonne grâce	dəbɔngʀɑs
Croissant	kʀwasɑ̃	De haut en bas	də'otɑ̃ba
Croix de guerre	kʀwad(ə)gɛʀ	De luxe	dəlyks
Croque-monsieur	kʀɔkməsjø	De mal en pis	dəmalɑ̃pi
Croquette	kʀɔket	De pis en pis	dəpiɑ̃pi
Croquis	kʀɔki	De règle	dəʀɛgl

De retour	dərətuʀ	*Dénouement*	denumɑ̃
De rigueur	dəʀigœʀ	*Dépassé*	depase
De trop	dətʀo	*Dépêche*	depeʃ
Débâcle	debɑkl	*Déraciné*	deʀasine
Débonnaire	debɔneʀ	*Dérailleur*	deʀɑjœʀ
Débouché	debuʃe	*Dernier cri*	dɛʀnjekʀi
Débris	debʀi	*Dernier mot*	dɛʀnjemo
Début	deby	*Dernier ressort*	dɛʀnjeʀ(ə)sɔʀ
Débutant	debytɑ̃	*Derrière*	dɛʀjeʀ
Débutante	debytɑ̃t	*Déshabillé*	dezabije
Déclassé	deklɑse	*Désorienté*	dezɔʀjɑ̃te
Décolletage	dekɔltaʒ	*Détaché*	detaʃe
Décolleté	dekɔlte	*Détente*	detɑ̃t
Décor	dekɔʀ	*Détenu*	det(ə)ny
Découpage	dekupaʒ	*Détour*	detuʀ
Défilé	defile	*Devoir*	dəvwaʀ
Dégagé	degaʒe	*Diable*	djɑbl
Dehors	dəɔʀ	*Diamanté*	djɑmɑ̃te
Déjà-vu	deʒavy	*Dieu avec vous*	djøavɛkvu
Déjeuner	deʒœne	*Dieu et mon droit*	djøemɔ̃dʀwa
Délégué	delege	*Digestif*	diʒɛstif
Déluge	delyʒ	*Dilettante*	diletɑ̃t
Démarche	demaʀʃ	*Discothèque*	diskɔtek
Demi-jour	dəmiʒuʀ	*Diseuse*	dizøz
Demi-lune	dəmilyn	*Distingué*	distɛ̃ge
Demi-sec	dəmisek	*Divan*	divɑ̃
Demi-tasse	dəmitas	*Divertissements*	divɛʀtismɑ̃
Démodé	demode	*Divorcé (e)*	divɔʀse
Demoiselle	dəmwazɛl	*Domaine*	dɔmen

Donjon	dõʒõ	Ecru	ekʀy
Dormeuse	dɔʀmøz	Edition de luxe	edisjõd(ə)lyks
Dos-à-dos	dozado	Egalité	egalite
Dossier	dosje	Egarement	egaʀmã
Douane	dawn	Eglantine	eglãtin
Douanier	dwanje	Elan	elã
Douceur de vivre	dusœʀdəvivʀ	Elégante	elegãt
Dragée	dʀaʒe	Elève	elɛv
Dramaturge	dʀamatyʀʒ	Elite	elit
Drap	dʀa	Eloge	elɔʒ
Drapé	dʀape	Embarras	ãbaʀa
Dressage	dʀesaʒ	Embarras du choix	ãbaradyʃwa
Droit du seigneur	dʀwadysɛɲœʀ	Embouchure	ãbuʃyʀ
Du jour	dyʒuʀ	Embrasure	ãbʀazyʀ
Du tac au tac	dytakotak	Emeute	emøt
Duchesse	dyʃɛs	Emigré	emigʀe
		En ami	ãnami
E		En arrière	ãnaʀjɛʀ
Eau de Cologne	od(ə)kɔlɔɲ	En attendant	ãnatãdã
Eau de Javelle	od(ə)ʒavɛl	En avant	ãnavã
Eau-de-toilette	od(ə)twalɛt	En bloc	ãblɔk
Eau-de-vie	od(ə)vi	En brosse	ãbʀɔs
Ebauche	eboʃ	En cocotte	ãkɔkɔt
Ebéniste	ebenist	En croûte	ãkʀut
Éclair	eklɛʀ	En dedans	ãd(ə)dã
Eclaircissement	eklɛʀsismã	En dehors	ãdəɔʀ
Eclat	ekla	En déshabillé	ãdezabije
Ecole	ekɔl	En échelon	ãneʃ(ə)lõ
Ecorché	ekɔʀʃe	En effet	ãnefɛ

En évidence	ãnevidãs	En vogue	ãvɔg
En face	ãfas	Enceinte	ãsɛ̃t
En famille	ãfamij	Enclave	ãklav
En fête	ãfɛt	Encore	ãkɔʀ
En gelée	ãʒ(ə)le	Enfant gâté	ãfãgate
En grande tenue	ãgʀãd(ə)təny	Enfant perdu	ãfãpɛʀdy
En gros	ãgʀo	Enfant terrible	ãfãtɛʀibl
En l'air	ãlɛʀ	Enfantillage	ãfãtijaʒ
En masse	ãmas	Enfin	ãfɛ̃
En noir	ãnwaʀ	Engagement	ãgaʒmã
En papillotte	ãpapijɔt	Enluminure	ãlyminyʀ
En passant	ãpɑsã	Ennui	ãnɥi
En pension	ãpãsjɔ̃	Ensemble	ãsãbl
En permanence	ãpɛʀmanãs	Ensuite	ãsɥit
En place	ãplas	Entente	ãtãt
En plein air	ãplɛ̃nɛʀ	Entente cordiale	ãtãtkɔʀdjal
En plein jour	ãplɛ̃ʒuʀ	Entourage	ãtuʀaʒ
En pointe	ãpwɛ̃t	Entr'acte	ãtʀakt
En prince	ãpʀɛ̃s	Entrain	ãtʀɛ̃
En principe	ãpʀɛ̃sip	Entre deux vins	ãtʀədøvɛ̃
En queue	ãkø	Entre nous	ãtʀənu
En rapport	ãʀapɔʀ	Entrechat	ãtʀəʃa
En règle	ãʀɛgl	Entrecôte	ãtʀəkot
En retour	ãʀətuʀ, ãʀ(ə)tuʀ	Entrée	ãtʀe
En revanche	ãʀəvãʃ	Entrelac	ãtʀəla
En route	ãʀut	Entremets	ãtʀəmɛ
En tout cas	ãtukɑ	Entrepôt	ãtʀəpo
En vérité	ãveʀite	Entrepreneur	ãtʀəpʀənœʀ
En ville	ãvil	Entresol	ãtʀəsɔl

Entrez	ãtʀe	Extraordinaire	ɛkstʀaɔʀdinɛʀ
Epatant	epatã		
Epaulette	epolɛt	**F**	
Eponge	epɔ̃ʒ	Fabliau	fablijo
Epure	epyʀ	Façade	fasad
Equipe	ekip	Facile	fasil
Escargot	ɛskaʀgo	Façon de parler	fasɔ̃d(ə)paʀle
Espadrille	ɛspadʀij	Façonné	fasɔne
Espalier	ɛspalje	Fagot	fago
Espionnage	ɛspjɔnaʒ	Faïence	fajãs
Esplanade	ɛsplanad	Faille	faj
Esprit de corps	ɛspʀid(ə)kɔʀ	Fainéant	feneã
Esprit d'escalier	ɛspʀidɛskalje	Fait-accompli	feakɔ̃pli
Esquisse	ɛskis	Faites vos jeux	fetvoʒø
Estouffade	ɛstufad	Faits divers	fedivɛʀ
Estrade	ɛstʀad	Falbala	falbala
Etage	etaʒ	Fanfaron	fãfaʀɔ̃
Etagère	etaʒɛʀ	Farandole	faʀãdɔl
Etalage	etalaʒ	Farce	faʀs
Etamine	etamin	Farceur	faʀsœʀ
Etape	etap	Farci	faʀsi
Etiquette	etikɛt	Fatigue	fatig
Etoile	etwal	Faubourg	fobuʀ
Etourdi	etuʀdi	Faute de mieux	fotdəmjø
Etude	etyd	Fauteuil	fotœj
Etui	etɥi	Fauvette	fovɛt
Expertise	ɛkspɛʀtiz	Faux amis	fozami
Exposé	ɛkspoze	Faux cul	foky
Extrados	ɛkstʀado	Faux marbre	fomaʀbʀ

Faux pas	fopɑ	*Finesse*	finɛs
Femme de chambre	famdəʃɑ̃bʀ	*Flacon*	flakɔ̃
Femme de ménage	famdəmenaʒ	*Flambeau*	flɑ̃bo
Femme du monde	famdymɔ̃d	*Flamboyant*	flɑ̃bwajɑ̃
Femme fatale	famfatal	*Flânerie*	flɑnʀi
Femme incomprise	famɛ̃kɔ̃pʀiz	*Flâneur*	flɑnœʀ
Femme savante	famsavɑ̃t	*Flèche*	flɛʃ
Fête	fɛt	*Fleur-de-lys*	flœʀdəlis
Fête champêtre	fɛtʃɑ̃pɛtʀ	*Flic flac*	flikflak
Fête galante	fɛtgalɑ̃t	*Flûtes*	flyt
Feu d'artifice	fødaʀtifis	*Folie*	fɔli
Feu de joie	fødʒwa	*Folie de grandeur*	fɔlid(ə)gʀɑ̃dœʀ
Feu follet	føfɔlɛ	*Fonctionnaire*	fɔ̃ksjɔnɛʀ
Feuille-morte	fœjmɔʀt	*Fondue*	fɔ̃dy
Fiancé (e)	fjɑ̃se	*Fortune*	fɔʀtyn
Fichu	fiʃy	*Fou rire*	fuʀiʀ
Figurine	figyʀin	*Fouetté*	fwete
Filet	filɛ	*Foulard*	fulaʀ
Filet de boeuf	filɛd(ə)bœf	*Fourchette*	fuʀʃet
Filet mignon	filemiɲɔ̃	*Fourreau*	fuʀo
Fille d'honneur	fijdɔnœʀ	*Foyer*	fwaje
Fille de joie	fijdəʒwa	*Fracas*	fʀaka
Fillette	fijet	*Fraîcheur*	fʀeʃœʀ
Film noir	filmnwaʀ	*Fraise*	fʀez
Fils	fis	*Framboise*	fʀɑ̃bwaz
Fin de siècle	fɛ̃d(ə)sjɛkl	*Frangipane*	fʀɑ̃ʒipan
Financier	finɑ̃sje	*Frappé*	fʀape
Fine Champagne	finʃɑ̃paɲ	*Frère*	fʀɛʀ
Fines herbes	finzɛʀb	*Fricassée*	fʀikase

Fripon	fʀipɔ̃	Gamin	gamɛ̃
Frisé (e)	fʀize	Gamine	gamin
Frisette	fʀizet	Gaminerie	gaminʀi
Frisson	fʀisɔ̃	Gamme	gam
Frisure	fʀizyʀ	Ganache	ganaʃ
Fromage blanc	fʀɔmaʒblɑ̃	Garage	gaʀaʒ
Fromage frais	fʀɔmaʒfʀɛ	Garçon	gaʀsɔ̃
Fronton	fʀɔ̃tɔ̃	Garçonne	gaʀsɔn
Frottage	fʀɔtaʒ	Garde du corps	gaʀd(d)ykɔʀ
Frottis	fʀɔti	Garderobe	gaʀdəʀɔb
Froufrou, frou-frou	fʀufʀu	Gasconnade	gaskɔnad
Fruits de mer	fʀɥid(ə)mɛʀ	Gastronome	gastʀɔnɔnı
Fumeuse	fymøz	Gâteau	gɑto
Fureur	fyʀœʀ	Gauche	gɔʃ
Fuseau	fyzo	Gaucherie	gɔʃʀi
Fuselage	fys(ə)laʒ	Gavotte	gavɔt
		Gazon	gazɔ̃
G		Gendarme	ʒɑ̃daʀm
Gabardine	gabaʀdin	Génoise	ʒenwaz
Gabelle	gabɛl	Gentilhomme	ʒɑ̃tijɔm
Gaffe	gaf	Gentillesse	ʒɑ̃tijɛs
Gage d'amour	gaʒ(ə)damuʀ	Gibus	ʒıbys
Gala	gala	Gigolo	ʒigɔlo
Galant	galɑ̃	Gigot	ʒigo
Galanterie	galɑ̃tʀi	Gigue	ʒig
Galantine	galɑ̃tin	Gilet	ʒilɛ
Galette	galet	Girandole	ʒiʀɑ̃dɔl
Galimatias	galimatja	Glace	glas
Galoche	galɔʃ	Glacé	glase

Glissade	glisad	Grille	gʀij
Glissé	glise	Grillé	gʀije
Gogo, à gogo	gogo, agogo	Grimace	gʀimas
Gondolier	gɔ̃dɔlje	Griotte	gʀijɔt
Gorge	gɔʀʒ	Grippe	gʀip
Gouache	gwaʃ	Grisaille	gʀizaj
Gourmand	guʀmɑ̃	Grisette	gʀizɛt
Gourmet	guʀmɛ	Gris-gris	gʀigʀi
Goût	gu	Gros	gʀo
Goutte	gut	Gros-grain	gʀogʀɛ̃
Grand	gʀɑ̃	Grotesque	gʀɔtɛsk
Grand Guignol	gʀɑ̃giɲɔl	Gruyère	gʀyjɛʀ
Grand mal	gʀɑ̃mal	Guêpière	gepjɛʀ
Grand Marnier	gʀɑ̃maʀnje	Guéridon	geʀidɔ̃
Grand monde	gʀɑ̃mɔ̃d	Guilloche	gijɔʃ
Grand prix	gʀɑ̃pʀi	Guillotine	gijɔtin
Grand siècle	gʀɑ̃sjɛkl	Guimpe	gɛ̃p
Grande dame	gʀɑ̃d(d)am	Guipure	gipyʀ
Grandeur	gʀɑ̃dœʀ		
Grandiose	gʀɑ̃djoz	**H**	
Gratin	gʀatɛ̃	Habit	abi
Gratiné	gʀatine	Habitant	abitɑ̃
Gratitude	gʀatityd	Habitué	abitɥe
Graves	gʀav	Hachis	ʼaʃi
Gravure	gʀavyʀ	Hachure	ʼaʃyʀ
Grenade	gʀənad	Haricot	ʼaʀiko
Grenadine	gʀənadin	Haut monde	ʼomɔ̃d
Grillade	gʀijad	Haut ton	ʼotɔ̃
Grillage	gʀijaʒ	Haute	ʼot

Haute bourgeoisie	'otbuʀʒwasi	Immortelle	imɔʀtɛl
Haute couture	'otkutyʀ	Impasse	ɛ̃pas
Haute cuisine	'otkɥizin	Impossible	ɛ̃pɔsibl
Hauteur	'otœʀ	Imprévu	ɛ̃pʀevy
Héritage	eʀitaʒ	Impromptu	ɛ̃pʀɔ̃pty
Hermitage	eʀmitaʒ	Impudence	ɛ̃pydɑ̃s
Hollandaise	'ɔ(l)lɑ̃dɛz	Incapable	ɛ̃kapabl
Homme	ɔm	Inconnu (e)	ɛ̃kɔny
Homme d'affaires	ɔmdafɛʀ	Inédit	inedi
Homme d'esprit	ɔmdɛspʀi	Infernal	ɛ̃fɛʀnal
Homme d'état	ɔmdeta	Ingénue	ɛ̃ʒeny
Homme de bien	ɔmdəbjɛ̃	Insolence	ɛ̃sɔlɑ̃s
Homme de lettres	ɔmdəletʀ	Insolent	ɛ̃sɔlɑ̃
Homme de robe	ɔ̃ndərɔb	Insouciance	ɛ̃susjɑ̃s
Hors de combat	ɔmdəkɔ̃ba	Insouciant	ɛ̃susjɑ̃
Hors de question	'ɔʀdəkɛstjɔ̃	Insouciante	ɛ̃susjɑ̃t
Hors de saison	'ɔʀdəsezɔ̃	Interlude	ɛ̃tɛʀlyd
Hors la loi	'ɔʀlalwa	Intrados	ɛ̃tʀado
Hors série	'ɔʀseʀi	Intrigant	ɛ̃tʀigɑ̃
Hors-d'oeuvre	'ɔʀdœvʀ	Intrigante	ɛ̃tʀigɑ̃t
Hôtel de ville	ɔtɛldəvil	Intrigue	ɛ̃tʀig
Houppelande	'uplɑ̃d		

J

		Jabot	ʒabo
I			
Ici on parle français	isiɔ̃paʀl(ə)fʀɑ̃sɛ	Jacquard	ʒakaʀ
Idée fixe	idefiks	Jalousie	ʒaluzi
Ignoble	iɲɔbl	Jardin anglais	ʒaʀdɛ̃ɑ̃glɛ
Illumination	i(l)lyminasjɔ̃	Jardinière	ʒaʀdinjɛʀ
Imbécile	ɛ̃besil	Je ne sais quoi	ʒənəsɛkwa

Jet d'eau	ʒɛdo	Laine	lɛn
Jeté	ʒəte	Laisser-aller	leseale
Jeu d'esprit	ʒødɛspʀi	Laisser-faire	lesefɛʀ
Jeu de mots	ʒød(ə)mo	Laissez-passer	lesepase
Jeu de théâtre	ʒød(ə)teɑtʀ	Lamé	lame
Jeune fille	ʒœnfij	Langouste	lɑ̃gust
Jeunesse dorée	ʒœnɛsdɔʀe	Langoustine	lɑ̃gustin
Jeux	ʒø	Langue de chat	lɑ̃gdəʃa
Jeux de société	ʒød(ə)sɔsjete	Lard	laʀ
Joie de vivre	ʒwad(ə)vivʀ	Lardon	laʀdɔ̃
Jolie laide	ʒɔlilɛd	Largesse	laʀʒɛs
Jongleur	ʒɔ̃glœʀ	Lavallière	lavaljɛʀ
Jonquille	ʒɔ̃kij	Layette	lɛjet
Jour	ʒuʀ	Le monde savant	ləmɔ̃dsavɑ̃
Jour de fête	ʒuʀdəfet	Le point du jour	ləpwɛ̃dyʒuʀ
Journal	ʒuʀnal	Léotard	leɔtaʀ
Jupe	ʒyp	Lèse-majesté	lɛzmaʒeste
Jupon	ʒypɔ̃	Levant	ləvɑ̃
Justaucorps	ʒystokɔʀ	Lever de rideau	ləvedyʀido
Juste-milieu	ʒystəmiljø	Liaison	ljezɔ̃
		Liberté Egalité Fraternité	libɛʀte egalite fʀatɛʀnite

K

Képi	kepi	Lieu	ljø
Kilogramme	kilɔgʀam	Limousine	limuzin
Kilomètre	kilɔmetʀ	Lingerie	lɛ̃ʒ(ə)ʀi
		Liqueur	likœʀ

L

L'avenir	lav(ə)niʀ	Lisière	lizjɛʀ
La soupe du jour	lasupdyʒuʀ	Livre de chevet	livʀdəʃ(ə)vɛ
		Livre de poche	livʀdəpɔʃ

Loge	lɔʒ	*Maison de santé*	mezɔ̃d(ə)sɑ̃te
Lorgnette	lɔʀɲet	*Maison de ville*	mezɔ̃d(ə)vil
Lorgnon	lɔʀɲɔ̃	*Maisonnette*	mezɔnet
Louche	luʃ	*Maître*	metʀ
Louis d'or	lwidɔʀ	*Maître Ballet*	metʀəbalɛ
Loup	lu	*Maître d'hôtel*	metʀədotel
Loup-garou	lugaʀu	*Maîtresse*	metʀɛs
Louvre	luvʀ	*Maîtresse femme*	metʀɛsfam
Lucarne	lykaʀn	*Mal à propos*	malapʀopo
Lunette	lynet	*Mal de mer*	maldɔmɛʀ
Lycée	lise	*Mal de tête*	maldətet
		Mal du pays	maldypci
M		*Mal du siècle*	maldysjekl
Ma vieille	mavjej	*Mal élevé*	malel(ə)ve
Ma chère	maʃeʀ	*Mal vu*	malvy
Ma foi	mafwa	*Malade imaginaire*	maladimaʒineʀ
Macabre	makabʀ	*Maladresse*	maladʀɛs
Macédoine	masedwan	*Malaise*	malez
Macramé	makʀame	*Malentendu*	malɑ̃tɑ̃dy
Madame	madam	*Malgré lui*	malgʀelɥi
Madeleine	madlen	*Manchette*	mɑ̃ʃet
Mademoiselle	mad(ə)mwazel	*Manège*	manɛʒ
Madrilène	madʀilɛn	*Mange-tout*	mɑ̃ʒtu
Maigre	megʀ	*Mannequin*	mankɛ̃
Maillot	majo	*Manoeuvre*	manœvʀ
Maison	mezɔ̃	*Manoir*	manwaʀ
Maison de campagne	mezɔ̃d(ə)kɑ̃paɲ	*Manqué*	mɑ̃ke
Maison de couture	mezɔ̃d(ə)kutyʀ	*Mansard*	mɑ̃saʀ
Maison de passe	mezɔ̃d(ə)pɑs	*Manteau*	mɑ̃to

Manteau de zibeline	mᾶtod(ə)ziblin	*Matelassé*	mat(ə)lase
Mantelet	mᾶt(ə)lɛ	*Matelote*	mat(ə)lɔt
Maquette	makɛt	*Matériel*	mateʀjɛl
Maquillage	makijaʒ	*Matinée*	matine
Maquillé	makije	*Mauvais goût*	mɔvɛgu
Maquis	maki	*Mauvais sujet*	mɔvɛsyʒɛ
Maraud	maʀo	*Mauve*	mov
Marceline	maʀsəlin	*Mayonnaise*	majɔnɛz
Mardi Gras	maʀdigʀɑ	*Méchant*	meʃᾶ
Marguerite	maʀgəʀit	*Méchante*	meʃᾶt
Mariage de convenance	maʀjaʒdəkõv(ə)n	*Médaillon*	medajõ
Marinade	maʀinad	*Médoc*	medɔk
Marionnette	maʀjɔnɛt	*Méfiance*	mefjᾶs
Marivaudage	maʀivodaʒ	*Mélange*	melᾶʒ
Marmite	maʀmit	*Mêlée*	mele
Marmotte	maʀmɔt	*Ménage à trois*	menaʒatʀwa
Marocain	maʀɔkɛ̃	*Ménage*	menaʒ
Marotte	maʀɔt	*Mentonnière*	mᾶtɔnjɛʀ
Marquis	maʀki	*Merci beaucoup*	mɛʀsiboku
Marquise	maʀkiz	*Merde*	mɛʀd
Marquisette	maʀkizɛt	*Meringue*	məʀɛ̃g
Marron	maʀõ	*Merveilleux*	mɛʀvɛjø
Marron glacé	maʀõglase	*Mes amis*	mezami
Martinet	maʀtinɛ	*Mésalliance*	mezaljᾶs
Martingale	maʀtɛ̃gal	*Messaline*	mesalin
Massage	masaʒ	*Méthode champenoise*	metɔdʃᾶpənwaz
Masseur	masœʀ	*Métier*	metje
Masseuse	masøz	*Métis*	metis
Massif	masif	*Métro*	metʀo

Meursault	mœʀso	*Mondaine*	mɔ̃dɛn
Mezzanine	medzanin	*Monde*	mɔ̃d
Midi	midi	*Monsieur*	məsjø
Midinette	midinɛt	*Montage*	mɔ̃taʒ
Mignon	miɲɔ̃	*Montagnard*	mɔ̃taɲaʀ
Mignonne	miɲɔn	· *Montagne russe*	mɔ̃taɲʀys
Mignonnette	miɲɔnɛt	*Mont-de-piété*	mɔ̃d(ə)pjete
Milieu	miljø	*Moquette*	mɔkɛt
Millefeuille	milfœj	*Morceau*	mɔʀso
Minauderie	minodʀi	*Mordoré*	mɔʀdɔʀe
Minaudière	minodjɛʀ	*Morgue*	mɔʀg
Miniature	minjatyʀ	*Mot juste*	mɔʒyst
Mirabelle	miʀabɛl	*Mots d'usage*	modyzaʒ
Mise-au-point	mizopwɛ̃	*Motif*	mɔtif
Mise-en-scène	mizɑ̃sen	*Mouchard*	muʃaʀ
Mise-en-page	mizɑ̃paʒ	*Mouche*	muʃ
Miséricorde	mizeʀikɔʀd	*Mouchoir*	muʃwaʀ
Mistral	mistʀal	*Moue*	mu
Mode	mɔd	*Moulage*	mulaʒ
Modiste	mɔdist	*Moule*	mul
Module	mɔdyl	*Moulin*	mulɛ̃
Moi	mwa	*Moulure*	mulyʀ
Moiré (e)	mwaʀe	*Mousquetaire*	muskətɛʀ
Moire	mwaʀ	*Mousse*	mus
Mon ami (e)	mɔ̃nami	*Mousseline*	muslin
Mon cher	mɔ̃ʃɛʀ	*Mousseline de laine*	muslindəlɛn
Mon Dieu	mɔ̃djø	*Mousseline de soie*	muslindəswa
Mon vieux	mɔ̃vjø	*Mousseux*	musø
Mondain	mɔ̃dɛ̃	*Moustache*	mustaʃ

Mule	myl	Nicotine	nikɔtin
Muscadet	myskadɛ	Noblesse	nɔblɛs
Muscat	myska	Noblesse oblige	nɔblɛsɔbliʒ
Muscatel	myskatɛl	Nocturne	nɔktyʀn
Musette	myzɛt	Noël	nɔɛl
Musique	myzik	Noir	nwaʀ
Musique concrète	myzik(k)ɔ̃kʀɛt	Noisette	nwazɛt
		Noix	nwa
N		Noix de Grenoble	nwad(ə)gʀənɔbl
N'est-ce pas	nɛspa	Nom de guerre	nɔ̃d(ə)gɛʀ
N'importe	nɛ̃pɔʀt	Nom de plume	nɔ̃d(ə)plym
Nacarat	nakaʀa	Nom de théâtre	nɔ̃d(ə)teɑtʀ
Nacelle	nasɛl	Non pareil	nɔ̃paʀɛj
Nacré	nakʀe	Nonchalance	nɔ̃ʃalɑ̃s
Naïf	naif	Nonchalant	nɔ̃ʃalɑ̃
Naïve	naiv	Notre-Dame	nɔtʀədam
Naïveté	naivte	Nougat	nuga
Napoléon	napɔleɔ̃	Nouveau	nuvo
Nature morte	natyʀmɔʀt	Nouveau riche	nuvoriʃ
Navarin	navaʀɛ̃	Nouveauté	nuvote
Navette	navɛt	Nouvelle (s)	nuvɛl
Né (e)	ne	Nouvelle vague	nuvɛlvag
Nécessaire	nesesɛʀ	Noyau	nwajo
Négligé	negliʒe	Nuance	nyɑ̃s
Négociant	negɔsjɑ̃	Nuisance	nɥizɑ̃s
Neuchâtel	nøʃatɛl	Nuit blanche	nɥiblɑ̃ʃ
Névé	neve		
Ni l'un ni l'autre	nilœ̃nilotʀ	**O**	
Niche	niʃ	Objet d'art	ɔbʒedaʀ

Objet trouvé	ɔbʒetʀuve	Panne	pan
Oeil-de-boeuf	œjdəbœf	Pantomime	pãtɔmim
Oeil-de perdrix	œjdəpeʀdʀi	Pantoufles	pãtufl
Oeillade	œjad	Papa	papa
Oeuf en cocotte	œfãkɔkɔt	Paperasserie	papʀasri
Oeuvre (s)	œvʀ	Papeterie	papetʀi
Ogive	ɔgiv	Papier	papje
Ombré	ɔ̃bʀe	Papier collé	papjekɔle
Ombres chinoises	ɔ̃bʀəʃinwaz	Papier mâché	papjemaʃe
Opéra bouffe	ɔpeʀabuf	Papillote	papijɔt
Opéra comique	ɔpeʀakɔmik	Par accident	paʀaksidã
Ordures	ɔʀdyʀ	Par avion	paʀavjɔ̃
Ortolan	ɔʀtɔlã	Par dépit	paʀdepi
Osier	ozje	Par excellence	paʀekselãs
Oubliette	ublijet	Par exemple	paʀegzãpl
Ouï-dire	widiʀ	Par faveur	paʀfavœʀ
Outrance	ulʀãs	Par force	paʀfɔʀs
Outré (e)	utʀe	Par hasard	paʀ'azaʀ
		Par rapport	paʀ(ʀ)apɔʀ
P		Parachute	paʀaʃyt
Paille	paj	Parapet	paʀapɛ
Paillette	pajet	Par-ci par là	paʀsipaʀla
Pain perdu	pɛ̃peʀdy	Pardessus	paʀdəsy
Paletot	palto	Pardon	paʀdɔ̃
Palette	palet	Parfait	paʀfɛ
Palmette	palmet	Parfaitement bien	paʀfetmãbjɛ̃
Panache	panaʃ	Parfumerie	paʀfymʀi
Panetière	pan(ə)tjeʀ	Pari mutuel	paʀimytɥel
Panier	panje	Parisienne	paʀizjen

Parloir	paʀlwaʀ	Passe-partout	pɑspaʀtu
Parmesan	paʀmǝzɑ̃	Passe-pied	pɑspje
Parole d'honneur	paʀɔldɔnœʀ	Pastel	pastɛl
Parquet	paʀkɛ	Pastiche	pastiʃ
Parsemé	paʀsǝme	Pastis	pastis
Parterre	paʀtɛʀ	Pastoral	pastɔʀal
Parti pris	paʀtipʀi	Pâté	pɑte
Partie	paʀti	Pâte à choux	pɑtaʃu
Partisan	paʀtizɑ̃	Pâte brisée	pɑtbrize
Partout	paʀtu	Pâté de campagne	pɑted(ǝ)kɑ̃paɲ
Parure	paʀyʀ	Pâté de foie gras	pɑted(ǝ)fwagʀɑ
Parvenu	paʀvǝny	Pâte de verre	pɑtdǝvɛʀ
Parvis	paʀvi	Pâte dure	pɑtdyʀ
Pas	pɑ	Pâté en croûte	pɑteɑ̃kʀut
Pas de	pɑdǝ	Pâté maison	pɑtemɛzɔ̃
Pas de basque	pɑd(ǝ)bask	Pâte tendre	pɑt(t)ɑ̃dʀ
Pas de bourrée	pɑd(ǝ)buʀe	Pâtissier	pɑtisje
Pas de chat	pɑd(ǝ)ʃa	Patois	patwa
Pas de cheval	pɑd(ǝ)ʃǝval	Patron	patʀɔ̃
Pas de ciseaux	pɑd(ǝ)sizo	Patte	pat
Pas de deux	pɑd(ǝ)dø	Patte de velours	patdǝv(ǝ)luʀ
Pas de quatre	pɑd(ǝ)katʀ	Pattes-d'oie	patdwa
Pas de trois	pɑd(ǝ)tʀwa	Paupiette	popjɛt
Pas du tout	pɑdytu	Pavane	pavan
Pas seul	pɑsøl	Paysage	peizaʒ
Passade	pɑsad	Peau d'Espagne	podɛspaɲ
Passe	pɑs	Peau d'orange	podɔʀɑ̃ʒ
Passé	pɑse	Peau de soie	pod(ǝ)swa
Passementerie	pɑsmɑ̃tʀi	Peignoir	pɛɲwaʀ

Pêle-mêle	pɛlmɛl	Petit mal	p(ə)timal
Pélerine	pelʀin	Petit pain	p(ə)tipɛ̃
Pelisse	pəlis	Petit point	p(ə)tipwɛ̃
Peloton	p(ə)lɔtɔ̃	Petit verre	p(ə)tivɛʀ
Pelouse	p(ə)luz	Petit-beurre	p(ə)tibœʀ
Pelure	p(ə)lyʀ	Petit-bourgeois	p(ə)tibuʀʒwa
Pelure d'oignon	p(ə)lyʀdɔɲɔ̃	Petite-bourgeoise	p(ə)titbuʀʒwaz
Penchant	pɑ̃ʃɑ̃	Petit-four	p(ə)tifuʀ
Penché	pɑ̃ʃe	Petits-pois	p(ə)tipwa
Pendant	pɑ̃dɑ̃	Petit-suisse	p(ə)tisɥis
Pendeloque	pɑ̃dl(ə)lɔk	Petite amie	p(ə)titami
Pensée	pɑ̃se	Pétrin	petʀɛ̃
Pension	pɑ̃sjɔ̃	Peu à peu	pøapø
Pensionnaire	pɑ̃sjɔnɛʀ	Peu de chose	pød(ə)ʃoz
Percale	pɛʀkal	Picot	piko
Percaline	pɛʀkalin	Pièce à thèse	pjɛsatez
Père	pɛʀ	Pièce d'occasion	pjɛsdɔkazjɔ̃
Permis de séjour	pɛʀmid(ə)seʒuʀ	Pièce de circonstance	pjɛsdəsiʀkɔ̃stɑ̃s
Perron	peʀɔ̃	Pièce de résistance	pjɛsdəʀezistɑ̃s
Perruque	peʀyk	Pièce montée	pjɛsmɔ̃te
Perruquier	peʀykje	Pièce noire	pjɛsnwaʀ
Persiennes	pɛʀsjen	Pied-à-terre	pjetatɛʀ
Persiflage	pɛʀsiflaʒ	Pied-noir	pjenwaʀ
Persifleur	pɛʀsiflœʀ	Pierrette	pjeʀet
Personnel	pɛʀsɔnel	Pierrot	pjeʀo
Pervenche	pɛʀvɑ̃ʃ	Pilotis	pilɔti
Pétard	petaʀ	Pinard	pinaʀ
Pétillant	petijɑ̃	Pince-nez	pɛ̃sne
Petit	p(ə)ti	Pinot noir	pinonwaʀ

Piquant	pikɑ̃	*Point de repère*	pwɛ̃d(ə)ʀəpɛʀ
Piquante	pikɑ̃t	*Pointe (s)*	pwɛ̃t
Piqué	pike	*Pointillisme*	pwɛ̃tijism
Pirogue	piʀɔg	*Polisson*	pɔlisɔ̃
Pirouette	piʀwɛt	*Polissonne*	pɔlisɔn
Pis-aller	pizale	*Politesse*	pɔlitɛs
Pisé	pize	*Polonaise*	pɔlɔnɛz
Pissaladière	pisaladjɛʀ	*Pomerol*	pɔmʀɔl
Pissoir	piswaʀ	*Pomme*	pɔm
Pivot	pivo	*Pomme frite*	pɔmfʀit
Placard	plakaʀ	*Pompadour*	pɔ̃paduʀ
Plafond	plafɔ̃	*Pompier*	pɔ̃pje
Plaque	plak	*Pompon*	pɔ̃pɔ̃
Plastique	plastik	*Pont l'Evêque*	pɔ̃levɛk
Plastron	plastʀɔ̃	*Port Salut*	pɔʀsaly
Plat du jour	pladyʒuʀ	*Portail*	pɔʀtaj
Plat	pla	*Porte cochère*	pɔʀt(ə)kɔʃɛʀ
Plateau	plato	*Porte-bonheur*	pɔʀt(ə)bɔnœʀ
Plein air	plɛnɛʀ	*Porte-bouquet*	pɔʀt(ə)bukɛ
Plié	plije	*Portefeuille*	pɔʀtəfœj
Plissé	plise	*Porte-monnaie*	pɔʀt(ə)mɔnɛ
Plombière	plɔ̃bjɛʀ	*Portière*	pɔʀtjɛʀ
Plongeur	plɔ̃ʒœʀ	*Posé*	poze
Pochette	pɔʃɛt	*Pose plastique*	poz(ə)plastik
Poète maudit	pɔɛtmodi	*Poseur*	pozœʀ
Poignant	pwaɲɑ̃	*Pot de chambre*	pod(ə)ʃɑ̃bʀ
Point	pwɛ̃	*Potable*	pɔtabl
Point d'appui	pwɛ̃dapɥi	*Potage*	pɔtaʒ
Point de départ	pwɛ̃d(ə)depaʀ	*Potager*	pɔtaʒe

Pot-au-feu	potofø	Promenade	pʀɔm(ə)nad
Potiche	pɔtiʃ	Protégé	pʀɔteʒe
Pot-pourri	popuʀi	Prunelle	pʀynɛl
Poudreuse	pudʀøz		
Pouf	puf	**Q**	
Poulaine	pulɛn	Quadrille	kadʀij
Poule au pot	pulopo	Quadrillé	kadʀije
Poulet	pulɛ	Quartier	kaʀtje
Poulette	pulɛt	Quatre-couleur	katʀkulœʀ
Pour rire	puʀ(ʀ)iʀ	Quelque chose	kɛlkəʃoz
Pourboire	puʀbwaʀ	Quenelle	kənɛl
Pourparler	puʀpaʀle	Queue	kø
Pourpoint	puʀpwɛ̃	Qui va là	kivala
Pour-soi	puʀswa	Quiche	kiʃ
Pousse-café	puskafe	Quinzaine	kɛ̃zɛn
Poussette	pusɛt	Qui-vive	kiviv
Praline	pʀalin		
Précis	pʀesi	**R**	
Premier danseur	pʀəmjedɑ̃sœʀ	Raclette	ʀɑklɛt
Première	pʀəmjɛʀ	Raconteur	ʀakɔ̃tœʀ
Première danseuse	pʀəmjɛʀdɑ̃søz	Raconteuse	ʀakɔ̃tøz
Prestige	pʀɛstiʒ	Radeau	ʀado
Prêt-à-porter	pʀɛtapɔʀte	Raffiné (e)	ʀafine
Prie-Dieu	pʀidjø	Ragoût	ʀagu
Princesse	pʀɛ̃sɛs	Railleur	ʀɑjœʀ
Prix fixe	pʀifiks	Railleuse	ʀɑjøz
Procédé	pʀɔsede	Raison d'état	ʀɛzɔ̃deta
Profession	pʀɔfesjɔ̃	Raison d'être	ʀɛzɔ̃dɛtʀ
Profiterole	pʀɔfitʀɔl	Ramequin	ʀamkɛ̃

Rampant	ʀɑ̃pɑ̃	*Régisseur*	ʀeʒisœʀ
Rangé	ʀɑ̃ʒe	*Regret*	ʀəgʀɛ, ʀ(ə)gʀɛ
Rappel	ʀapɛl	*Reinette*	ʀɛnɛt
Rapport	ʀapɔʀ	*Relais*	ʀəlɛ, ʀ(ə)lɛ
Rapprochement	ʀapʀɔʃmɑ̃	*Relief*	ʀəljɛf
Ratafia	ʀatafja	*Religieuse*	ʀ(ə)liʒjøz
Rataplan	ʀɑ̃tɑ̃plɑ̃	*Religieux*	ʀ(ə)liʒjø
Ratatouille	ʀatatuj	*Rémoulade*	ʀemulad
Râté	ʀate	*Renaissance*	ʀ(ə)nesɑ̃s
Ratine	ʀatin	*Rencontre*	ʀɑ̃kɔ̃tʀ
Ravage	ʀavaʒ	*Rendez-vous*	ʀɑ̃devu
Ravigote	ʀavigɔt	*Rentier*	ʀɑ̃tje
Ravissant	ʀavisɑ̃	*Rentrée*	ʀɑ̃tʀe
Rayonnant	ʀɛjɔnɑ̃	*Répertoire*	ʀepɛʀtwaʀ
Rayonnante	ʀɛjɔnɑ̃t	*Réplique*	ʀeplik
Reblochon	ʀəblɔʃɔ̃	*Répondez s'il-vous-plaît*	ʀepɔ̃desilvuplɛ
Récamier	ʀekamje	*Reportage*	ʀ(ə)pɔʀtaʒ
Réchaud	ʀeʃo	*Repoussé*	ʀ(ə)puse
Réchauffé	ʀeʃofe	*Répudiation*	ʀepydjasjɔ̃
Recherché (e)	ʀəʃɛʀʃe,	*Réseau*	ʀezo
Récit	ʀesi	*Restaurant*	ʀɛstɔʀɑ̃
Réclame	ʀeklɑm	*Restaurateur*	ʀɛstɔʀatœʀ
Recueil	ʀəkœj	*Résumé*	ʀezyme
Redingote	ʀ(ə)dɛ̃gɔt	*Réticule*	ʀetikyl
Réduit	ʀedɥi	*Retroussé*	ʀ(ə)tʀuse
Reflet	ʀəflɛ, ʀ(ə)flɛ	*Réveillon*	ʀevejɔ̃
Refrain	ʀəfʀɛ̃, ʀ(ə)fʀɛ̃	*Revenant*	ʀəv(ə)nɑ̃
Refuge	ʀəfyʒ, ʀ(ə)fyʒ	*Révérence*	ʀeveʀɑ̃s
Régime	ʀeʒim	*Rêverie*	ʀɛvʀi

Revers	ʀ(ə)vɛʀ	Roman de geste	ʀɔmɑ̃d(ə)ʒɛst
Rêveur	ʀɛvœʀ	Roman noir	ʀɔmɑ̃nwaʀ
Rhône	ʀɔn	Roman policier	ʀɔmɑ̃pɔlisje
Ricochet	ʀikɔʃe	Romance	ʀɔmɑ̃s
Rideau	ʀido	Roman-fleuve	ʀɔmɑ̃flœv
Rien ne va plus	ʀjɛ̃n(ə)vaply	Rond de jambe	ʀɔ̃d(ə)ʒɑ̃b
Rillettes	ʀijɛt	Rond-de-cuir	ʀɔ̃d(ə)kɥiʀ
Riposte	ʀipɔst	Ronde	ʀɔ̃d
Risqué	ʀiske	Rondeau	ʀɔ̃do
Rissole	ʀisɔl	Rond-point	ʀɔ̃pwɛ̃
Rissoler	ʀisɔle	Roquefort	ʀɔfɔʀ
Rite de passage	ʀitdəpasaʒ	Rose	ʀoz
Rivière	ʀivjɛʀ	Rosé	ʀoze
Robe	ʀɔb	Rose bonbon	ʀozbɔ̃bɔ̃
Robe à fourreau	ʀɔbafuro	Rosette	ʀozɛt
Robe à l'anglaise	ʀɔbalɑ̃glɛz	Rôti	ʀoti, ʀɔti
Robe bustier	ʀɔb(b)ystje	Rôtisserie	ʀɔtisʀi
Robe chasuble	ʀɔbʃazybl	Rôtisseur	ʀɔtisœʀ
Robe chemise	ʀɔbʃəmiz	Roturier	ʀɔtyʀje
Robe de chambre	ʀɔbdəʃɑ̃bʀ	Roué	ʀwe
Robe du soir	ʀɔbdyswaʀ	Rouge	ʀuʒ
Robe sac	ʀɔbsak	Rouge-et-noir	ʀuʒenwaʀ
Rocaille	ʀɔkaj	Roulade	ʀulad
Rococo	ʀɔkɔko	Roulade au	ʀuladoʃɔkɔla
Roi fainéant	ʀwafɛneɑ̃	Rouleau	ʀulo
Roi soleil	ʀwasɔlej	Roulette	ʀulɛt
Romaine	ʀɔmɛn	Routier	ʀutje
Roman à clef	ʀɔmɑ̃akle	Routine	ʀutin
Roman à thèse	ʀɔmɑ̃atɛz	Roux	ʀu

Ruse	ʀyz	*Sans façon*	sɑ̃fasɔ̃
Ruse de guerre	ʀyzdəgeʀ	*Sans pareil*	sɑ̃paʀej
		Sans peur	sɑ̃pœʀ
S		*Sans recours*	sɑ̃ʀ(ə)kuʀ
S'il vous plaît	silvuple	*Sans reproche*	sɑ̃ʀ(ə)pʀɔʃ
Sablé	sɑble	*Sans sérif*	sɑ̃serif
Sabot	sabo	*Sans souci*	sɑ̃susi
Sabotage	sabɔtaʒ	*Sans tache*	sɑ̃taʃ
Saboteur	sabɔtœʀ	*Sans-culottes*	sɑ̃kylɔt
Sachet	saʃɛ	*Sans-gêne*	sɑ̃ʒɛn
Sain-et-sauf	sɛ̃esof	*Sarabande*	saʀabɑ̃d
Saint-Emilion	sɛ̃temiljɔ̃	*Satin*	satɛ̃
Saint-Honoré	sɛ̃tɔnɔʀe	*Satinette*	satinɛt
Salade niçoise	saladniswaz	*Saucier*	sosje
Salle à manger	salamɑ̃ʒe	*Saucisse*	sosis
Salle d'attente	saldatɑ̃t	*Saut*	so
Salle de jeux	saldəʒø	*Sauté*	sote
Salle des pas perdus	saldepapeʀdy	*Sauternes*	sotɛʀn
Salon	salɔ̃	*Sautoir*	sotwaʀ
Salon des refusés	salɔ̃deʀ(ə)fyze	*Sauve-qui-peut*	sovkipø
Salopettes	salɔpɛt	*Sauvignon Blanc*	soviɲɔ̃blɑ̃
Sancerre	sɑ̃sɛʀ	*Savant*	savɑ̃
Sang-froid	sɑ̃fʀwɑ	*Savarin*	savaʀɛ̃
Sanglier	sɑ̃glije	*Savate*	savat
Sanguine	sɑ̃gin	*Savoir-faire*	savwaʀfɛʀ
Sans	sɑ̃	*Savoir-vivre*	savwaʀvivʀ
Sans blague	sɑ̃blag	*Sculpture*	skyltyʀ
Sans cérémonie	sɑ̃seʀemɔni	*Séance*	seɑ̃s
Sans doute	sɑ̃dut	*Secret de Polichinelle*	səkʀed(ə)poliʃinel

Secrétaire	sǝkʀetɛʀ	Sottise	sɔtiz
Semainier	s(ǝ)menje	Sou	su
Sequin	sǝkẽ	Soubise	subis
Sérénade	seʀenad	Soubrette	subʀɛt
Serge	sɛʀʒ	Soufflé	sufle
Serin	s(ǝ)ʀẽ	Soupçon	supsɔ̃
Sermon	sɛʀmɔ̃	Soupe	sup
Serpette	sɛʀpɛt	Soupe à l'oignon	supalɔɲɔ̃
Servante	sɛʀvɑ̃t	Soupe printanière	sup(p)ʀẽtanjɛʀ
Serviette	sɛʀvjɛt	Soupirant	supiʀɑ̃
Servitude	sɛʀvityd	Sourdine	suʀdin
Siècle	sjɛkl	Sous-chef	suʃɛf
Siècle d'or	sjɛkldɔʀ	Sous-entendu	suzɑ̃tɑ̃dy
Siffleur	siflœʀ	Soutane	sutan
Signature	siɲatyʀ	Souteneur	sut(ǝ)nœʀ
Silhouette	silwɛt	Souterrain	suteʀẽ
Singerie	sẽʒʀi	Souvenir	suv(ǝ)niʀ
Sobriquet	sɔbʀikɛ	Sportif	spɔʀtif
Soi-disant	swadizɑ̃	Sportive	spɔʀtiv
Soigné	swaɲe	Statuette	statɥet
Soirée	swaʀe	Suave	sɥav
Soirée dansante	swaʀedɑ̃sɑ̃t	Suède	sɥɛd
Soirée musicale	swaʀemyzical	Suprême	sypʀɛm
Soit	swa	Surtout	syʀtu
Solitaire	sɔlitɛʀ	Svelte	svɛlt
Sommelier	sɔmǝlje		
Son et lumière	sɔ̃elymjɛʀ	**T**	
Sondage	sɔ̃daʒ	Table ambulante	tablɑ̃bylɑ̃t
Sorbetière	sɔʀbǝtjɛʀ	Table d'hôte	tablǝdot

Tableau	tablo	*Tête-bêche*	tɛtbeʃ
Tableau vivant	tablovivã	*Tête-de-pont*	tɛtdəpɔ̃
Tablier	tablije	*Tic*	tik
Tabouret	tabuʀɛ	*Tic douloureux*	tikduluʀø
Tac au tac	takotak	*Tiers Monde*	tjɛʀmɔ̃d
Taille	tɑj	*Tignon*	tiɲɔ̃
Tailleur	tɑjœʀ	*Tilleul*	tijœl
Tailloir	tɑjwaʀ	*Timbale*	tɛ̃bal
Talon	talɔ̃	*Timbre*	tɛ̃bʀ
Tambour	tãbuʀ	*Tirade*	tiʀad
Tambourin	tãbuʀɛ̃	*Tisane*	tizan
Tant mieux	tãmjø	*Toile*	twal
Tant pis	tãpi	*Toilette de soirée*	twalɛtdəswaʀe
Tapis	tapi	*Ton*	tɔ̃
Tartare	taʀtaʀ	*Tonne*	tɔn
Tarte	taʀt	*Tonneau*	tɔno
Tarte Tatin	taʀt(t)atɛ̃	*Tonsure*	tɔ̃syʀ
Tartelette	taʀtəlɛt	*Toque*	tɔk
Taupe	top	*Torchère*	tɔʀʃɛʀ
Tempête	tãpɛt	*Torchon*	tɔʀʃɔ̃
Temps	tã	*Torsade*	tɔʀsad
Tendu	tãdy	*Touché*	tuʃe
Terrain	teʀɛ̃	*Toupet*	tupɛ
Terrasse	teʀas	*Tour*	tuʀ
Terre à terre	teʀateʀ	*Tour de force*	tuʀdəfɔʀs
Terrine	teʀin	*Tourbillon*	tuʀbijɔ̃
Terroir	teʀwaʀ	*Tournedos*	tuʀnədo
Tête folle	tɛtfɔl	*Tourniquet*	tuʀnikɛ
Tête-à-tête	tɛtatɛt	*Tourtière*	tuʀtjɛʀ

Tout	tu	Troupe	tʀup
Tout à fait	tutafɛ	Trousseau	tʀuso
Tout à l'heure	tutalœʀ	Trou-trou	tʀutʀu
Tout à vous	tutavu	Truite au bleu	tʀɥitoblø
Tout au contraire	tutokɔ̃tʀɛʀ	Trumeau	tʀymo
Tout court	tukuʀ	Tulle	tyl
Tout de même	tud(ə)mɛm	Tuque	tyk
Tout de suite	tud(ə)sɥit	Turban	tyʀbɑ̃
Tout le monde	tul(ə)mɔ̃d	Turpitude	tyʀpityd
Tout Paris	tupaʀi	Tutu	tyty
Tragédie lyrique	tʀaʒediliʀik		
Tragédienne	tʀaʒedjen	**U**	
Traiteur	tʀɛtœʀ	Unique	ynik
Tranche de vie	tʀɑ̃ʃdəvi	Urinoir	yʀinwaʀ
Travail	tʀavaj	Usage	yzaʒ
Treillis	tʀeji		
Tremblement	tʀɑ̃bləmɑ̃	**V**	
Très	tʀɛ	Vagabond	vagabɔ̃
Très chic	tʀeʃik	Vaisselier	vɛsəlje
Triage	tʀijaʒ	Valet	valɛ
Tricorne	tʀikɔʀn	Valise	valiz
Tricot	tʀiko	Valse	vals
Tringle	tʀɛ̃gl	Vaudeville	vod(ə)vil
Tripes	tʀip	Vaurien	voʀjɛ̃
Triste	tʀist	Vedette	vədɛt
Tristesse	tʀistɛs	Veilleuse	vɛjøz
Trompe-l'oeil	tʀɔ̃plœj	Velours	v(ə)luʀ
Trottoir	tʀɔtwaʀ	Velouté	vəlute
Trou Normand	tʀunɔʀmɑ̃	Vendangeur	vɑ̃dɑ̃ʒœʀ

Vendeuse	vãdøz	*Vin fou*	vẽfu
Vengeance	vãʒãs	*Vin gris*	vẽgʀi
Verdure	veʀdyʀ	*Vin jaune*	vẽʒon
Vermeil	veʀmej	*Vin mousseux*	vẽmusø
Vermillion	veʀmijɔ̃	*Vin oeil-de-perdrix*	vẽœjdəpeʀdʀi
Vernissage	veʀnisaʒ	*Vin ordinaire*	vẽoʀdineʀ
Verre églomisé	veʀeglomize	*Vin rosé*	vẽʀoze
Vers de société	veʀdəsɔsjete	*Vin rouge*	vẽʀuʒ
Vers libre	veʀlibʀ	*Vin sec*	vẽsek
Vert	veʀ	*Vinaigrette*	vinegʀet
Verve	veʀv	*Vinasse*	vinas
Vestibule	vestibyl	*Visage*	vizaʒ
Veuve	vœv	*Vis-à-vis*	vizavi
Vichyssoise	viʃiswaz	*Vitrine*	vitʀin
Vie de Bohème	vid(ə)bɔem	*Vive la bagatelle*	vivlabagatel
Vie de château	vid(ə)ʃato	*Vive la différence*	vivladiferãs
Vie en rose	viãʀoz	*Vive le roi*	vivlərwa
Vieux jeu	vjøʒø	*Vive*	viv
Vieux rose	vjøʀoz	*Voilà tout*	vwalatu
Vigneron	viɲ(ə)ʀɔ̃	*Voilà*	vwala
Vignette	viɲet	*Voile*	vwal
Vignoble	viɲɔbl	*Voir dire*	vwaʀdiʀ
Ville lumière	vil(l)ymjeʀ	*Voisinage*	vwazinaʒ
Vin blanc	vẽblã	*Voiture*	vwatyʀ
Vin compris	vẽkɔ̃pʀi	*Voiturette*	vwatyʀet
Vin cuit	vẽkɥi	*Voix céleste*	vwaselest
Vin d'honneur	vẽdɔnœʀ	*Volage*	vɔlaʒ
Vin de paille	vẽd(ə)paj	*Volant*	vɔlã
Vin doux	vẽdu	*Vol-au-vent*	vɔlovã

Volte-face	vɔltəfas
Voltigeur	vɔltiʒœʀ
Voluble	vɔlybl
Volute	vɔlyt
Voussoir	vuswaʀ
Vouvray	vuvʀɛ
Voyage	vwajaʒ
Voyageur	vwajaʒœʀ
Voyant	vwajã
Voyeur	vwajœʀ
Voyou	vwaju
Vue d'ensemble	vydãsãbl

W

Wagon-lit	vagɔ̃li
Wagon-restaurant	vagɔ̃ʀɛstɔʀã

Y

Yé-yé	ʹjeje

Z

Zazou	zazu
Zibeline	ziblin
Zouave	zwav
Zut	zyt

BE A SNOB

FRENCH PHRASES:

CHAPTERS I TO IV

A l'oeil	alœj
A la belle étoile	alabɛletwal
A lécher les vitrines	aleʃelevitʀin
Alors là, c'est le bouquet	alɔʀlasɛl(ə)bukɛ
Andouille! Quelle andouille	ãduj, kɛlãduj
Armoire à glace	aʀmwaʀaglas
Au diable; Va au diable!	odjabl; vaodjabl
Aux frais de la princesse	ofʀɛd(ə)lapʀɛsɛs
Avoir le béguin, J'ai le béguin	avwaʀləbœgɛ̃, ʒɛl(ə)begɛ̃
Battre la breloque	batʀlabʀəlɔk
Beau comme un jour	bokɔmœ̃ʒuʀ
Bête comme un chou	bɛtkɔmœ̃ʃu
Bien balancé	bjɛ̃balãse
Bon dos	bɔ̃do
Bon pied, bon oeil	bɔ̃pjebɔnœj
Bonjour vieille noix	bɔ̃ʒuʀvjɛjnwa
C'est bibi; coucou c'est bibi	sɛbibi; kukusɛbibi
C'est du gâteau	sɛdygato
C'est du guignol	sɛdyɡiɲɔl
C'est la misère noire	selamizɛʀnwaʀ
C'est le bouquet mon ami	sɛl(ə)bukɛmɔ̃nami
C'est le pompon mon cher	sɛl(ə)pɔ̃pɔ̃mɔ̃ʃɛʀ

C'est son papa gâteau	sesɔ̃papagato	De la galette	d(ə)lagalɛt
C'est très chou; très chou	sɛtʀɛʃu; tʀɛʃu	De ta lucarne	dətalykaʀn
C'est un roman pour midinettes	sɛtœ̃ʀɔmɑ̃puʀmidinɛt	Des cancans	dekɑ̃kɑ̃
		Des contes de bonnes femmes	dekɔ̃tdəbɔnfam
C'est une petite midinette	setynp(ə)titmidinɛt	
Ce n'est pas du gâteau	s(ə)nɛpadygato	Des idées noires	dezidenwaʀ
Ceinture! je fais ceinture	sɛ̃tyʀ; ʒ(ə)fɛsɛ̃tyʀ	Des niches	deniʃ
Chapeau bas!	ʃapoba(ɑ)	Du béton	dybetɔ̃
Chaussure à mon pied	ʃosyʀamɔ̃pje	Du bien au soleil	dybjẽ sɔlɛj
Comme un éclair	kɔmœ̃neklɛʀ	Du coffre	dykɔfʀ
Comme un sabot	kɔmœ̃sabo	Du réchauffé	dyʀeʃofe
Comme une éponge	kɔmynepɔ̃ʒ	Du toupet	dytupɛ
Comme une pantoufle	kɔmyn(ə)pɑ̃tufl	Du velours	dyv(ə)luʀ
Complètement frappé	kɔ̃plɛtmɑ̃fʀape	Elle refait la façade	ɛlʀəfɛlafasad
Conte à dormir debout	kɔ̃tadɔʀmiʀdəbu	En béton	ɑ̃betɔ̃
Coucou, c'est bibi	kukusebibi	En carafe	ɑ̃kaʀaf
Courir le cotillion; Il court le cotillion	kuʀiʀləkɔtijɔ̃; ilkuʀləkɔtijɔ̃	En chien de faïence	ɑ̃ʃjẽd(ə)fajɑ̃s
		En compote	ɑ̃kɔ̃pɔt
Dans de beaux draps	dɑ̃d(ə)bodʀa	En Suisse	ɑ̃sɥis
Dans la lune	dɑ̃lalyn	Entre deux chaises	ɑ̃tʀədøʃɛz
Dans la peau	dɑ̃lapo	Entre deux vins	ɑ̃tʀədøvẽ
Dans le décor	dɑ̃l(ə)dekɔʀ	Faire le saut	fɛʀləso
Dans le même sabot	dɑ̃l(ə)mɛmsabo	Faux jeton	foʒ(ə)tɔ̃
Dans mon assiette	dɑ̃mɔ̃nasjet	Filer à l'anglaise; Il file à l'anglaise	filealɑ̃glez; ilfilalɑ̃glez
Dans un beau pétrin	dɑ̃zœ̃bopetʀẽ	
Dans une impasse	dɑ̃zynẽpas	Froid de canard	fwʀad(ə)kanaʀ
De la brioche	d(ə)labʀiɔʃ	Fumer la moquette	fymelamɔkɛt
De la comédie	d(ə)lakɔmedi	Gravure de mode	gʀavyʀdəmɔd
De la daube	d(ə)ladob	Gros bonnet	gʀobɔnɛ

Gros lard	gʀolaʀ	Mon pompon	mɔ̃pɔ̃pɔ̃
Gros plein de soupe	gʀoplɛ̃d(ə)sup	Occupe-toi de tes oignons	ɔkyptwad(ə)tezɔɲɔ̃
Il/elle a la corde au cou	il/ɛlalakɔʀdoku	Panier percé	panjepɛʀse
Il/elle a un fil a la patte	il/ɛlaœ̃filalapat	Pas un radis	pazœ̃ʀadi
Il, elle sucre les fraises	il/ɛlsykʀ(ə)lɛfʀɛz	Pas un sou	pazœ̃su
Je connais la musique	ʒ(ə)kɔnɛlamyzik	Peau de vache	pod(ə)vaʃ
Je suis sur la paille	ʒ(ə)sɥsyʀlapɑj	Pique-assiette	pikasjet
La bague au doigt	labagodwa	Pommes de terre en robe de chambre	pɔmdətɛʀɑ̃ʀɔbdə-ʃɑ̃bʀ
La fin des haricots	lafɛ̃de'aʀiko		
La grasse matinée	lagʀɑsmatine	Pompette	pɔ̃pet
La gueule de bois	lagœldəbwa	Poule mouillée	pulmuje
La mème chanson	lamɛmʃɑ̃sɔ̃	Pour bibi, c'est pour bibi	puʀbibi; ʒepuʀbibi
La mème histoire	lamemistwaʀ	Pour la façade	puʀlafasad
La misère noire	lamizɛʀnwaʀ	Près du bonnet	pʀɛdybɔne
La peau des fesses	lapodefɛs	Quel bonnet de nuit	kɛlbɔned(ə)nɥi
La prunelle de mes yeux	lapʀynɛldəmezjø	Quel chantier	kɛlʃɑ̃tje
La tête farcie	latɛtfaʀsi	Quel cornichon	kɛlkɔʀniʃɔ̃
La vie en rose	laviɑ̃ʀoz	Quel toupet	kɛltupe
Langue de vipère	lɑ̃gdəvipɛʀ	Quelle boudeuse	kɛlbudøz
Le grand saut	ləgʀɑ̃so	Quelle caqueteuse	kɛlkaktøz
Les yeux de la tête	lezjød(ə)latet	Quelle cloche	kɛlklɔʃ
Ma croûte	makʀut	Quelle croûte	kɛlkʀut
Ma petite cuisine	map(ə)titkɥizin	Quelle cuisine	kɛlkɥizin
Maigre comme un clou	mɛgʀ(ə)kɔmœ̃klu	Quelle grande gigue	kɛlgʀɑ̃dʒig
Mal au citron	malositʀɔ̃	Quelle macédoine	kɛlmasedwan
Mauvaise langue	movezlɑ̃g	Quelle noix	kɛlnwa
Mon béguin	mɔ̃begɛ̃	Quelle potiche	kɛlpotiʃ
Mon oeil	mɔ̃nœj	Quelle tarte	kɛltaʀt
		Quel vieux tableau	kɛlvjøtablo

Rendre son tablier	ʀɑ̃dʀ(ə)sɔ̃tablije	Travaille du chapeau	tʀavajdyʃapo
Rien dans le buffet	ʀjɛ̃dɑ̃l(ə)byfɛ	Un bon boulevard	œ̃bɔ̃bulvaʀ
Rond comme un petit pois	ʀɔ̃kɔmœ̃p(ə)tipwa	Un bon coup de fourchette	œ̃bɔ̃kud(ə)fuʀʃet
Rouge comme un coquelicot	ʀuʒkɔmœ̃kɔkliko	Un bon diable	œ̃bɔ̃djabl
		Un casse-croûte	œ̃kaskʀut
Son béguin	sɔ̃begɛ̃	Un coup de barre	œ̃kud(ə)baʀ
Son panache	sɔ̃panaʃ	Un gros bonnet; c'est un gros bonnet	œ̃gʀobɔnɛ; setœ̃gʀobɔnɛ
Son pompon; Il/elle a son pompon	sɔ̃pɔ̃pɔ̃; il/ɛlasysɔ̃pɔ̃pɔ̃		
		Un Malabar	malabaʀ
Sorti de l'auberge	sɔʀtid(ə)lobɛʀʒ	Un gros buffet	œ̃gʀobyfɛ
Soupe à la grimace	supalagʀimas	Un petit bout de chou	œ̃p(ə)tibud(ə)ʃu
Soupe au lait	supolɛ	Un petit noir	œ̃p(ə)tinwaʀ
Sous le manteau	sul(ə)mɑ̃to	Un rond	œ̃ʀɔ̃
Sur la paille	syʀlapɑj	Un sac de pommes de terre	œ̃sakdəpɔmdətɛʀ
Tête de lard	tetdəlaʀ		
Tête de papier mâché	tetdəpapjemaʃe	Une bonne pâte; c'est une bonne pâte	ynbɔnpat; setynbɔnpat
Tomber du ciel; il/elle tombe du ciel	tɔ̃bedysjɛl; il/ɛltɔ̃bdysjɛl		
		Une noix de beurre	yn(n)wad(ə)bœʀ
Tout en noir	tutɑ̃nwaʀ	Une petite bagatelle	ynp(ə)titbagatel
Tout le bataclan	tulbataklɑ̃	Une petite midinette	ynpətitmidinet
Tout le bazar	tulbazaʀ	Une peur bleue	ynpœʀblø
Tout le tralala	tultʀalala	Va au diable	vaodjabl
Tout le tremblement	tultʀɑ̃bləmɑ̃	Vieille ganache	vjɛjganaʃ
Tout un fromage	tutœ̃fʀɔmaʒ	Vieille peau	vjɛjpo
Tout un roman	tutœ̃ʀɔmɑ̃	Vieux croûton	vjøkʀutɔ̃

PROVERBS

CHAPTER I

Cerise	C'est la cerise sur le gâteau	sɛlas(ə)ʀizsyʀləgɑto
Chinois	C'est du chinois	sɛdyʃlnwa
Madeleine	Elle pleure comme une Madeleine	ɛlplœ̃ʀkɔmynmadlɛn
Mousse	Pierre qui roule n'amasse pas mousse	pjɛʀkiʀulnamaspɑmus

CHAPTER II

Art nouveau (nouveau)	Tout nouveau, tout beau!	tunovo, tubo
Chanson de geste (chanson)	Tout fini par des chansons	tufiniparde ʃɑ̃sɔ̃
Oeuvre	A L'oeuvre on commaît l'ouvrier	alœvʀɔ̃kɔnɛluvʀije
Tempête	Qui sème le vent, récolte la tempête	kisɛmləvɑ̃, ʀekɔltlatɑ̃pet
Temps	Le temps perdu ne se rattrape jamais	lətɑ̃pɛʀdynəs(ə)ʀatʀapʒamɛ

CHAPTER III

Habit	L'habit ne fait pas le moine	labin(ə)fɛpɑlmwan
Cloche	Qui n'entend qu'une cloche, n'entend qu'un son	kinɑ̃tɑ̃kynklɔʃ, nɑ̃tɑ̃kœ̃ sɔ̃
Revers	Toute médaille a son revers	tutmedajasɔ̃ʀ(ə)vɛʀ
	(Il n'y a pas de rose sans épines)	ilniɑpɑd(ə)ʀozsɑ̃zepin
Rivière	Les petits ruisseaux font les grandes rivières	lep(ə)tiʀɥisofɔ̃legʀɑ̃d(ə) ʀivjɛʀ

CHAPTER IV

ENGLISH PHRASES À LA FRANÇAISE Examples of *English phrases à la française* and the phonetic for these expressions are given below. However, creative English speakers can pick and choose to arrange loanwords together as they see fit.

English Phrases à la française	Phonetic	Other English version
A bientôt mon cher	abjɛ̃ɔtomɔ̃ʃɛʀ	Until later, see you soon my dear
A la bonne heure, mon ami	alabɔnœʀmɔ̃ami	Right on, my friend
A moi, mon cher!	amwamɔ̃ʃɛʀ	Help, my dear!
A mon avis, ma chère	amɔ̃avimaʃɛʀ	In my opinion, my dear
A propos, Mademoiselle	apʀɔpomad(ə)mwazɛl	By the way, Miss
A quoi bon, méchant	akwabɔ̃meʃɑ̃	What's the good of it, bad boy!
A tout prix, ma chère	atupʀimaʃɛʀ	At all cost, my dear
Adieu, mon cher ami	adjømɔ̃ʃɛʀami	Farewell, my dear friend
Ainsi va la vie, mon amie	ɛ̃sivalavimɔ̃ami	So goes life, my friend
Allez-vous, en vaurien	alevuzɑ̃vɔʀjɛ̃	Go away, good for nothing
Allons Mademoiselle	alɔ̃mad(ə)mwazɛl	Come on Miss
Au contraire, mon cher ami	okɔ̃tʀɛʀmɔ̃ʃɛʀami	On the contrary, my dear fellow
Au fait, ma chère	ofɛtmaʃɛʀmadam	Incidentally, my dear
Au revoir, polisson	oʀ(ə)vwaʀpɔlisɔ̃	Good-bye, naughty boy
Au secours, cher confrère	os(ə)kuʀʃɛʀkɔ̃fʀɛʀ	Help! dear fellow
Avec votre permission, ma chère	avɛkvɔtʀəpɛʀmisjcmaʃɛʀ	With your permission, my dear

B

Bien entendu, vaurien	bjɛ̃nɑ̃tɑ̃dyvɔʀje	Of course, good for nothing
Bienvenue fainéant	bjɛ̃v(ə)yfɛneɑ̃	Welcome lazy-bones!
Bon appétit, ma chère Madame	bɔnapetimaʃɛʀmadam	Bon appétit, my dear Madam
Bon gré, mal gré, mon frère	bɔ̃gʀemalgʀemɔ̃fʀɛʀ	Willing or not, brother
Bon voyage, mes amis	bɔ̃vwajaʒ(ə)mezami	Bon voyage, my friends
Bonjour, méchante	bɔ̃ʒuʀmeʃɑ̃t	Good morning, bad girl
Bonne chance, mon cher ami	bɔnʃɑ̃smɔ̃ʃeʀami	Good luck, my dear friend
Bonsoir polissonne	bɔ̃swaʀpɔlisɔn	Good night, naughty girl

C

C'est à dire, mon vieux	sɛtadiʀmɔ̃vjø	That is to say, old chap
C'est la guerre, mon cher	sɛlagɛʀmɔ̃ʃeʀ	It's war my dear
C'est la vie, chère Madame	sɛlaviʃɛʀmadam	It's life, dear Madam!
C'est magnifique, mes amis	semaɲifikmezami	It's wonderful, my friends
Cela va sans dire, canaille	s(ə)lavasɑ̃diʀkanaj	That goes without saying, scoundrel!
Chacun son goût, mes amis	ʃakœsɔ̃gumezami	To each their own taste, my friends
Chez moi, mon ami	ʃemwamɔ̃ami	At my house, my friend
Comme ci comme ça, mon chou	kɔmsikɔmsamɔ̃ʃu	So so, my darling
Comme il faut, cher Monsieur	kɔmilfoʃɛʀməsjø	As it should be, dear Sir
Coûte que coûte, ma chère amie	kutkəkutmaʃɛʀami	Whatever it takes, my dear friend

D

D'accord, mon cher ami	dakɔrmɔ̃ʃɛrami	Agreed, my dear friend
Déjà-vu, mon cher confrère	deʒavymɔ̃ʃɛrkɔ̃frɛr	Déjà-vu, my dear fellow
De mal en pis, ma chère	dəmalɑ̃pimaʃɛr	From bad to worse, my dear
Du tac au tac, mon cher	dytakotakmɔ̃ʃɛr	Tit for tat, my dear

E

Encore s'il vous plaît mon ami	ɑ̃kɔrsilvuplɛmɔ̃ami	Once more, please my friend
Enfin chère amie	ɑ̃fɛ̃ʃɛrami	At last, dear friend
Ensuite Monsieur	ɑ̃sɥitməsjø	After that, (next) Sir
Entre nous, chère amie	ɑ̃trənuʃɛrami	Between you and me, dear friend
Entrez s.v.p. Monsieur	ɑ̃trɛsilvuplɛməsjø	Enter, if you please, Sir
En avant, mes amis	ɑ̃navɑ̃mezami	Off we go, my friends!
En effet, ma mignonne	ɑ̃nefɛmamiɲɔn	Indeed, my sweet darling
En passant, cher confrère	ɑ̃pasɑ̃ʃɛrkɔ̃frɛr	In passing, by the way, dear colleague
En tout cas, mes amis	ɑ̃tukɑmezami	In any case, my friends
Epatant, mon chou	epatɑ̃mɔ̃ʃu	Wonderful my darling!
Extraordinaire, mes amis	ɛkstraɔrdinɛrmezami	Outstanding, my friends!

F

Façon de parler, cher Monsieur	fasɔ̃d(ə)parleʃɛrməsjø	Manner of speaking, dear Sir
Faute de mieux, Mademoiselle	fotdəmjømad(ə)mwazɛl	For lack of something better, Miss
Faux pas ma chère	fopamaʃɛr	Social blunder, my dear

H-I-J-L-M-N-P-R

Hors de question, mon ami	ˈɔʀdəkɛstjɔ̃mɔ̃ami	Out of the question, my friend
Ici on parle français, mon cher	isiɔ̃paʀl(ə)fʀɑ̃sɛmɔ̃ʃɛʀ	French is spoken here, my dear
Je ne sais quoi, ma chère	ʒən(ə)sɛkwamaʃɛʀami	I know not what, my dear
Joie de vivre cher	ʒwad(ə)vivʀʃɛʀ	Zest for life, my dear
Laissez-faire, chère Madame	lesefɛʀʃemadam	Let it be, dear Madam
Ma foi, mes amis	mafwamezami	Upon my faith, my friends!
Merci beaucoup, canaille	mɛʀsibokukanaj	Thank you very much, scoundrel
Mon Dieu! mon cher ami	mɔ̃djømɔ̃ʃɛʀami	My God! my dear friend
N'est-ce pas? mon cher	nɛspamɔ̃ʃɛʀ	Isn't it, my dear?
N'importe, mon vieux	nɛ̃pɔʀtmɔ̃vjø	It does not matter, old pal
Ni l'un ni l'autre, mon ami	nilœ̃nilotʀmɔ̃ami	Neither one, nor the other, my friend
Noblesse oblige, cher Monsieur	nɔblɛsɔbliʒʃɛʀməsjø	Nobility obliges, dear Sir
Pardon, mon petit chou	paʀdɔ̃mɔ̃p(ə)tiʃup	Excuse-me my little darling, sweet thing
Pas du tout, chère Madame	pɑdytuʃɛʀmadam	Not at all, dear Madam
Répondez s.v.p., ma chère amie	ʀepɔ̃desilvuplemaʃɛʀami	Answer please, my dear friend

S

Sans arrière-pensée, ma chère	sɑ̃zaʀjɛʀpɑ̃semaʃɛʀ	Without ulterior motive, my dear
Sans blague, mon cher	sɑ̃blagmɔ̃ʃɛʀ	No kidding, my dear
Sans cérémonie, mes amis	sɑ̃seʀemɔnimezami	Without formality, my friends

Sans chichi, mon vieux	sãʃiʃimɔ̃vjø	Without *chichi* (*froufrou*), old chap
Sans doute, Mademoiselle	sãdutmad(ə)mwazɛl	Without doubt, Miss
Sans façon, ma chère amie	sãfasɔ̃maʃɛʀami	Without ceremony, my dear friend
Sans gêne, Madame! Monsieur	sãʒɛnmadam	Lots of nerve, Madam! Monsieur
Sans panache, ma mignonne	sãpanaʃmamiɲɔn	Without *panache*, my darling

T-V

Tant mieux, mes amis	tãmjømezami	So much the better, my friends
Tant pis, mon frère	tãpimɔ̃fʀɛʀ	Too bad, brother
Touché, mon ami	tuʃemɔ̃nami	*Touché*, my friend
Tout à fait femme du monde	tutafɛfamdymɔ̃d	Entirely a woman of the world
Tout à vous, ma mignonne	tutavumamiɲɔn	All yours, my darling
Tout de suite, mon beau	tud(ə)sɥitmɔ̃bo	Right away, good looking
Tout le monde, ma chère	tul(ə)mɔ̃dmaʃɛʀ	Everybody, my dear
Très distingué, cher ami	tʀɛ distɛ̃geʃɛʀami	Very distinguished, dear friend
Vive la différence, mes amis	vivladiferãsmezami	*Vive la différence*, my friends
Voilà, mon cher	vwalamɔ̃ʃɛʀ	There it is, my dear
Voilà tout, mes chers amis	vwalatumeʃɛʀzami	Nothing more to say, my dear friends

FOR FRANCOPHILES ONLY

French Expressions	Phonetic		
Mon petit chat (m,f)	mɔ̃p(ə)tiʃa	Ma petite puce (f)	map(ə)titpys
Ma chérie (f), Mon chéri (m)	maʃeʀi, mɔ̃ʃeʀi	Ma biche, ma bibiche, ma bichette (f)	mabiʃ, mabibiʃ, mabiʃet
Mon amour (m,f)	mɔ̃namuʀ	Mon loulou, mon petit loulou (m)	mɔlulu, mɔ̃p(ə)tilulu
Mon petit lapin (m,f)	mɔ̃p(ə)tilapɛ̃		
Mon poulet (m), ma poulette (f)	mɔ̃pulɛ, mapulet	Petit mioche (m,f)	p(ə)timjɔʃ
		Petit lardon (m,f)	p(ə)tilaʀdɔ̃
Ma poule (f)	mapul	Mon coeur, Mon petit coeur (m)	mɔ̃kœʀ, mɔ̃p(ə)tikœʀ
Mon petit poussin (m,f)	mɔ̃p(ə)tipusɛ̃	Mon trésor (m,f)	mɔ̃tʀezɔʀ
Petit cochon (m,f)	p(ə)tikɔʃɔ̃	Mon ange (m,f)	mɔ̃nɑ̃ʒ
Petit démon (m,f)	p(ə)tidemɔ̃	Mon chérubin (m,f)	mɔ̃ʃeʀybɛ̃
Petit diable (m,f)	p(ə)tidjɑbl	Ma cocotte (f)	makɔkɔt
Petit drôle (m,f)	p(ə)tidʀol	Foufou (m); Fofolle (f)	fufu, fɔfɔl
Petit coquin (m), Petite coquine (f)	p(ə)tikɔkɛ̃, p(ə)titkɔkin	Dodo (m,f)	dodo
		Bisou (m)	bizu